Frommer's®

Puerto
Rico

Here's what the critics say about Frommer's:

"Amazingly easy to use. Very portable, very complete."
—*Booklist*

♦

"Complete, concise, and filled wih useful information."
—*New York Daily News*

♦

"Hotel information is close to encyclopedic."
—*Des Moines Sunday Register*

♦

"The only mainstream guide to list specific prices. The Walter Cronkite of guidebooks—with all that implies."

Other Great Guides for Your Trip:

Frommer's Caribbean

Frommer's Caribbean rom $60 a Day

Frommer's Caribbean Cruises and Ports of Call

Frommer's Caribbean Ports of Call

Frommer's Born to Shop Caribbean Ports of Call

The Unofficial Guide to Cruises

Frommer's Caribbean Hideaways

Puerto Rico

by Darwin Porter
& Danforth Prince

MACMILLAN • USA

ABOUT THE AUTHORS

Ever since the age of 17, when **Darwin Porter** sold his first article on Puerto Rico to a travel magazine, he has been visiting and writing about the island. A bureau chief of *The Miami Herald* at the age of 21, Porter has traveled frequently and extensively throughout Puerto Rico and the rest of the Caribbean. His coauthor is **Danforth Prince,** formerly of the Paris bureau of *The New York Times.* Together they share their secrets and discoveries of travel to Puerto Rico with you.

MACMILLAN TRAVEL

A Simon & Schuster Macmillan Company
1633 Broadway
New York, NY 10019
Find us online at **www.frommers.com**

ISBN 0-02862271-5
ISSN 1062-4775

Editors: Bill Goodwin, Kelly Regan
Production Editor: Robyn Burnett
Design by Michele Laseau
Digital Cartography by Raffaele DeGennaro and John Decamillis
Photo Editor: Richard Fox
Page creation by Toi Davis and Trudy Coler

SPECIAL SALES

Bulk purchases (10+ copies) of Frommer's and selected Macmillan travel guides are available to corporations, organizations, mail-order catalogs, institutions, and charities at special discounts, and can be customized to suit individual needs. For more information write to Special Sales, Macmillan General Reference, 1633 Broadway, New York, NY 10019.

Manufactured in the United States of America

Contents

List of Maps

An Invitation to the Reader

In researching this book, we discovered many wonderful places—hotels, restaurants, shops, and more. We're sure you'll find others. Please tell us about them so that we can share the information with your fellow travelers in upcoming editions. If you were disappointed with a recommendation, we'd love to know that, too. Please write to:

Frommer's Puerto Rico
Macmillan Travel
1633 Broadway
New York, NY 10019

An Additional Note

Please be advised that travel information is subject to change at any time—and this is especially true of prices. We therefore suggest that you write or call ahead for confirmation when making your travel plans. The authors, editors, and publisher cannot be held responsible for the experiences of readers while traveling. Your safety is important to us, however, so we encourage you to stay alert and be aware of your surroundings. Keep a close eye on cameras, purses, and wallets, all favorite targets of thieves and pickpockets.

What the Symbols Mean

✪ **Frommer's Favorites**

Our favorite places and experiences—outstanding for quality, value, or both.

The following abbreviations are used for credit cards:

AE American Express	DISC Discover
CB Carte Blanche	MC MasterCard
DC Diners Club	V Visa

Find Frommer's Online

Arthur Frommer's Outspoken Encyclopedia of Travel (www.frommers.com) offers more than 6,000 pages of up-to-the-minute travel information—including the latest bargains and candid, personal articles updated daily by Arthur Frommer himself. No other Web site offers such comprehensive and timely coverage of the world of travel.

The Best of Puerto Rico

Whatever you want to do on a tropical vacation or business trip—play on the beach with the kids (or gamble away their college fund), enjoy a romantic honeymoon, or have a little fun after a grueling negotiating session—you'll find it in Puerto Rico. But you don't want to waste precious hours once you get here searching for the best deals and the best experiences. We've done that work for you. During our years of traveling through the islands that form the Commonwealth of Puerto Rico, we've tested the beaches, toured the sights, reviewed countless restaurants, inspected hotels, and sampled the best scuba, hikes, and other outdoor adventures. We've even learned where to get away from it all when you want to escape the crowds.

Here's what we consider to be the best that Puerto Rico has to offer.

1 The Best Beaches

White, sandy beaches put Puerto Rico and its offshore islands on world tourist maps in the first place. This is not true of many other Caribbean islands with only jagged coral outcroppings or black volcanic-sand beaches that get very hot in the noonday sun.

- **Luquillo Beach:** About 30 miles east of San Juan, Luquillo Beach sits in a crescent-shaped bay edged by a vast coconut grove, which makes it not only the best in Puerto Rico, but one of the finest beaches in the entire Caribbean. Coral reefs protecting the crystal-clear lagoon subdue the often-fierce Atlantic waters that can batter this coast. Much photographed because of its white sands, it also has tent sites and other facilities, including picnic areas with changing rooms, lockers, and showers. Regrettably, Luquillo Beach isn't as well maintained as it used to be, although it remains the favorite of beach buffs from San Juan. In winter, it's also inhabited by "snowbirds" (condo owners from up north who live nearby). See chapter 7.
- **Condado Beach:** San Juan's Condado Beach may not be the best, but it is the Caribbean's most famous—which helps explain why it often is overcrowded in winter. Once the stamping ground of the rich, including the Vanderbilts and the Rockefellers, it has long bands of white sand bordering some of the Caribbean's finest resort hotels. When the Condado comes to an end as it

stretches toward the airport, the beaches of Isla Verde come into the picture. See chapter 7.

- **Playa Dorado:** West of San Juan, Playa Dorado actually is a term for six white-sand beaches along the northern coast, reached by a series of winding roads. This is the setting for the Hyatt hotel resorts. Although not as famous as Luquillo, the beaches here are better maintained and are a real family favorite. See chapter 8.

- **Palmas del Mar** (Humacao; ☎ 800/725-6273 in the U.S., or 787/852-6000): The huge Palmas del Mar resort near Humacao on the eastern coast of Puerto Rico has been called "the new American Riviera." The architectural dream of this 2,750-acre playground resort built on a former coconut plantation hasn't been realized yet, but the site sports 3 miles of white-sand beaches. Unlike some of the rough-water beaches near Rincón in the west, the sea here is tranquil and calm year-round. There's also a water-sports center and marina. See chapter 8.

- **Playa de Ponce:** The beaches on the southeast coast west of Ponce, the "second city" of Puerto Rico, are far less crowded than those of the Condado, Luquillo, and Dorado. This long strip of white sand opens onto the tranquil waters of the Caribbean. Several very good seafood restaurants are found in the vicinity. See chapter 9.

- **Boquerón Beach:** South of Mayagüez, in the town of the same name, Boquerón Beach is the Cape Cod of Puerto Rico. The town itself stands at the heart of a 3-mile bay, with palm-fringed white sand curving away on both sides. Fishermen and women, sailors, scuba divers, and windsurfers, as well as beach devotees, are attracted to this beach, where fresh oysters shucked on the spot and doused with Tabasco are sold from shacks. Here the ice cream is made with sweet corn and dusted with paprika (it sounds awful, but tastes good). See chapter 9.

- **The Secret Beaches:** The main island is filled with isolated sandy coves that only the locals seem to know about. The best, all guaranteed to delight the escapist in you, stretch between Cabo Rojo (the southwesterly tip of Puerto Rico) all the way east to Ponce. Beginning in the west, directly east of Cabo Rojo, you'll dis-cover Bahia Sucia Beach, Rosada Beach, Santa Beach, Manglillos Beach (with a recreation area), Caña Gorda Beach, Tamarindo Beach, and Ballena Beach. Access to many of these beaches is limited because of poor roads, but the effort to reach them is worth it. Bring along what supplies you'll need. See chapter 10.

- **The Beaches of Vieques & Culebra:** To escape the crowds head for the isolated beaches of the offshore islands of Vieques and Culebra. In Vieques alone there are some 40 beaches, most of them unnamed even though U.S. sailors have nick-named their favorites—everything from Green Beach to Orchid. Sun Bay (Sombe), a public beach on Vieques, is one of our favorites—a splendid crescent of sand with picnic tables and a bathhouse. The beaches of the less-visited island of Culebra are known to savvy aficionados. Here you will find white-sand strips studding the island and opening onto coral reefs and clear waters. Playa Fla-menco Beach is the best, lying on the north shore of the island. This 3-mile-long crescent has shade trees and facilities including picnic tables. It's popular with day-trippers from Fajardo, especially on weekends. See chapter 11.

2 The Best Scuba Diving

With the continental shelf surrounding it on three sides, Puerto Rico has an abun-dance of coral reefs, caves, sea walls, and trenches to be explored by divers of all levels of experience. See "The Active Vacation Planner," in chapter 3, for detailed information.

- **Metropolitan San Juan:** More convenient if not as spectacular as those mentioned below is an easy beach dive off the Condado district in San Juan. Lava reefs sculptured with caverns, tunnels, and overhangs host hiding areas for schools of snapper, grunts, and copper sweepers. The inner and outer reefs here are active breeding spots where divers of all levels can mingle with an impressive array of small tropical fish—French angels, jacks, bluehead wrasse, butterfly fish, and sergeant majors, among them—along with sea horses, arrow crabs, coral shrimp, octopuses, batfish, and flying gunards. Visibility is about 10 to 20 feet. The Condado reef is also ideal for resort courses, certification courses, and night dives. See chapters 3 and 7.
- **Fajardo:** This coastal town in eastern Puerto Rico offers divers the opportunity to explore ringing reefs, small caverns, miniwalls, and channels below a string of palm-tufted islets. The reefs are decked in an array of corals ranging from delicate gorgonians to immense coral heads. Visibility usually exceeds 50 feet. You can hand-feed some of the full assortment of reef fish that inhabit the corals. Sand channels and a unique double barrier-reef system surround Palomino Island, where bandtailed puffers and parrot-fish harems are frequently sighted. Cayo Diablo farther to the east provides a treasure box of corals and marine animals, from green moray eels and barracudas to octopuses and occasional manatees. See chapters 3 and 8.
- **Humacao Region:** South of Fajardo are some 24 dive sites in a 5-mile radius of the shore. Overhangs, caves, and tunnels perch in 60 feet of water along mile-long Basslet Reef, where dolphins visit in spring. At "The Cracks," a jigsaw of caves, alleyways, and boulders hosts an abundance of goby-cleaning stations and shelters a number of lobsters. With visibility often exceeding 100 feet, the Reserve offers a clear look at corals. At the Drift, divers float along with nurse sharks and angelfish into a valley of swim-throughs and ledges. For the experienced diver, "Red Hog" is the newest site in the area, with a panoramic wall that drops from 80 to 1,160 feet. See chapters 3 and 8.
- **Southern Puerto Rico:** The continental shelf drops off precipitously several miles off the southern coast, producing a dramatic wall 20 miles long and teeming with marine life. Compared favorably to the Cayman Islands' wall, the Puerto Rican version has become the Caribbean's newest world-class dive destination. Paralleling the coast from the seaside village of La Parguera to the city of Ponce, the wall descends in slopes and sheer drops from 60 to 120 feet before disappearing into 1,500 feet of sea. Scored with valleys and deep trenches, it is cloaked in immense gardens of staghorn and elkhorn coral, deep-water gorgonians, and other exquisite coral formations. Visibility can exceed 100 feet. There are more than 50 dive sites around Parguera alone. See chapters 3 and 9.
- **Mona Island:** Mona Island, 40 miles west of the city of Mayagüez in western Puerto Rico, is considered to be the Caribbean version of the Galápagos Islands. Renowned for its pirate tales, cave-pocked cliffs, 3-foot-long iguanas, and other works of nature, its waters are among the cleanest in Puerto Rico, with horizontal visibility at times exceeding 200 feet. More than 270 species of fish have been found in Mona waters, including more than 60 reef-dwelling species. Larger marine animals, such as sea turtles, whales, dolphins, and marlins, visit the region during migrations. Various types of coral reefs, underwater caverns, drop-offs, and deep vertical walls ring the island. The most accessible reef dives are along the southern and western shores. Getting there is a pain, however. You must brave a 5-hour boat ride across the often rough Mona Passage. See chapters 3 and 9.

3 The Best Golf & Tennis

- **Rio Mar Golf Course** (Palmer; ☎ **787/888-8811**): A 45-minute drive from San Juan on the northeast coast, the 6,145-yard Rio Mar Golf Course is shorter than those at both Palmas del Mar and Dorado East. One avid golfer recommended it to "those whose games and egos have been bruised by the other two courses." Wind here can seriously influence the outcome of your game. The greens fees here are also a lot less expensive than those of its two major competitors. See chapter 7.

- **Hyatt Resorts Caribbean** (Dorado; ☎ **800/233-1234** in the U.S., or 787/796-1234): With 72 holes, Dorado has the highest concentration of golf on the island. Two courses—east and west—belong to the Hyatt Regency Cerromar and the Hyatt Dorado Beach resorts. Dorado East is our favorite. Designed by Robert Trent Jones, Sr., it has been the site of the Senior PGA Tournament of Champions all during the 1990s.

    And true tennis buffs head here, too. The Dorado courts are the best on the island, and both hotels sponsor tennis weeks and offer special tennis packages. The Hyatt Regency Cerromar has 14 Laykold courts alone, two of them lit for night play. The Hyatt Regency Dorado weighs in with five Laykold courts, two of them lighted. See chapter 8.

- **El Conquistador Resort & Country Club** (Las Croabas; ☎ **800/468-5228** in the U.S., or 787/863-1000): This sprawling resort east of San Juan is one of the island's finest tennis retreats, with seven Har-Tru courts and a pro on hand to offer guidance and advice. If you don't have a partner, the hotel will find one for you. Only guests of the hotel are allowed to play here. See chapter 8.

- **The Club de Golf at Palmas del Mar** (Humacao; ☎ **800/725-6273** in the U.S., or 787/852-6000): Lying on the southeast coast on the grounds of a former coconut plantation, the Palmas del Mar resort complex sports the second-leading course in Puerto Rico—a par-72, 6,803-yard layout designed by Gary Player. Crack golfers consider holes 11 through 15 the toughest five successive holes in the Caribbean. See chapter 8.

- **Palmas del Mar** (Humacao; ☎ **800/725-6273** or 787/852-0000): On the eastern coastline, this resort complex on the grounds of a former coconut plantation has 20 courts, of which 5 are Har-Tru and 15 are Tenneflex (a harder surface). Seven of the courts are lighted. The resort offers tennis packages, and an on-site pro conducts private lessons. See chapter 8.

4 The Best Hikes

Bring your boots, for Puerto Rico's mountainous interior offers ample opportunity for hiking and climbing, with many trails presenting spectacular panoramas at the least-expected moments. See "The Active Vacation Planner," in chapter 3, for detailed information.

- **El Yunque** (☎ **787/888-1810** for information): Containing the only rain forest on U.S. soil, this Caribbean National Forest east of San Juan offers a number of walking and hiking trails. The rugged El Toro trail passes through four different forest systems en route to the 3,523-foot Pico El Toro, the highest peak in the forest. El Yunque trail leads to three of the recreation area's most panoramic lookouts, and the Big Tree Trail is an easy walk to La Mina Falls. Just off the main road is La Coca Falls, a sheet of water cascading down mossy cliffs. See chapters 2 and 10.

- **Guánica State Forest** (☎ 787/724-3724 for information): At the opposite extreme of El Yunque's lush and wet rain forest, Guánica State Forest's climate is dry and arid, its Arizona-like landscape riddled with cacti. The area, cut off from the Cordillera Central mountain range, gets little rainfall. Yet it's home to some 50% of all the island's terrestrial bird species, including the rare Puerto Rican nightjar, once thought to be extinct. The forest has 36 miles of trails through four forest types. We prefer the mile-long Cueva Trail, where hikers look for the endangered bufo lemur toad, another species thought to be extinct but still jumping in this area. Within the forest, El Portal Tropical Forest Center offers 10,000 square feet of exhibition space about the forest and provides information. See chapter 9.

- **Mona Island:** Off the western coast of Puerto Rico, this fascinating island noted for its scuba-diving sites also provides hiking opportunities found nowhere else in the Caribbean. Called the Galápagos of Puerto Rico because of its unique wildlife, Mona is home to giant iguanas and three species of endangered sea turtles. Some 20 endangered animals also have been spotted here. Eco-tourists like to hike among Mona's mangrove forests, coral reefs, cliffs, and complex honeycomb of caves, ever on the alert for the diversity of both plant and animal life, including 417 plant and tree species, some of which are unique and 78 of which are rare or endangered. More than 100 bird species have been documented, 2 of which are unique. Hikers can camp out at Mona for $1 a night. Contact the **Puerto Rico Department of Natural Resources** (☎ 787/724-3724) for more information. See chapter 9.

5 The Best Natural Wonders

- **El Yunque** (☎ 787/888-1810 for information): Lying 45 minutes by road east of San Juan in the Luquillo Mountains, and protected by the U.S. Forest Service, El Yunque is Puerto Rico's greatest natural attraction. Some 100 billion gallons of rain fall annually on this home to four forest types containing 240 species of tropical trees. Families can walk one of the dozens of trails that wind past waterfalls, dwarf vegetation, and miniature flowers, while the island's colorful parrots fly overhead. You can hear the sound of Puerto Rico's mascot, the *coquí,* a small frog. See chapters 2 and 10.

- **Río Camuy Cave Park** (☎ 787/898-2770): Some 2½ hours west of San Juan, visitors board a tram to descend into this forest-filled sinkhole at the mouth of the Clara Cave. They walk the footpaths of a 170-foot-high cave to a deeper sinkhole. Once they're inside, a 45-minute tour helps everyone, including kids, learn to differentiate stalactites from stalagmites. At the Pueblos sinkhole a platform overlooks the Camuy River, passing through a network of cave tunnels. See chapter 10.

- **Las Cabezas de San Juan Nature Reserve** (☎ 787/722-5834): This 316-acre nature reserve lying only 45 minutes from San Juan encompasses seven different ecological systems, including forest land, mangroves, lagoons, beaches, cliffs, and offshore coral reefs. Visitors may tour the reserve's nature center and 19th-century working lighthouse, El Faro, offering a view of distant Caribbean islands, but call before going, because reservations are required. See chapter 10.

6 The Best Family Resorts

Puerto Rico has a bounty of attractions, natural wonders, and resorts welcoming families who choose to play together.

- **Condado Plaza Hotel & Casino** (San Juan; ☎ **800/468-8588** in the U.S., or 787/721-1000): This resort offers Camp Taíno, a regular program of activities and special events for children ages 4 to 12. The cost of $25 per child includes lunch. The main pool has a kids' water slide starting in a Spanish-castle turret, plus a toddler pool. For teenagers, the hotel has a video game room, tennis courts, and various organized activities. For the whole family, the resort offers two pools and opens onto a public beach. It also has the best collection of restaurants of any hotel on the Condado. See chapter 5.
- **El San Juan Hotel & Casino** (San Juan; ☎ **800/468-2818** in the U.S., or 787/791-1000): The grandest hotel in Puerto Rico lies on Isla Verde, the less-famous beach strip connecting with El Condado in San Juan. Its Kids Klub features trained counselors and group activities for the 5-to-13 age set. A daily fee of $28 buys lunch and an array of activities. The hotel opens onto a good beachfront and has some of the best restaurants in San Juan. See chapter 5.
- **Hyatt Resorts Caribbean** (Dorado; ☎ **800/233-1234** in the U.S., or 787/796-1234): Sitting 18 miles west of San Juan, the Hyatt Regency Cerromar Beach Resort & Casino and the Hyatt Dorado Beach Resort & Casino share a Camp Hyatt program available for guests ages 3 to 12. Certified counselors direct programs of educational, environmental, and cultural activities. In the evening, movies, talent shows, and video games occupy the agenda. All this costs $40 a day per kid. Parents find one of the largest beaches and resort complexes in the Caribbean, including the world's longest freshwater river pool. See chapter 8.
- **El Conquistador Resort & Country Club** (Las Croabas; ☎ **800/468-5228** in the U.S., or 787/863-1000): Located 31 miles east of San Juan, this resort offers Camp Coquí on Palomino Island for children 3 to 12 years of age. The hotel's water taxi takes kids there for a half or full day of water sports, nature hikes, and island crafts, costing $19 for a half day or $38 for a full day. This resort has some of the best facilities and restaurants in eastern Puerto Rico. See chapter 8.
- **Palmas del Mar Resort** (Humacao; ☎ **800/725-6273** in the U.S., or 787/852-6000): The major rival in the east to El Conquistador, this sprawling resort has an Adventure Club for children ages 3 to 13. Supervised activities include arts, crafts, and sports, plus horseback riding for those old enough. For nonguests, the cost is $22 per half day or $28 daily, including lunch. Hotel guests may enroll their children free. Family packages are sold for as low as $100 per person per night, based on four-person occupancy of a room. The resort is one of the most extensive in the Caribbean, with beaches, restaurants, and lots of water sports. See chapter 8.

7 The Best Honeymoon Resorts

- **El San Juan Hotel & Casino** (San Juan; ☎ **800/468-2818** in the U.S., or 787/791-1000): If you want Vegas-style shows, gambling, nightlife, great restaurants, and the most famous beach in Puerto Rico, El San Juan is at your disposal. It has the most glamorous lobby in the Caribbean and is set on 12 acres at Isla Verde. Options include a suite in the main tower with a whirlpool or your own private casita with a sunken Roman bath. The best deal is a package, costing from

$290 to $460 per night for 6 nights, with the 7th night free. A lot of freebies are thrown in, including champagne and strawberries, daily tennis, free continental breakfast, two free massages, and free admission to the disco and fitness center. See chapter 5.

- **Hyatt Dorado Beach Resort** (Dorado; ☎ **800/233-1234** in the U.S., or 787/796-1234): This resort offers a more tranquil atmosphere than the nearby Hyatt Regency Cerromar, yet guests here can partake of all the facilities and attractions of its neighbor. You can book one of the elegantly furnished upper-level rooms in the Oceanview Houses and enjoy romantic vistas of two crescent-shaped beaches. There's casino and disco action, plus a spa, a health club, jogging trails, and 14 tennis courts. Packages in low season begin at $1,635 for two for the week, including one breakfast, one dinner, and transfers to and from the airport. In high season the tab rises by $300 a week per honeymooning couple, but breakfast and dinner are included. See chapter 8.

- **El Conquistador Resort & Country Club** (Las Croabas; ☎ **800/468-5228** in the U.S., or 787/863-1000): If you'd like lots of good food and plenty of diversions on your honeymoon instead of a romantic tranquil retreat, El Conquistador is the best sprawling big-time resort on the island. Atop a 300-foot bluff in eastern Puerto Rico, it has virtually everything when you want to play outside, including golf and tennis, but when you want seclusion you can post the PRIVADO sign and the world is yours. It offers a $460 per night honeymoon package (based on 3 nights and 4 days), with many specials such as champagne, a golf clinic, a half-day snorkeling trip, nonmotorized water sports, and even transfers to and from the airport. If you stay a full week, the cost of this package is reduced to $395 per honeymooning night. See chapter 8.

- **Palmas del Mar Resort** (Humacao; ☎ **800/725-6273** in the U.S., or 787/852-6000): This luxury resort complex sits on 2,750 acres of a former coconut plantation on Puerto Rico's sheltered southeast coast. It takes only about an hour's drive from San Juan for another world to unfold, with Mediterranean villas, cobblestone plazas, condos, and Spanish-style fountains. The Palmas Inn suites are best for honeymooners, unless you want to rent a private villa. You get some of the best golf on the island here, along with 20 tennis courts, a spa and health club, and miles of hiking and jogging trails. Honeymoon packages for 7 nights and 8 days begin in the range of $1,165 to $1,628. Of course, you can live more luxuriously here, but included in this package are champagne, a fruit basket, and a free continental breakfast daily, plus one dinner and one lunch. See chapter 8.

- **Ponce Hilton and Casino** (Ponce; ☎ **800/HILTONS** in the U.S., or 787/259-7676): A first-class act at Puerto Rico's "second city" on the south coast, this sprawling resort is set in an 80-acre garden. There are both a casino and a disco, plus lots of amusements, including a Jacuzzi, tennis courts, and a fitness room. Eight suites are ideal for honeymoons. Its two restaurants also serve the best food on the south coast. The first night costs $209, including a bottle of champagne, truffles, chocolates, and fresh strawberries as a gift. Each additional night is only $160. See chapter 9.

- **Horned Dorset Primavera** (Rincón; ☎ **787/823-4030**): The most romantic place for a honeymoon on the island unless you stay in a private villa somewhere, this small, tranquil estate lies on the Mona Passage in western Puerto Rico, a pocket of posh where privacy is almost guaranteed. Accommodations are luxurious in the Spanish neocolonial style. The property opens onto a long secluded beach of white sand. There are no phones, TVs, or radios in the rooms to interfere with the soft sounds of pillow talk. This is a retreat for adults only, with no facilities for children. Seven-night packages, including a bottle of champagne, breakfast, dinner, and airport transfers, range from $2,000 to $4,000, depending on the season. See chapter 9.

8 The Best Big Resort Hotels

- **El San Juan Hotel & Casino** (San Juan; ☎ **800/468-2818** in the U.S., or 787/791-1000): An opulent circular lobby sets the haute style at the Caribbean's most elegant resort. From its location along Isla Verde Beach, it houses some of the capital's finest restaurants and is the city's major entertainment venue. Guest rooms are tropically designed and maintained in state-of-the-art condition. See chapter 5.

- **The Ritz-Carlton** (San Juan; ☎ **800/241-3333** or 787/253-1700): At last Puerto Rico has a Ritz-Carlton, and this truly deluxe hostelry on prime oceanfront property is one of the island's most spectacular resorts. Guests are pampered in a setting of elegance and beautifully furnished guest rooms. Hotel dining is second only to that at El San Juan, and a European-style spa features 11 treatments "for body and beauty." See chapter 5.

- **Hyatt Dorado Beach Resort** (Dorado; ☎ **800/233-1234** in the U.S., or 787/796-1234): Lying on the former stamping grounds of the Rockefellers, these low-rise buildings blend into their tropical setting in lush surroundings on the site of a grapefruit and coconut plantation. Spacious rooms open onto a long stretch of secluded beach, and grounds include an 18-hole, Robert Trent Jones–designed championship golf course. Tennis, windsurfing, pool swimming, and dozens of water sports are available, as well as the most elegant dining in Dorado. See chapter 8.

- **El Conquistador Resort & Country Club** (Las Croabas; ☎ **800/468-5228** in the U.S., or 787/863-1000): The finest in Puerto Rico, this is a world-class destination—a sybaritic haven for golfers, honeymooners, families, and anyone else. Three intimate "villages" combine with one grand hotel, draped along 300-foot bluffs overlooking both the Atlantic and the Caribbean at Puerto Rico's northeastern tip. The 500 landscaped acres include tennis courts, an 18-hole Arthur Hills–designed championship golf course, and a marina filled with yachts and charter boats. See chapter 8.

- **Westin Rio Mar Beach Resort & Casino** (Rio Grande; ☎ **800/4-Riomar** or 787/888-6000): This $180 million, 481-acre resort, 19 miles east of the San Juan airport, is one of the three largest hotels in Puerto Rico. In spite of its size, personal service and style are hallmarks of the property. Twelve restaurants and lounges boast an array of different cuisines. Along with its proximity to two golf courses, entertainment is a key ingredient in the hotel's success. See chapter 8.

- **Palmas del Mar Resort** (Humacao; ☎ **800/725-6273** in the U.S., or 787/852-6000): Although not as impressive as El Conquistador, this sprawling complex evokes a Mediterranean village, opening onto 3⅓ miles of beach on the east coast of Puerto Rico. Palm trees grow everywhere. The complex boasts the largest tennis center in the Caribbean, plus an 18-hole Gary Player championship golf course, a horseback riding center for beach rides, water sports galore, and an outstanding scuba-diving program, along with deep-sea fishing charters. There's even a casino, plus nine restaurants. See chapter 8.

9 The Best Moderately Priced Hotels

- **Gallery Inn at Galería San Juan** (San Juan; ☎ 787/722-1808): The most whimsically bohemian hotel in the Caribbean sits in the heart of the historic city. Once the home of an aristocratic Spanish family, it is today filled with verdant courtyards and adorned with sculpture, silk screens, and original paintings. Staying in one of these comfortable rooms is like living in an art gallery. See chapter 5.
- **Empress Oceanfront Hotel** (San Juan; ☎ 800/678-0757 or 787/791-3083): Far removed from the deluxe megaresorts along the Condado and Isla Verde beaches, this comfortable establishment is run by a local Anglo-Latino family. Its quiet neighborhood is on 2½ acres of rocky headlands jutting out from the coastline. There are a swimming pool, good spareribs in the hotel restaurant, and a tropical decor. See chapter 5.
- **Copamarina Beach Resort** (Caña Gorda; ☎ 800/468-4553 in the U.S., or 787/821-0505): Near Ponce, this resort was once the private vacation retreat of those local cement barons, the de Castro family. Today it's been converted into one of the best beach hotels along Puerto Rico's southern shore. In fact, its beach is one of the island's best. Set in a palm grove, the resort is handsomely decorated and comfortably furnished, with a swimming pool and two tennis courts. See chapter 9.
- **Hotal Paradores Joyuda Beach** (Cabo Rojo; ☎ 787/851-5650): South of Mayagüez in scenic Cabo Rojo, this idyllic little beachfront hotel is far removed from the tourist-trodden districts. It's on one of the island's finest beaches, and it offers well-furnished and air-conditioned bedrooms. It's a favorite with Puerto Rican honeymooners. See chapter 9.
- **La Casa del Francés** (Vieques Island; ☎ 787/741-3751): A retired French general built this house in 1905, but it now welcomes the few visitors who show up at this remote island outpost. Bedrooms are high-ceilinged and old-fashioned. If you like a funky, laid-back retreat from the world, this is it. See chapter 11.

10 The Best Attractions

- **The Historic District of Old San Juan:** There's nothing like it in the Caribbean. Partially enclosed by old walls dating from the 17th century, Old San Juan has been designated a U.S. National Historic Zone since 1950. Chockablock with shops, tree-shaded squares, monuments, and open-air cafes, along with restaurants and bars, it is filled with some 400 beautifully restored buildings. If you're interested in history, there is no better stroll in the West Indies. See chapter 7.
- **Castillo San Felipe del Morro:** In Old San Juan and nicknamed El Morro, this fort was originally built in 1540. It stands on a rocky promontory on the northwestern tip of the old city guarding the bay. It covers enough territory to accommodate a nine-hole golf course. The place is rich in history and legend. See chapter 7.
- **The Historic District of Ponce:** Second only to Old San Juan, the central district of Ponce is a blend of Ponce Créole and art deco architectural styles, dating mainly from the 1890s to the 1930s. One street, Calle Isabel, offers a textbook of the different Ponceño architectural styles, which often borrowed upon neoclassic details. The city has undergone a massive restoration preceding the celebration of its 300th anniversary in 1996. See chapter 9.

- **Museo de Arte de Ponce:** Also in Ponce, this museum has the finest collection of European and Latin American art in the Caribbean. The building itself was designed by Edward Durell Stone, who also designed the Museum of Modern Art in New York. Contemporary work by Puerto Ricans is displayed, as is an array of old masters, including Renaissance and baroque works from Italy. See chapter 9.
- **Tropical Agriculture Research Station** (Mayagüez): These tropical gardens contain one of the largest collection of tropical species useful to people in the western hemisphere. These include cacao, fruit trees, spices, timbers, and ornamentals. Adjacent to the Mayagüez campus of the University of Puerto Rico, the site attracts botanists from around the world. See chapter 9.
- **The City of San Germán:** In the southwestern corner of Puerto Rico, and founded in 1512, the small town of San Germán is Puerto Rico's second-oldest city. Its 36-acre historic zone is filled with buildings and monuments of historic interest. Surrounded by mountains, San Germán is justly nicknamed the city of the hills. Today's residents are descendants from the smugglers, poets, priests, and politicians of days past. Thanks to the breadth of architectural styles on display on its streets and plazas, San Germán is the second Puerto Rican city (San Juan is the other) to be included in the National Register of Historic Places. See "Driving Tour 2" in chapter 10.
- **Iglesia Porta Coeli** (San Germán): The main attraction of this ancient town is the oldest church in the New World. It was originally built by Dominican friars in 1606. The church is constructed to resemble a working chapel, although mass is held here only three times a year. Along the sides of the church are treasures gathered from all over the world. See "Driving Tour 2" in chapter 10.

11 The Best Restaurants

- **Chef Marisoll** (San Juan; ☎ 787/725-7454): One of Puerto Rico's best chefs, Marisoll Hernández, prepares Old Town's finest cuisine in this Spanish colonial building in the heart of the historic district. With a strong background in classic cooking, she has expanded her repertoire to include innovative and memorable dishes, including her curried chicken with fried sweet bananas, homemade mango chutney, and a saffron risotto. Or try her grilled swordfish with calamata olives. See chapter 6.

- **Parrot Club** (San Juan; ☎ 787/725-7370): This recent addition to the San Juan scene has already been claimed as one of the finest and most innovative restaurants on the island. Its chef serves a Nuevo Latino cuisine that is a happy medley of Puerto Rican delights, drawing upon Spanish, African, and even the Taíno influences of the island. Menu items are based on updated interpretations of old-fashioned regional dishes—everything from *criola*-styled flank steak to a pan-seared tuna served with a sauce of dark rum and essence of oranges. See chapter 6.

- **Ramiro's** (San Juan; ☎ 787/721-9049): Chef Jesús Ramiro has some of the most innovative cookery along the Condado beachfront strip, along with the city's best wine list. Ramiro has made his culinary reputation with such dishes as quail stuffed with lamb in a port sauce and lamb loin in a tamarind coriander sauce, both equally delectable. His dessert menu is two pages long, including the town's best soufflés. His death-by-chocolate mousse on a green grape leaf is equaled only by his caramelized fresh mango Napoleon. See chapter 6.

- **Ajili Mójili** (San Juan; ☎ **787/725-9195**): Also on the Condado beachfront, Ajili Mójili provides the most refined interpretation of classic Puerto Rican cookery on the island. Locals find it evocative of the food they enjoyed at their mother's table. Examples include *mofongos,* green plantains stuffed with veal, chicken, shrimp, or pork. The chefs take that cliché dish, *arroz con pollo* (stewed chicken with saffron rice), and raise it to celestial levels. The restaurant takes its name from the lemon-garlic sweet chili salsa that's traditionally served here with fish or meat. See chapter 6.
- **Augusto's Cuisine** (San Juan; ☎ **787/725-7700**): Originally from Austria, much-awarded chef August Schreiner is a five-time winner of *El Nuevo Día's* Five Fork Award, honoring the island's great chefs. Try any of his lobster or game dishes, such as venison. His chocolate soufflé Grand Marnier is the island's finest. His mother may not have taught him to make one of the city's best seafood paellas, but somebody did—or else he invented it himself. See chapter 6.
- **Aquarela** (in El San Juan Hotel, San Juan; ☎ **787/253-5566**): This charming, award-winning restaurant specializes in modern interpretations of traditional Latin dishes. Its guiding light is chef Douglas Rodriguez, acclaimed with justification as one of the island's finest culinary stars. He adds a personal, innovative touch to almost every dish he touches—even a "twisted" version of skirt steak served with mashed root vegetables and a black-bean broth. See chapter 6.
- **El Ancla** (Ponce; ☎ **787/840-2450**): One of the best restaurants along the southern coast, this is the best place to go for regional specialties and fresh seafood. The cuisine is prepared with zest and flavor, as exemplified by its red snapper stuffed with shrimp and lobster. The chef specializes in paella for two persons and makes a wicked sautéed conch, which one frequent habitué calls "sexy conch." See chapter 9.
- **La Cava** in the Ponce Hilton (Ponce; ☎ **787/259-7676**): The stellar restaurant of this first-class hotel, La Cava is designed like a series of rooms within a 19th-century coffee plantation. It's the most elegant restaurant along the southern tier, and it serves a delectable international cuisine. From the ever-changing menu you are likely to be served everything from grilled lamb sausage on a bed of couscous to tuna loin seared with sesame oil. See chapter 9.

12 The Best Offbeat Travel Experiences

- **Attending a Cockfight:** Although a brutal sport that many find distasteful, cockfighting is legal in Puerto Rico and has its devotees. The most authentic cockfights are in the town of Salinas in the southeast. But it's not necessary to go that far to witness one of these bouts. Three fights a week are held at the **Coliseo Gallistico,** Route 37 (☎ **787/791-6005**) in San Juan. Betting is heavy when these roosters take to the ring. See chapter 7.
- **Taking an Excursion to Monkey Island** (off Palmas del Mar Resort, Humacao): Reached from the marina at Palmas del Mar, the 39-acre islet of Cayo Santiago lies off the eastern shore of Puerto Rico. A boat, *Shagrada,* takes snorkelers and the merely curious over to see an island colony of rhesus monkeys whose ancestors were brought here from India in 1938 for study. Many significant breakthroughs in human medicine have been attributed to observing the behavioral patterns of these rambunctious primates. Passengers aren't allowed to actually go on the island, but you can see the monkeys on the shore, swinging through the trees, playing the mating game, nursing their young, or just "going bananas." See chapter 8.

- **Doing the "Wet and Dry Tour" in Guánica** (near Ponce): Southern Puerto Rico is the site of the world's largest remaining tract of dry coastal forest, and this part of the island allows you to explore miles of mangrove channel systems. **Tropix Wellness Tours** (☎ **787/268-2173**) takes you into a part of the island rarely explored by visitors. Two expeditions combine a dry forest hike with mangrove kayaking at sunset. After traversing waterways by kayaks, you're led to secluded island beaches. It's a 4-day, 3-night adventure that is fully escorted. See chapters 3 and 9.

- **Diving off Mona Island** (Mayagüez): Surrounded by some of the most beautiful coral reefs in the Caribbean, Mona Island has the most pristine, extensive, and well-developed reefs in Puerto Rican waters. In fact, they have been nominated as a U.S. National Marine Sanctuary. The tropical marine ecosystem around Mona includes patch reefs, black coral, spore and groove systems, underwater caverns, deep-water sponges, fringing reefs, and algal reefs. The lush environment attracts octopuses, lobster, queen conch, rays, barracuda, snapper, jack, grunt, angelfish, trunkfish, filefish, butterfly fish, dolphin, parrot fish, tuna, flying fish, and more. The crystal waters afford exceptional horizontal vision from 150 to 200 feet, as well as good views down to the shipwrecks that mark the site—including some Hispanic galleons. Five species of whales visit the island's offshore waters. See chapter 9.

- **Visiting Vieques & Culebra:** Puerto Rico's offshore islands—still relatively undiscovered by the modern world—remain an offbeat adventure, and they've got great beaches too. The most developed is Vieques, off the east coast (as is Culebra). Vieques attracts with its gorgeous stretches of sand with picnic facilities and shade trees. It is an ideal retreat for snorkelers and for tranquillity seekers. Although nearly three-quarters of the island is owned by the U.S. Navy, you'll never know you're visiting a military complex. The beaches are nearly always deserted, and they are among the Caribbean's loveliest. Culebra is even less developed, yet its Playa Flamenco is also one of the Caribbean's finest beaches. In addition to its lovely sand beaches, Culebra has a wildlife refuge and coral reefs. And is it ever sleepy here! See chapter 11.

- **Spending the Evening at Mosquito (Phosphorescent) Bay** (Vieques Island): At any time except when there's a full moon, you're taken out in a boat to swim in glowing waters that are lit by dinoflagellates called *pyrodiniums* (whirling fire). These creatures light up the waters like fireflies, and swimming among them is one of the most unusual things to do in Puerto Rico—truly a magical, almost psychedelic experience. It's estimated that a gallon of bay water might contain about three quarters of a million of these little glowing creatures. See chapter 11.

- **Sampling the Island's Nosh Pits:** Think of Puerto Rico as one gigantic fast-food joint, for no other island in the Caribbean offers such a delectable array of roadside eats. Snack food lies in wait around virtually every turn in the road in Puerto Rico. As you drive throughout the island, stop and take your pick of the roadside dives. They may look junky, even trashy, but the food is often a delight—and cheap too.

  You'll find succulent barbecued pig, *pastelillos* (pastry turnovers filled with meat, cheese, or seafood), *surullitos* (deep-fried cornmeal sticks), *alcapurrias* (a filling of fish or meat in a deep-fried casing of finely grated green plantains and taro root), *bacalaitos* (deep-fried codfish fritters), *papas rellenas* (stuffed potatoes), and *arañitas* ("little spiders"—actually, deep-fried clusters of shredded green plantains).

You don't have to go far for barbecued pig—just head to the roadside food stands in Luquillo Beach, to the east of San Juan. It makes for a great picnic at the beach.

A truck stop, **Café Restaurant La Nueva Union,** 35 miles west of San Juan at the junction of Carretera 2 and Highway 22 between Arecibo and Hatillo (☎ **787/878-2353**), serves the most succulent of traditional fare. Sample its fresh octopus salad, its meaty goat stew, and definitely its *guisados,* or beef stew. Don't leave without an order of coconut flan.

If you make it all the way around the island to La Parguera, stop at **El Quenepo,** a towable lunch wagon parked under a towering *quenepa* (a tropical fruit tree). It sits on Route 116 between routes 304 and 324. Usually you can spot it by a line of cars letting passengers out to sample the delights from its crowded peanut-size kitchen. El Quenepo offers a vast array of Puerto Rican specialties, many of which you may never have sampled before: cold codfish soup, even a green bean omelette, and *piononos* (a "mountain" composed of fried eggs, plantain strips, and seasoned meat filling).

2 Getting to Know Puerto Rico

"It's heaven and hell—all rolled into one tiny island," a Trenton, New Jersey, woman confided to us about Puerto Rico on a return flight from San Juan to Miami. "My husband loved it. I couldn't wait to get back home. But then he's a golfer and a fisherman, and while he was doing that, there were only so many crafts I could buy."

The woman saw only the island's crime, unemployment, bad traffic, and what to her was "poor food." But in spite of its many critics, Puerto Rico must be doing something right. Of course, you can get bad food here, but in many places the island's cuisine, an adaptation of many cooking styles, is the finest in the Caribbean.

Ever since Castro in the early 1960s started chasing the gringos out of Havana, Puerto Rico has blossomed as a tourist destination, with its towering mountains, rain forests, long beaches, and vibrant Spanish culture.

"If you want your Caribbean with a Latin beat, come here," one tour operator told us. "There's nobody who does it better than us." And he's basically right.

History buffs will get more ancient buildings and monuments here than anywhere else in the entire Caribbean, many of them dating back to the Spanish conquistadores some 500 years ago. Add some of the best golf and tennis in the West Indies, posh beach resorts, tranquil and offbeat (though not luxurious) government *paradores* (guest houses), and lots of Las Vegas–type gambling, glitter, and even extravagant shows, and you've got a formidable attraction.

Yes, there are problems here. As in many major cities, you could be mugged or have your car stolen or even hijacked. Service personnel are often gruff and unhelpful. Although there are country retreats where you can escape the masses, San Juan and most of the rest of the island is simply overcrowded.

There is also some anti-American sentiment here. Not all locals passionately embrace Uncle Sam. When we were seeking some real lowdown salsa joints away from the tourist hordes, a taxi driver told us, "I can take you to a club—maybe several clubs—but I'm not sure you'd get back in one piece."

Yet for all its drawbacks, we still love Puerto Rico and rate it as one of the top destinations in the Caribbean, right up there with Aruba, St. Thomas, Jamaica, Barbados, and all the other front-running islands. Visit after visit over so very many years confirms our original impression: Puerto Rico wakes up life in the sleepy Caribbean.

1 The Natural Environment: Beaches, Mountains, the Rain Forest & More

Roughly half the size of New Jersey, this American commonwealth with 272 miles of Atlantic and Caribbean coastline sits strategically some 1,000 miles southeast of Florida at the hub of the Caribbean chain of islands. You'll probably fly in and out of San Juan at least once if you're doing much touring in the region. And with a 2-year, $2.8 million project having restored its waterfront, this oldest capital city under the U.S. flag is also the world's second-largest home port for cruise-ship passengers.

Puerto Rico has experienced many political changes since the days of its first Spanish governor, Juan Ponce de León, the conquistador who sailed with Columbus and who tried in vain to find a fountain of youth in Florida. With nearly 500 years reflected in its restored Spanish colonial architecture, Old San Juan is the Caribbean's greatest historic center.

Puerto Rico is the most easterly and the smallest of the four major islands that form the Greater Antilles. The other three are Cuba, Jamaica, and Hispaniola (which is home to two nations, Haiti and the Dominican Republic). Surrounded by the Atlantic Ocean to the north and the Caribbean Sea to the south, Puerto Rico is flanked by a trio of smaller islands—Vieques and Culebra to the east and Mona to the west—which are its political and geologic satellites.

The island's terrain ranges from palm-lined beaches on four coastlines to rugged mountain ranges, gently rolling hills, and dry desert-like areas. There are 20 designated forest reserves in Puerto Rico, and 6 more may be added.

BEACHES

The island has dozens of miles of sandy beaches, some long and straight, others broken into coves by headlands. On the northern coast, the Atlantic waters are often more turbulent than those along the more tranquil southern coast. Some stretches near San Juan and the major resorts are incredibly crowded, but it's still possible to find a quiet, remote beach. The big resorts have claimed the most ideal beaches, but even so, they are still open to the public. Public bathing beaches in Puerto Rico are called *balnearios*. These are government-run, with lifeguards, parking, and dressing rooms. For more information about Puerto Rico's beaches, refer to the **Department of Recreation and Sports** (☎ 787/722-1551).

In the northeast of the island are 6 miles of relatively unspoiled beaches, with waters ranging from calm to raging. Visits to El Yunque, the rain forest, are often combined with a stopover at the most popular (and the best) beach in the northeast, **Luquillo Beach,** a balneario. There's a huge stand of majestic coconut palms that shade more than a mile of sand. Dressing facilities, parking, and lockers are found here. It is the major beach used by residents of San Juan, and it tends to be overcrowded on weekends, especially at places where the most facilities are located.

Some of the best beaches of Puerto Rico are in the east—but offshore—on the two small islands of **Culebra** and **Vieques.** In Culebra, the white-sand beaches, particularly Flamenco Beach, have clear waters and scenic coral reefs, including a mile-long formation off Culebrita, where there is also a lighthouse.

The adjoining island, Vieques, contains numerous scalloped beaches along the north and northwest coasts, all of which lie on U.S. Navy land and are open to the public when no military maneuvers are going on.

On the south coast, the best beaches are centered near the fishing village of **La Parguera,** which becomes busy and bustling on weekends, when locals pour in for fun in the sun. Numerous mangrove cays and islets here form ornate channels in places, attracting boaters. Swimmers and picnickers prefer **Rosada Beach** or **Mata de la Gata Cay,** the best beaches in the area. Snorkelers and scuba divers explore the reefs and the outer shelf walls that lie 7 miles offshore.

On the west coast the best beach is along the bay at **Boquerón,** part of the municipality of Cabo Rojo. The area opens onto a mile of white sand bordered by clear water. Long a balneario, it is frequented mainly by locals. The beach is popular for swimming and picnicking under coconut palms. Nearby is the Boquerón Lagoon, a refuge for ducks and other birds.

In the northwest, rough Atlantic waters deter bathers but attract surfers. Scuba divers and snorkelers also gravitate to a beach here known as "**The Shacks,**" lying near Isabela. They swim among its coral caverns and reefs, whereas surfers head for **Jobos Beach.**

TOWERING MOUNTAINS

Other than these beaches, the island's most noteworthy geological feature is the **Cordillera**—the towering mountains that rise high above its central region. Geologists have identified the island's summits as the high parts of a chain of mountains whose mass is mostly submerged beneath the sea. These mountains, the oldest of the many land masses of the West Indies, form a dramatic relief in Puerto Rico.

What makes mountains' altitudes even more impressive is the existence, about 75 miles to the island's north, of one of the deepest depressions in the Atlantic, the Puerto Rico Trough. Running more or less parallel to the island's northern shoreline, it plunges to depths of up to 30,000 feet. Although not as obvious as this trench near the northern coastline, the sea floor a few miles from the island's southern coast also drops off, to nearly 17,000 feet below sea level. Geologists have calculated that if the base of this mountain chain were at sea level, it would be one of the highest land masses in the world. Puerto Rico's highest summit—Cerro de Punta at 4,389 feet—would exceed in altitude even Mt. Everest, the world's tallest peak.

Most of Puerto Rico's geology, especially its mountain peaks, resulted from volcanic activity that deposited lava and igneous rock in consecutive layers. To a lesser degree, the island is also composed of quartz, diomites, and, along some of its edges, coral limestone.

EL YUNQUE & THE RAIN FORESTS

The mountains are home to the island's greatest natural attraction, ✪ **El Yunque** (☎ **787/887-2875** for information), a 45-minute drive east of San Juan. Given national park status by President Theodore Roosevelt, this 28,000-acre preserve is the only tropical rain forest on U.S. soil and is protected by the U.S. Forest Service. On these soaring peaks, the virgin forest remains much like it was in 1493 when Columbus first sighted Puerto Rico.

Today, El Yunque offers its visitors close encounters of the natural kind, from picnics amid rare flora and fauna to hikes along the scenic trails. Encompassing four distinct forest types, it is home to 240 species of tropical trees; flowers, including more than 20 kinds of orchids; and other wildlife, including millions of tiny tree frogs whose distinctive cry of *coquí* (pronounced *ko-kee*) has given them their name. Tropical birds include the lively, greenish blue- and red-fronted Puerto Rican parrot, once nearly extinct and now making a comeback. Other rare animals include the Puerto Rican boa, which grows to 7 feet, and 26 animal species found nowhere else in the world.

El Yunque also offers a number of walking and hiking trails, including the rugged "El Toro," which passes through four different forest systems en route to the 3,523-foot Pico El Toro, the highest peak in the forest. El Yunque Trail leads to three of the recreation area's most spectacular lookouts, and Big Tree Trail is an easy walk to the panoramic La Mina Falls. Just off the main road is La Coca Falls, a sheet of water cascading down mossy cliffs.

Puerto Rico also has 19 other forest preserves. Directly east of San Juan lies **Piñones Forest,** which contains the island's largest mangrove forest. West of Ponce, **Guánica Forest** borders several white-sand beaches and the historic bay where U.S. troops first landed in 1898 during the Spanish-American War. **Cambalache Forest,** east of Arecibo, contains plantations of eucalyptus, teak, and mahoe trees. The driest vegetation is found in **Maricao Forest,** which also has a new visitor center and expansive views to the west coast. **Toro Negro Forest,** which straddles the peaks of the Cordillera in the center of the island, boasts the island's tallest peak with stunning drops to the Caribbean and the Atlantic. All these forests are open to visitors, and several have picnic areas and campsites.

THE KARST COUNTRY & CAVES

One of the most interesting areas of Puerto Rico to explore is the "**Karst Country.**" One of the world's strangest rock formations, karst is formed by the process of water sinking into limestone. As time goes by, larger and larger basins are eroded, forming sinkholes. Mogotes or karstic hillocks are peaks of earth where the land didn't sink into the erosion pits. The Karst Country lies along the island's north coast, directly northeast of Mayagüez in the foothills between Quebradillas and Manatí. The region is filled with an extensive network of caves. One sinkhole contains the 20-acre dish of the world's largest radio/radar telescope at the Arecibo Observatory. For the best way to see this region, refer to Driving Tour 2 in chapter 10, "Island Drives."

Reached by Route 446, the **Guajataca Forest Reserve** is found here, offering some 25 miles of trails that take you through some of the most rugged part of this country.

Eons ago, one of the world's largest underground rivers carved the **Rio Camuy Caves** in northwest Puerto Rico, which experts today consider to be among the most spectacular on earth. Although relatively new to today's visitors, the Rio Camuy Caves contain evidence of occupation long before the island was sighted by Columbus in 1493. The first professional explorers of the system were led to the site by local boys already familiar with some of the entrances.

Camuy Cave Park opens access to **Tres Pueblos Sinkhole,** measuring 65 feet in diameter with a depth of 400 feet—room enough to fit in all of El Morro Fortress in San Juan. Tres Pueblos, located on the boundaries of the Camuy, Hatillo, and Lares municipalities, is one of two sinkholes in the Rio Camuy Cave system now adapted for visitors. The other, Cueva Clara de Empalme, opened in 1986 and has been the park's featured attraction for the past 7 years.

In Tres Pueblos, visitors can walk along two platforms—one on the Lares side facing the town of Camuy and the other on the Hatillo side overlooking Tres Pueblos Cave and the Rio Camuy.

2 The Regions in Brief

Although the many geological divisions of Puerto Rico might not be immediately apparent to the ordinary visitor, its people take great pride in stressing the island's diversity. Its most important geological and political divisions are detailed next.

SAN JUAN

The largest and best-preserved complex of Spanish colonial architecture in the Caribbean, Old San Juan (founded in 1521) is the oldest capital city under the U.S. flag. Once a linchpin of Spanish dominance in the Caribbean, it has three major fortresses, miles of solidly built stone ramparts, a charming collection of antique buildings, and a modern business center. The city's economy is the most stable and solid in all of Latin America.

San Juan is the site of the official home and office of the governor of Puerto Rico (La Fortaleza), the 16th-century residence of Ponce de León's family, and several of the oldest places of Christian worship in the western hemisphere. Its bars, restaurants, shops, and nightclubs attract an animated group of patrons and fans as well. In recent years, the old city has become surrounded by acres of densely populated modern buildings, including an ultramodern airport, which makes San Juan one of the most dynamic cities in the West Indies.

THE NORTHEAST: EL YUNQUE, A NATURE RESERVE, FAJARDO & MORE

The capital city of San Juan (see above) dominates Puerto Rico's northeast. Despite the region's congestion, there are still many remote areas, including some of the island's most important nature reserves. Among the region's most popular towns, parks, and attractions are the following:

EL YUNQUE   In the Luquillo Mountains, 35 miles east of San Juan, El Yunque is a favorite escape from the capital. Teeming with plant and animal life, it is a sprawling tropical forest (actually a national forest) whose ecosystems are strictly protected. Some 100 billion gallons of rainwater fall here each year, allowing about 250 species of trees and flowers to flourish.

LAS CABEZAS DE SAN JUAN NATURE RESERVE   About an hour's drive from San Juan, this is one of the island's newest ecological refuges. It was established in 1991 on 316 acres of forest, mangrove swamp, offshore cays, coral reefs, and freshwater lagoons—a representative sampling of virtually every ecosystem on Puerto Rico. There is a visitor center, a 19th-century lighthouse (El Faro) that still works, and ample opportunity to forget the pressures of urban life.

LOÍZA ALDEA   Located about 12 miles east of San Juan, this coastal town is the center of an area whose population is largely composed of descendants of African, specifically Yoruba, slaves. During the 16th century, African slaves were imported to pan for gold in the nearby watercourse, the Río Grande de Loíza, and to work the sugarcane fields. Later, slaves from other Caribbean islands—either escapees who had been recaptured or spoils of war taken from rival British plantations—were added to the region's cultural mix. The town was founded in 1719, but the foundations of one church were laid about 70 years before that. Loíza Aldea today is one of the three poorest municipalities on Puerto Rico. The region, with about 50,000 inhabitants, is the center of African-Hispanic culture on Puerto Rico.

FAJARDO   Small and sleepy, this town was originally established as a supply depot for the many pirates who plied the nearby waters. Today, a host of private

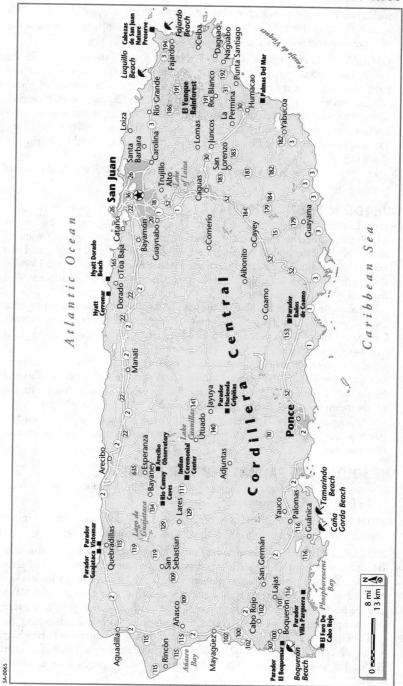

SA-0065

yachts bob at anchor in its harbor, and the many offshore cays provide visitors with secluded beaches. From Fajardo, ferryboats make choppy but frequent runs to the offshore islands of Vieques and Culebra.

CAGUAS   Located 20 miles south of San Juan, Caguas is the largest city in the interior and the focal point of the broad and fertile Turabo Valley. Ringed by mountain peaks, the city has a population of around 120,000 residents, many of whom commute to work in San Juan. The city was named after Caguax, the 16th-century Taíno chief who ruled the valley during the Spanish Conquest and whose peace-making efforts eventually led, according to legend, to his conversion to Christianity. The town's central square, Plaza Palmer, with its 19th-century cathedral, is quite charming.

For more attractions—still in the northeast—refer to "Dorado & the North Coast," below.

DORADO & THE NORTH COAST

Playa Dorado, directly east of San Juan at Dorado, is actually a term for a total of six white-sand beaches along the northern coast, reached by a series of winding roads. Dorado is the island's oldest resort town, the center of golf, casinos, and two major Hyatt resorts (see chapter 8). At the Hyatt Resorts Puerto Rico at Dorado, you'll find 72 holes of golf, the greatest concentration in the Caribbean—all designed by Robert Trent Jones.

The complex is quite family-friendly, with its Camp Hyatt that offers programs for children 3 to 15. There is also a water playground at the Hyatt Regency Cerromar Beach Hotel, with a 1,776-foot-long fantasy pool—the world's longest freshwater swimming pool.

Another resort of increasing importance is also found along the north coast: El Conquistador at Palomino Island, a private island paradise with sandy beaches and recreational facilities. This resort lies near Las Croabas, a fishing village on the northeasternmost tip of Puerto Rico's north coast.

Challenging both the Hyatt Resorts and El Conquistador is the Westin Rio Mar Beach Resort & Country Club, lying 19 miles to the east of the San Juan international airport.

THE SOUTHEAST: PALMAS DEL MAR & MORE

The southeastern quadrant has some of the most heavily developed, as well as some of the least developed, sections of the island.

HUMACAO   Because of its easy access to San Juan, this small, verdant inland town has increasingly become one of the capital's residential suburbs.

PALMAS DEL MAR   This sprawling vacation and residential resort community is located near Humacao. A splendid golf course covers some of the grounds. Palmas del Mar is at the center of what has been called "the New American Riviera"—3 miles of white-sand beaches on the eastern coast of the island. Palmas del Mar is also the largest resort in Puerto Rico, lying to the south of Humacao on 2,800 acres of a former coconut plantation—now devoted to luxury living and the sporting life.

The Equestrian Center at Palmas is the finest riding headquarters in Puerto Rico, with trails cutting through an old plantation and jungle along the beach. The resort is ideal for families and has a supervised summer activities program for children 5 to 12.

THE RESERVA FORESTAL CARLTE   This 6,000-acre nature reserve is known simply as Guavate. Its relatively cool temperatures (averaging 72°F) and frequent rainfall sustain acres of teak, mahogany, and sierra palm trees. A radio/television tower sits atop the park's highest peak, the 3,000-foot Cerro La Santa.

ARROYO   This village on Puerto Rico's southwestern coast was founded in 1855 and has slumbered ever since in quiet obscurity, a favorite retreat of escapists. It was visited in 1848 by Samuel F. B. Morse, the inventor of the Morse code, who personally installed the local telegraph line. The town's main street, Calle Morse, is named in his honor. Several of the town's most impressive houses were built by New England sea captains who—perhaps piqued by the calm, tropical beauty of the place—decided to settle here.

BARRANQUITAS   Set inland at an altitude of more than 1,800 feet and capped by a dramatically situated Catholic church, Barranquitas is one of the most photogenic towns on Puerto Rico. Its houses rise almost on top of one another, in a style similar to that of a fortified village in Spain. Barranquitas's most famous son was the statesman Luís Muñoz Rivera, who is honored by a small museum in the house where he was born in 1859. Near Barranquitas is one of Puerto Rico's deepest and most spectacular gorges, the nearly inaccessible canyon of San Cristóbal. Here, cliffs nearly 500 feet high overlook the raging waters of the Usabon River.

COAMO   Although today Coamo is a bedroom community for San Juan, originally it was the site of two different Taíno communities. Founded in 1579, it now has a main square draped with bougainvillea and one of the best-known Catholic churches on Puerto Rico. Even more famous, however, are the mineral springs whose therapeutic warm waters helped President Franklin D. Roosevelt during his recovery from polio. (Some historians claim that these springs inspired the legend of the Fountain of Youth, which in turn set Ponce de León off on his vain search of Florida.)

THE SOUTHWEST: PONCE, MAYAGÜEZ, SAN GERMÁN & MORE

One of Puerto Rico's most beautiful regions, the southwest is rich in local lore, civic pride, and natural wonders.

PONCE   Puerto Rico's second-largest city, Ponce has always prided itself on its independence from the Spanish-derived laws and taxes that governed San Juan and the rest of the island. Long-ago home of some of the island's shrewdest traders, merchants, and smugglers, it is enjoying a renaissance as citizens and visitors rediscover its unique cultural and architectural charms. Located about 90 minutes by car from the capital on Puerto Rico's southern coast, Ponce contains a handful of superb museums, one of the most charming main squares in the Caribbean, an ancient cathedral, dozens of authentically restored colonial-era buildings, and a number of outlying mansions and villas that, at the time of their construction, were among the most opulent on the island.

MAYAGÜEZ   The third-largest city on Puerto Rico, Mayagüez is named after the *majagua*, the Amerindian word for a tree that grows abundantly in the area. Because of an earthquake that destroyed almost everything in town in 1917, few old buildings remain. The town is known as the commercial and industrial capital of Puerto Rico's western sector. Its botanical garden is among the finest on the island.

SAN GERMÁN   Located on the island's southwestern corner, small, sleepy, and historic San Germán was named after Ferdinand of Spain's second wife, Germaine de Foix, whom he married in 1503. San Germán's central church, Porta Coeli, was built in 1606. At one time much of the populace was engaged in piracy, pillaging the ships that sailed off the nearby coastline. The central area of this village is still sought out for its many reminders of the island's Spanish heritage and colonial charm.

YAUCO   Established relatively late in the island's history (in 1756), Yauco immediately attracted a population of Corsicans and Haitian French, who grew a distinctive brand of coffee known for its low caffeine and mild flavor. By 1900, ravaged by hurricane damage and competition from other coffee-producing countries such as Colombia, the town had declined into obscurity. Today it retains its steeply sloping streets, a handful of old houses, aromatic coffee, and a distinctive air of faded Spanish grandeur.

CABO ROJO   Established in 1772, Cabo Rojo reached the peak of its prosperity during the 19th century, when immigrants from around the Mediterranean, fleeing revolutions in their own countries, arrived to establish sugarcane plantations. Today, cattle graze peacefully on land originally devoted almost exclusively to sugarcane, while the area's many varieties of exotic birds draw bird-watchers from throughout North America. Even the offshore waters are fertile; it's estimated that nearly half of all the fish consumed on Puerto Rico are caught in waters near Cabo Rojo.

BOQUERÓN   Famous for the beauty of its beach and the abundant birds and wildlife in the nearby Boquerón Forest Reserve, this small and sleepy village is now ripe for large-scale tourism-related development. During the early 19th century, the island's most-feared pirate, Roberto Cofresi, terrorized the Puerto Rican coastline from a secret lair in a cave nearby.

LA PARGUERA   Named after a breed of snapper (*pargos*) that abounds in the waters nearby, La Parguera is a quiet coastal town best known for the phosphorescent waters of La Bahía Fosforescente (Phosphorescent Bay). Here, sheltered from the waves of the sea, billions of plankton (luminescent dinoflagellates) glow dimly when they are disturbed by movements of the water. The town comes alive on weekends, when crowds of young people from San Juan arrive to party the nights away. Filling modest rooming houses, they temporarily change the texture of the town as bands produce long and loud sessions of salsa music.

THE NORTHWEST: ARECIBO, RÍO CAMUY, RINCÓN & MORE

A fertile area with many rivers bringing valuable water for irrigation from the high mountains of the Cordillera, the northwest also offers abundant opportunities for sightseeing. The region's principal districts include the following:

ARECIBO   Located on the northern coastline a 2-hour drive west of San Juan, Arecibo was originally founded in 1556. Although little remains of its original architecture, the town is well-known to physicists and astronomers around the world because of the radar/radio-telescope that fills a concave depression between six of the region's hills. Equal in size to 13 football fields and operated jointly by the National Science Foundation and Cornell University, it studies the shape and formation of the galaxies by accumulating and deciphering radio waves from space.

RÍO CAMUY CAVE PARK   Located near Arecibo, this park's greatest attraction is underground, where a network of underground rivers and caves provides some of the most enjoyable spelunking in the world. At its heart lies one of the largest known underground rivers. Covering 300 acres above ground, the park is sought out by cave explorers the world over.

RINCÓN   Named after the 16th-century landowner Don Gonzalo Rincón, who donated its site to the poor of his district, the tiny town of Rincón is famous throughout Puerto Rico for its world-class surfing and beautiful beaches. The lighthouse that warns ships and boats away from dangerous offshore reefs is one of the most powerful on Puerto Rico.

AGUADILLA   Christopher Columbus landed near Aguadilla during his second voyage to the New World in 1493. Today the town has a busy airport, fine beaches, and a growing tourism-based infrastructure. It is also the center of Puerto Rico's tiny lace-making industry, a craft imported here many centuries ago by immigrants from Spain, Holland, and Belgium.

UTUADO   Small, sunny, and nestled amid the hills of the interior, Utuado is famous as the center of the *jíbaro* (hillbilly) culture of Puerto Rico. Some of Puerto Rico's finest mountain musicians have come from Utuado and mention the town in many of their ballads. The surrounding landscape is sculpted with caves and lushly covered with a variety of tropical plants and trees.

THE OFFSHORE ISLANDS: CULEBRA, VIEQUES & MORE

Few *norteamericanos* realize that Puerto Rico has at least four well-known islands and a multitude of tiny cays lying offshore. The most famous of these include:

CAYO SANTIAGO   Lying off the southeastern coast is the small island of Cayo Santiago. Home to a group of about two dozen scientists and a community of rhesus monkeys originally imported from India, the island is a medical experimentation center run by the U.S. Public Health Service. Monkeys are studied in a "wild" but controlled environment both for insights into the behavioral sciences and for possible cures for such maladies as diabetes and arthritis. Casual visitors are not permitted on Cayo Santiago, but they can cruise along the shore and watch the monkeys.

CULEBRA & VIEQUES   Located off the eastern coast, these two islands are among the most unsullied and untrammeled areas in the West Indies. Come here for sun, almost no scheduled activities, fresh seafood, clear waters, sandy beaches, and teeming coral reefs. Vieques is especially proud of its phosphorescent bay.

MONA   Remote, uninhabited, and teeming with bird life, this barren island off the western coast is ringed by soaring cliffs and finely textured white beaches. The island has almost no facilities, so visitors seldom stay for more than a day of swimming and picnicking. The currents that surround Mona on all sides are legendary for their dangerous eddies, undertows, and sharks.

3 Puerto Rico Today

In the late 1990s Puerto Rico continues to make headlines in mainland newspapers. Sometimes the news is good; at other times, troubling.

First the good. In 1997, the island saw an increase of 4.3% in tourism over the previous year, so the island's hotel and marketing promotion is paying off. Travelers from the United States alone climbed 8.2%. Canada registered a whopping 17.1% increase, with Latin America growth rising even more, up 19.1%.

Indeed, the island's 3.56 million people—including a million in the San Juan metropolitan area—have forged ahead economically and made rapid strides. Their annual income is now the highest in Latin America, and their average life expectancy has risen to 73.8 years. And with the island's economy evolving from agriculture to manufacturing and tourism, a demand for an educated workforce has resulted in the ordinary worker having at least 12 years of schooling.

Tourism represents about 6% of the gross national product. Puerto Rico's present governor, Dr. Pedro Rosselló, has challenged both the private and public sectors of the tourism industry to double that contribution to the GNP within the next decade. At once both labor intensive and environmentally friendly, tourism is seen as the island's best alternative to continued heavy industrialization in pursuit of new jobs for its people.

Rosselló isn't just talking. He recently announced the development of a new $173 million tourism project on nearly 600 acres of land located in the municipalities of Rio Grande and Luquillo right outside San Juan. Here will be developed a 600-room hotel, two 18-hole golf courses, 13 tennis courts, a 20,000-square-foot clubhouse, swimming pools, a health club, and sporting facilities for children and teens.

Talk of making Puerto Rico the 51st state also continues in the news. At press time, Congress was considering a bill giving the territory's nearly 4 million residents a "once and for all" choice of their political relationship with the United States. This old question was raised again as the centennial of the Spanish-American War approached. To some islanders, 100 years of U.S. sovereignty over a territory denied full rights has gone on long enough. While those people advocate full statehood or even independence, others are quite content with the present commonwealth status.

Now the bad. As part of legislation raising the nation's minimum wage in 1996, President Clinton vetoed a set of tax breaks for U.S. companies operating on the island. That ended 75 years of federal incentives that attracted Stateside industries and helped make Puerto Rico the industrial powerhouse in the West Indies. For example, it produces about half the prescription drugs sold in the United States. What impact losing its special tax status will have in the long run remains to be seen.

Even with the tax breaks, Puerto Rico struggled with a 14% unemployment rate and a per capita income of $7,500, about half the level of America's poorest state, Mississippi.

Mirroring the U.S. mainland, rising crime, drugs, the AIDS crisis, chronic unemployment, overpopulation, and more troubles plague Puerto Rico. The island has America's third-highest AIDS rate and the dubious distinction of being a major gateway into the United States for drugs from Latin America. All the violence and social ills associated with drugs have beset the island. A newspaper headline said it best: "Puerto Rico Reeling Under Scourge of Drugs and Rising Gang Violence." Although the drug issue is still of epidemic horror, you can visit Puerto Rico and be completely unaware that all this criminal activity is going on around you, especially if you're heading to one of the big, self-sufficient resorts. And efforts are being made to solve the drug problem. In the mid-1990s the government increased the number of police officers, enacted harsher prison sentences for drug dealers, and conducted arms and drug raids—all part of a continuing battle to stop the flow of illegal drugs into the United States.

Even in the now-prosperous tourism industry, storm clouds loom. The unspoken fear among developers of megaresorts is the possible impact of Cuba reopening to the American tourism market. Before Fidel Castro took over Cuba in 1959, Americans by the thousands flocked to Havana, and Puerto Rico was a mere dot on the tourist map. The island's growth was fueled enormously by the embargo imposed on Castro's communist government.

4 History 101

IN THE BEGINNING

Although the Spanish occupation was the decisive factor defining Puerto Rico's current culture, the island was settled many thousands of years ago by Amerindians. The oldest archaeological remains yet discovered were unearthed in 1948. Found in a limestone cave a few miles east of San Juan, in Loíza Aldea, the artifacts consisted of conch shells, stone implements, and crude hatchets deposited here by tribal peoples during the first century of the Christian Era. These people belonged to an archaic, seminomadic, cave-dwelling culture that had not developed either agriculture or pottery. Some ethnologists suggest that these early inhabitants originated in Florida, immigrated to Cuba, and from there began a steady migration along the West Indian archipelago.

Around A.D. 300, a different group of Amerindians, the Arawaks, migrated to Puerto Rico from the Orinoco Basin in what is now Venezuela. Known by ethnologists as the Saladoids, they were the first of Puerto Rico's inhabitants to make and use pottery, which they decorated with exotic geometric designs in red and white. Subsisting on fish, crabs, and whatever else they could catch, they populated the big island and the offshore island of Vieques as well.

By about A.D. 600, this culture had disappeared, bringing to an end the island's historic era of pottery making. Ethnologists' opinions differ as to whether the tribes were eradicated by new invasions from South America, succumbed to starvation or plague, or simply evolved into the next culture that dominated Puerto Rico—the Ostionoids.

Much less skilled at making pottery than their predecessors but more accomplished at polishing and grinding stones for jewelry and tools, the Ostionoids were the ethnic predecessors of the tribe that became the Taínos. The Taínos inhabited Puerto Rico when it was explored and invaded by the Spanish beginning in 1493. The Taínos were spread throughout the West Indies but reached their greatest development in Puerto Rico and neighboring Hispaniola (the island shared by Haiti and the Dominican Republic).

Taíno culture has impressed both the colonial Spanish and modern sociologists. This people's achievements included construction of ceremonial ballparks whose boundaries were marked by upright stone dolmens, development of a universal language, and creation of a complicated religious cosmology. There was a hierarchy of deities who inhabited the sky. The god Yocahu was the supreme creator. Another, Jurancán, was perpetually angry and ruled the power of the hurricane. Myths and traditions were perpetuated through ceremonial dances (*areytos*), drumbeats, oral traditions, and a ceremonial ball game played between opposing teams (of 10 to 30 players per team) with a rubber ball; winning this game was thought to bring a good harvest and strong, healthy children.

Skilled at agriculture and hunting, the Taínos were also good sailors, canoe makers, and navigators.

About 100 years before the Spanish invasion, the Taínos were challenged by an invading South American tribe—the Caribs. Fierce, warlike, sadistic, and adept at using poison-tipped arrows, the Caribs raided Taíno settlements for slaves (especially female) and bodies for the completion of their rites of cannibalism. Some ethnologists argue that the preeminence of the Taínos, shaken by the attacks of the Caribs, was already jeopardized by the time of the Spanish occupation. In fact, it was the Caribs who fought the most effectively against the Europeans; their

Ponce de León: Man of Myth & Legend

For an explorer of such myth and legend, Juan Ponce de León still remains an enigma to many historians, his exploits subject to as much myth as fact.

It is known that he was born around 1460 in San Tervas de Campos, a province of Valladolid in Spain, to a noble Castilian family. The red-haired youth grew into an active, aggressive, and perhaps impulsive young man, similar in some respects to Sir Francis Drake in England. After taking part in Spain's Moorish wars, Ponce de León sailed to America with Columbus on his second voyage, in 1493.

In the New World, Ponce de León served as a soldier in the Spanish settlement of Hispaniola, now the island home of Haiti and the Dominican Republic. From 1502 to 1504 he led Spanish forces against Indians in the eastern part of the island, finally defeating them.

In 1508, he explored Puerto Rico, discovering gold on the island and conquering its native tribes within a year. A year later he was named governor of Puerto Rico and soon rose to become one of the most powerful Europeans in the Americas. From most accounts Ponce de León was a good governor of Puerto Rico before his political rivals forced him from office in 1512.

At that time he received permission from King Ferdinand to colonize the island of Bimini in the Bahamas. In searching for Bimini, he came upon the northeast coast of Florida, which he at first thought was an island, in the spring of 1513. He named it "La Florida" because he discovered it at the time of Pascua Florida or "Flowery Easter." He was the first explorer to claim some of the North American mainland for Spain.

The following year he sailed back to Spain, carrying with him 5,000 gold pesos. King Ferdinand ordered him back to Puerto Rico with instructions to colonize both Bimini and Florida. Back in Puerto Rico, he ordered the building of the city of San Juan. In 1521, he sailed to Florida with 200 men and supplies to start a colony. This was to be his downfall. Wounded by a poison arrow in his thigh, he was taken back to Cuba in June of 1521 and there died from his wound.

Legend says Ponce de León searched in vain for the so-called Fountain of Youth, first in Bimini and then later in Florida. He never once mentioned it in any of his private or official writings—at least those writings that still exist—and historians believe his goal was gold and other treasures, and perhaps to convert the natives to Catholicism.

His legacy lives on at the Casa Blanca in Old San Juan (see "Seeing the Sights" in chapter 7). Casa Blanca is the oldest continuously occupied residence in the western hemisphere and the oldest of about 800 Spanish Colonial buildings in Old San Juan's National Historic Zone. In 1968, it became a historic national monument placed in the care of the Institute of Puerto Rican culture. Today the building is the site of the Juan Ponce de León Museum. The carved conquistador's coat of arms greets visitors at the entrance.

behavior led the Europeans to unfairly attribute warlike tendencies to all of the island's tribes. A dynamic tension between the Taínos and the Caribs certainly existed when Christopher Columbus landed on Puerto Rico.

To understand Puerto Rico's prehistoric era, it is important to know that the Taínos, far more than the Caribs, contributed greatly to the everyday life and language that evolved during the Spanish occupation. Taíno place names are still used for such towns as Utuado, Mayagüez, Caguas, and Humacao. Many Taíno implements and techniques were copied directly by the Europeans, including the *bohío* (straw hut) and the *hamaca* (hammock), the musical instrument known as the maracas, and the method of making bread from the starchy cassava root. Also, many Taíno superstitions and legends were adopted and adapted by the Spanish and still influence the Puerto Rican imagination.

SPAIN, SYPHILIS & SLAVERY

Christopher Columbus became the first European to land on the shores of Puerto Rico, on November 19, 1493, near what would become the town of Aguadilla, during his second voyage to the New World. Giving the island the name San Juan Bautista, he sailed on in search of shores with more obvious riches for the taking. A European foothold on the island was established in 1508 when Juan Ponce de León, the first governor of Puerto Rico, imported colonists from the nearby island of Hispaniola. They founded the town of Caparra, which lay close to the site of present-day San Juan. The town was almost immediately wracked with internal power struggles among the Spanish settlers, who pressed the native peoples into servitude, evangelized them, and frantically sought for gold, thus quickly changing the face of the island.

Meanwhile, the Amerindians began dying at an alarming rate, victims of imported diseases such as smallpox and whooping cough, against which they had no biologic immunity. The natives also paid the Spanish back, giving them diseases such as syphilis against which they had little immunity. Both communities reeled, disoriented, from their contact with one another. In 1511, the Amerindians rebelled against attempts by the Spanish to enslave them. The rebellion was brutally suppressed by the Spanish forces of Ponce de León, whose muskets and firearms were vastly superior to the hatchets and arrows of the native peoples. In desperation, the remnants of the Taínos joined forces with their traditional enemies, the Caribs, but even that belated union did little to check the inexorable growth of European power.

Because the Indians languished in slavery, sometimes preferring mass suicide to imprisonment, their work in the fields and mines of Puerto Rico was soon taken over by Africans who were imported by Spanish, Danish, Portuguese, British, and American slavers.

By 1521 the island had been renamed Puerto Rico (Rich Port) and was one of the most strategic islands in the Caribbean, which was increasingly viewed as a Spanish sea. Officials of the Spanish Crown dubbed the island "the strongest foothold of Spain in America" and hastened to strengthen the already impressive bulwarks surrounding the city of San Juan.

PIRATES & PILLAGING ENGLISHMEN

Within a century, Puerto Rico's position at the easternmost edge of what would become Spanish America helped it play a major part in the Spanish expansion toward Florida, the South American coast, and Mexico. It was usually the first port of call for Spanish ships arriving in the Americas; recognizing that the island was a strategic keystone, the Spanish decided to strengthen its defenses. By 1540, La Fortaleza, the first of three massive fortresses built in San Juan, was completed. By 1600, San Juan was completely enclosed by some of the most formidable ramparts in the Caribbean, whereas, ironically, the remainder of Puerto Rico was almost defenseless. In 1565, the King of Spain ordered the governor of Puerto Rico to provide men and material to strengthen the city of San Agustin (St. Augustine) in Florida.

By this time, the English (and to a lesser extent, the French) were seriously harassing Spanish shipping in the Caribbean and North Atlantic. At least part of the French and English aggression was in retaliation for the 1493 Papal Bull dividing the New World between Portugal and Spain—an arrangement that eliminated all other nations from the spoils and colonization of the New World.

Queen Elizabeth I's most effective weapon against Spanish expansion in the Caribbean wasn't the Royal Navy; rather, it was buccaneers such as John Hawkins and Sir Francis Drake. Their victories included the destruction of St. Augustine in Florida, Cartagena in Colombia, and Santo Domingo in what is now the Dominican Republic, and the general harassment and pillaging of many Spanish ships and treasure convoys sailing from the New World to Europe with gold and silver from the Aztec and Inca empires. The Royal Navy did play an important role, however, for its 1588 defeat of the Spanish Armada marked the rise of the English as a major maritime power. The Spanish then began to aggressively fortify such islands as Puerto Rico.

In 1595, Drake and Hawkins persuaded an uncertain Queen Elizabeth to embark on a bold and daring plan to invade and conquer Puerto Rico. An English general, the Earl of Cumberland, urged his men to bravery by "assuring your selves you have the maydenhead of Puerto Rico and so possesse the keyes of all the Indies." Confident that the island was "the very key of the West Indies which locketh and shutteth all the gold and silver in the continent of America and Brasilia," he brought into battle an English force of 4,500 soldiers and eventually captured La Fortaleza.

Although the occupation lasted a full 65 days, the English eventually abandoned Puerto Rico when their armies were decimated by tropical diseases and the local population, which began to engage in a kind of guerrilla warfare against the English. After pillaging and destroying much of the Puerto Rican countryside, the English left. Their short but abortive victory compelled the Spanish king, Philip III, to continue construction of the island's defenses. Despite these efforts, Puerto Rico retained a less-than-invincible aspect as Spanish soldiers in the forts often deserted or succumbed to tropical diseases.

A DUTCH TREAT

In 1625, Puerto Rico was covetously eyed by Holland, whose traders and merchants desperately wanted a foothold in the West Indies. Spearheaded by the Dutch West India Company, which had received trading concessions from the Dutch Crown covering most of the West Indies, the Dutch armies besieged El Morro Fortress in San Juan in one of the bloodiest assaults the fortress ever sustained. When the commanding officer of El Morro refused to surrender, the Dutch burned San Juan to the ground, including all church and civil archives and the bishop's library, by then the most famous and complete collection of books in America. Fueled by rage and courage, the Spanish rallied their forces and soon threw out the Dutch.

In response to the widespread destruction of the strongest link in the chain of Spanish defenses, Spain threw itself wholeheartedly into improving and reinforcing the defenses around San Juan. King Philip IV justified his expenditures by declaring Puerto Rico the "front and vanguard of the Western Indies and, consequently, the most important of them and most coveted by the enemies of Spain."

Within 150 years, after extravagant expenditures of time and money, the city's walls were considered almost impregnable. Military sophistication was added during the 1760s, when two Irishmen, Tomas O'Daly and Alejandro O'Reilly, surrounded the city with some of Europe's most technically up-to-date defenses. Despite the thick walls, however, the island's defenses remained precarious because of the frequent tropical epidemics that devastated the ranks of the soldiers; the chronically late pay, which weakened the soldiers' morale; and the belated and often wrong-minded priorities of the Spanish monarchy, which were decided upon thousands of miles away.

A CATHOLIC CRUSADE

From the earliest days of Spanish colonization, an army of priests and missionaries embarked on a vigorous crusade to convert Puerto Rico's Taínos to Roman Catholicism. King Ferdinand himself paid for the construction of a Franciscan monastery and a series of chapels, and required specific support of the church from the aristocrats who had been awarded land grants in the new territories. They were required to build churches, provide Christian burials, and grant religious instruction to both Taíno and African slaves.

Among the church's most important activities were the Franciscan monks' efforts to teach the island's children how to read, write, and count. In 1688, Bishop Francisco Padilla, who is now included among the legends of Puerto Rico, established one of the island's most famous schools. When it became clear that local parents were too poor to provide their children with appropriate clothing, he succeeded in persuading the King of Spain to pay for their clothes.

Puerto Rico was declared by the pope as the first *see*—ecclesiastical headquarters—in the New World. In 1519, it became the general headquarters of the Inquisition in the New World. (About 70 years later, the Inquisition's headquarters was transferred to the important and well-defended city of Cartagena, in Colombia.)

FROM SMUGGLING TO SUGAR

The island's early development was shackled by Spain's insistence on a centrist economy. All goods exported from or imported to Puerto Rico had to pass through Spain itself, usually through Seville. In effect, this policy prohibited any trade (officially, at least) between Puerto Rico and its island neighbors.

In response, a flourishing black market developed. Cities such as Ponce, became smuggling centers. This black market was especially prevalent after the Spanish colonization of Mexico and Peru, when many Spanish goods, which once would have been sent to Puerto Rico, ended up in those more immediately lucrative colonies instead. Although smugglers were punished if caught, nothing could curb this illegal (and untaxed) trade. Some historians estimate that almost everyone on the island—including priests, citizens, and military and civic authorities—was actively involved.

By the mid-1500s, the several hundred settlers who had immigrated to Puerto Rico from Spain heard (and sometimes believed) rumors of the fortunes to be made in the gold mines of Peru. When the island's population declined because of the ensuing mass exodus, the king enticed 500 families from the Canary Islands to settle on Puerto Rico between 1683 and 1691. Meanwhile, an active trade in slaves—imported as labor for fields that were increasingly used for sugarcane and tobacco production—swelled the island's ranks. This happened despite the Crown's imposition of strict controls on the number of slaves that could be brought in. Sugarcane earned profits for many islanders, but Spanish mismanagement, fraud within the government bureaucracy, and a lack of both labor and ships to transport the finished product to market discouraged the fledgling industry. Later, fortunes were made and lost in the production of ginger, an industry that died as soon as the Spanish government raised taxes on ginger imports to exorbitant levels. Despite the arrival of immigrants to Puerto Rico from many countries, diseases such as spotted fever, yellow fever, malaria, smallpox, and measles wiped out the population almost as fast as it grew.

MORE SMUGGLING

As the philosophical and political movement known as the Enlightenment swept both Europe and North America during the late 1700s and the 1800s, Spain moved to improve Puerto Rico's economy through its local government. The island's defenses were beefed up, roads and bridges were built, and a public education program was launched. The island remained a major Spanish naval stronghold in the New World. Immigration from Europe and other places more than tripled the population. It was during this era that Puerto Rico began to develop a unique identity of its own, a native pride, and a consciousness of its importance within the Caribbean.

The heavily fortified city of San Juan, the island's civic centerpiece, remained under Spain's rigid control. The outlying countryside, without the benefit of encircling ramparts and victim occasionally of raids by both pirates and the forces of England and France, was usually left alone to develop its own local power centers. The city of Ponce, for example, flourished under the Spanish Crown's lax supervision and grew wealthy from the tons of contraband and the high-quality sugar that passed through its port. This trend was also encouraged by the unrealistic law that declared San Juan the island's only legal port. Contemporary sources, in fact, cite the fledgling United States as among the most active of Ponce's early contraband trading partners.

RISING POWER

During the 18th century the number of towns on the island grew rapidly. There were five settlements in Puerto Rico in 1700; 100 years later there were almost 40 settlements, and the island's population had grown to more than 150,000.

Meanwhile, the waters of the Caribbean increasingly reflected the diplomatic wars unfolding in Europe. In 1797, the British, after easily capturing Trinidad (which was poorly defended by the Spanish), failed in a spectacular effort to conquer Puerto Rico. The *criollos,* or native Puerto Ricans, played a major role in the island's defense and later retained a growing sense of their own cultural identity.

The islanders were becoming aware that Spain could not enforce the hundreds of laws it had previously imposed to support its centrist trade policies. Thousands of merchants, farmers, and civil authorities traded profitably with privateers from various nations, thereby deepening the tendency to evade or ignore the laws imposed by Spain and its colonial governors. The attacks by privateers on British shipping were especially severe, since pirates based in Puerto Rico ranged as far south as Trinidad, bringing dozens of captured British ships into Puerto Rican harbors. (Several decades earlier, British privateers operating out of Jamaica had endlessly harassed Spanish shipping; the tradition of government-sanctioned piracy was well established.)

It was during this period that coffee—which would later play an essential role in the island's economy—was introduced to the Puerto Rican highlands from the nearby Dominican Republic.

Despite the power of San Juan and its Spanish institutions, 18th-century Puerto Rico was predominantly rural. The report of a special emissary of the Spanish king,

Marshal Alejandro O'Reilly, remains a remarkably complete analysis of 18th-century Puerto Rican society. It helped promote a more progressive series of fiscal and administrative policies that reflected the Enlightenment ideals found in many European countries.

Suddenly, Puerto Rico began to be viewed as a potential source of income for the Spanish Empire, rather than a drain on income. One of O'Reilly's most visible legacies was his recommendation that people live in towns rather than be scattered about the countryside. Shortly after this, seven new towns, some in the island's interior, were established.

Meanwhile, as the island prospered and its bourgeoisie became more numerous and affluent, daily life became more refined. New public buildings were erected; concerts were introduced; and the everyday aspects of life—such as furniture and social ritual—grew more ornate. Insights into Puerto Rico's changing life can be seen in the works of its most famous 18th-century painter, José Campeche, whose portraits, religious frescoes, and landscapes are among his era's most distinctive legacies.

THE LAST BASTION

Much of the politics of 19th-century Latin America cannot be understood without a review of Spain's problems at that time. Up until 1850 there was political and military turmoil in Spain, a combination that eventually led to the collapse of its empire. Since 1796, Spain had been a military satellite of post-revolutionary France, an alliance that brought it into conflict with England. In 1804, Admiral Horatio Lord Nelson's definitive victory for England over French and Spanish ships during the Battle of Trafalgar left England in supreme control of the international sea lanes and interrupted trade and communications between Spain and its colonies in the New World.

These events led to important changes for Spanish-speaking America. The revolutionary fervor of Simón Bolívar and his South American compatriots spilled over to the entire continent, embroiling Spain in a desperate attempt to hold onto the tattered remains of its empire at any cost. Recognizing that Puerto Rico and Cuba were probably the last bastions of Spanish Royalist sympathy in the Americas, Spain liberalized its trade policies, decreeing that goods no longer had to pass through Seville.

The sheer weight and volume of illegal Puerto Rican trade with such countries as Denmark, France, and—most important—the United States, forced Spain's hand in establishing a realistic set of trade reforms. A bloody revolution in Haiti, which had produced more sugarcane than almost any other West Indies island, spurred sugarcane and coffee production in Puerto Rico. Also important was the introduction of a new and more prolific species of sugarcane, the Otahiti, which helped increase production even more.

By the 1820s, the United States was providing ample supplies of such staples as lumber, salt, butter, fish, grain, and foodstuffs, while huge amounts of Puerto Rican sugar, molasses, coffee, and rum were consumed in the United States. Meanwhile, the United States was increasingly viewed as the keeper of the peace in the Caribbean, suppressing the piracy that flourished while Spain's navy was preoccupied with its European wars.

During Venezuela's separation from Spain, Venezuelans loyal to the Spanish Crown fled en masse to the remaining Royalist bastions in the Americas—Puerto Rico and, to a lesser extent, Cuba. Although many arrived penniless, having forfeited their properties in South America in exchange for their lives, their excellent understanding of agriculture and commerce probably catalyzed much of the era's economic development in Puerto Rico. Simultaneously, many historians argue, their unflinching loyalty to the Spanish Crown contributed to one of the most conservative and reactionary social structures anywhere in the Spanish-speaking Caribbean. In any event, dozens of Spanish naval expeditions that were intended to suppress the revolutions in Venezuela were outfitted in Puerto Rican harbors during this period.

A REVOLT SUPPRESSED & SLAVERY ABOLISHED

During the latter half of the 19th century, political divisions were drawn in Puerto Rico reflecting both the political instability in Spain and the increasing demands of Puerto Ricans for some form of self-rule. As governments and regimes in Spain rose and fell, Spanish policies toward its colonies in the New World changed, too.

In 1865, representatives from Puerto Rico, Cuba, and the Philippines were invited to Madrid to air their grievances as part of a process of liberalizing Spanish colonial policy. Reforms, however, did not follow as promised, and a much-publicized and very visible minirevolt (during which the mountain city of Lares was occupied) was suppressed by the Spanish governors in 1868. Some of the funds and much of the publicity for this revolt came from expatriate Puerto Ricans living in Chile, St. Thomas, and New York.

Slavery was abolished in March 1873, about 40 years after it had been abolished throughout the British Empire. About 32,000 slaves were freed following years of liberal agitation. Abolition was viewed as a major victory for liberal forces throughout Puerto Rico, although cynics claim that slavery was much less entrenched in Puerto Rico than in neighboring Cuba, where the sugar economy was far more dependent on slave labor.

The 1895 revolution in Cuba increased the Puerto Rican demand for greater self-rule; during the ensuing intellectual ferment, many political parties emerged. The Cuban revolution provided part of the spark that led to the Spanish-American War, Cuban independence, and U.S. control of Puerto Rico, the Philippines, and the Pacific island of Guam.

THE YANKS ARE COMING, THE YANKS ARE COMING!

In 1897, faced with intense pressure from sources within Puerto Rico, a weakened Spain granted its colony a measure of autonomy, but it came too late. Other events were taking place between Spain and the United States that would forever change the future of Puerto Rico.

On February 15, 1898, the U.S. battleship *Maine* was blown up in the harbor of Havana, killing 266 men. The so-called "yellow press" in the United States, especially the papers owned by the tycoon William Randolph Hearst, aroused Americans' emotions into a fever pitch for war, with the rallying cry "Remember the *Maine*."

On April 20 of that year, President William McKinley signed a resolution demanding Spanish withdrawal from Cuba. The president ordered a blockade of Cuba's ports, and on April 24, Spain, in retaliation, declared a state of war with the United States. On April 25 the U.S. Congress declared war on Spain. In Cuba, the naval battle of Santiago was won by American forces, and in another part of the world, the Spanish colony of the Philippines was also captured by U.S. troops.

On July 25, after their victory at Santiago, American troops landed at Guánica, Puerto Rico, and several days later took over Ponce. U.S. Navy Capt. Alfred T. Mahan later wrote that the United States viewed Puerto Rico, Spain's remaining colonial outpost in the Caribbean, as vital to American interests in the area. Puerto Rico could be used as a military base to help the United States maintain control of the isthmus and to keep communications and traffic flowing between the Atlantic and the Pacific.

Spain offered to trade other territory for Puerto Rico, but the United States refused and demanded Spain's ouster from the island. Left with little choice against superior U.S. forces, Spain capitulated. The Spanish-American War ended on August 31, 1898, with the surrender of Spain and the virtual collapse of the once-powerful Spanish Empire. Puerto Rico, in the words of McKinley, was to "become a territory of the United States."

Although the entire war lasted just over 4 months, the invasion of Puerto Rico took only 2 weeks. "It wasn't much of a war," remarked Theodore Roosevelt, who had led the Rough Riders cavalry outfit in their charge up San Juan Hill, "but it was all the war there was." The United States had suffered only four casualties while acquiring Puerto Rico, the Philippines, and the island of Guam. The Treaty of Paris, signed on December 10, 1898, settled the terms of Spain's surrender.

A DUBIOUS PRIZE

Some Americans looked on Puerto Rico as a "dubious prize." One-third of the population consisted of mulattoes and blacks, descended from slaves, who had no money or land. Only about 12% of the population could read or write. About 8% were enrolled in school. It is estimated that a powerful landed gentry—only about 2% of the population—owned more than two-thirds of the land.

Washington set up a military government in Puerto Rico, headed by the War Department. A series of governors-general were appointed to rule the island, with almost the authority of a dictator. Although ruling over a rather unhappy populace, these governors-general brought about much-needed change, including tax and public health reforms. But most Puerto Ricans wanted autonomy, and many leaders, including Luís Muñoz Rivera, tried to persuade Washington to compromise. However, their protests generally fell on deaf ears.

The island's beleaguered economy was further devastated by an 1899 hurricane that caused millions of dollars' worth of property damage, killed 3,000 people, and left one out of four people homeless. Belatedly, Congress allocated the sum of $200,000, but this did little to relieve the suffering.

Tensions mounted between Puerto Ricans and their new American governors. In 1900, U.S. Secretary of War Elihu Root decided that military rule of the island was inadequate; he advocated a program of autonomy that won the endorsement of President McKinley.

Thus began a nearly 50-year colonial protectorate relationship as Puerto Rico was recognized as an unincorporated territory with its governor named by the President of the United States. Only the president had the right to override the veto of the island's governors. The legislative branch was composed of an 11-member executive committee appointed by the president, plus a 35-member chamber of delegates elected by popular vote. A resident commissioner, it was agreed, would represent Puerto Rico in Congress, "with voice but no vote."

As the United States prepared to enter World War I in 1917, Puerto Ricans were granted American citizenship and thus were subject to military service. The people of Puerto Rico were allowed to elect their legislature, which had been reorganized into a Senate and a House of Representatives. The President of the United States continued to appoint the governor of the island and retained the power to veto any of the governor's actions.

FROM HARVARD TO REVOLUTION

Many Puerto Ricans continued, at times rather violently, to agitate for independence. Requests for a plebiscite were constantly turned down. Meanwhile, economic conditions improved, as the island's population began to grow dramatically. Government revenues increased as large corporations from the U.S. mainland found Puerto Rico a profitable place in which to do business. There was much labor unrest, and by 1909, a labor movement demanding better working conditions and higher wages was gaining momentum.

The emerging labor movement showed its strength by organizing a cigar workers' strike in 1914 and a sugarcane workers' strike the following year. The 1930s proved to be disastrous for Puerto Rico, since it suffered greatly from the worldwide depression. To make matters worse, two devastating hurricanes—one in 1928 and another in 1932—destroyed millions of dollars' worth of crops and property. There was also an outbreak of disease that, along with starvation, demoralized the population. Some relief came in the form of food shipments authorized by Congress.

As tension between Puerto Rico and the United States intensified, there emerged Pedro Albizu Campos, a graduate of Harvard Law School and a former U.S. army officer. Leading a group of militant anti-American revolutionaries, he held that America's claim to Puerto Rico was illegal, since the island had already been granted autonomy by Spain. Terrorist acts by his followers, including assassinations, led to Albizu's imprisonment, but terrorist activities still continued.

In 1935, President Franklin D. Roosevelt launched the Puerto Rican Reconstruction Administration, which provided for agricultural development, public works, and electrification of the island. The following year, Sen. Millard E. Tidings of Maryland introduced a measure to grant independence to the island. His efforts were cheered by a local leader, Luís Muñoz Marín, son of the statesman Luís Muñoz Rivera. The young Muñoz founded the Partida Popular Democratica (Popular Democratic Party) in 1938, which adopted the slogan "Bread, Land, and Liberty." By 1940 this new party had gained control of more than 50% of the seats of both the upper and the lower houses of government, and the young Muñoz was elected leader of the Senate.

Roosevelt appointed Rexford Guy Tugwell as governor of Puerto Rico; he spoke Spanish and seemed to have a genuine concern for the plight of the islanders. Muñoz met with Tugwell and convinced him that Puerto Rico was capable of electing its own governor. As a step in that direction, Roosevelt appointed Jesús Piñero as the first resident commissioner of the island.

In 1944, the U.S. Congress approved a bill granting Puerto Rico the right to elect its own governor. This was the beginning of the famed Operation Bootstrap, a pump-priming fiscal and economic aid package designed to improve the island's standard of living.

SHOOTING AT HARRY

In 1946, President Harry S. Truman appointed native-born Piñero as governor of Puerto Rico, and the following year the U.S. Congress recognized the right of Puerto Ricans to elect their own governor. In 1948, Luís Muñoz Marín became the first elected governor and immediately recommended that Puerto Rico be transformed into an "associated free state." Endorsement of his plan was delayed by Washington, but President Truman approved the Puerto Rican Commonwealth Bill in 1950, providing for a plebiscite in which voters would decide whether they would remain a colony or become a U.S. commonwealth. In June 1951, Puerto

Impressions

It is a kind of lost love-child, born to the Spanish Empire, and fostered by the United States.

—Nicholas Wollaston, *Red Rumba*, 1962

Ricans voted three to one for commonwealth status, and on July 25, 1952, the Commonwealth of Puerto Rico was born.

This event was marred by a group of nationalists who marched on the Governor's Mansion in San Juan, resulting in 27 deaths and hundreds of casualties. A month later, two Puerto Rican nationalists made an unsuccessful attempt on Truman's life in Washington, killing a policeman in the process. And in March 1954, four Puerto Rican nationalists wounded five U.S. congressmen when they fired down into the House of Representatives from the visitors' gallery.

In spite of this violence, during the 1950s Puerto Rico began to take pride in its own culture and traditions. In 1955, the Institute of Puerto Rican Culture was established in San Juan, and 1957 saw the inauguration of the Pablo Casals Festival, which launched a renaissance of classical music and a celebration of the arts, a tradition that continues to this day. In 1959, a wealthy industrialist, Luís A. Ferré, donated his personal art collection toward the establishment of the Museum of Fine Arts in Ponce.

GIVE ME LIBERTY OR GIVE ME STATEHOOD

Luís Muñoz Marín resigned from office in 1964, but his party continued to win subsequent elections. The independent party, which demanded complete autonomy, gradually lost power. An election on July 23, 1967, reconfirmed the desire of most Puerto Ricans to maintain commonwealth status. In 1968, Luís A. Ferré won a close race for governor, spearheading a pro-statehood party, the Partida Progressiva Nueva (New Progressive Party). It staunchly advocated statehood as an alternative to the island's commonwealth status, but in 1972, the Partida Popular Democratica returned to power; by then, the island's economy was based largely on tourism, rum, and industry. Operation Bootstrap had been successful in creating thousands of new jobs, although more than 100,000 Puerto Ricans moved to the U.S. mainland during the 1950s, seeking a better life. The island's economy continued to improve, although perhaps not as quickly as anticipated by Operation Bootstrap.

Puerto Rico grabbed the world's attention in 1979 with the launching of the Pan-American Games. It is vigorously attempting to bring the Summer Olympics there in 2004. The island's culture received a boost in 1981 with the opening of the Center of the Performing Arts in San Juan, which attracted world-famous performers and virtuosos. The international spotlight again focused on Puerto Rico at the time of the first papal visit there in 1986. John Paul II (or Juan Pablo II, as he was called locally) kindled a renewed interest in religion, especially among the Catholic youth of the island.

In 1996, Puerto Rico lost its special tax-break status, which had originally lured American industry to the island. Down the road some dire consequences to the island economy are predicted as a result of this loss. In 1998, Congress was considering legislation to authorize Puerto Ricans to choose—"once and forever"—among statehood, commonwealth, or independence. More important, it binds Congress to implement the results within 10 years. If passed, the bill will lead to Puerto Rico's most controversial election, one that is bound to spark bitter debate.

5 A Portrait of the Puerto Ricans

The people of Puerto Rico represent a mix of races, cultures, languages, and religions. They draw their unique heritage from the original native population, from Spanish royalists who sought refuge here, from African slaves imported to work the sugar plantations, and from other Caribbean islanders who have come here seeking jobs. The Spanish they speak is a mix, too, with many words borrowed from the pre-Columbian Amerindian tongue right up to modern-day English. Even the Catholicism they practice blends some Taíno and African traditions.

THE ISLANDERS

Some 3.56 million people inhabit the main island, making it one of the most densely populated in the world. It has an average of about 1,000 people per square mile, a ratio higher than that within any of the 50 states. It is estimated that if the some 2 million Puerto Ricans who have migrated to the United States (more Puerto Ricans are said to live in New York City than in San Juan) were to return home, the island would be so crowded that there would be virtually no room for them to live. There has been a reversal of this pattern in recent years, with many Puerto Ricans returning home.

When the United States acquired the island in 1898, most Puerto Ricans worked in agriculture, but today, most jobs are industrial and are situated in the cities. Today, one-third of the commonwealth's population is concentrated in the San Juan/Carolina/Bayamón metropolitan area.

The people of Puerto Rico represent a cultural and racial mix. When the Spanish forced the Taíno peoples into slavery, virtually the entire indigenous population was decimated, except for a few Amerindians who escaped into the remote mountains. Eventually they intermarried with the poor Spanish farmers and became known as *jíbaros*. Because of industrialization and migration to the cities, few jíbaros remain.

Besides the slaves imported from Africa to work on the plantations, other ethnic groups joined the island's racial mix. Fleeing Simón Bolívar's independence movements in South America, Spanish loyalists fled to Puerto Rico—a fiercely conservative Spanish colony during the early 1800s. French families also flocked here from both Louisiana and Haiti, as changing governments or violent revolutions turned their worlds upside down. Meanwhile, as word of the rich sugarcane economy reached economically depressed Scotland and Ireland, many farmers from those countries also journeyed to Puerto Rico in search of a better life.

During the mid-19th century, labor was needed to build roads. Initially, Chinese workers were imported for this task, followed by workers from such countries as Italy, France, Germany, and even Lebanon. American expatriates came to the island after 1898. Long after Spain had lost control of Puerto Rico, Spanish immigrants continued to arrive on the island. The most significant new immigrant population arrived in the 1960s, when thousands of Cubans fled from Fidel Castro's Communist state. The latest arrivals in Puerto Rico have come from the economically depressed Dominican Republic.

THEIR LANGUAGES

Spanish is the language of Puerto Rico, although English is widely spoken, especially in hotels, restaurants, shops, and nightclubs that attract tourists. In the hinterlands, however, Spanish prevails.

If you plan to travel extensively on Puerto Rico but don't speak Spanish, pick up a Spanish-language phrase book. The most popular is *Berlitz Spanish for Travelers,*

Sweet Songs of Love

The Spanish colonialists first recorded some of the Taíno tribespeople's legends, which they had passed down orally from generation to generation. Many of these were ghost tales about demons who roamed the island after dark, pursuing food or people or else protecting gold and loot that pirates long ago stashed away for safekeeping.

But one such tale, dated from about 1511, is the Puerto Rican version of *Romeo and Juliet* or the early Virginian legend of Capt. John Smith and his Native American bride, Pocahontas.

The story is called "Guanina" because it tells of Don Cristóbal de Sotomayor, a young man from Valladolid, Spain, who was enchanted by a graceful Amerindian girl, Guanina. At its end, the two are found dead, Guanina's head resting on his bloody chest.

It was said that a witch doctor buried their bodies under the roots of a towering ceiba tree, and that white lilies and red poppies grew from their graves. Locals claimed to hear sweet songs of love rustling through the leaves of the giant ceiba.

Some people on the island say the lovers still come out on moonlit nights to renew their vows of devotion.

---

published by Collier Macmillan. The University of Chicago's *Pocketbook Dictionary* is equally helpful. If you already have a basic knowledge of Spanish and want to improve both your word usage and your sentence structure while in Puerto Rico, consider purchasing a copy of *Spanish Now,* published by Barron's.

Many Amerindian words from pre-Columbian times have been retained in the language. For example, the Puerto Rican national anthem, titled "La Borinqueña," refers to the Arawak name for the island, Borinquen, while Mayagüez, Yauco, Caguas, Guaynabo, and Arecibo are all pre-Columbian place names.

Many Amerindian words were borrowed to describe the phenomena of the New World. The natives slept in *hamacas,* and today Puerto Ricans still lounge in hammocks. The god Juracán was feared by the Arawaks just as much as contemporaries fear autumn hurricanes. African words were also added to the linguistic mix, and Castilian Spanish was significantly modified.

With the American takeover in 1898, English became the first Germanic language to be introduced into Puerto Rico. This linguistic marriage led to what some scholars call Spanglish, a colloquial dialect blending English and Spanish into forms not considered classically correct in either linguistic tradition.

The bilingual confusion was also greatly accelerated by the mass migration to the U.S. mainland of thousands of Puerto Ricans, who quickly altered their speech patterns to conform to the language used in the urban Puerto Rican communities of such cities as New York.

THEIR RELIGIONS

The majority of Puerto Ricans are Roman Catholic, but religious freedom for all faiths is guaranteed by the Commonwealth Constitution. Catholic services are conducted throughout the island in both English and Spanish. There is a Jewish Community Center in Miramar, plus a Jewish Reformed Congregation in Santurce. There are English-speaking Protestant services for Baptists, Episcopalians, Lutherans, and Presbyterians, and other interdenominational services.

Although predominantly Catholic, Puerto Rico does not follow Catholic dogma and rituals as assiduously as do the churches of Spain and Italy. Because the church supported slavery, there was a long-lasting resentment against the all-Spanish clergy of colonial days. Island-born men were excluded from the priesthood. When Puerto Ricans eventually took over the Catholic churches on the island, they followed some guidelines from Spain and Italy but modified or ignored others. For example, many Catholic couples in Puerto Rico practice birth control and are married outside the Catholic church.

Following the U.S. acquisition of the island in 1898, Protestantism grew in influence and popularity. There were Protestants on the island before the invasion, but their numbers increased after Puerto Rico became an American colony. Many islanders liked the idea of separation of church and state, as provided for in the U.S. Constitution. In recent years, a Pentecostal fundamentalism has swept across the island. There are perhaps some 1,500 evangelical churches in Puerto Rico today.

As throughout Latin America, the practice of Catholicism in Puerto Rico blends certain native Taíno and African traditions with mainstream tenets of the faith. It has been said that the real religion of Puerto Rico is *espiritismo* (spiritualism), a quasi-magical belief in occult forces. Spanish colonial rulers outlawed spiritualism, but under the U.S. occupation it flourished in dozens of isolated pockets of the island.

Students of religion trace spiritualism to the Taínos, and to their belief that *jípia* (the spirits of the dead—somewhat like the legendary vampire) slumbered by day and prowled the island by night. Instead of looking for bodies, the jípia were seeking wild fruit to eat. Thus arose the Puerto Rican tradition of putting out fruit on the kitchen table. Even in modern homes today, you'll often find a bowl of plastic, flamboyantly colored fruit resting atop a refrigerator.

Many islanders still believe in the "evil eye," or *mal de ojo.* To look on a person or a person's possessions covetously, according to believers, can lead to that individual's sickness or perhaps death. Little children are given bead charm bracelets to guard against the evil eye. Spiritualism also extends into healing, folk medicine, and food. Some spiritualists, for example, believe that cold food should never be eaten with hot food. Various island plants, herbs, and oils are believed to have certain healing properties, and spiritualist literature is available throughout the island.

6　Puerto Rican Handcrafts

SANTOS

The most impressive of the island's crafts are the *santos,* carved religious figures that have been produced since the 1500s. Craftspeople who make these are called *santeros;* using clay, gold, stone, or cedarwood, they carve figurines representing saints, usually from 8 to 20 inches tall. Before the Spanish colonization, small statues called *zemi* stood in native tribal villages and camps as objects of veneration, and Puerto Rico's santos may derive from that pre-Columbian tradition. Every town has its patron saint, and every home has its santos to protect the family. For some families, worshipping the santos replaces a traditional mass.

Art historians view the carving of santos as Puerto Rico's greatest contribution to the plastic arts. The earliest figures were richly baroque, indicating a strong Spanish influence, but as the islanders began to assert their own identity, the carved figures often became simpler.

In carving santos, craftspeople often used handmade tools. Sometimes such natural materials as vegetable dyes and even human hair were used. The saints represented by most santos can be identified by their accompanying symbols; for example, Saint Anthony is usually depicted with the infant Jesus and a book. The most popular group of santos is the Three Kings. The Trinity and the Nativity also are depicted frequently.

Art experts claim that santos making approached its zenith at the turn of the century, although hundreds of *santeros* (santos makers) still practice their craft throughout the island. Serious santos collectors view the former craftsmen of old as the true artists in the field. However, many skilled santeros still practice this art, and take it most seriously. To pick up a list of these artisans, you can visit the **Popular Arts and Crafts Center,** Calle Cristo 253 (☎ 787/722-0621), run by the Institute of Puerto Rican Culture in Old San Juan. They will provide you with contacts of studios where visitors are welcomed. Also see "Shopping" in chapter 7 for outlets selling these santos figures.

Some of the best santos on the island can be seen at the Capilla del Cristo in Old San Juan. Perhaps at some future date a museum devoted entirely to santos will open on Puerto Rico.

OLD LACE

Another Puerto Rican craft has undergone a big revival just as it seemed that it would disappear forever: lace. Originating in Spain, *mundillos* (tatted fabrics) are the product of a type of bobbin lace making. This craft, 5 centuries old, exists today only in Puerto Rico and Spain.

The first lace made in Puerto Rico was called *torchon* (beggar's lace). Early examples of beggar's lace were considered of inferior quality, but artisans today have transformed this fabric into a delicate art form, eagerly sought by collectors. Lace bands called *entrados* have two straight borders, whereas the other traditional style, *puntilla,* has both a straight and a scalloped border.

The best place to see the craft of the mundillo is the **Folk Arts Center** at the Dominican Convent at Calle Norzagaray 98 in Old San Juan (☎ 787/721-6866). This center has information on island shops that make and sell mundillos. You can also attend the Puerto Rican Weaving Festival, held annually at the end of April in the town of Isabela. For more information on how to purchase Puerto Rican lace, refer to "Shopping" in chapter 7.

GROTESQUE MASKS

The most popular of all Puerto Rican crafts are the frightening *caret-as—papier-mâché* masks worn at island carnivals. Tangles of menacing horns, fang-toothed leering expressions, and bulging eyes of these half-demon, half-animal creations send children running screaming to their parents. At carnival time, they are worn by costumed revelers called *vejigantes.* Vejigantes often wear bat-winged jumpsuits and roam the streets either individually or in groups.

The origins of these masks and carnivals may go back to medieval Spain and/or tribal Africa. A processional tradition in Spain, dating from the early 17th century, was intended to terrify sinners with marching devils in the hope that they would return to church. Cervantes described it briefly in *Don Quijote.* Puerto Rico blended this Spanish procession with the masked tradition brought by slaves from Africa. Some historians believe that the Taínos also were accomplished mask makers, which would make this a very ancient tradition indeed.

The predominant mask colors, at least traditionally, were black, red, and yellow, all symbols of hellfire and damnation. Today, pastels are more likely to be used. Each vejigante sports at least two or three horns, although some masks have

---

Impressions

A machete is the only instrument used in their work. With it, they cut the sticks, vines, and palm leaves to build their houses and also clear the ground and plant and cultivate their crops.

—Fray Inigo Abbad

---

hundreds of horns in all shapes and sizes. Mask making in Ponce, the major center for this craft, and in Loíza Aldea, a palm-fringed town on the island's northeastern coast, has since led to a renaissance of Puerto Rican folk art.

You can purchase these masks year-round at various places, even in the homes of the mask makers, providing that you have their addresses. Although many masks are extremely elaborate and expensive, they typically range in price from $15 to $100. The premier store selling these masks is **Puerto Rican Art and Crafts,** at Calle Fortaleza 204 in Old San Juan (☎ 787/725-5596). Masks can be seen in action at the three big masquerade carnivals on the island: the Ponce Festival in February, the Festival of Loíza Aldea in July, and the Día de las Mascaras at Hatillo in December.

WHERE TO SEE THE BEST ARTS & CRAFTS

Serious students of Puerto Rican art always go to the **Folk Arts Center** at the Dominican Convent at Calle Norzagaray 98 in Old San Juan (☎ 787/721-6866). It's the best source of information on the island about Puerto Rican arts and crafts. For actual purchases of Puerto Rican crafts, the best outlet is **Puerto Rican Arts and Crafts** at Calle Fortaleza 204 (☎ 787/725-5596), also in Old San Juan.

With its dozen or so museums and even more art galleries, Old San Juan is the greatest repository of Puerto Rican arts and crafts. Galleries sell everything from pre-Columbian artifacts to paintings by relatively contemporary artists such as Angel Botello, who died in 1986. The **Galleria Botello,** at Calle del Cristo 208, was his former home. He restored the colonial mansion himself; now his paintings and sculptures are on display here.

Another good place to see Puerto Rican art is the **Museum of the University of Puerto Rico** in Río Piedras. Because of space limitations, the museum's galleries can exhibit only a fifth of their vast collection at one time, but the work is always of top-notch quality. The collection ranges from pre-Columbian artifacts to works by today's major painters.

The greatest art on the island is at the **Museo de Arte de Ponce,** Avenida de las Americas, in Puerto Rico's second-largest city. The collection, donated by former governor Luís A. Ferré, ranges from Jan van Eyck's *Salvatore Mundi* to Rossetti's confrontational *Daughters of King Lear*. The museum building was designed by Edward Durell Stone, who also designed New York's Museum of Modern Art. Works are displayed here in a honeycomb of skylit hexagonal rooms. Puerto Rican artists who are represented include José Campeche (see above) and Francisco Oller. In addition to such European masters as Reubens, van Dyck, and Murillo, the museum features works by Latin American artists, including some by the Mexican Diego Rivera.

7 Puerto Rico's Exotic Bill of Fare

Although Puerto Rican cooking is somewhat similar to both Spanish and Mexican cuisine, it has a unique style, using such indigenous seasonings and ingredients as coriander, papaya, cacao, nispero, apio, plantains, and yampee.

Cocina Criolla (Creole cooking) can be traced back to the Arawaks and Taínos, the original inhabitants of the island, who thrived on a diet of corn, tropical fruit, and seafood. When Ponce de León arrived with Columbus in 1493, the Spanish added beef, pork, rice, wheat, and olive oil to the island's foodstuffs.

The Spanish soon began planting sugarcane and importing slaves from Africa, who brought with them okra and taro (known in Puerto Rico as *yautia*). The mingling of flavors and ingredients passed from generation to generation among the different ethnic groups that settled on the island, resulting in the exotic blend of today's Puerto Rican cuisine.

APPETIZERS & SOUPS

Lunch and dinner generally begin with sizzling-hot appetizers such as *bacalaítos,* crunchy cod fritters; *surullitos,* sweet plump cornmeal fingers; and *empanadillas,* crescent-shaped turnovers filled with lobster, crab, conch, or beef.

Soups also are a popular beginning. There is a debate about whether one of the world's best-known soups, *frijoles negros,* is Cuban or Puerto Rican in origin. Wherever it started, black-bean soup makes a savory if filling opening to a meal. Another classic soup is *sopón de pollo con arroz*—chicken soup with rice—which manages to taste somewhat different in every restaurant. One traditional method of preparing this soup calls for large pieces of pumpkin and diced potatoes or yautias (the starchy root of a large-leaved tropical plant whose flesh is usually yellow or creamy white).

The third classic soup is *sopón de pescado* (fish soup), prepared with the head and tail intact. Again, this soup varies from restaurant to restaurant and may depend on the catch of the day. Traditionally, it is made with garlic and spices plus onions and tomatoes, the flavor enhanced by a tiny dash of vinegar and a half cup of sherry. Galician broth (*caldo gallego*) is a dish imported from Spain's northwestern province of Galicia. It is prepared with salt pork, white beans, ham, and *berzas* (collard greens) or *grelos* (turnip greens), and the whole kettle is flavored with spicy chorizos (Spanish sausages).

Garbanzos (chickpeas) are often added to give flavor, body, and texture to Puerto Rican soups. One of the most authentic versions of this is *sopón de garbanzos con patas de cerdo* (chickpea soup with pig's feet). Into this kettle is added a variety of ingredients, including pumpkin, chorizos, salt pork, chile peppers, cabbage, potatoes, tomatoes, and fresh cilantro leaves.

Not really a soup, the most traditional Puerto Rican dish is *asopao,* a hearty gumbo made with either chicken or shellfish. One well-known version, consumed when the food budget runs low, is *asopao de gandules* (pigeon peas). Every Puerto Rican chef has his or her own recipe for asopao. *Asopao de pollo* (chicken asopao) takes a whole chicken, which is then flavored with spices such as oregano, garlic, and paprika, along with salt pork, cured ham, green peppers, chile peppers, onions, cilantro, olives, tomatoes, chorizos, and pimientos. For a final touch, green peas or asparagus might be added.

MAIN COURSES

The aroma that wafts from kitchens throughout Puerto Rico comes from *adobo* and *sofrito*—blends of herbs and spices that give many of the native foods their distinctive taste and color. Adobo, made by crushing together peppercorns, oregano, garlic, salt, olive oil, and lime juice or vinegar, is rubbed into meats before they are roasted. Sofrito, a potpourri of onions, garlic, and peppers browned in either olive oil or lard and colored with *achiote* (annatto seeds), imparts the bright yellow color to the island's rice, soups, and stews.

Strange Fruit

Reading of Capt. James Cook's explorations of the South Pacific in the late 1700s, West Indian planters were intrigued by his accounts of the breadfruit tree, which grew in abundance on Tahiti. Seeing that it as a source of cheap food for their slaves, they beseeched King George III to sponsor an expedition to bring the trees to the Caribbean.

In 1787, the king put Capt. William Bligh in command of H.M.S. *Bounty* and sent him to do just that. One of Bligh's lieutenants was a former shipmate named Fletcher Christian. They became the leading actors in one of the great sea yarns when Christian overpowered Bligh, took over the *Bounty*, threw the breadfruit trees into the South Pacific Ocean, and disappeared into oblivion.

Bligh survived by sailing the ship's open longboat 3,000 miles to the East Indies, where he hitched a ride back to England on a Dutch vessel. Later he was given command of another ship and sent to Tahiti to get more breadfruit. Although he succeeded on this second attempt, the whole operation went for naught when the West Indies slaves refused to eat the strange fruit of the new tree, preferring instead their old, familiar rice.

Descendants of those trees still grow in the Caribbean, and the islanders prepare the head-size fruit in a number of ways. A thick green rind covers its starchy, sweet flesh whose flavor is evocative of a sweet potato. *Tostones*—fried green breadfruit slices—accompany most meat, fish, or poultry dishes served today in Puerto Rico.

Stews loom large in the Puerto Rican diet. They are usually cooked in a *caldera* (heavy kettle). A popular one is *carne guisada puertorriqueña* (Puerto Rican beef stew). The ingredients that flavor the chunks of beef vary according to the cook's whims or whatever happens to be in the larder. These might include green peppers, sweet chile peppers, onions, garlic, cilantro, potatoes, olives stuffed with pimientos, or capers. Seeded raisins may be added on occasion.

Meat pies (*pastelon de carne*) are the staple of many Puerto Rican dinners. Salt pork and ham are often used for the filling and are cooked in a *caldero* (small cauldron). This medley of meats and spices is covered with a pastry top and baked.

Other typical main dishes include fried beefsteak with onions (*carne frita con cebolla*), veal (*ternera*) à la parmesana, and roast leg of pork, fresh ham, lamb, or veal, à la criolla. These roasted meats are cooked in the Creole style, flavored with adobo. *Chicharrónes* is very popular, especially around Christmastime—fried pork with the crunchy skin left on top for added flavor.

Puerto Ricans also like such dishes as breaded calf's brains (*sesos empanados*), calf's kidney stew (*riñones guisados*), and stuffed beef tongue (*lengua rellena*).

A festive island dish is *lechón asado*, or **barbecued pig**, which is usually cooked for a party of 12 to 15. It is traditional for picnics and alfresco parties; one can sometimes catch the aroma of this dish wafting through the palm trees, a smell that must have been familiar to the Taíno peoples. The pig is basted with *jugo de naranja agria* (sour orange juice) and achiote coloring. Green plantains are peeled and roasted over hot stones, then served with the barbecued pig as a side dish. The traditional dressing served with the pig is *aji-li-mojili*, a sour garlic sauce. The sauce combines garlic, whole black peppercorns, and sweet seeded chile peppers, flavored further with vinegar, lime juice, salt, and olive oil.

Puerto Ricans adore **chicken,** which they flavor with various spices and seasonings. *Arroz con pollo* (chicken with rice) is the most popular chicken dish on the island, and it was brought long ago to the U.S. mainland. Other favorite preparations include *pollo al Jerez* (chicken in sherry), *pollo en agridulce* (sweet-and sour chicken), and *pollitos asados à la parrilla* (broiled chickens).

Most visitors to the island prefer the fresh **fish and shellfish.** A popular dish is fried fish with Puerto Rican sauce (*mojo isleno*). The sauce is made with olives and olive oil, onions, pimientos, capers, tomato sauce, vinegar, and a flavoring of garlic and bay leaves. Fresh fish is often grilled, and perhaps flavored with garlic and an overlay of freshly squeezed lime juice—a very tasty dinner indeed. Caribbean lobster is usually the most expensive item on any menu, followed by shrimp. Puerto Ricans often cook shrimp in beer (*camarones en cerveza*). Another delectable shellfish dish is boiled crab (*jueyes hervidos*).

Many tasty **egg dishes** are served, especially *tortilla española* (Spanish omelette), cooked with finely chopped onions, cubed potatoes, and olive oil.

The rich and fertile fields of Puerto Rico produce a wide variety of **vegetables.** A favorite is the *chayote,* a pear-shaped vegetable called *christophine* throughout most of the English-speaking Caribbean. Its delicately flavored flesh is often compared to that of summer squash.

Fried *tostones* are made with both **breadfruit** (see box) and **plantains.** In fact, the plantain is the single most popular side dish served on the island. Plantains are a variety of banana that cannot be eaten raw. They are much coarser in texture than ordinary bananas and are harvested while green, then baked, fried, or boiled. When made into tostones, they are usually served as an appetizer with before-dinner drinks. Fried to a deep golden yellow, plantains may accompany fish, meat, or poultry dishes.

THE AROMA OF COFFEE

It is customary for most Puerto Ricans to finish their meal with the strong, black aromatic coffee grown here. Originally imported from the nearby Dominican Republic, coffee beans have been produced in the island's high-altitude interior for more than 300 years and still rank among the island's leading exports.

Puerto Rican coffee, in the view of many connoisseurs, rivals that of the more highly touted product from Colombia. Coffee has several degrees of quality, of course, the lowest ranking one being *café de primera,* which is typically served at the ordinary family table. The top category is called *café super premium.* Only three coffees in the world belong to super premium class: Blue Mountain coffee of Jamaica, kona coffee from Hawaii, and Puerto Rico's homegrown Alto Grande, platinum coffee beans sought by coffee connoisseurs around the world.

The best brand names for Puerto Rican coffee are Café Crema, Café Rico, Rioja, and Yaucono.

You can ask for your brew *puya* (unsweetened), *negrito con azúcar* (black and sweetened), *cortao* (black with a drop of milk), or *con leche* (with milk).

RUM: KILL-DEVIL OR WHISKY-BELLY VENGEANCE

Rum is the national drink, and you can buy it in almost any shade. Since the island is the world's leading rum producer, it's little wonder that every Puerto Rican bartender worthy of the profession likes to concoct his or her own favorite rum libation.

All resorts offer the *piña colada,* made with cream of coconut, white Puerto Rican rum, and canned pineapple juice. The ingredients are thoroughly blended and served frappé style in a tall, cool glass, usually garnished with a maraschino cherry and a small paper parasol. But you may want to be more adventurous and sample some of the island's other cocktails, many of which are made with fresh fruit juices. Planter's punch, served over cracked ice, is the second-most-popular mixed rum drink for tourists. Often, it combines dark Puerto Rican rum, dark brown Jamaican rum, citrus juice, and Angostura bitters.

Of course, you can call for Puerto Rican rum in many mixed drinks such as rum collins, rum sour, rum screwdriver, and rum and tonic. The classic sangría, which is prepared in Spain with dry red wine, sugar, orange juice, and other ingredients, may be given a thoroughly Puerto Rican twist with a hefty dose of the island's rum.

Today's version of rum bears little resemblance to the raw and grainy beverage consumed by the renegades and pirates of the Spanish Main. Christopher Columbus brought sugarcane, from which rum is distilled, to the Caribbean on his second voyage to the New World, and in virtually no time it became *the* regional drink.

It is believed that Ponce de León introduced rum to Puerto Rico during his governorship, which began in 1508. In time, there emerged large sugarcane plantations. From Puerto Rico and other West Indian islands, rum was shipped to colonial America, where it lent itself to such popular and hair-raising 18th-century drinks as Kill-Divil and Whistle-Belly Vengeance. After America became a nation, rum was largely displaced as the drink of choice by whisky, distilled from grain grown on the American plains.

It took almost a century before Puerto Rico's rum industry regained its former vigor. This occurred during a severe whisky shortage in the U.S. at the end of World War II. By the 1950s, sales of rum had fallen off again, as more and different kinds of liquor became available on the American market.

The local brew had been a questionable drink because of inferior distillation methods and quality. Recognizing this problem, the Puerto Rican government drew up rigid standards for producing, blending, and aging rum. Rum factories were outfitted with the most modern and sanitary equipment, and sales figures (encouraged by aggressive marketing campaigns) began to climb.

No one will ever agree on what "the best" rum is in the Caribbean. There are just too many of them to sample. Some are so esoteric as to be unavailable in your local liquor store. But if popular tastes mean anything, then Puerto Rican rums, especially Bacardi, head the list. There are 24 different rums from Puerto Rico sold in the United States under 11 brand names—not only Bacardi, but Ron Bocoy, Ronrico, Don Q, and many others.

Puerto Rican rums are generally light, gold, or dark. Usually white or silver in color, the biggest seller is light in body and dry in taste. Its subtle flavor and delicate aroma make it ideal for many mixed drinks, including the daiquiri, rum collins, rum mary, and rum and tonic or soda. It also goes with almost any fruit juice, or on the rocks with a slice of lemon or lime. Gold or amber rum is aromatic and full-bodied in taste. Aging in charred oak casks adds color to the rum.

Gold rums are usually aged longer for a deeper and more mellow flavor than light rums. They are increasingly popular on the rocks, straight up, or in certain mixed drinks in which extra flavor is desired—certainly in the famous piña colada, rum and coke, or eggnog.

Finally, dark rum is full-bodied with a deep, velvety, smooth taste and a complex flavor. It can be aged for as long as 15 years. Enjoy it on the rocks, with tonic or soda, or in mixed drinks when you want the taste of rum to stand out.

Your best introduction to Puerto Rican rum making is to visit the Bacardi distillery in Cataño, just a short ferryboat ride across the San Juan harbor.

8 Salsa & Bomba: Dancing to the Beat

One of Puerto Rico's notable exports is its music, which along with that of Jamaica is the predominant Caribbean music heard in the United States. Few if any American ears haven't been exposed to the vibrant Latin beats of the salsa, the bomba, and the plena.

Regrettably, you can often go to more Puerto Rican clubs in New York than you can in San Juan to hear this music. You would think that since Puerto Ricans like music so much, San Juan would be filled with dives offering a Latin beat. There are many dives in San Juan with music, but it's usually recorded. The best artists are hired to perform at the hotels, and even so, performances are irregular. Live music is heard more frequently in the winter than in the summer months, when there are fewer visitors.

Why so few clubs? Puerto Ricans often hear their music on radio or recorded instead of going to clubs. It's a way for them to listen to good music without paying high tabs. For a representative sampling of what's available—and admittedly it's limited—see "San Juan After Dark" in chapter 7.

At least some of the unique sounds of salsa, bomba, and the plena come from instruments that originated with the Taíno peoples. Most noteworthy is the *güicharo,* or *güiro,* a notched, hollowed-out gourd, which was adapted from pre-Columbian days. The musical traditions of the Spanish and Africans can also be heard in Puerto Rico's music. At least four different instruments were adapted from the six-string Spanish classical guitar: the *requinto,* the *bordonua,* the *cuatro,* and the *tiple,* each of which produces a unique tone and pitch. The most popular of these, and the one for which the greatest number of adaptations and compositions have been written, is the cuatro, a guitar-like instrument with 10 strings (arranged in five pairs). Usually carved from solid blocks of laurel wood and known for resonances and pitches different from those produced by its Spanish counterpart, this instrument's graceful baroque body has been revered for decades as the national instrument of Puerto Rico.

Also prevalent on the island are such percussion instruments as *tambours* (hollowed tree trunks covered with stretched-out animal skin), *maracas* (gourds filled with pebbles or dried beans and mounted on handles), and a variety of drums whose original designs were brought from Africa by the island's slaves. All these instruments contribute to the rich variety of folk music with roots in the cultural melting pot of the island's Spanish, African, and Taíno traditions.

PUERTO RICAN FOLK MUSIC

During Puerto Rico's colonial years, a series of musical traditions evolved based on the folk songs and romantic ballads of 18th- and 19th-century Spain. Eventually, these became fused with music either imported or native to the Hispanic New World. Dealing with life, death, and everyday events of an agrarian society far removed from the royal courts of Europe, this music has been studiously collected and reorchestrated for modern audiences.

One collector of this music was Don Felo, whose 19th-century compositions were based on the melodic traditions of both Spain and the Spanish-speaking Caribbean. In the 20th century, Narciso Figueroa continued the tradition of collecting folk songs and reorchestrating them for chamber orchestras; his recordings have been sponsored by the Institute of Puerto Rican Culture.

Today, the most widely applauded—and, to many, most enjoyable—of the island's folk music are the hillbilly pieces created by the mountain-dwelling jíbaros. Using the full array of stringed and percussion instruments described above, they give lyrical performances whose live or recorded versions are popular at everything from island weddings to commencement exercises. Despite the appeal of other island musical forms, such as salsa, it could be argued that the jíbaro tradition of cuatro with drums is the island's most notable—and the one most likely to evoke homesickness in the hearts of any expatriate Puerto Rican.

Puerto Rico, unfortunately, doesn't have clubs featuring folk music on a regular basis. It's a "sometimes" thing. However, folk music is often incorporated into shows presented by music groups that seem to float from one hotel to another.

SALSA

The major type of music coming out of Puerto Rico is salsa, *the* rhythm of the islands. Its name literally translates as the "sauce" that makes parties happen. Originally developed within the Puerto Rican community of New York, it draws heavily from the musical roots of the Cuban and the African-Caribbean experience. Highly danceable, its rhythms are hot, urban, rhythmically sophisticated, and compelling. Today, the center of salsa has probably shifted from New York back to Puerto Rico, where local musicians compete fiercely with those from Cuba for the most infectious melodies.

Cuban salsa tends to be less avant-garde than the constantly mutating versions produced in Puerto Rico. Even within the salsa tradition, different groups adhere more or less fervently to the traditions of mainstream jazz, popular Latin song, and African inspirations.

Salsa is not an old form of music at all. Music critics claim that it originated in New York City nightclubs in the years following World War II, an evolution of the era's Big Band tradition. The first great salsa musician was Tito Puente, who, after a stint with the U.S. Navy, studied percussion at New York's Juilliard School of Music. He went on to organize his own band, Puente's Latin Jazz Ensemble, which has been heard by audiences around the world. One critic said that the music is what results when the sounds of Big Band jazz meet African-Caribbean rhythms. Other critics say that salsa is a combination of fast Latin music that embraces the rumba, mambo, cha-cha, guaguancho, and merengue.

Salsa has definitely made Puerto Rico famous in the world of international music. Salsa bands require access to a huge array of percussion instruments, including güiros, the gourds on which the Taíno peoples may have played music. Other instruments include maracas, bongos, timbales, conga drums, and claves—and to add the jíbaro touch, a clanging cowbell. Of course, it also takes a bass, a horn section, a chorus, and a lead vocalist to get the combination right.

No one quite agrees about who is the king of salsa today, but Willie Colón, El Gran Combo de Puerto Rico, and Hector Lovoe are on everyone's list as the "Grand Masters of today's salsa beat." Chances are you won't get to see them on their home turf because they may be touring internationally. However, appearances on the island by one of these stars are widely heralded in the media, and tickets are hard to come by. Hundreds of young *salseros* are waiting to take their thrones as the popularity (and income levels) of the emerging salsa stars continues to climb.

BOMBA & PLENA

Although usually grouped together, *bomba y plena* are actually two entirely different types of music that are coupled with dance. Pure African, **bomba** was brought over by black slaves who worked on the island's sugar plantations. It's a rhythmic music using barrel-shaped drums covered with tightly stretched animal skins and played by hand. This form of music is produced by one large drum plus a smaller drum called a *subidor.* The drums are accompanied by the rhythmical beating of sticks and maracas to create a swelling tide of drumbeats, in which aficionados can hear the drummers bang out a series of responses one to another.

Bomba is described as a dialogue between dancer and drummer. It's as if the drummer were challenging the dancer to a rhythmic duel. The dance can go on just as long as the dancer can continue. Although critics are uncertain about the exact origins of bomba, it is divided into different rhythmic backgrounds and variations, such as the Euba, Cocobale, and Sica. As the dance and the drummer's beat continue, the music grows more spirited and more complex. Bomba is sometimes incorporated into folkloric shows presented infrequently in San Juan. Otherwise, it's nearly impossible to find a club presenting it with regularity. Count yourself fortunate if you get to see a performance.

Whereas bomba is purely African in origin, **plena** blends elements from Puerto Ricans' wide cultural backgrounds, including music that the Taíno tribes may have used during their ceremonies. This type of music first appeared in Ponce, where performing the plena became a hallmark of Spanish tradition and coquetry.

Instruments used in plena include the güiro, a dried-out gourd whose surface is cut with parallel grooves and, when rubbed with a stick, produces a raspy and rhythmical percussive noise. The Taínos may have invented this instrument. From the guitars brought to the New World by the Spanish conquistadores emerged the 10-stringed cuatro. To the güiro and cuatro is added the tambourine, known as *panderos,* originally derived from Africa. Dancing plena became a kind of living newspaper. Singers recited the events of the day and often satirized local politicians or scandals. Sometimes plenas were filled with biting satire; at other times, they commented on major news events of the day, such as a devastating hurricane.

Bomba y plena remain the most popular forms of folk music on the island, and many cultural events highlight this music for entertainment. In a somewhat commercialized form, *bomba y plena* shows are often presented at resort hotels along San Juan's Condado beachfront strip. It may not be "the real thing," but often it's just as good even if presented at a hotel instead of a local dive in some forgotten Puerto Rican village.

3

Planning a Trip to Puerto Rico

This chapter discusses the where, the when, and the how of your trip to Puerto Rico—everything required to plan your trip and get it on the road. Here we've concentrated on what you need to do *before* you go.

In addition to helping you decide when to take your vacation, we've put a wealth of insider information at your fingertips. This chapter also explores different possibilities for getting to Puerto Rico, including not only the most obvious ones but also some that may not have crossed your mind. We also discuss various ways to travel around the island and suggest an itinerary to help you get the most out of a week's vacation. You'll find tips on deciding where to stay, where to dine, and what to buy. Capping off the chapter is a quick-reference list of helpful "Fast Facts" about Puerto Rico.

1 Visitor Information, Entry Requirements & Money

VISITOR INFORMATION

For information before you leave home, contact one of the following **Puerto Rico Tourism Company** offices: 575 Fifth Ave., New York, NY 10017 (☎ **800/223-6530** or 212/599-6262); 3575 W. Cahuenga Blvd., Suite 405, Los Angeles, CA 90068 (☎ **800/874-1230** or 213/874-5991); or 901 Ponce de León Blvd., Suite 604, Coral Gables, FL 33134 (☎ **800/815-7391** or 305/445-9112).

In Canada contact the company at 41-43 Colbourne St., Suite 301, Toronto, ON M5E 1E3 (☎ **800/667-0394** or 416/368-2680).

If you have Internet access, visit **City.Net** (www.city.net). City.Net lists links, organized by location and then by subject, to sites with information about many destinations. To find Puerto Rico, click on the "Caribbean" heading; when a map of the region appears, click on the island. This site has a number of links to other sources for Puerto Rico info. Another worthwhile site is **"My Puerto Rico Homepage"** (gwis2.circ.gwu.edu/~jacobino/puerto-rico.html). It, too, serves as a hotlist of other sites with Puerto Rico content, plus links to individual homepages that include Puerto Rico in some way.

One of the best Caribbean Web sites is **Caribbean-On-Line** (www.webcom. com/earleltd/), a series of virtual guidebooks full of information on hotels, restaurants, and shopping, along with sights and detailed maps of the islands. The site is still a work in progress, and at press time Puerto Rico information was not yet accessible. However, the site also includes links to travel agents and cruise lines that are up on the Web.

You may also want to contact the U.S. State Department for background bulletins. Write the Superintendent of Documents, **U.S. Government Printing Office,** Washington, DC 20402 (☎ **202/512-1800**).

A good travel agent can be a source of information. Make sure your agent is a member of the American Society of Travel Agents (ASTA). If you get poor service from an ASTA agent, you can write to the **ASTA Consumer Affairs Department,** 1101 King St., Alexandria, VA 22314 (☎ **703/739-8739**).

ENTRY REQUIREMENTS

DOCUMENTS   Americans who fly from the mainland to Puerto Rico and return to the mainland don't need passports because Puerto Rico is a territory of the United States. If they visit no other country from a land base in Puerto Rico, however, they are asked if they are U.S. citizens upon flying back to the mainland. A simple "yes" will do. In other words, Americans don't have to prove citizenship or produce documents.

Canadians, however, should carry some form of identification. Acceptable documents include an ongoing or a return ticket, plus a current voter registration card or a birth certificate. In addition, you will need some photo ID, which could be a driver's license or an expired passport. Driver's licenses alone are not acceptable as ID. Visitors from the United Kingdom, New Zealand, Ireland, and most western European nations need only a valid passport as long as they plan to stay in Puerto Rico 90 days or less. Citizens of Australia need just a passport to enter Puerto Rico.

Before leaving home, make two copies of your most valuable documents, including your passport, your driver's license, or any other identity document; your airline ticket; and any hotel vouchers. If you're on medication, you should also make copies of prescriptions.

VACCINATIONS   Vaccinations are not required for entry to Puerto Rico if you're coming from the United States or Canada.

Infectious hepatitis has been reported on other Caribbean islands but less frequently on Puerto Rico. Consult your doctor about the advisability of getting a gamma-globulin shot before you leave home.

Typhoid, poliomyelitis, and tetanus are not common diseases on the island, and inoculations against them are recommended mainly to visitors who plan to rough it in the wilds. If you're staying in a regular Puerto Rican hotel, such preventive measures are generally not needed, but your doctor can advise you, based on your destination and travel plans.

CUSTOMS

U.S. citizens do not need to clear Puerto Rican Customs upon arrival by plane or ship from the mainland. All non-U.S. citizens must clear Customs and are permitted to bring in items intended for their personal use, including tobacco, cameras, film, and a limited supply of liquor (usually 40 oz.).

U.S. CUSTOMS   On departure, U.S.-bound travelers must have their luggage inspected by the U.S. Agriculture Department because laws prohibit bringing certain fruits and plants to the U.S. mainland. Fruits and vegetables are not allowed, but otherwise, you can bring back as much as you want without paying duty.

For more specifics, write to the **U.S. Customs Service**, 1301 Constitution Ave., P.O. Box 7407, Washington, DC 20044 (☎ 202/927-6724; www.customs. ustreas.gov/), and request the free pamphlet *Know Before You Go*.

CANADIAN CUSTOMS   Canadians who have spent 24 hours or less outside the country are allowed a C$50 exemption from taxation goods they've bought, but any tobacco or liquor products purchased abroad are subject to Canadian duty. For Canadians who have spent more than 48 hours outside the Canadian border, a C$300 exemption is granted on goods they've purchased, and they're allowed to bring back duty-free 200 cigarettes, 200 grams of tobacco, 40 imperial ounces of liquor, and 50 cigars. For Canadians who have spent 7 days or more outside the country, the exemption is raised to C$500, and the same quantities of tobacco and liquor mentioned above can be brought in duty-free.

In addition to the exemptions noted above, and regardless of the amount of time they spend away from Canada, Canadians are allowed to mail gifts from abroad to friends, clients, and relatives in Canada (but not to themselves), at the rate of C$60 per day, provided that the gifts are unsolicited and aren't alcohol or tobacco products. Be sure to write "Unsolicited gift, under C$60 value" on the outside of the package.

All valuables such as expensive cameras and jewelry should be declared on the Y-38 Form before your departure from Canada, and, whenever it's possible, with the notation of the article's serial number. When serial numbers aren't available, as in the case of jewelry, it's wise to carry a photocopy of either the original bill of sale or a bona fide appraisal.

For more information, contact Revenue Canada, 2265 St. Laurent Blvd., Ottawa, ON K1G 4K3 (☎ 613/993-0534), and ask for the free booklet *I Declare*.

BRITISH CUSTOMS   On returning from the Caribbean, British subjects who either arrive directly in the United Kingdom or arrive via a port in another European Community (EC) country and who did not pass through Customs controls with all their baggage must go through U.K. Customs and declare any goods in excess of 200 cigarettes or 50 cigars or 250 grams of tobacco; 2 liters of still table wine and 1 liter of spirits or strong liqueurs over 22% volume, or 2 liters of fortified or sparkling wine or other liqueurs; 60cc (ml) of perfume; 250cc (ml) of toilet water; and £145 worth of all other goods, including gifts and souvenirs. (No one under 17 years of age is entitled to a tobacco or alcohol allowance.) Only go through the green "nothing to declare" line if you're sure that you have no more than the Customs allowances and no prohibited or restricted goods. For further details on U.K. Customs, contact **H.M. Customs and Excise Office,** Dorset House, Stamford St., London SE1 9PY, England (☎ **0171/202-4227**; fax 0171/202-4216; www.open.gov.uk/customs/c&ehome.htm).

AUSTRALIAN CUSTOMS   The duty-free allowance in Australia is A$400 or, for those under 18, A$200. Personal property mailed back from Puerto Rico should be marked "Australian goods returned" to avoid payment of duty. Upon returning to Australia, citizens can bring in 250 cigarettes or 250 grams of loose tobacco, and 1125ml of alcohol. If you're returning with valuable goods you already own, including foreign-made cameras, you should file Form B263. A helpful brochure, available from Australian consulates or Customs offices, is *Know Before You Go*. For more information, contact **Australian Customs Services**, GPO Box 8, Sydney, NSW 2001 (☎ **02/92/32000**).

NEW ZEALAND CUSTOMS   The duty-free allowance for New Zealand is NZ$700. Citizens over 17 years of age can bring in 200 cigarettes, or 50 cigars, or 250 grams of tobacco (or a mixture of all three if their combined weight doesn't exceed 250g); plus 4.5 liters of wine and beer, or 1.125 liters of liquor. There is no limit on how much currency you can carry in or out of New Zealand. Fill out a certificate of export, listing the valuables you are taking out of the country; that way, you can bring them back without paying duty. Most questions are answered in a free pamphlet available at New Zealand consulates and Customs offices: *New Zealand Customs Guide for Travellers,* Notice no. 4. For more information, contact **New Zealand Customs**, 50 Anzac Ave., P.O. Box 29, Auckland, New Zealand (☎ 09/359-66-55).

MONEY

CURRENCY   The U.S. dollar is the coin of the realm. Keep in mind that once you leave Ponce or San Juan, you might have difficulty finding a place to exchange foreign money (unless you're staying at a large resort), so it's wise to handle your exchange needs before you head off into rural parts of Puerto Rico.

CURRENCY EXCHANGE   The currency exchange facilities at any large international bank within Puerto Rico's larger cities can exchange non-U.S. currencies for dollars. You can also exchange money at the Luis Muñoz Marín International Airport. In Old San Juan, go to Thomas Cook, Calle Tetuan 201B (☎ 787/791-6015). Hours are Monday through Friday from 8am to 5pm and Saturday from 9am to 5pm. Also, you'll find foreign-exchange facilities in large hotels and at the many banks in Old San Juan or along Ashford Avenue in Condado. In Ponce, look for foreign exchange facilities at large resorts and at banks such as Banco Popular, Plaza Las Delicias (☎ 787/843-8000).

TRAVELER'S CHECKS   Although it's now perfectly easy to find ATM machines in Puerto Rico and get cash from them as you would at home (see "ATM Networks," below), some travelers still like the security of carrying traveler's checks so that they can get a refund in the event of theft.

Most large banks sell traveler's checks, charging fees that average between 1% and 2% of the value of the checks you buy, although some out-of-the-way banks, in rare instances, have charged as much as 7%. If your bank wants more than a 2% commission, it may pay to call the traveler's check issuers directly for the address of outlets where this commission will be less.

American Express (☎ 800/221-7282 in the U.S. and Canada, with many regional representatives around the world) is one of the largest issuers of traveler's checks. American Express platinum card holders get traveler's checks issued commission free at American Express offices or through the American Express service number (☎ 800/553-6782). Gold card holders can get commission-free checks only through the American Express service number; other cardholders pay a commission. The **American Automobile Association (AAA)** does not charge its members a fee for American Express traveler's checks purchased at AAA offices.

Citicorp (☎ 800/645-6556 in the U.S. and Canada, or 813/623-1709, collect, from other parts of the world) is another major issuer. **Thomas Cook** (☎ 800/223-7373 in the U.S. and Canada, or 609/987-7300 collect from other parts of the world) issues MasterCard traveler's checks, and **Interpayment Services** (☎ 800/221-2426 in the U.S. and Canada, or 212/858-8500 collect from other parts of the world) sells Visa traveler's checks.

CREDIT CARDS   Credit cards are widely used in Puerto Rico. VISA and MasterCard are the major cards, although American Express and, to a lesser extent, Diners Club are also popular. We've noted which cards are accepted at every hotel and restaurant we've reviewed in this book.

ATM NETWORKS   Plus, Cirrus, and other automated-teller machine (ATM) networks operate in Puerto Rico. Before departing, check to see if your PIN number must be reprogrammed for use at Caribbean ATMs to withdraw money on either your ATM or your credit card.

Always determine what the frequency limits for withdrawals and cash advances are on your bank or credit card. For locations of Cirrus abroad, call ☎ 800/424-7787 in the United States. For Plus usage abroad, dial ☎ 800/843-7587. ATMs give a better exchange rate than banks, but some ATMs exact a service charge on every transaction.

MONEYGRAMS   Sponsored by American Express, **Moneygram** (☎ 800/926-9400) is the fastest-growing money-wiring service in the world. Funds can be transferred from one individual to another in less than 10 minutes from any of thousands of locations to any of thousands of other locations throughout the world. An American Express phone representative will give you the names of four or five offices near you. (You don't have to go to an American Express office; some locations are pharmacies or convenience stores in small communities.) Acceptable forms of payment include cash, Visa, MasterCard, or Discover, and occasionally, a personal check. Service charges collected by AmEx are $40 for the first $500 sent, with a sliding scale of commissions for larger sums. Included in the transfer is a 10-word telex-style message. The deal also includes a free 3-minute phone call to the recipient. Funds are transferred within 10 minutes, and they can then be retrieved by the beneficiary at the most convenient location when proper photo ID, and in some cases, a security code established by whoever provides the funds, is presented.

2 When to Go

CLIMATE

Puerto Rico has one of the most unvarying climates in the world. Temperatures year-round range from 75°F to 85°F (24°C to 29°C). The island is wettest and hottest in August, averaging 81°F (27°C) and 7 inches of rain. San Juan and the northern coast seem to be cooler and wetter than Ponce and the southern coast. The coldest weather is in the high altitudes of the Cordillera. Puerto Rico's lowest temperature—39°F (4°C)—was recorded there.

THE HURRICANE SEASON

The curse of Puerto Rican weather, the hurricane season lasts—officially, at least—from June 1 to November 30. But there's no cause for panic. In general, satellite forecasts give adequate warnings so that precautions can be taken.

If you're heading for Puerto Rico during the hurricane season, you can call your local branch of the **National Weather Service** (listed in your phone directory under the U.S. Department of Commerce) for a weather forecast.

It'll cost 95¢ per query, but you can get information about the climate conditions in any city you plan to visit by calling ☎ 800/WEATHER. When you're prompted, enter your Visa or MasterCard account number and then punch in the name of any of 1,000 cities worldwide whose weather is monitored by the **Weather Channel** (www.weather.com).

Average Temperatures on Puerto Rico

	Jan	Feb	Mar	Apr	May	June	July	Aug	Sept	Oct	Nov	Dec
Temp. (°F)	75	75	76	78	79	81	81	81	81	81	79	77
Temp. (°C)	25	24	24	24.4	25.6	26	27	27	27	27	27	26

THE "SEASON"

In Puerto Rico, hotels charge their highest prices during the peak winter period from mid-December to mid-April, when visitors fleeing from cold north winds flock to the islands. Winter is the driest season along the coasts but can be wet in mountainous areas.

If you plan to travel in the winter, make reservations 2 to 3 months in advance. At certain hotels it's almost impossible to book accommodations for Christmas and the month of February.

SAVING MONEY IN THE OFF-SEASON

Puerto Rico is a year-round destination. The island's "off-season" runs from late spring to late fall, when temperatures in the mid-80s (about 29°C) prevail throughout most of the region. Trade winds ensure comfortable days and nights, even in accommodations without air-conditioning. Although the noonday sun may raise the temperature to around 90°F (32°C), cool breezes usually make the morning, late afternoon, and evening more comfortable here than in many parts of the U.S. mainland.

Dollar for dollar, you'll spend less money by renting a summer house or fully equipped unit in Puerto Rico than you would on Cape Cod, Fire Island, Laguna Beach, or the coast of Maine.

The off-season in Puerto Rico—roughly from mid-April to mid-December (rate schedules vary from hotel to hotel)—amounts to a summer sale. In most cases, hotel rates are slashed from 20% to a startling 60%. It's a bonanza for cost-conscious travelers, especially families who like to go on vacations together. In the chapters ahead, we'll spell out in dollars the specific amounts hotels charge during the off-season.

OTHER OFF-SEASON ADVANTAGES

Although Puerto Rico may appear inviting in the winter to those who live in northern climates, there are many reasons why your trip may be much more enjoyable if you go in the off-season:

- After the winter hordes have left, a less-hurried way of life prevails. You'll have a better chance to appreciate the food, culture, and local customs.
- Swimming pools and beaches are less crowded—perhaps not crowded at all.
- Year-round resort facilities are offered, often at reduced rates, that may include snorkeling, boating, and scuba diving.
- To survive, resort boutiques often feature summer sales, hoping to clear the merchandise they didn't sell in February to accommodate stock they've ordered for the coming winter.
- You can often appear without a reservation at a top restaurant and get a table for dinner, a table that in winter would have required a reservation far in advance. Also, when waiters are less hurried, you'll get better service.
- The endless waiting game is over: no waiting for a rented car (only to be told none is available), no long wait for a golf course tee time, and quicker access to tennis courts and water sports.
- The atmosphere is more cosmopolitan in the off-season than it is in winter, mainly because of the influx of Europeans. You'll no longer feel as if you're at a

What Things Cost in Puerto Rico	U.S. $
Taxi from the airport to Condado	12.00
Average taxi fare within San Juan	12.00
Typical bus fare	.25–.50
Local telephone call	.10
Double room at the Caribe Hilton (very expensive)	340.00
Double room at El Canario by the Lagoon (moderate)	105.00
Double room at Windchimes Inn (inexpensive)	65.00
Lunch for one at Amadeus (moderate)	15.00
Lunch for one at La Bombonera (inexpensive)	12.00
Dinner for one at Ramiro's (very expensive)	46.00
Dinner for one at El Patio de Sam (moderate)	28.00
Dinner for one at Tony Roma's (inexpensive)	16.00
Draft beer in a bar	3.75
Coca-Cola in a cafe	1.50
Glass of wine in a restaurant	3.75
Roll of ASA 100 color film, 36 exposures	8.00
Admission to Castillo San Felipe del Morro	Free
Movie ticket	5.00
Theater ticket	15.00–38.00

Canadian or American outpost. Also, since the Puerto Ricans themselves travel in the off-season, your holiday will become more of a multicultural experience.

- Some package-tour fares are as much as 20% lower, and individual excursion fares are also reduced between 5% and 10%.
- All accommodations and flights are much easier to book.
- Summer is an excellent time for family travel, not usually possible during the winter season.
- Finally, the very best of Puerto Rican attractions remain undiminished in the off-season—sea, sand, and surf, with lots of sunshine.

Off-Season Disadvantages

Let's not paint too rosy a picture. Although the advantages of off-season travel far outweigh the disadvantages, there are nevertheless drawbacks to traveling in summer:

- You might be staying at a construction site. Hoteliers save their serious repairs and their major renovations until the off-season when they have fewer clients. That means you might wake up early in the morning to the sound of the hammer.
- Single tourists find the cruising better in winter when there are more clients, especially the unattached. Families predominate in summer and there are fewer chances to meet fellow singles than in the winter months.
- Services are often reduced. In the peak of winter, everything is fully operational. But in summer many of the programs such as water sports might be curtailed. Also, not all restaurants and bars are fully operational at all resorts. For example,

for lack of business, certain gourmet or specialty dining rooms might be shut down until house count merits reopening them. In all, the service atmosphere is more laid-back when a hotel or resort might also be operating with a reduced staff.

HOLIDAYS

Puerto Rico has many public holidays when stores, offices, and schools are closed: New Year's Day, January 6 (Three Kings Day), Washington's Birthday, Good Friday, Memorial Day, July 4th, Labor Day, Thanksgiving, Veterans' Day, and Christmas, plus such local holidays as Constitution Day (July 25) and Discovery Day (November 19). Remember, U.S. federal holidays are holidays in Puerto Rico too.

PUERTO RICO CALENDAR OF EVENTS

January
- **Three Kings Day,** island-wide. On this traditional gift-giving day in Puerto Rico, there are festivals with lively music, dancing, parades, puppet shows, caroling troubadours, and traditional feasts. January 6.

February
- **San Blas de Illescas Marathon,** Coamo. International and local runners compete in a challenging 13.1-mile half-marathon in the hilly south-central town of Coamo. February 9. Call Delta Phi Delta Fraternity (☎ 787/825-2775 or 787/825-4077).
- **Coffee Harvest Festival,** Maricao. Folk music, a parade of floats, typical foods, crafts, and demonstrations of coffee preparation in Maricao, a 1-hour drive east of Mayagüez in the center of one of the island's coffee-growing districts. February 13 to 15. For more information, call ☎ 787/838-2290 or 787/856-1345.
- **Carnival Ponce.** The island's Carnival celebrations feature float parades, dancing, and street parties. One of the most vibrant festivities is held in Ponce, known for its masqueraders wearing brightly painted horned masks. Live music includes the folk rhythms of the *plena,* which originated in Africa. Festivities include the crowning of a Carnival queen and the closing "burial of the sardine." February 5 to 14. For more information, call ☎ 787/840-4141.
- **Coffee Harvest Festival,** Yauco. Music, crafts, foods, coffee, and demonstrations of coffee preparation. Events take place in the main square of this southwestern town in the heart of the island's coffee-growing region. For more information, call ☎ 787/856-1345.

March
- **Feria Dulce Sueño,** Guayama. A 2-day competition held in the southern city of Guayama features Puerto Rico's finest Paso Fino steeds, the island's own breed of smooth-gaited horses. First of March. For more information, call Juan E. Villanueva (☎ 787/864-1866).
- **Regional Crafts Fair,** Ponce. The largest artisans' fair on the south coast, this event features folkloric shows, typical Puerto Rican food, and a children's troubadour (folk music) contest. March 22 to 24. For more information, contact Maria Rosello, Institute of Puerto Rican Culture (☎ 787/844-2540 or 787/843-2300).
- **Emancipation Day,** island-wide. Commemoration of the emancipation of Puerto Rico's slaves in 1873, held at various venues. March 22.

- **Good Friday and Easter,** island-wide. Celebrated with colorful ceremonies and processions. Date varies.

April
- **José de Diego Day,** island-wide. Commemoration of the birthday of José de Diego, a patriot, lawyer, writer, orator, and political leader who was the first president of the Puerto Rico House of Representatives under U.S. rule. April 17.
- **Maví Carnival,** at the town plaza in Juana Díaz. Traditional carnival in this southern coastal town honors *maví* (pronounced mah-*vee*), a fermented drink made from the bark of the ironwood tree (*Colubrina reclinata*). Daytime and evening festivities, a parade, floats, costumes, live music, typical food, plenty of *maví*, and a carnival queen contest. For more information, contact Elenia Acosta (☎ 787/837-2185, ext. 2201).
- **Sugar Harvest Festival,** in the western town of San Germán. Festival marks the end of the island's sugar harvest, with live music, crafts, and typical foods, as well as exhibitions of sugarcane plants and past and present harvesting techniques. Late April. For more information, contact Luis Cruz (☎ 787/892-5574).

May
- **Virgin del Pozo Marathon,** in the southwestern town of Sabana Grande. The annual 13.1-mile half-marathon starts in front of the sanctuary of the Virgin del Rosario. Mid-May. For more information, contact Ismael Nazario (☎ 787/ 873-2093).
- **Danza Week,** Ponce. A week of historical and cultural events commemorating the *danza,* the popular turn-of-the-century ballroom dance. Developed in Ponce, it is slightly similar to the waltz. Conferences, *danza* concerts by string quartets, a parade, a *danza* competition, and demonstrations by senior couples who danced *danza* in their youth in period dress. The main event is a concert by the Ponce Municipal Band on the last day at La Perla Theater. Early May. For more information, call ☎ 787/284-4141.

June
- **San Juan Bautista Day.** Puerto Rico's capital and other cities celebrate the island's patron saint with weeklong festivities. At midnight, Sanjuaneros walk backward into the sea (or nearest body of water) three times to renew good luck for the coming year. June 21.
- **Aibonito Flower Festival,** at Road 722 next to the City Hall Coliseum, in the central mountain town of Aibonito. This annual flower-competition festival features acres of lilies, anthuriums, carnations, roses, gardenias, and begonias. Late June. For more information, call ☎ 787/735-3871.

July
- **Barranquitas Artisans' Fair.** The island's oldest crafts fair marks its 35th year in 1999 with craft exhibitions by more than 130 artisans from around Puerto Rico; also features traditional music and food. For more information, call Orlando Torres at ☎ 787/857-0520.
- **Luis Muñoz Rivera's Birthday,** island-wide. A birthday celebration commemorating Luis Muñoz Rivera (1829 to 1916), statesman, journalist, poet, and resident commissioner in Washington, D.C. July 15.
- **Vieques Patron Saint Festival,** on the eastern coast island of Vieques. The festival is a favorite of residents on the Puerto Rican "mainland," who often stay at inns and beach houses, or camp out that weekend in Vieques, an island with a population of 8,000. July 15 to 25. For more information, call ☎ 787/ 741-5000.

LeLoLai: Saving Money in Puerto Rico

For $10 you can join the ✪ **LeLoLai VIP** (Value in Puerto Rico) program and get the equivalent of up to $250 in travel benefits. Free admission to folkloric shows and discounts on guided tours of historic sites, natural attractions, lodgings, meals, shopping, outdoor activities, and more can add up to significant savings. Most of the experiences linked to LeLoLai are rather touristy, but participation in the program is a worthy investment nonetheless.

The *paradores puertorriqueños,* the island's modestly priced network of country inns, give cardholders 10% to 20% lower room rates Monday to Thursday. Discounts of 10% to 20% are offered at many restaurants, from San Juan's toniest hotels to several *mesones gastronómicos,* government-sanctioned restaurants out on the island serving Puerto Rican fare. Shopping discounts are offered at many stores and boutiques, and, best yet, cardholders get 10% to 20% discounts at many island attractions.

Among the island's folkloric shows, the card entitles you to free admission to *Jolgorio,* presented every Wednesday at 8:30pm at the Caribe Terrace of the Caribe Hilton (check to make sure of the schedule).

For more information about the LeLoLai card, call ☎ **787/723-3135** or 787/722-1513, or go to the El Centro Convention Center at Ashford Avenue on the Condado. Although you can call before you leave home, especially about current offerings, you can sign up for this program only after you reach Puerto Rico. Many hotels, however, include participation in this program as part of their package deals.

- **Loíza Carnival.** An annual folk and religious ceremony honoring St. James the Apostle. Colorful processions take place, with costumes, masks, and bomba dancers. A jubilant celebration reflecting the African and Spanish heritage of the northeastern town of Loíza. Late July. For more information, call ☎ **787/876-3570**.

August
- **Fishing Tournament,** Boca de Cangrejos Marina, between Isla Verde and Piñones in the northeast coastal city of Carolina. Early August. For more information about this deep-sea fishing event, contact Humberto Donato (☎ **787/781-8105**).

September
- **International Light Tackle Tournament,** a blue marlin fishing competition off the southwestern coastal town of Cabo Rojo. It's sponsored by the three west coast deep-sea fishing clubs: Club Náutico de Boquerón, Club Náutico de Rincón, and Club Deportivo del Oeste. Late September to early October. For more information, contact Marta T. Guzmán (☎ **787/851-8880**).

October
- **La Raza Day (Columbus Day),** island-wide. Commemoration of Columbus' landing in the New World. October 12.
- ✪ **National Plantain Festival,** in the northern town of Corozal. Annual festivity with crafts, paintings, agricultural products, exhibition, and sale of plantain dishes; *neuva trova* music and folk ballet are performed. October 30 to November 2. For more information, call ☎ **787/859-1259**.

November
- **Puerto Rican Day of Bomba and Plena,** Ponce. Festivities celebrate two local rhythms and dances, the bomba and plena, which are still popular today. Groups from all over the island present their repertoires. A colorful parade, handcraft exhibits, and typical food. Dates vary. For more information, call ☎ 787/842-6727.
- **Start of Baseball Season,** in Hiram Bithorn Park in San Juan and throughout the island. Six Puerto Rican professional clubs compete. Professionals from North America also play here through February. Usually November 2, lasting until February.
- **Puerto Rico Discovery Day,** island-wide. This commemorates the "discovery" by Columbus of the already inhabited island of Puerto Rico in 1493. He is thought to have come ashore at the northwestern municipality of Aguadilla, although the exact location is unknown. November 19.
- **Jayuya Indian Festival,** at Jayuya. This fiesta features the culture and tradition of the island's original inhabitants, the Taíno Indians, and their music, food, and games. More than 100 artisans exhibit and sell their works. There is also a Miss Taíno Indian Pageant, in which contestants are judged by their features and garments that are designed to evoke—both in style and materials—the typical dress of a Taíno woman. Late November. For more information, call ☎ 787/828-5010.

December
- **Las Mañanitas,** Ponce. A religious procession starts out from Lolita Tizol Street toward the city's Catholic church, led by mariachis singing songs to honor Our Lady of Guadeloupe, the city's patron saint. The lead song is the traditional Mexican birthday song, *Las Mañanitas.* There's a 6am mass. Mid-December. For more information, contact the Ponce City Hall (☎ 787/284-4141).
- **Hatillo Masks Festival,** at the northwestern coastal town of Hatillo. A tradition celebrated since 1823 represents the Biblical story of King Herod's ordering the death of all infant boys in an attempt to kill the baby Jesus. Men with colorful masks and costumes represent the soldiers, who run or ride through the town from early morning looking for the children. Food, music, and crafts exhibits in the town square. Late December. For more information, call ☎ 787/898-3835.

SAN JUAN CALENDAR OF EVENTS

January
- **San Sebastián Street Festival,** Calle San Sebastián in Old San Juan. Nightly celebrations with music, processions, crafts, and typical foods, as well as graphic arts and handcraft exhibitions. January 17 to 20. For more information, call ☎ 787/724-7171.

May
- **Artisan Mothers' Day.** Fifty or more artisans from all over the island participate with their children, showing and selling their crafts at the Plaza de la Dársena and Paseo de la Princesa in Old San Juan. May 2 to 3. For more information, call Raquel Tirado or Carmen Vargas (☎ 787/721-2891 or 787/723-0692).

June
- ✪ **Casals Festival.** Sanjuaneros and visitors alike eagerly look forward to the annual Casals Festival, the Caribbean's most celebrated cultural event. The bill at San Juan's Performing Arts Center includes a glittering array of international guest

conductors, orchestras, and soloists. They come to honor the memory of Pablo Casals, the renowned cellist who was born in Spain to a Puerto Rican mother. When Casals died in Puerto Rico in 1973 at the age of 97, the Casals Festival was 16 years old and attracting the same class of performers who appeared at the Pablo Casals Festival he founded in France after World War II. When he moved to Puerto Rico in 1957 with his wife, Marta Casals Istomin (past artistic director of the John F. Kennedy Center for the Performing Arts), he founded not only this festival but also the Puerto Rico Symphony Orchestra to foster musical development on the island.

Where: Performing Arts Center in San Juan. **When:** June 1 to 20. **How:** Ticket prices for the Casals Festival range from $20 to $40. A 50% discount is offered to students, senior citizens over 60, and persons with disabilities. Tickets are available through the Performing Arts Center in San Juan (☎ **787/721-7727**). Information is also available from the Puerto Rico Tourism Company, 575 Fifth Ave., New York, NY 10017 (☎ **800/223-6530** in the U.S., or 212/599-6262).

August

- **International Billfish Tournament,** at Club Náutico. This is one of the premier game-fishing tournaments and the longest consecutively held billfish tournament in the world. Fishers from many countries angle for blue marlin that can weigh up to 900 pounds. Late August to early September. For further information contact the International Billfish Tournament, c/o Pesca Deportiva, Club Náutico, The Boardwalk, La Guancha, Ponce, PR 00731 (☎ **787/841-6720**).

September

- **Inter-American Festival of the Arts,** at the Luis A. Ferré Performing Arts Center. A 3-week series of musical art performances that includes classical, popular, and folk music; ballet and modern dance productions; and musical theater. Approximately September 20 to October 10. Call ☎ **787/721-7727** for more information.

November

- **Festival of Puerto Rican Music.** Annual classical and folk music festival. One of its highlights is a cuatro-playing contest. Mid-November. For more information, call ☎ **787/724-0700**.

December

- **Puerto Rico International Offshore Cup,** in San Juan Bay. First of its kind on the island, this competition matches local speedboat racing teams with some of the best offshore teams from the United States and the Caribbean. December 14. For more information, call Pepe Llama, the Puerto Rico Offshore Association (☎ **787/753-7715**).
- **Bacardi Artisans' Fair.** The best and largest artisans' fair on the island is held the first two Sundays in December, when more than 100 artisans turn out to exhibit and sell their wares. The fair includes shows for both adults and children, a Puerto Rican troubadour contest, rides, typical food and drink—all sold by nonprofit organizations. On the grounds of the world's largest rum-manufacturing plant, in early Cataño. For more information, call ☎ **787/788-1500**.
- **Old San Juan's White Christmas Festival,** Old San Juan. Special musical and artistic presentations take place in stores, with window displays. December 1–January 12.
- **Lighting of the Town of Bethlehem,** between San Cristóbal Fort and Plaza San Juan Bautista in Old San Juan. During the Christmas season.

YEAR-ROUND FESTIVALS

In addition to the individual events described above, Puerto Rico has two year-long series of special events.

Many of Puerto Rico's most popular events are during the **Patron Saint Festivals** (*fiestas patronales*) in honor of the patron saint of each municipality. The festivities, held in each town's central plaza, include religious and costumed processions, games, local food, music, and dance.

At **Festival La Casita** prominent Puerto Rican musicians, dance troupes, and orchestras perform; puppet shows are staged; and painters and sculptors display their works. It's on every Saturday at Puerto Rico Tourism's "La Casita" Tourism Information Center, Plaza Darsenas, across from Pier 1, Old San Juan.

For more information about all these events, contact the **Puerto Rico Tourism Company,** 575 Fifth Ave., New York, NY 10017 (☎ **800/223-6530** or 212/599-6262).

3 The Active Vacation Planner

Puerto Rico offers a wide variety of participant and spectator sports, including golf, tennis, horseback riding, and all kinds of water sports—from scuba diving to deep-sea fishing.

Many resorts offer a large choice of sports activities, and various all-inclusive sports-vacation packages are available from hotels and airlines serving Puerto Rico.

Dorado Beach, Cerromar Beach, and Palmas del Mar are the chief centers for golf, tennis, and beach life. San Juan's hotels on the Condado/Isla Verde coast also generally offer a complete array of water sports.

BEACHES

With 272 miles of Atlantic and Caribbean coastline, Puerto Rico obviously has plenty of beaches. **The Condado** and **Isla Verde** beaches in San Juan are the most frequented. Good snorkeling is possible, and rental equipment is available for water sports at both. These and other beaches, such as the excellent **Luquillo**, 30 miles east of San Juan (see chapter 10), are overcrowded, especially on Saturday and Sunday. On the other hand, others are practically deserted. The public beaches on the north shore of San Juan at **Ocean Park** and **Park Barbosa** are good and can be reached by bus.

Some of the best deserted beaches stretch between Cabo Rojo, on the southwesterly tip of Puerto Rico, eastward all the way to Ponce. Beginning in the west, directly east of Cabo Rojo, you'll discover **Bahia Sucia Beach, Rosada Beach, Santa Beach, Manglillos Beach** (with a recreation area), **Caña Gorda Beach, Tamarindo Beach,** and **Ballena Beach.** Access to many of these beaches is limited because of poor roads, but the effort to reach them is worth it. Bring along what supplies you'll need.

The best surfing beaches in the Caribbean are on the west coast north of Mayagüez, including the beach at **Punta Higuero,** on Route 413 near the town of Rincón, which is said to be one of the finest surfing spots in the world (see chapter 9).

Puerto Rico's public beaches are open to the public, and some of them are practically deserted. You will be charged for parking and for use of *balneario* facilities, such as lockers and showers, at the public beaches. They are closed on Monday (if Monday is a holiday, they are open then but closed on Tuesday). In winter, public beach hours are 9am to 5pm; in summer, from 9am to 6pm. For more information

Take Me Out to the *Beisbol* Game

Whereas the United States may claim baseball as its national pastime, the sport also has a long, illustrious history in Puerto Rico. Imported around the turn of the century by plantation owners as a leisure activity for workers, *beisbol* quickly caught fire, and local leagues have produced such major-league stars as Roberto Alomar, Carlos Balarga, and the late great Roberto Clemente.

A top-notch league of six teams—featuring many rising professionals honing their skills during the winter months—begins its season in October and plays in ballparks throughout the island. Many baseball fans from the U.S. mainland come down specifically to see these teams play. For a chance to see good baseball in a more intimate setting than is afforded in the major leagues, call **Professional Baseball of Puerto Rico** (☎ 787/765-6285) for information about professional games and, if available, a schedule.

about the island's many beaches, call the **Department of Sports and Recreation** (☎ 787/722-1551).

The following public beaches have balnearios:

Punta Salinas (Route 868, Cataño)
Escambron (Puerta de Tierra, San Juan)
Isla Verde (Route 187, Isla Verde)
Luquillo (Highway 3, Luquillo)
Seven Seas (Route 987, Fajardo)
Sun Bay (Route 997, Vieques)
Punta Santiago (Highway 3, Humacao)
Punta Guilarte (Highway 3, Humacao)
Punta Guilarte (Highway 3, Arroyo)
Cana Gora (Route 333, Guánica)
Boquerón (Route 101, Boquerón)
Añasco (Route 410, Añasco)
Cerro Gordo (Route 690, Vega Baja)
Sardinera (Route 698, Dorado)

Warning: Don't go walking along the beaches at night. Even if you find that secluded, hidden beach of your dreams, proceed with caution. On unguarded beaches you will have no way to protect yourself or your valuables should you be approached by a robber or mugger, which happens frequently.

BOATING & SAILING

The waters off Puerto Rico provide excellent boating in all seasons. For sailors, winds average 10 to 15 knots virtually year-round. Marinas provide facilities and services on a par with any in the Caribbean, and many have powerboats or sailboats for rent, crewed or bareboat charter.

Marinas include the **San Juan Bay Marina** (☎ 787/721-8062); **Marina Puerto Chico,** at Puerto Chico (☎ 787/863-0834); **Marina del Mar** at Palmas del Mar in Humacao (☎ 787/850-2065); and **Marina de Salinas** (☎ 787/752-8484) in Salinas. The Caribbean's largest and most modern marina, **Puerto del Rey** (☎ 787/860-1000), is located on the island's east coast in Fajardo.

Annual sailing regattas include the Copa Velasco Regatta for ocean racing, at Palmas del Mar Resort in Humacao.

CAMPING

The island abounds in sandy beaches and forested hillsides suitable for erecting a tent. More protected and much safer are sites throughout the island where simple cabins, sometimes with fireplaces, are maintained by the **Recreational Development Company of Puerto Rico.** Although accommodations are bare-boned minimalist, the costs are much less than those charged by hotels. For more information and an application to rent one of the units, call ☎ **787/722-1551** or 787/722-1771. It is better and safer to camp only in sites maintained by the government. Some of these are simple places where you erect your own tent, although they are outfitted with electricity and running water. Showers are communal. To stay at a campsite costs between $10 and $17 per night per tent.

Many sites offer very basic cabins for rent. Each cabin is equipped with a full bathroom, a stove, a refrigerator, two beds, and a table and chairs. However, most of your cooking will probably be tastier if you do it outside at one of the on-site barbecues. In nearly all cases you must provide your own sheets and towels. Nearly all cabins rent for $55.40 daily for 2 to 6 people.

The loveliest campsites in Puerto Rico include **Maricao,** deep in the cool mountains. Each cabin here comes with a fireplace at no extra charge. Or you might like to camp along or near a lovely beach. If so, the best sites are **Añasco** and **Humacao,** which are right on the beach. Añasco provides campsites; cabins and campsites are available at Humacao. **Arroyo** is another beach site offering both cabins and regular campsites. The most expensive site is at **Boquerón Beach.** These cabins are the most luxurious in Puerto Rico; they come with air-conditioning but they cost $109 per night for up to 6 people.

An official from one of the park departments will provide you with a map and detailed instructions about how to reach each of these sites. Additional information may be available from the **Parks and Recreation Association of Puerto Rico** (☎ 787/721-2800).

DEEP-SEA FISHING

The offshore fishing here is top-notch! Allison tuna, white and blue marlin, sailfish, wahoo, dolphin, mackerel, and tarpon are some of the fish that can be caught in Puerto Rican waters, where 30 world records have been broken.

Charter arrangements can be made through most major hotels and resorts. In San Juan, **Capt. Mike Benitez** sets the standard by which to judge other captains (see chapter 7). In Palmas del Mar, which has some of the best year-round fishing in the Caribbean, you'll find **Capt. Bill Burleson** (see chapter 8).

GOLF

Home to 13 golf courses, including 8 championship links, Puerto Rico justifiably is known as the "Scotland of the Caribbean." In fact, the 72 holes at the Hyatt resorts at Dorado offer the greatest concentration of golf in the Caribbean.

The courses at the **Hyatt Dorado Beach Hotel** and the **Hyatt Regency Cerromar** are among the 25 best created by Robert Trent Jones. Jack Nicklaus rates the challenging 13th hole at the Hyatt Dorado as one of the top 10 in the world. On the southeast coast, crack golfers consider holes 11 through 15 at **The Golf Club at Palmas del Mar** to be the toughest five successive holes in the Caribbean. At **El Conquistador Resort and Country Club,** the spectacular $250 million resort at Las Croabas east of San Juan, the course's 200-foot changes in elevation provide panoramic vistas. At Palmer on the northeast coast, inexperienced golfers prefer the **Rio Mar Golf Course** to the more challenging courses at Dorado.

With the exception of the El Conquistador Resort and Country Club, these courses are open to the public. See chapter 8 for more details.

HIKING

The mountainous interior of Puerto Rico provides ample opportunities for hill climbing and nature treks. These are especially appealing because panoramas open at the least-expected moments, often revealing spectacular views of the faraway sea.

The most popular, most beautiful, and most spectacular trekking spots include **El Yunque,** the sprawling jungle maintained by the U.S. Forest Service, and the only rain forest on U.S. soil.

El Yunque is part of the **Caribbean National Forest,** lying a 30-minute drive east of San Juan. More than 250 species of trees and some 200 types of fern have been identified here. Some 60 species of birds inhabit El Yunque, including the increasingly rare Puerto Rican parrot. Such rare birds as the elfin wods warbler, the green mango hummingbird, and the Puerto Rican lizard-cuckoo live here.

Park rangers have clearly marked the trails that are ideal for walking. Our favorite, taking 2 hours for the round-trip jaunt, is called La Mina & Big Tree Trail, which is actually two trails combined. The La Mina trail is paved and signposted, beginning at the picnic center adjacent to the visitor center and running parallel to La Mina River. It is named for gold once discovered on the site. After you reach La Mina Falls, the Big Tree Trail begins (also signposted). It winds a route through the towering trees of Tabonuco Forest until it approaches Route 191. Along the trail you might spot such native birds as the Puerto Rican woodpecker, the tanager, the screech owl, and the bullfinch.

Those with twice the time might opt for the El Yunque Trail, which takes 4 hours round-trip to traverse. This trail—signposted from El Caimitillo Picnic Grounds—takes you on a steep, winding path. Along the way you pass natural forests of sierra palm and palo colorado before descending into the dwarf forest of Mount Britton, which is often shrouded in clouds. Your major goal, at least for panoramic views, will be the lookout peaks of Roca Marcas, Yunque Rock, and Los Picachos. On a bright, clear day you can see all the way to the eastern shores of the Atlantic.

If you're not a hiker but you appreciate rain forests, there's an easy way out here. You can drive through the forest on Route 191, a tarmac road. This trail goes from the main highway of Route 3 penetrating deep into El Yunque. You can actually see ferns that grow some 120 feet tall, and at any minute you expect a hungry dinosaur to peek between the fronds looking for a snack—namely you. You're also treated to lookout towers offering panoramic views, waterfalls, picnic areas, and even a restaurant.

El Yunque is not the only forest reserve in Puerto Rico. Others range from coastal mangrove swamps teeming with bird life to densely forested palm groves in the high-altitude interior.

A lesser forest, but one that is still intriguing to visit, is the **Maricao Forest Reserve**, near the coffee town of Maricao. This forest is in western Puerto Rico, east of the town of Mayagüez. Take Route 105 east from Mayagüez to explore it. Trails are signposted here, and your goal might be the highest peak in the forest, Las Tetas de Cerro Gordo, at 2,625 feet. A panoramic view unfolds from here, including a spotting of the offshore island of Mona. Nearly 50 species of birds live in this forest, including the Lesser Antillean pewee and the scaly naped pigeon. Nature watchers will delight to know that there are some 280 tree species in this reserve. Some 38 of the tree species are found only in Maricao.

North of Ponce, **Toro Negro Forest Reserve** (take Route 139) lies along the Cordillera Central, the cloud-shrouded Panoramic Route that follows the Cordillera Central as it goes from the southeast town of Yabucoa all the way to Mayagüez on the west coast. This 7,000-acre park, ideal for hikers, straddles the highest peak of the Cordillera Central in the very heart of Puerto Rico. A forest of lush trees, the reserve also contains the headwaters of several main rivers.

The lowest temperatures recorded on the island—some 40°F (4°C)—were measured at **Lake Guineo,** the island's highest lake, which lies within the reserve. The best trail to take here is a short, paved, and wickedly steep path on the north side of Route 143 going up to the south side of Cerro de Punta, which at 4,390 feet is the highest peak in Puerto Rico. Allow about half an hour for an ascent up this peak. Once at the top, you'll be rewarded with Puerto Rico's grandest view, sweeping across the lush interior from the Atlantic to the Caribbean coasts. Other peaks in the reserve also offer hiking possibilities.

For information about other forest reserves, specifically **Guánica State Forest** and the **Carite Forest Reserve**, refer to chapter 9 on Ponce, Mayagüez, and Rincón.

Equally suitable for hiking are the protected lands (especially the **Río Camuy Caves**) whose topography is characterized as "karst"—that is, limestone riddled with caves, underground rivers, and natural crevasses and fissures. Although these regions pose additional risks and technical problems for trekkers, some people prefer the opportunities they provide for exploring the territory both above and below its surface. See chapter 10 for details about El Yunque and the Río Camuy Caves.

A word of warning: When you hike in the tropics, you can quickly become dehydrated and also sustain more serious insect bites and sunburn than you would while hiking in more temperate climes. Take plenty of water and drink it frequently, wear a sun hat, and consider the advisability of long-sleeved shirts and sunscreen to protect yourself from heat exhaustion and sunstroke.

For more information about any of the national forest reserves of Puerto Rico, call the **Department of Sports & Recreation** at ☎ 787/721-2800.

NATURE TOURS

Lectures on wildlife and the environment are offered by the Commonwealth of Puerto Rico Department of Natural Resources, especially for scientists and students. Also, tours of the nature reserves and forests on the island can be arranged in advance. You need to specify the name of the reserve or forest you'd like to visit. For a description of the best of these forest reserves, refer to "Hiking," above. Contact the **Department of Natural Resources,** Forest, Reserves and Refuge Area, P.O. Box 5887, San Juan, PR 00906 (☎ 787/721-5495 for the reserve and refuge; 787/723-1717 for the forest).

Despite the lushness, forest reserves, rain forest, and plant, bird, and animal life here, nature-oriented clubs such as Sierra Club and the Audubon Society do not have organized nature tours to Puerto Rico. On the other hand, the local **Tropix Wellness Tours** (☎ 787/268-2173; fax 787/268-1722) offers five major excursions, including the exploration of sea turtles' nesting sites in Culebra, the Phosphorescent Bay in Vieques, the Rio Camuy Cave system in Camuy, and the dry, desert-like forest in Guánica.

Its **Happy Turtle Tour,** or *la tortuga Feliz,* on Culebra includes a half-day kayaking/snorkeling expedition and a visit to the sea turtles' nesting sites during the spring/summer season. The cost includes 4 days and 3 nights of accommodations at a villa with a view and air-conditioning. The tour starts at Rivas Dominici

Airport in Miramar, and interisland air transportation to Culebra Airport is included. Rates are $473 per person, based on double occupancy, and include continental breakfast, three boxed lunches, and equipment for escorted expeditions.

Vieques, Puerto Rico's other major offshore island, is the focus of its **Bioluminescent Bay Tour,** which includes an expedition to the Isla Nena, home to one of the most panoramic bioluminescent bays in the world. Additional attractions on Vieques include reefs, bird sanctuaries, and deserted sandy beaches. The tour includes 4 days and 3 nights of accommodations at the Crows Nest and interisland air transportation to Vieques. Rates are $368.75 per person, based on double occupancy, and include full breakfast, three boxed lunches, and all equipment.

The **Caveman Tour,** or *Tour Cavernicola,* in Camuy includes an expedition through one of the world's largest underground cave river systems. Miles of natural waterways are surrounded by stalagmites, stalactites, sunless vegetation, and 20 species of marsupials. The tour includes 3 days and 2 nights of accommodations at the Parador Guajataca in Quebradillas. Rates are $243 per person, based on double occupancy, and include two full breakfasts, one full lunch, and equipment.

The **Express Tour** in Maricao includes a full-day hiking expedition in the mountains and natural spring-water pools of the area. The Express Tour costs $243 per person, including 3 days and 2 nights double occupancy at the Hacienda Juanita, a restored coffee plantation turned hotel.

The **Wet & Dry Tour** in Guánica includes two expeditions: a dry forest hike and mangrove kayaking in the clear waters of a mangrove swamp. Southwestern Puerto Rico is home to the world's largest remaining tract of tropical dry coastal forest. This part of the island also features miles of mangrove channel systems. Visitors can explore these waterways by kayak as they are led to secluded Puerto Rican beaches. The tour includes 4 days and 3 nights of accommodations at the Compamarina Hotel. Rates are $518 per person, based on double occupancy, and include three full breakfasts and equipment.

Tropix Wellness Tours will customize an itinerary for those traveling to Puerto Rico alone, or for groups of six or more. "Add-ons" to the fixed tours, such as body-rafting expeditions through underground cave rivers and hiking excursions, can also be arranged.

SCUBA DIVING & SNORKELING

The continental shelf, which surrounds Puerto Rico on three sides, is responsible for an abundance of coral reefs, caves, sea walls, and trenches for scuba diving and snorkeling.

Open-water reefs off the southeastern coast near **Humacao** are visited by migrating whales and manatees. Many caves are located near Isabela on the west coast. The **Great Trench,** off the island's south coast, is ideal for experienced open-water divers. Caves and the sea wall at **La Parguera** are also favorites. **Vieques and Culebra islands,** off the east coast, have coral formations. ♦ **Mona Island,** off the west coast, offers unspoiled reefs at depths averaging 80 feet; seals are one of the attractions. Uninhabited islands, such as **Icacos,** off the northeastern coast near Fajardo, are also popular with both snorkelers and divers.

These sites are now within reach since many of Puerto Rico's dive operators and resorts offer packages that may include daily or twice-daily dives, scuba equipment, instruction, and excursions to the island's popular attractions.

In San Juan, the **Caribbean School of Aquatics** offers an array of sailing, scuba, and snorkeling trips, as well as boat charters and fishing. **Karen Vega's Caribe Aquatic Adventures,** in the lobby of the Radisson Normandie Hotel, teaches PADI and NAUI diving certification courses (see chapter 7). At the Palmas del Mar resort, **Coral Head Divers & Water Sports Center** offers daily two-tank open-water dives for certified divers, plus snorkeling trips to Monkey Island and Vieques (see chapter 8).

Elsewhere on the island, several other companies offer scuba and snorkeling instruction. We provide details in each section.

Because of its overpopulation, the waters around San Juan aren't the most ideal for **snorkeling.** In fact, the entire north shore of Puerto Rico fronts the Atlantic, where the waters are often turbulent. Windsurfers—not snorkelers—gravitate to the waves and surf in the northwest.

The most ideal conditions for snorkeling in Puerto Rico are along the shores of the remote islands of Vieques and Culebra (see chapter 11).

The best snorkeling on the main island is found near the town of **Fajardo,** to the east of San Juan and along the tranquil eastern coast.

The calm, glasslike quality of the clear Caribbean along the south shore also is ideal for snorkeling. The most developed tourist mecca here is the city of Ponce. Few rivers empty their muddy waters into the sea along the south coast, resulting in gin-clear waters offshore. You can snorkel off the coast without having to go on a boat trip. One good place is at **Playa La Parguera,** where you can rent snorkeling equipment from kiosks along the beach. This beach lies east of the town of Guánica, to the east of Ponce. Here tropical fish add to the brightness of the water, which is generally turquoise itself. The addition of mangrove cays in the area also makes La Parguera more of an allure for snorkelers. Another good spot for snorkelers is **Caja de Muertos** off the coast of Ponce. Here a lagoon coral reef boasts a large number of fish species.

For reservations or more information about Puerto Rico diving packages, contact Kathy Rothschild at **Rothschild Enterprises** (☎ **800/359-0747,** or 212/662-4858 in New York City).

SURFING

Puerto Rico's northwest beaches attract surfers from around the world. Called the Hawaii of the East, the island has hosted a number of international competitions. October through February are the best surfing months, but the sport is enjoyed in Puerto Rico from August through April. The most popular areas are from Isabela around Punta Borinquén to Rincón—with beaches such as Wilderness, Surfers, Crashboat, Los Turbos in Vega Jaja, Pine Grove in Isla Verde, and La Pared in Luquillo. Surfboards are available at many water-sports shops.

International competitions held in Puerto Rico have included the 1968 and the 1988 World Amateur Surfing Championships, the annual Caribbean Cup Surfing Championship, and the 1989 and 1990 Budweiser Puerto Rico Surfing Challenge events, stops on the professional tour.

TENNIS

Puerto Rico has approximately 100 tennis courts. Many are at hotels and resorts; others are in public parks throughout the island. Several paradores also have courts. A number of courts are lighted for nighttime play.

In San Juan, the **Caribe Hilton,** the **Condado Plaza Hotel & Casino,** and the **Carib Inn** all have tennis courts. Also in the area is a **public court** at the old navy base, Isla Grande, in Miramar. The entrance is from Avenida Fernández Juncos at bus stop 11. See chapter 7.

The twin **Hyatt Resorts Caribbean** at Dorado and Cerromar maintain a total of 21 courts between them. The **Tennis Center** at Palmas del Mar in Humacao, the largest in Puerto Rico, features 20 courts. See chapter 8.

WINDSURFING

Windsurfing is a popular water sport on Puerto Rico, with the sheltered waters of the Condado Lagoon in San Juan a favorite spot. Other sites include Ocean Park, Ensenada, Boquerón, Honda Beach, and Culebra. Puerto Rico hosted its first major windsurfing tournament, the Ray Ban Windsurfing World Cup, in June 1989.

Throughout the island, many companies offering snorkeling and scuba also provide windsurfing equipment and instruction, and dozens of hotels have facilities on their own premises.

One of the best places to arrange for windsurfing in San Juan is at **Caribe Aquatic Adventures,** whose main office is in the lobby of the Radisson Normandie Hotel (see chapter 7). Along the north shore, windsurfing is excellent at the beachfront of the Hyatt Dorado Beach Hotel, where the **Penfield Island Adventures** offers lessons and rentals (see chapter 8).

4 Health & Insurance

STAYING HEALTHY

Finding a good doctor in Puerto Rico is easy, and most speak English. See "Fast Facts: Puerto Rico," below, for the locations of hospitals.

POTENTIAL PROBLEMS   It's best to stick to bottled mineral water here. Although tap water is said to be safe to drink, many visitors experience diarrhea, even if they follow the usual precautions. The illness usually passes quickly without medication if you eat simply prepared food and drink only mineral water until you recover. If symptoms persist, consult a doctor.

The sun can be brutal, especially if you haven't been exposed to it in some time. Experts advise that you limit your time on the beach the first day. If you do overexpose yourself, stay out of the sun until you recover. If your exposure is followed by fever or chills, a headache, or a feeling of nausea or dizziness, see a doctor.

Sandflies (or "no-see-ums") are one of the biggest insect menaces in Puerto Rico. They appear mainly in the early evening, and even if you can't see these tiny bugs, you sure can "feel-um," as any native Puerto Rican will attest. Screens can't keep them out, so you'll need to use your favorite insect repellent.

Although mosquitoes are a nuisance, they do not carry malaria in Puerto Rico.

Hookworm and other intestinal parasites are relatively common in the Caribbean, though you are less likely to be affected on Puerto Rico. Hookworm can be contracted by just walking barefoot on an infected beach. Schistosomiasis (also called bilharzia), caused by a parasitic fluke, can be contracted by submerging your feet in rivers and lakes infested with a certain species of snail.

And don't forget that Puerto Rico has been especially hard hit by AIDS. Exercise *at least* the same caution in choosing your sexual partners, and in practicing safe sex, as you would at home.

For conditions such as epilepsy, a heart condition, diabetes, or allergies, consider wearing a **Medic Alert Identification Tag.** For a lifetime membership, the cost is $35 for a steel tag, $45 if silver plated, and $60 if gold plated. In addition, there is a $15 annual fee. Contact the Medic Alert Foundation, P.O. Box 1009, Turlock, CA 95381-1009 (☎ **800/825-3785;** fax 209/669-2495). Medic Alert's 24-hour hotline enables a foreign doctor to obtain your medical records.

Take along an adequate supply of any **prescription medications** you need and a written prescription specifying the generic name of the drug—not the brand name. However, U.S. brand names are commonly available at most pharmacies. You may also want to take such over-the-counter items as first-aid cream, insect repellent, aspirin, and Band-Aids.

INSURANCE

Before purchasing insurance, check your current homeowner's, automobile, and medical insurance policies, as well as the membership contracts of automobile and travel clubs and credit/charge cards, for any coverage extended to you while you travel.

Many credit- and charge-card companies insure their users in case of a travel accident when the travel cost was paid with their card. Sometimes fraternal organizations have policies that protect members in case of sickness or accidents abroad.

Many homeowner's insurance policies cover theft of luggage during foreign travel and loss of such documents as your passport and your airline ticket. Coverage is usually limited to about $500. Remember that to submit a claim on your insurance, you'll need police reports or a statement from a local medical authority that you did suffer the loss or experience an illness. Some policies provide advances in cash or arrange for immediate transferals of funds.

Companies offering special travel insurance policies include the following:

Travel Guard International, 1145 Clark St., Stevens Point, WI 54481-9970 (☎ **800/826-1300** outside Wisconsin, or 715/345-0505), offers a comprehensive travel protection policy that covers lost luggage, emergency assistance, accidental death, trip cancellation, and medical coverage abroad. Package costs start at $45 and are based on your total trip cost. Children under 16 are automatically covered if accompanying adults have purchased a policy.

Travelers Insurance PAK, Travel Insured International, P.O. Box 280568, East Hartford, CT 06128-0568 (☎ **800/243-3174**), offers illness and accident coverage costing from $10 for 6 to 10 days. For lost or damaged luggage, $500 worth of coverage costs $20 for 6 to 10 days. Trip cancellation insurance is $5.50 per $100 of coverage to a limit of $10,000 per person.

Wallach and Co., 107 W. Federal St., P.O. Box 480, Middleburg, VA 20118-0480 (☎ **800/237-6615** or 540/687-3172), offers coverage for between 10 and 120 days at $4 per day; this policy includes accident and sickness coverage up to $250,000. Medical evacuation is also included, along with $25,000 accidental death and dismemberment compensation. Provisions for trip cancellation can also be written into this policy at a nominal cost.

Travelex, P.O. Box 9408, Garden City, NJ 11530 (☎ **800/228-9792**), offers insurance packages priced from $10 to $59 per person for a trip lasting between 1 and 31 days. Included in these packages are travel-assistance services and financial protection against trip cancellation, trip interruption, bankruptcy, flight and baggage delays, accident and sickness, and medical evacuation. Major credit card holders can file their application for insurance over the phone at the number listed above.

5 Tips for Travelers with Special Needs

FOR TRAVELERS WITH DISABILITIES

The Americans with Disabilities Act is enforced as strictly in Puerto Rico as it is on the U.S. mainland—in fact, a telling example of the act's enforcement can be found in Ponce, where the sightseeing trolleys come equipped with ramps and extra balustrades to accommodate travelers with disabilities. Unfortunately, hotels rarely give much publicity to the facilities they offer persons with disabilities, so it's always wise to contact the hotel directly, in advance. Tourist offices usually have little data about such matters.

You can obtain a free copy of *Air Transportation of Handicapped Persons,* published by the U.S. Department of Transportation. Write for Free Advisory Circular No. AC12032, Distribution Unit, U.S. Department of Transportation, Publications Division, 3341Q 75 Ave., Landover, MD 20785 (☎ **301/322-4961;** fax 301/386-5394). Only written requests are accepted.

For names and addresses of operators of tours specifically for visitors with disabilities, and other relevant information, contact the **Society for the Advancement of Travel for the Handicapped (SATH),** 347 Fifth Ave., Suite 610, New York, NY 10016 (☎ **212/447-7284;** fax 212/725-8253). Yearly membership dues in the society are $45, $30 for senior citizens and students. Send a self-addressed, stamped envelope. SATH will also provide you with hotel/resort accessibility for Caribbean destinations.

For blind or visually impaired persons, the best source of information is the **American Foundation for the Blind,** 11 Penn Plaza, Suite 300, New York, NY 10001 (☎ **800/232-5463** or 212/502-7600). It acts as a referral source for travelers and can offer advice on the transport and border formalities for Seeing Eye dogs.

One of the best organizations serving the needs of persons with disabilities is **Flying Wheels Travel,** 143 West Bridge (P.O. Box 382), Owatoona, MN 55060 (☎ **800/535-6790** or 507/451-5005), offering various customized, all-inclusive vacation packages in the Caribbean.

For a $25 annual fee, you can join **Mobility International USA,** P.O. Box 10767, Eugene, OR 97440 (☎ **541/343-1284** voice and TDD; fax 541/343-6812). It answers questions on various destinations and also offers discounts on its programs, videos, and publications. Its quarterly newsletter, *Over the Rainbow,* provides information on Caribbean hotel chains, accessibility, and transportation.

TIPS FOR BRITISH TRAVELERS WITH DISABILITIES The **Royal Association for Disability and Rehabilitation (RADAR),** Unit 12, City Forum, 250 City Rd., London, EC1V 8AF (☎ **0171/250-3222;** fax 0171/250-0212), publishes holiday "fact packs," three in all, which sell for £2 each or all three for £5. The first one provides general information, including planning and booking a holiday, insurance, finances, and useful organization and holiday providers. The second outlines transportation available abroad and equipment for rent. The third deals with specialized accommodations.

FOR GAY & LESBIAN TRAVELERS

Puerto Rico is the most gay-friendly destination in the Caribbean, with lots of accommodations, restaurants, clubs, and bars that actively cater to a gay clientele. A free monthly newsletter, *Puerto Rico Breeze,* lists items of interest to the island's gay community; it's distributed at the Atlantic Beach Hotel (see chapter 5) and many of the gay-friendly clubs mentioned in this book (see chapter 7).

Men can order *Spartacus,* the international gay guide ($32.95), or *Odysseus, The International Gay Travel Planner,* a guide to international gay accommodations ($27). Both lesbians and gay men might want to pick up a copy of *Ferrari Travel Planner* ($16), which specializes in general information, as well as listings of bars, hotels, restaurants, and places of interest for gay travelers throughout the world. These books and others are available from **Giovanni's Room,** 1145 Pine St., Philadelphia, PA 19107 (☎ **215/923-2960**).

Our World, 1104 N. Nova Rd., Suite 251, Daytona Beach, FL 32117 (☎ **904/441-5367**), is a magazine devoted to options and bargains for gay and lesbian travel worldwide. It costs $35 for 10 issues. *Out and About,* 8 W. 19th St., Suite 401, New York, NY 10011 (☎ **800/929-2268**), has been hailed for its "straight" reporting about gay travel. It profiles the best gay or gay-friendly hotels, restaurants, gyms, clubs, and other places, with coverage of destinations throughout the world. The cost is $49 a year for 10 information-packed issues, plus four events calendars. It aims for the more upscale gay male and lesbian traveler, and it has been praised by everybody from *Travel and Leisure* to the *New York Times.* Both of these publications are also available at most gay and lesbian bookstores.

The **International Gay and Lesbian Travel Association (IGLTA),** 4331 N. Federal Hwy., #304, Ft. Lauderdale, FL 33308 (☎ **800/448-8550** or 954/776-2626), encourages gay and lesbian travel worldwide. With more than 1,300 member agencies, it specializes in networking, providing the information travelers would need to link up with the appropriate gay-friendly service organization or tour specialist. It offers quarterly newsletters, marketing mailings, and a membership directory that's updated four times a year. Travel agents who are IGLTA members will be tied into this organization's vast information resources.

FOR SENIORS

Though much of the island's sporting and nightlife activity is geared toward more youthful travelers, Puerto Rico also has much to offer the senior citizen. The best source of information for seniors is the Puerto Rico Tourism Company (see "Visitor Information," above), or, if you're staying in a large resort hotel, the activities director or the concierge.

For information before you go, obtain a free copy of *101 Tips for the Mature Traveler,* available from Grand Circle Travel, 347 Congress St., Suite 3A, Boston, MA 02210 (☎ **800/221-2610** or 617/350-7500). This tour operator offers extended vacations, escorted programs, and cruises that feature unique learning experiences for seniors at competitive prices.

SAGA International Holidays, 222 Berkeley St., Boston, MA 02115 (☎ **800/343-0273**), is known for its all-inclusive tours and cruises for seniors, preferably those 50 years of age or older. Both medical insurance and trip-cancellation insurance are included in the net price of any of its tours, except cruises.

AARP (American Association of Retired Persons) is the best organization in the United States for seniors. It offers discounts on car rentals and hotels. For more information, contact AARP at 601 E St., NW, Washington, DC 20049 (☎ **202/434-AARP**).

Information is also available from the **National Council of Senior Citizens,** 8403 Colesville Rd., Suite 1200, Silver Spring, MD 20910 (☎ **301/578-8800;** fax 301/578-8999). For a fee of $13 per person or couple, you receive a monthly newsletter, part of which is devoted to travel tips. Reduced discounts on hotel and auto rentals are available.

Mature Outlook, P.O. Box 9390, Des Moines, IA 50306-9519 (☎ **800/ 336-6330;** fax 515/252-7855), is a travel organization for people over 50. Members receive a bimonthly magazine and are offered discounts at ITC-member hotels. ITC is an international hotel club offering discounts to members. Annual membership is $14.95 to $19.95.

FOR SINGLES

Puerto Rico's thriving nightlife makes it a stellar destination for singles looking for romance. Two of the best clubs for meeting people are Club Egipto (if you're straight) and Eros (if you're gay). See the write-up of each club in "San Juan After Dark" in chapter 7.

Unfortunately for the 85 million or so single Americans, the travel industry is far more geared toward couples, so singles often wind up paying the penalty. It pays to travel with someone. One company that resolves this problem is Travel Companion, which matches single travelers with like-minded companions. It's headed by Jens Jurgen, who charges $99 for a 6-month listing in his well-publicized records. People seeking travel companions fill out forms stating their preferences and needs and receive a listing of potential travel partners. Companions of the same or opposite sex can be requested. A bimonthly newsletter averaging 46 large pages also gives numerous money-saving travel tips of special interest to solo travelers. A sample copy is available for $5. For an application and more information, contact Jens Jurgen at **Travel Companion**, P.O. Box P-833, Amityville, NY 11701 (☎ **516/454-0880;** fax 516/454-0170).

Golden Companions, part of the larger Travel Companion Exchange, has helped travelers 45 and older find compatible companions since 1987. The organization offers a 6-month introductory membership for $99. The membership includes a bimonthly newsletter, with travel tips for singles and listings of others seeking travel partners. Newsletter-only subscriptions cost $48 for 12 months. For a free brochure, write **Golden Companions,** P.O. Box 833, Amityville, NY 11701 (☎ **800/392-1256** or 516/454-0170).

Since single supplements on tours carry a hefty price tag, some tour companies will arrange for you to share a room with another single traveler of the same gender. One such company that offers a "guaranteed-share plan" is Cosmos. Book through your travel agent or call ☎ **800/221-0090.**

FOR FAMILIES

Puerto Rico is a terrific family destination. The smallest toddlers can spend blissful hours on sandy beaches and in the shallow seawater or pools specifically constructed for them. There's no end to the fascinating pursuits available for older children, ranging from boat rides to shell collecting to horseback riding and hiking. Perhaps your children are old enough to learn to snorkel and explore the wonderland of underwater Puerto Rico. Skills such as swimming and windsurfing are taught here, and there is a variety of activities unique to the islands. Most resort hotels will advise you of what there is in the way of fun for the young, and many have play directors and supervised activities for various age groups. Look for the "Family-Friendly Hotels" and "Family-Friendly Restaurants" boxes we've included throughout the book, pointing you to places that cater to kids.

Family Travel Times, which is published 10 times a year by Travel With Your Children (TWYCH), includes a weekly call-in service for subscribers. Subscriptions cost $40 a year and can be ordered by contacting TWYCH, 40 5th Ave., New York, NY 10011 (☎ **212/477-5524**).

6 Getting There: Flying to Puerto Rico

Puerto Rico is by far the most accessible of the Caribbean islands, with frequent airline service. It's also the major airline hub of the Caribbean Basin.

THE AIRLINES

With San Juan as its hub for the entire Caribbean, **American Airlines** (☎ 800/433-7300) offers nonstop daily flights to San Juan from Baltimore, Boston, Chicago, Dallas–Fort Worth, Hartford, Miami, Newark, New York (JFK), Orlando, Philadelphia, Tampa, Fort Lauderdale, and Washington (Dulles), plus flights to San Juan from both Montréal and Toronto with changes in Chicago or Miami. There are also at least two daily flights from Los Angeles to San Juan that touch down in Dallas or Miami.

American, because of its wholly owned subsidiary, **American Eagle,** also is the undisputed leader among the short-haul local commuter flights of the Caribbean. It usually flies in propeller planes carrying between 34 and 64 passengers. Collectively, American Eagle, along with its larger associate, American Airlines, offers service to 37 destinations on 31 islands of the Caribbean and the Bahamas, more than any other carrier.

Delta (☎ 800/221-1212) has four daily nonstop flights from Atlanta Monday to Friday, nine nonstop on Saturday, and seven nonstop on Sunday. Flights into Atlanta from around the world are frequent, with excellent connections from points throughout Delta's network in the South and Southwest.

United Airlines (☎ 800/241-6522) offers daily nonstop flights from Chicago to San Juan. **Northwest** (☎ 800/447-4747) has one daily nonstop flight to San Juan from Detroit, as well as at least one (and sometimes more) connecting flights to San Juan from Detroit. United also offers flights to San Juan, some of them nonstop, from both Memphis and Minneapolis, with a schedule that varies according to the season and the day of the week.

TWA (☎ 800/892-4141) offers three daily nonstop flights throughout the year between New York's JFK and San Juan. There are also daily nonstop flights to San Juan from St. Louis in winter, but none in summer.

US Airways (☎ 800/428-4322) also competes, with daily direct flights between Baltimore and San Juan, in which flights make an intermediate stop in Charlotte, North Carolina, before continuing nonstop to San Juan. The airline also offers three daily nonstop flights to San Juan from Philadelphia, and one daily nonstop flight to San Juan from Pittsburgh.

Kiwi (☎ 800/JET-KIWI-) offers daily non-stop flights to San Juan from both Newark and Orlando. They also recently instituted daily non-stop service from Newark and Orlando to Aguadill—a convenient option if you're staying on the West coast of the island.

British travelers can take a **British Airways** (☎ 0345/222111 in the U.K.) weekly flight direct from London to San Juan on Sunday. **Lufthansa** (☎ 01/803-803-803 in Germany) passengers can fly on Saturday (one weekly flight) from Frankfurt to San Juan via Condor (a subsidiary operating the flight). And **Iberia** (☎ 1/587-8156 in Spain) has two weekly flights from Madrid to San Juan, leaving on Thursday and Saturday.

SAVING ON AIRFARES

In recent years, the traditional expectation that winter fares to the Caribbean were higher than those in summer has changed. On their island routes, most airlines now divide their year into peak season and basic season, eliminating what used to be known as shoulder season. **Peak season** for fares between North America and Puerto Rico now generally means midwinter and midsummer, whereas the less expensive **basic season** covers spring and fall.

Also noteworthy is the fact that most airlines are eliminating business class on their routes from North America to Puerto Rico. Instead, they are offering only economy class and first class. (On most American Eagle flights, first class has been eliminated entirely in favor of single-service flights; since most intra-Caribbean American Eagle flights rarely exceed 90 minutes, no one seems to mind.)

OTHER WAYS TO SAVE

Proceed with caution through the next suggestions. What constitutes good value changes almost daily in the airline industry. It's hard to keep up, even if you are a travel agent or regularly surf the net (see the "Cyber Deals for Net Surfers" box, below). Fares, especially to Puerto Rico, change all the time—what was the lowest possible fare one day can change the very next day when a new promotional fare is offered.

CHARTER FLIGHTS   These flights allow you to travel at rates lower than those of regularly scheduled flights. Many of the major carriers offer charter flights at rates that can cost 30% less than the regular airfare.

There are some drawbacks to charter flights that you need to consider. Advance booking, for example, of up to 45 days or more may be required, and there are hefty cancellation penalties, although you can take out insurance against emergency cancellation. Also, you must depart and return on your scheduled dates or else you'll lose your money. If you don't have proper insurance, it will do you no good to call the airline and tell them you've had a ski accident in Aspen. If you're not on the plane, you can kiss your money good-bye.

Since charter flights are so complicated, it's best to go to a good travel agent and ask him or her to explain the problems and advantages. Sometimes charters require ground arrangements, such as prebooking hotel rooms.

One company that arranges charters is the **Council Travel,** 205 E. 42nd St., New York, NY 10017 (☎ **800/800-8222** in the U.S., or 212/661-1414).

Another is **Travac**, 989 Sixth Ave., New York, NY 10018 (☎ **800/TRAV-800** or 212/563-3303). Other Travac offices include 2601 E. Jefferson St., Orlando, FL 32803 (☎ **407/896-0014**).

BUCKET SHOPS (CONSOLIDATORS)   In its purest sense, a bucket shop acts as a clearinghouse for blocks of tickets that airlines discount and consign during normally slow periods of air travel (for Puerto Rico, that usually means from mid-April to mid-December). Charter operators and bucket shops used to perform separate functions, but their offerings have often become blurred in recent years. Many outfits perform both functions.

Tickets are sometimes—but not always—discounted as much as 20% to 35%. Terms of payment can vary, from perhaps 45 days prior to departure to the last minute. Some consolidators require you to buy their discounted tickets through a regular travel agent, who usually marks up the ticket 8% to 10%, maybe more, thereby greatly reducing your discount. If you go through an agent, ask him or her to comparison-shop for you, since prices can vary from consolidator to consolidator.

A survey conducted of flyers who use consolidator tickets found only one major complaint: such a ticket doesn't qualify you for an advance seat assignment, so you are likely to be assigned a poor seat on the plane at the last minute.

Another possible hitch: many people who booked consolidator tickets reported no savings at all, since the airlines will sometimes match the price of the consolidator ticket by announcing a promotional fare. Because the situation is a bit tricky, you need to investigate carefully just how much you can expect to save.

Cyber Deals for Net Surfers

It's possible to get some great deals on airfare, hotels, and car rentals via the Internet. So go grab your mouse and start surfing before you hit the real waves—you could save a bundle on your trip. The Web sites highlighted below are worth checking out, especially since all services are free.

Microsoft Expedia (www.expedia.com) The best part of this multipurpose travel site is the "Fare Tracker": you fill out a form on the screen indicating that you're interested in cheap flights from your hometown, and, once a week, they'll e-mail you the best airfare deals. The site's "Travel Agent" will steer you to bargains on hotels and car rentals, and you can book everything, including flights, right online. This site is useful even once you're booked: Before you go, log on to Expedia for oodles of up-to-date travel information, including weather reports and foreign exchange rates.

Preview Travel (www.reservations.com and www.vacations.com) Another useful travel site, Reservations.com has a "Best Fare Finder," which will search the Apollo computer reservations system (a huge database used by travel agents worldwide) for the three lowest fares for any route on any days of the year. Say you want to go from Chicago to Orlando and back between December 6 and 13: Just fill out the form on the screen with times, dates, and destinations, and within minutes, Preview will show you the best deals. If you find an airfare you like, you can book your ticket right online—you can even reserve hotels and car rentals on this site. If you're in the preplanning stage, head to Preview's Vacations.com site, where you can check out the latest package deals around the world by clicking on "Hot Deals."

Travelocity (www.travelocity.com) This is one of the best travel sites out there. In addition to its "Personal Fare Watcher," which notifies you via e-mail of the lowest airfares for up to five destinations, Travelocity will track the three lowest fares for any routes on any dates in minutes. You can book a flight right then and there, and if you need a rental car or hotel, Travelocity will find you the best deal via the SABRE computer reservations system (another huge travel-agent database). Click on "Last Minute Deals" for the latest travel bargains, including a link to **H.O.T. Coupons (www.hotcoupons.com)**, where you can print electronic coupons for travel in the United States and Canada.

Trip.Com (www.thetrip.com) This site is really geared toward the business traveler, but vacationers-to-be can also use Trip.Com's valuable fare-finding engine, which will e-mail you every week with the best city-to-city airfare deals on your selected route or routes.

Discount Tickets (www.discount-tickets.com) Operated by the European Travel Network (ETN), this site offers discounts on airfares, accommodations,

To be doubly cautious, since some bucket shops have proved dishonest in the past, you should confirm your flight with the airline to make sure that the bucket shop actually made the reservation for you. Do not rely solely on the word of the bucket shop. Bucket shops can ticket you on both charters and scheduled flights. Even though a scheduled flight may cost more, you have a greater assurance that it will leave on time.

One more bit of advice: inquire as to any and all restrictions, and always pay by credit card.

car rentals, and tours. It deals in flights between the United States and other countries, not domestic U.S. flights, so it's most useful for foreign travelers.

E-Savers Programs Several major airlines offer a free e-mail service known as **E-Savers,** via which they'll send you their best bargain airfares on a weekly basis. Here's how it works: Once a week (usually Wednesday), subscribers receive a list of discounted flights to and from various destinations, both international and domestic. Now here's the catch: These fares are available only if you leave the very next Saturday (or sometimes Friday night) and return on the following Monday or Tuesday. It's really a service for the spontaneously inclined and travelers looking for a quick getaway. But the fares are cheap, so it's worth taking a look. If you have a preference for certain airlines (in other words, the ones you fly most frequently), sign up with them first. Another caveat: You'll get frequent-flier miles if you purchase one of these fares, but you can't use miles to buy the ticket.

Here's a list of airlines and their Web sites, where you can not only get on the e-mailing lists, but also book flights directly:

- **American Airlines:** www.americanair.com
- **Continental Airlines:** www.flycontinental.com
- **TWA:** www.twa.com
- **Northwest Airlines:** www.nwa.com
- **US Airways:** www.usairways.com

Other airlines also maintain Web sites worth browsing, including **British Airways** (www.british-airways.com), **Lufthansa** (www.lufthansa-usa.com), and **Iberia** (www.iberia.com).

Travel and Booking Agencies **Preview Travel** (www.previewtravel.com) is the most user-friendly of several travel agency sites, offering some incredible vacation, airline, and hotel deals and updating its offerings every day. It even lets you book your vacation online. **Moments Notice** (www.moments-notice.com) promotes itself as a travel service, not an agency, providing a vacation bargain hunter's dream. The Web site, updated each morning, advertises many deals that are snapped up by the end of the day. A drawback is that many of these vacations require you to drop everything and go almost immediately. **180096hotel.com** offers budget reservations at prestigious hotels all over the world, many accommodations up to 65% off. Booking can be done online. **America Online** (www.aol.com) is the most comprehensive site online, offering direct links to many of these sites and others.

Although bucket shops abound from coast to coast (look for their usually small ads in your local newspaper's Sunday travel section), few specialize in the highly competitive Caribbean market. One of these is **TFI Tours International,** 34 W. 32nd St., 12th Floor, New York, NY 10001 (☎ **800/745-8000** in the U.S., or 212/736-1140 in New York state).

REBATERS To make matters even more confusing, rebaters also compete in the low-airfare market. Rebaters are organizations that pass along to the passenger part of their commission, although many of them assess a fee for their services. And although rebaters are not the same as travel agents, they sometimes offer roughly similar services. Sometimes a rebater will sell you a discounted travel ticket and also offer discounted land arrangements, including hotels and car rentals. Most rebaters offer discounts averaging anywhere from 10% to 25% (but this varies from place to place), plus a $25 handling charge.

Travel Avenue, 10 S. Riverside Plaza, Suite 1404, Chicago, IL 60606 (☎ **800/333-3335** in the U.S., or 312/876-6866), is one of the oldest agencies of its kind. It offers up-front cash rebates on every airline ticket over $350 it sells. It sells airline tickets to independent travelers who have already worked out their travel plans. Also available are tour and cruise fares, plus hotel bookings.

Another major rebater is **The Smart Traveller,** 3111 SW 27th Ave. (P.O. Box 330010), Miami, FL 33133 (☎ **800/448-3338** in the U.S., or 305/448-3338; fax 305/443-3544). This agency offers discounts on package tours, Caribbean cruises, dive packages, and villa and condo rentals.

TRAVEL CLUBS   Travel clubs supply an unsold inventory of tickets that are discounted from 20% to 60%. After you pay an annual fee, you're given a hotline number to call to find out what discounts are available. Some discounts become available a few days in advance of actual departure, some a week in advance, and some as much as a month. Of course, you're limited to what's available, so you have to be flexible. Some of the best of these clubs are listed below.

Moment's Notice, 7301 New Utrecht Ave., Brooklyn, NY 11204 (☎ **718/ 234-6295;** fax 718/234-6450), charges $25 per year for membership, which allows spur-of-the-moment participation in dozens of tours. Its discounted air-and-land packages to all Caribbean islands sometimes represent substantial savings over what you'd have paid through more conventional channels. Members can call the hotline (☎ **212/873-0908**) to learn what options are available. Most of the company's best-valued tours depart from the northeast.

Travelers Advantage, 3033 South Parker Rd., Suite 900, Aurora, CO 80014 (☎ **800/548-1116**), offers a 3-month trial participation for $1 and an annual membership fee starting at $49. You'll get offers for members-only vacation packages at reductions of 5% to 30%. For specific information about prices, call ☎ **800/TEL-TRIP.**

Another club, **Encore Travel Club,** 4501 Forbes Blvd., Lanham, MD 20706 (☎ **800/638-8976** in the U.S.), charges $59.95 a year for membership, which offers up to 50% discounts at more than 4,000 hotels. It also offers discounts on airfare, cruises, and car rentals through its volume purchase plans. Membership includes a travel package outlining the company's many services and use of a toll-free phone number.

7 Package Tours

If you want everything done for you and want to save money as well, consider taking a package tour. Besides general tours, many have specific themes—tennis, golf, scuba and snorkeling, and honeymoons. Puerto Rico is prominently featured by most package tour companies.

Economy and convenience are the chief advantages of a package tour—the costs of transportation (usually by plane), a hotel room, food (sometimes), and sightseeing (sometimes) are combined and neatly tied up with a single price tag. There are extras, of course, but in general you'll know in advance roughly what the cost of your vacation will be, and you can budget accordingly. The disadvantage is that you may find yourself, for example, in a hotel you dislike but cannot leave because you've already paid for it.

If you're a serious foodie who likes to dine around, beware of packages that include all meals. Eating all your meals at one hotel on a package plan is almost always cheaper than if you dine around à la carte. However, if you're seeking variety in your dining experiences, you won't find it unless your hotel is particularly adept at creating new taste sensations nightly. To still save money and to savor different dining experiences, ask if you can opt for a Modified American Plan (MAP) that will allow you to eat breakfast at your hotel and either lunch or dinner, at your choice. That way, you're free to have either lunch or dinner outside your hotel. On the MAP we'd opt for a "free" lunch at the hotel, then go out for dinner at one of the many restaurants recommended in this guide.

Choosing the right package can be a bit of a problem. It's best to go to a travel agent, tell him or her what island (or islands) you'd like to visit, and see what's currently offered.

Packages are available because tour operators can mass-book hotels and make volume purchases. You generally have to pay the cost of the total package in advance. Transfers between your hotel and the airport are often included (this may be more of a break than it sounds at first since some airports are situated a $40-or-more taxi ride from a resort). Many packages carry several options, including the possibility of low-cost car rentals. Nearly all tour packages are based on double occupancy.

To save time comparing the price and value of all the package tours out there, consider calling **TourScan Inc.,** P.O. Box 2367, Darien, CT 06820 (☎ **800/962-2080** in the U.S., or 203/655-8091; fax 203/655-6689). Every season, the company gathers and computerizes the contents of about 200 brochures containing 10,000 different vacations in the Caribbean, the Bahamas, and Bermuda. TourScan selects the best value at each hotel and condo. Two catalogs are printed each year. Each lists a broad-based choice of hotels on most of the islands of the Caribbean, in all price ranges. Write to TourScan for their catalogs costing $4 each, the price of which is credited to any TourScan vacation.

Some of the leading tour operators to the Caribbean include the following:

Caribbean Concepts Corp., 1428 Brickell Ave., Suite 402, Miami, FL 33131 (☎ **888/741-7711** in the U.S., or 305/373-8687; fax 305/373-8310), offers all-inclusive low-cost air-and-land packages to the islands, including apartments, hotels, villas, or condo rentals.

Another good deal might be a combined land-and-air package offered by one of the major U.S. carriers. Call their toll-free numbers for more information: **American Airlines Fly-Away Vacations** (☎ 800/321-2121), **Delta's Dream Vacations** (☎ 800/872-7786), **TWA Getaway Vacations** (☎ 800/GETAWAY), and **United Airlines Vacations** (☎ 800/328-6877).

Other options for general independent packages include:

Horizon Tours, 1634 Eye St., NW, Suite 301, Washington, DC 20006 (☎ **888/SUN-N-SAND** in the U.S., or 202/393-8390; fax 202/393-1547), specializes in all-inclusive upscale resorts in Puerto Rico. Finally, **Liberty Travel**, 69 Spring St., Ramsey, NJ 07446 (☎ **201/934-3500;** fax 201/934-3888), advertises more packages to the Caribbean than any other agency.

PACKAGES FOR BRITISH TRAVELERS

British travelers can contact **Caribbean Connection,** Concorde House, Forest Street, Chester, England CH1 1QR (☎ **01244/341131**), which offers all-inclusive packages (airfare and hotel) to the Caribbean and customizes tours for independent travel. It publishes two catalogs of Caribbean offerings, one featuring more than 160 properties on all the major islands, and a 50-page catalog of luxury all-inclusive properties.

Other Caribbean specialists operating out of England include **Kuoni Travel,** Kuoni House, Dorking, Surrey RH5 4AZ (☎ **01306/740-888**). **Caribtours,** 161 Fulham Rd., London SW3 6SN (☎ **0171/581-3517**), a small, very knowledgeable organization, also specializes in Caribbean travel and will tailor itineraries.

Although Australians are welcome to visit Puerto Rico, as are New Zealanders and other nationals, there are no special packages or deals for them.

8 For the Cruise-Ship Traveler

If you'd like to sail the Caribbean in a hotel with an ocean view, a cruise ship might be for you. Cruises are slow and easy and are no longer enjoyed only by the idle rich who have months to spend away from home. In fact, most cruises today appeal to the middle-income traveler who probably has no more than 1 or 2 weeks of vacation.

Miami is the cruise capital of the world, but San Juan is second. Unless you have never visited Miami and would like to include it as part of your extended Caribbean itinerary, there is justification in flying directly to San Juan by plane and beginning your cruise here. It puts you immediately in the Caribbean, which means you save a 2-day ocean voyage just to get here. Instead of sailing from Florida, you can spend the time getting to know Puerto Rico.

Most cruise-ship operators emphasize the concept of a total vacation. Some are mostly activity centered; others offer the chance to do nothing but relax. Cruise ships are self-contained resorts, offering a large variety of services and activities on board and sightseeing once you arrive in a port of call.

For those who don't want to spend all their time at sea, some lines offer a fly-and-cruise vacation. You spend a week cruising the Caribbean and another week staying at an interesting hotel at reduced prices. These total packages should cost less than the cruise and air portions purchased separately.

Another version of fly-and-cruise is to fly to and from the cruise. Most plans offer a package deal from the principal airport closest to your residence to the major airport nearest to the cruise-departure point. It's possible to purchase your air ticket on your own and book your cruise ticket separately, but you'll save money by combining the fares in a package deal.

Most cruise ships travel at night, arriving the next morning at the day's port of call. In port, passengers can go ashore for sightseeing, shopping, and a local meal. Cruise prices vary widely. Sometimes the same route with the same ports of call can carry different fares, depending on the ship's luxury (as well as your accommodations on board). Consult a good travel agent for the latest offerings.

Some of the most likely contenders include the following: **Ambassador Tours,** 120 Montgomery St., Suite 400, San Francisco, CA 94104 (☎ **800/989-9000** or 415/357-9876); **Cruises Inc.,** 5000 Campuswood Dr. E., Syracuse, NY 13057 (☎ **800/854-0500** or 315/463-9695); **Cruises of Distinction,** 2750 S. Woodward Ave., Bloomfield Hills, MI 48304 (☎ **800/634-3445** or 810/332-3030); **Cruise Fairs of America,** Century Plaza Towers, 2029 Century Park E., Suite 950, Los Angeles, CA 90067 (☎ **800/456-4FUN** or 310/556-2925); **Kelly Cruises,** 1315 W. 22nd St., Suite 105, Oak Brook, IL 60521 (☎ **800/837-7447** or

708/990-1111); and **Hartford Holidays Travel,** 626 Willis Ave., Williston Park, NY 11596 (☎ **800/828-4813**). Any of these stay tuned to last-minute price wars brewing among such megacarriers as Carnival, Princess, Royal Caribbean, and Holland America, as well as such low-budget contenders as Premier.

Vacations to Go, 1502 Augusta Dr., Suite 415, Houston, TX 77057 (☎ **800/338-4962** in the U.S.), provides catalogs and information on discount cruises through the Atlantic, the Caribbean, and the Mediterranean. Annual membership costs $6.95 per family.

WHILE WAITING FOR YOUR SHIP TO SAIL

While waiting for the departure of your cruise vessel, you might spend the day enjoying the historic district of Old San Juan with its endless sightseeing possibilities and merchandise-crammed shops. Another day can be devoted to the Condado with its beaches, gambling casinos, and sporting possibilities in the Greater San Juan area, including almost unlimited golf, tennis, and water sports. Even if you have only hours to spend before your ship's departure, you can explore the historic old city, either taking a tour or going on your own. You'll find beaches galore on upcoming islands, but nothing to equal this historic sector.

WHEN YOUR SHIP COMES IN

The Port of San Juan is the busiest ocean terminal in the West Indies, with an estimated half of the Caribbean's trade passing through here. There are about 710 cruise-ship arrivals every year, bringing nearly 860,000 passengers.

A spacious walkway connects the piers to the cobblestone streets of Old San Juan, so you can walk over there to shop. You can also take a waiting taxi to the beaches of Condado. For advice and maps, contact the **Tourist Information Center** at La Casita, near Pier 1 in Old San Juan (☎ **787/721-2400**). The dock area, now restored, is an attractive place for strolling, with its plazas, fountains, promenades, and beaches.

THE CRUISE LINES

Here's a brief rundown of some of the cruise lines serving San Juan and the Caribbean. For far-more-detailed information, pick up a copy of our companion guide in this series, *Frommer's Caribbean Cruises and Ports of Call.*

- **American Canadian Caribbean** (☎ **800/556-7450**) is a Rhode Island–based cruise outfit whose shallow-draft, small-scale coastal cruisers have been studied with almost obsessive interest by most of its competitors. They embark on 7- to 12-day excursions through complicated shoals, including some off the shores of Puerto Rico, near Caribbean landmasses where larger ships cannot go. Although itineraries at this small-scale outfitter, whose level of repeat passengers is exceptionally high, are likely to change, look for at least one of its trio of ships to spend part of its winter touching down at isolated coasts of Puerto Rico within the context of cruises that also stop in the Bahamas, the Virgin Islands, the Panama Canal, and the coasts of Central America.

- **Carnival Cruise Lines** (☎ **800/438-6744**), a specialist in the maintenance of some of the biggest and most brightly decorated ships afloat, is the richest, boldest, brashest, and most successful mass-market cruise line in the world. Nine of its vessels depart from Florida or Caribbean ports that include, among others, San Juan, Miami, Tampa, and New Orleans. Two of the ships (*Carnival Inspiration* and *Carnival Fascination*) define San Juan as their home port, from which 7-day excursions are made to such southern Caribbean ports as St. Thomas, Sint

Maarten, Dominica, Barbados, Guadeloupe, Martinique, Grenada, St. Lucia, and Santo Domingo. If you prefer to depart from one of the ports of Florida (especially Miami), know in advance that many of the company's cruises make San Juan a focal point of their stopovers. Most of the company's Caribbean cruises offer good value, last between 4 and 11 days (in most cases 7 days), and feature nonstop activities, lots of glitter, and the hustle and bustle of armies of clients and crew members embarking and disembarking at every port. Cuisine and party-colored drinks are plentiful, although with vessels of this size, they are, by necessity, mass-produced. The overall atmosphere is comparable to that of a floating theme park with hordes of visitors, loaded with whimsy, and with lots of emphasis on partying in a style you might have expected in Atlantic City. Lots of single passengers, some of them with gleams in their eye, opt for this line, and some actually get lucky. Despite the presence of lots of unattached or loosely attached adults, the line makes special efforts to amuse and entertain children between 2 and 17. The average onboard age ranges from 38 to 42, although individual passengers range from 3 to 95.

- **Celebrity Cruises** (☎ 800/437-3111) maintains five newly built, medium-to-large ships offering cruises of between 7 and 15 nights to such ports as Key West, Grand Cayman, St. Thomas, Ocho Rios, Antigua, and Cozumel, Mexico, among others. Passengers interested in maximum exposure to Puerto Rico usually opt to cruise aboard *Galaxy,* a 77,000-ton megaship that's based (October to April only) in San Juan, and which embarks every week throughout the year for tours to such southern Caribbean islands as Barbados, Martinique, and Antigua. Alternatively, passengers might opt for a 10- or 11-night Panama Canal cruise that involves either eastbound or westbound treks between San Juan and Acapulco. Pre- or post-cruise vacation extenders allow additional days in Puerto Rico as an add-on bonus to your trip.

    Despite a recent merger of Celebrity with the larger and better-financed Royal Caribbean International, Celebrity will maintain its own identity and corporate structure within the larger framework. The niche this line has created is unpretentious but classy, several notches above mass-market, but with pricing that's nonetheless relatively competitive. Accommodations are roomy and well equipped, and the cuisine is among the most intensely cultivated of any of its competitors afloat.

- **Costa Cruise Lines** (☎ 800/462-6782), the U.S.-based branch of an Italian cruise line that has thrived for about a century, maintains hefty-to-megasize vessels that are newer than those of many other lines afloat. Two of these offer virtually identical jaunts through the western and eastern Caribbean on alternate weeks, each of them departing from Fort Lauderdale. Ports of call during the eastern Caribbean itineraries of both vessels include a stopover in San Juan, followed by visits to St. Thomas, Serena Cay (a private island off the coast of the Dominican Republic known for its beaches), and Nassau. There are an Italian flavor and lots of Italian design on board here, and an atmosphere of relaxed indulgence. The ships—*CostaRomantica* and *CostaVictoria*—feature tame versions of ancient Roman Bacchanalia, as well as such celebrations as *Festa Italiana,* and focaccia and pizza parties by the pool.

- **Norwegian Cruise Line** (☎ 800/327-7030), controller of the cruise world's most diverse collection of ships, appeals to all ages and income levels. Its collection of mostly midsized ships includes a roster of Scandinavian officers, an international staff, and a pervasive modern Viking theme. The company's most visible entry within the Puerto Rican market is the *Norwegian Sea,* which departs every

Sunday throughout the year from its home port of San Juan. Itineraries alternate between the "Barbados route" (which includes stops at Santo Domingo, Dominica, and St. Thomas) and the "Antigua route" (which includes stops at Santo Domingo, St. Lucia, Sint Maarten, and St. Thomas). NCL administers a snappy, high-energy array of onboard activities and, in many cases, a revolving array of international sports figures for game tips and lectures.

- **Princess Cruises** (☎ **800/421-0522**) has a large and far-flung fleet that during the life of this edition will total between 8 and 10 megavessels. Four of these cruise at various times of the year through Caribbean and Bahamian waters sometimes with stops at San Juan as part of the itinerary. The one most closely associated with Puerto Rico, however, is *Dawn Princess,* a state-of-the-art megaship that defines San Juan as its home port. Departing weekly, every Saturday, it pays calls at ports that include St. Thomas, Sint Maarten, Barbados, Martinique, and St. Lucia. On alternate weeks, it stops at Aruba, Caracas, Grenada, St. Thomas, and Dominica. The *Dawn Princess*'s sibling ship, *Sun Princess,* pinpoints San Juan and Acapulco as the beginning or end point of trans-Canal cruises that last between 10 and 11 days each. Princess is one of the very few in the world offering luxury accommodations and upscale service as a standard feature aboard its megaships. These usually carry a smaller number of passengers than similarly sized vessels on less-elegant lines. The company's clientele is upscale, with an average passenger age of 55 or over. A respectable percentage of the staff is British.

- **Radisson Seven Seas Cruises** (☎ **800/477-7500**) is noted for the level of glamour and prestige that permeates its cruises. It sends only one of its ships, the *Radisson Diamond,* into the Caribbean on a regular basis. Designed along lines distinctly different from those of every other cruise line afloat, it's a relatively slow but stable ship floating atop submerged pontoons similar to those used by catamarans or oil-drilling platforms in the North Sea. Despite the fact that its design is not likely to be duplicated anytime soon within the cruise industry, passengers appreciate it for its fine cuisine, upscale service, and suitability for corporate conventions at sea. Cruises are relatively expensive compared to those offered by less-prestigious lines, and roam freely, with less allegiance to a fixed home port than many other vessels. During a brief period of every year, the *Diamond* defines San Juan as its home port, but only between February and April, when it embarks on short-term cruises of no more than 6 days in duration. Stopovers include Tortola, St. Barts, and Sint Maarten. The rest of the time, the ship's Caribbean ports include cities along the coast of Costa Rica, as well as Curaçao, Aruba, Grand Cayman, Cayman Brac, Cartagena, St. Barts, Sint Maarten, St. Thomas, and Cozumel.

- **Royal Caribbean International** (☎ **800/327-6700**) leads the industry in the development of megaships. Most of this company's dozen or so vessels weigh in at around 73,000 tons, are among the largest of any line afloat, and represent a roster of floating hardware that's more impressive than that of many national navies. Marketed as a mainstream, mass-market cruise line whose components have been fine-tuned through endless repetition, the line encourages a restrained house-party theme that's somehow a bit less frenetic than that found aboard the more raucous megaships of other cruise lines. The company is well run, and there are enough onboard activities to suit virtually any taste and age level. Though accommodations and accouterments are more than adequate, they are not upscale, and cabins aboard some of the line's older vessels tend to be a bit more cramped than the industry norm. Using either Miami or San Juan as their home port, RCCL ships call regularly at such oft-visited ports as St. Thomas, Ocho Rios, Sint Maarten, Grand Cayman, St. Croix, and Curaçao. Most of the company's cruises last for 7 days, although some weekend jaunts from San Juan to St. Thomas are available for 3 nights, and some Panama Canal crossings last for 11 and 12 nights. Royal Caribbean is the only cruise line in the business that owns, outright, two tropical beaches (one in the Bahamas, the other along an isolated peninsula in northern Haiti) whose sands and water-sports facilities are the focus of many of the company's Caribbean cruises.

- **Royal Olympic Cruises** (☎ **800/872-6400**), formed in 1995 from a merger between Sun Lines and Epirotiki Cruises, is a well-respected Greek shipping line that operates the only Greek-registered ship in the Caribbean, the aging but comfortable and well-maintained *Stella Solaris*. Many of this ship's stopovers at Caribbean ports (San Juan, Sint Maarten, St. Lucia, Antigua, and St. Thomas) are configured either as annual Christmas cruises or as visits en route to either the Amazon or the Panama Canal. Despite the age of the ship, its many restorations and the cheerfulness of one of the best staffs of any vessel afloat make this a consistently popular ship.

- **Windjammer Barefoot Cruises** (☎ **800/327-2601**) operates eight sailing ships, most of which are faithful renovations of antique schooners or sail-driven private yachts. Most have illustrious antecedents, including stints as the private getaway ships of sometimes notorious billionaires or wannabes. The company is proud of its role as purveyor of some of the least formal cruises afloat, with few passengers ever bringing more than a roster of shorts and T-shirts for their time aboard. The line specializes in visits to rarely visited Caribbean outposts, with special emphasis on the scattered reefs and cays of the Virgin Islands and the Grenadines. The ship that's most closely linked to Puerto Rico is *The Legacy*, a steel-hulled sailing vessel that was originally built in 1952 as a meteorological research ship for the French Navy. Today, from a base in Fajardo, Puerto Rico, it departs every Sunday for the offshore islands of Vieques or Culebra and isolated cays within the United States and British Virgin Islands.

9 Getting Around

BY PLANE

American Eagle (☎ **800/433-7300** or 787/749-1747) flies from Luis Muñoz Marín International Airport to Mayagüez, which can be your gateway to western Puerto Rico. Most round-trip fares are $95 to $136. It also offers two daily flights between San Juan and Ponce for $95 to $136 round-trip, depending on the ticket. However, prices are known to fluctuate, so call for last-minute details. For information about air connections to the offshore islands of Vieques and Culebra, see chapter 11.

BY RENTAL CAR

Rental cars are readily available, but many of your fellow readers have offered this advice: *Drive on Puerto Rico only if necessary.* They point out that local drivers are often dangerous, as evidenced by the number of fenders with bashed-in sides. The older coastal highways provide the most scenic routes but are often congested. Some of the roads, especially in the mountainous interior, are just too narrow for automobiles. Proceed with caution along these poorly paved and maintained roads, which most often follow circuitous routes. Cliffslides or landslides are not uncommon.

If you do rent a vehicle, some local agencies may tempt you with special reduced prices. But if you're planning to tour the island by car, you won't find any local branches to help you if you experience trouble. And some of the agencies widely advertising low-cost deals won't take credit cards and want cash in advance. Also, watch out for "hidden" extra costs, which sometimes proliferate among the smaller and not very well-known firms, and difficulties connected with resolving insurance claims.

If you do rent a vehicle, it's best to stick with the old reliables: **Avis** (☎ **800/ 331-2112** or 787/791-2500), **Budget** (☎ **800/527-0700** or 787/791-3685), or **Hertz** (☎ **800/654-3001** or 787/791-0840). Each of the "big three" companies offers minivan transport to its office and car depot. Be alert to the minimum age requirements for car rentals in Puerto Rico. Both Avis and Hertz require that renters be 25 or older, while at Budget, renters between the ages of 21 and 24 pay a $5 daily surcharge to the agreed-upon rental fee.

Alternatively, you can opt for a rental from **Kemwel Holiday Auto** (☎ **800/678-0678**). Based in Harrison, New York, their offerings in Puerto Rico consist of a standard roster of cars whose cheapest vehicle, a Toyota Tercel, rents for $195 per week, with unlimited mileage. More expensive vehicles, ranging upward to as much as $399 per week for a Ford Taurus, are also available. Additional insurance in the form of a collision damage waiver (CDW) is available at prices that begin at $63 a week (see "Insurance," below). Kemwel charges drivers between the ages of 21 and 24 an extra $6 per day.

None of these companies rents Jeeps, four-wheel-drive vehicles, or convertibles.

Added security comes from an antitheft double-locking mechanism that has been installed in most of the rental cars available in Puerto Rico. Car theft is high on Puerto Rico, so extra precaution is always needed.

Distances are often posted in kilometers rather than miles (1km = 0.62 mile), but speed limits are reckoned in miles per hour.

INSURANCE Each company offers an optional collision damage waiver priced at around $12 to $14 a day. Purchasing the waiver eliminates most or all of the financial responsibility you would face in case of an accident. With it, you can simply go home, leaving the rental company to sort it all out. Without it, you would be liable for up to the full value of the car in case it was damaged. Paying for the rental with certain credit or charge cards sometimes eliminates the need to buy this extra insurance. Also, your own automobile insurance policy may cover some or all of the damages. You should check with both your own insurer and your credit-card issuers before leaving home.

GASOLINE There is usually an abundant supply of gasoline in Puerto Rico, especially on the outskirts of San Juan, where you'll see all the familiar signs, such as Mobil. Gasoline stations are also plentiful along the main arteries traversing the island. However, if you're going to remote areas of the island, especially on Sunday, it's advisable to start out with a full tank. *Note:* In Puerto Rico, gasoline is sold by the liter, not by the gallon.

DRIVING RULES Driving rules can be a source of some confusion. Speed limits are often not posted on the island, but when they are, they're given in miles per hour. For example, the limit on the San Juan–Ponce *autopista* (superhighway) is 70 m.p.h. Speed limits elsewhere, notably in heavily populated residential areas, are much lower. Since you're not likely to know what the actual speed limit is in some of these areas, it's better to confine your speed to no more than 30 m.p.h. The

Highway Signs

Road signs using international symbols are commonplace in the San Juan metropolitan area and other urban centers, but they are written in Spanish. The following translations will also help you figure out what they mean:

Spanish	English
Autopista	Expressway
Balneario	Public beach
Calle sin salida	Dead end
Carretera cerrada	Road closed to traffic
Carretera dividida	Divided highway
Carretera estrecha	Narrow road
Cruce	Crossroad
Cruce de peatones	Pedestrian crossing
Cuesta	Hill
Desprendimiento	Landslide
Desvío	Detour
Estación de peaje	Toll station
Manténgase a la derecha	Keep right
No entre	Do not enter
No estacione	Do not park
Parada de guaguas	Bus stop
Peligro	Danger
Puente estrecho	Narrow bridge
Velocidad máxima	Speed limit
Zona escolar	School zone

highway department places *lomas* (speed bumps) at strategic points to deter speeders. Sometimes these are called "sleeping policemen."

Puerto Ricans drive, as do U.S. and Canadian motorists, on the right-hand side of the road.

ROAD MAPS   One of the best and most detailed road maps of Puerto Rico is published by **International Travel Maps,** 345 W. Broadway, Vancouver, BC, Canada V5Y 1P8 (☎ **604/879-3621**), and distributed in the United States by Rand McNally. It's available in some bookstores and is a good investment at $8.95. The **Gousha Puerto Rico Road Map,** which sells for $2.95 in the United States and Canada, has a good street map of San Juan but lacks detailed information about minor highways on the island and is very similar to the map of Puerto Rico distributed free at tourist offices.

BREAKDOWNS AND ASSISTANCE   All the major towns and cities have garages that will come to your assistance and tow your vehicle in for repairs if necessary. There's no national emergency number to call in the event of a mechanical breakdown. If you have a rental car, call the rental company first. Usually, someone there will bring motor assistance to you. If your car requires extensive repairs because of a mechanical failure, a new one will be sent to replace it.

BY PUBLIC TRANSPORTATION

Cars and minibuses known as *públicos* provide low-cost transportation around the island. Their license plates have the letters "P" or "PD" following the numbers. They serve all the main towns of Puerto Rico; passengers are let off and picked up along the way. Rates are set by the Public Service Commission. Públicos usually operate during daylight hours, departing from the main plaza (central square) of a town.

Information about público routes between San Juan and Mayagüez is available at **Lineas Sultana,** Calle Esteban González 898, Urbanización Santa Rita, Río Piedras (☎ 787/765-9377). Information about público routes between San Juan and Ponce is available from **Choferes Unidos de Ponce,** Terminal de Carros Públicos, Calle Vive in Ponce (☎ 787/764-0540).

Fares vary according to whether the público will make a detour to pick up or drop off a passenger at a specific locale. (If you want to deviate from the predetermined routes, you'll pay more than if you wait for a público beside the main highway.) Fares from San Juan to Mayagüez range from $16 to $30; from San Juan to Ponce, from $15 to $25. Be warned that although prices of públicos are admittedly low, the routes are slow, with frequent stops, often erratic routing, and lots of inconvenience.

10 Tips on Choosing Your Accommodations

HOTELS & RESORTS

There is no rigid classification of Puerto Rican hotels. The word "deluxe" is often used—or misused—when "first class" might be a more appropriate term. Self-described first-class hotels often aren't. We've presented fairly detailed descriptions of the hotels in this book, so you'll get an idea of what to expect once you're here.

Even in the real deluxe and first-class properties, however, don't expect top-rate service and efficiency. The slow tropical pace is what folks mean when they talk about "island time." Also, "things" often don't work as well in the tropics as they do in some of the fancy resorts of California or Europe. You may even experience power failures.

Ask detailed questions when booking a room. Don't just ask to be booked into a certain hotel, but specify your likes and dislikes. There are several logistics of getting the right room in a hotel. Entertainment in Puerto Rico is often alfresco, so light sleepers obviously won't want a room directly over a steel band. In general, back rooms cost less than oceanfront rooms, and lower rooms cost less than upper-floor units. Therefore, if budget is a major consideration with you, opt for the cheaper rooms. You won't have a great view but you'll pay less. Just make sure that it isn't next to the all-night drummers.

Transfers from the airport or the cruise dock are included in some hotel bookings, most often in a package plan but usually not in ordinary bookings. This is true of first-class and deluxe resorts but rarely of medium-priced or budget accommodations. Always ascertain whether transfers (which can be expensive) are included.

When using the facilities at a resort, make sure that you know exactly what is free and what costs money. For example, swimming in the pool is nearly always free, but you might be charged for use of a tennis court. Nearly all water sports cost extra, unless you're booked in on some special plan such as a scuba package. Some resorts seem to charge every time you breathe and might end up costing more than a deluxe hotel that includes most everything in the price.

What the Symbols Mean

First-time travelers to Puerto Rico may at first be confused by classifications on hotel-room rate sheets. We've used these same classifications in this guide. One of the most common rates is **MAP**, meaning Modified American Plan. Simply put, that means room, breakfast, and dinner, unless the room rate is quoted separately in a listing, and then it means only breakfast and dinner. **CP** means Continental Plan—that is, room and a light breakfast. **EP** is European Plan—room only. **AP**, American Plan, is the most expensive rate because it includes your room and three meals a day.

Some hotels are right on the beach. Others involve transfers to the beach by taxi or bus, so factor in transportation costs, which can mount quickly if you stay 5 days to a week. If you want to go to the beach every day, it might be wise to book a hotel on the Condado and not stay in romantic Old San Juan: you'll spend a lot of time and money transferring back and forth between your hotel and the beach.

Most hotels in Puerto Rico are on the windward side of the island, with lots of waves, undertow, and surf. If a glasslike smooth sea is imperative for your stay, you can book on the leeward or Caribbean side, which is better for snorkeling. That means the eastern shore of Puerto Rico and its southeast coast. The major centers here are the resort complex of Palmas del Mar and the "second city" of Ponce.

SPAS

The Penthouse spa—the best on island—at the **El San Juan Hotel & Casino** has full amenities for men and women, including fitness evaluations, supervised weight-loss programs, aerobics classes, sauna, steam room, and massage. It's open 7 days a week, year-round. A daily fee for individual services is assessed. See chapter 5.

The Plaza Spa at the **Condado Plaza Hotel & Casino** features Universal weight-training machines, video exercycles, sauna, whirlpool, facials, and massages. See chapter 5.

The fitness center at the **Palmas del Mar Resort** in Humacao features hydra-fitness exercise equipment, exercise programs, free-weight training, and computerized fitness evaluations. It's open 7 days a week. See chapter 8.

The Spa Caribe at the **Hyatt Regency Cerromar Beach** offers shape-up programs, including aerobics and "talking" Powercise machines, health evaluations, plus skin- and body-care treatments, such as massage facials. See chapter 8.

At the **Parador Baños de Coamo** in Coamo, there are therapeutic thermal springs—one hot, one cool. There are also two swimming pools (one for children) and a tennis court. It's open daily. See chapter 10.

THE PUERTO RICAN GUESTHOUSE

An entirely different type of accommodation is the guesthouse, where Puerto Ricans themselves usually stay when they travel. Ranging in size from 7 to 25 rooms, they offer a familial atmosphere. Many are on or near the beach, some have pools or sundecks, and a number serve meals.

In Puerto Rico, however, the term "guesthouse" has many meanings. Some guesthouses are like simple motels built around swimming pools. Others have small individual cottages with their own kitchenettes, constructed around a main building in which you'll often find a bar and a restaurant serving local food. Some are surprisingly comfortable, often with private baths and swimming pools. You may or may not have air-conditioning. The rooms are sometimes cooled by ceiling fans, or by the trade winds blowing through open windows at night.

For value, the guesthouse can't be topped. Staying at a guesthouse, you can journey over to a big beach resort, using its seaside facilities for only a small charge. Although bereft of frills, the guesthouses we've recommended are clean and safe for families or single women. However, the cheapest ones are not places where you'd want to spend a lot of time because of their modest furnishings.

For further information, contact the **Puerto Rico Tourism Company,** 575 Fifth Ave., New York, NY 10017 (☎ **800/223-6530** or 212/599-6262).

PARADORES

In an effort to lure travelers beyond the hotels and casinos of San Juan's historic district to the tranquil natural beauty of the island's countryside, the Puerto Rico Tourism Company offers *paradores puertorriqueños*—charming country inns—which are comfortable bases for exploring the island's varied attractions. Vacationers seeking a peaceful idyll can also choose from several privately owned and operated guesthouses.

Using Spain's parador system as a model, the Puerto Rico Tourism Company established the paradores in 1973 to encourage tourism across the island. Each of the paradores is situated in a historic place or site of unusual scenic beauty and must meet high standards of service and cleanliness.

Some of the paradores are located in the mountains and others by the sea. Most have swimming pools, and all offer excellent Puerto Rican cuisine. Many are within easy driving distance of San Juan (see chapter 10). To make a reservation at one of the paradores, call ☎ **800/443-0266** in the United States (8am to noon and 1 to 4:30pm Atlantic time).

VILLAS & VACATION HOMES

You can often secure good deals in Puerto Rico by renting privately owned villas and vacation homes.

Many villas have a staff, or at least a maid who comes in a few days a week, and they also provide the essentials of home life, including bed linen and cooking paraphernalia. Condos usually come with a reception desk and are often comparable to life in a suite at a big resort hotel. Nearly all condo complexes have swimming pools (some have more than one).

Private apartments are rented either with or without maid service. This is more of a no-frills option than the villas and condos. The apartments may not be in buildings with swimming pools, and they may not have a front desk to help you. Cottages offer the most free-wheeling way to live among the major categories of vacation homes. Most cottages are fairly simple, many opening in an ideal fashion onto a beach, whereas others may be clustered around a communal swimming pool. Many contain no more than a simple bedroom together with a small kitchen and bath. For the peak winter season, reservations should be made at least 5 or 6 months in advance.

Dozens of agents throughout the United States and Canada offer these types of rentals (see "Rental Agencies," below, for some recommendations). You can also write to local tourist information offices, which can advise you on vacation home rentals.

Travel experts agree that savings, especially for a family of three to six people, or two or three couples, can range from 50% to 60% of what a hotel would cost. If there are only two in your party, these savings probably don't apply.

RENTAL AGENCIES

Agencies specializing in renting properties in Puerto Rico include:

Villas of Distinction, P.O. Box 55, Armonk, NY 10504 (☎ **800/289-0900** in the U.S., or 914/273-3331; fax 914/273-3387), is one of the best rental agencies offering "complete vacations," including airfare, rental car, and domestic help. Some private villas have two to five bedrooms, and almost every villa has a swimming pool.

Caribbean Connections Plus Ltd., P.O. Box 261, Trumbull, CT 06611 (☎ **203/261-8603;** fax 203/261-8295), offers many apartments, cottages, and villas in the Caribbean. Caribbean Connections specializes in island hopping with JetAir, and it offers especially attractive deals for U.S. West Coast travelers. This is one of the few reservations services whose staff has actually been on the islands, so members can talk to people from experience and not from a computer screen.

VHR, Worldwide, 235 Kensington Ave., Norwood, NJ 07648 (☎ **800/633-3284** in the U.S. and Canada, or 201/767-9393; fax 201/767-5510), offers the most comprehensive portfolio of luxury villas, condominiums, resort suites, and apartments for rent in the Caribbean, including complete packages for airfare and car rentals. The company's more than 4,000 homes and suite resorts are handpicked by the staff, and accommodations are generally less expensive than comparable hotel rooms.

Hideaways International, 767 Islington St., Portsmouth, NH 03801 (☎ **800/843-4433** in the U.S., or 603/430-4433; fax 603/430-4444), provides a 144-page guide with illustrations of its accommodations in the Caribbean so that you'll get some idea of what you're renting. Most of its villas, which can accommodate up to three couples or a large family of about 10, come with maid service. You can also ask this travel club about discounts on plane fares and car rentals.

Rent-a-Home International, 7200 34th Ave., NW, Seattle, WA 98117 (☎ **800/488-RENT** or 206/789-9377; fax 206/789-9379), maintains an inventory of several thousand properties, specializing in condos and villas with weekly rates ranging from $700 to $50,000. It arranges weekly or longer bookings. For their color catalog including prices, descriptions, and pictures, send $15, which will be applied to your next rental.

Sometimes local tourist offices will also advise you on vacation-home rentals if you write or call them directly.

FAST FACTS: Puerto Rico

American Express See "Fast Facts: San Juan," in chapter 4.

Area Code The telephone area code for Puerto Rico is **787.** For calls on the island, the area code is not used.

Banks All major U.S. banks have branches on Puerto Rico; their hours are 8am to 2:30pm Monday through Friday and 9:45am to noon on Saturday.

Business Hours Regular business hours are Monday through Friday from 8am to 5pm. Shopping hours vary considerably. Regular shopping hours are Monday through Thursday and Saturday from 9am to 6pm. On Friday, stores have a long day: 9am to 9pm. Many stores also open on Sunday from 11am to 5pm.

Camera & Film Nearly all well-known brands of film are sold on Puerto Rico. Rolls of film cost about what they do on the U.S. mainland. It's relatively easy to get film processed on the island, especially in San Juan. It's important to protect

The Paradores of Puerto Rico

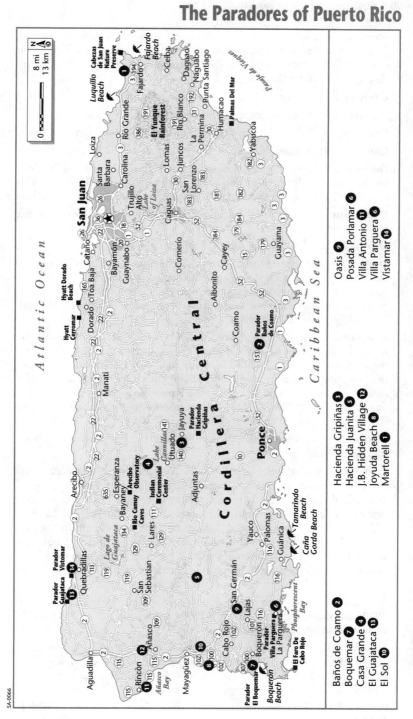

Baños de Coamo ❷
Boquemar ❼
Casa Grande ❹
El Guajataca ⓭
El Sol ❿

Hacienda Gripiñas ❸
Hacienda Juanita ❺
J.B. Hidden Village ⓬
Joyuda Beach ❽
Martorell ❶

Oasis ❾
Posada Porlamar ❻
Villa Antonio ⓫
Villa Parguera ❻
Vistamar ⓮

89

your camera not only from theft but also from saltwater and sand; furthermore, the camera can become overheated and ruin any film it contains if left in the sun or locked in the trunk of a car. For the best commercial camera stores in Puerto Rico, see "Fast Facts: San Juan," in chapter 4.

Car Rentals   See "Getting Around," earlier in this chapter.

Climate   See "When to Go," earlier in this chapter.

Currency   See "Visitor Information, Entry Requirements & Money," above.

Customs   See "Visitor Information, Entry Requirements & Money," above.

Dentists & Doctors   Dental emergencies can be taken care of at the **San Juan Health Center,** 150 Avenida de Diego, Santurce (☎ **787/725-0202**). This center also handles medical emergencies within the Greater San Juan area.

Documents   See "Visitor Information, Entry Requirements & Money," earlier in this chapter.

Driving Rules   See "Getting Around," earlier in this chapter.

Drugs   A branch of the Federal Narcotics Strike Force is permanently stationed on Puerto Rico, where illegal drugs and narcotics are a problem. Convictions for possession of marijuana can bring severe penalties, ranging from 2 to 10 years in prison for a first offense. Possession of hard drugs, such as cocaine or heroin, can lead to 15 years or more in prison.

Drugstores   It's a good idea to carry enough prescription medications with you to last the duration of your stay. If you're going into the hinterlands, take along the medicines you'll need. If you need any additional medications, you'll find many drugstores in San Juan and other leading cities. One of the most centrally located pharmacies in Old San Juan is the **Puerto Rican Drug Co.,** Calle San Francisco 157 (☎ **787/725-2202**); it's open Monday through Saturday from 7:30am to 9:30pm and on Sunday from 8am to 7:30pm.

Electricity   The electricity is 110 volts AC, as it is in the continental United States and Canada.

Embassies & Consulates   Since Puerto Rico is part of the United States, there is no U.S. embassy or consulate. Instead, there are branches of all the principal U.S. federal agencies. Canada has no embassy or consulate either. In case of a problem, citizens of the United Kingdom can call ☎ **787/721-5193** or 787/723-6355 to receive recorded directions to leave a message including their name, address, telephone number, and a brief description of their problem. A staff member will eventually return the call. Otherwise, there are no special provisions or agencies catering to British travel needs in Puerto Rico. There are no agencies serving Australian or New Zealand citizens.

Emergencies   In an emergency, dial 911. Or call the local **police** (☎ **787/343-2020**), **fire department** (☎ **787/343-2330**), **ambulance** (☎ **787/343-2550**), or **medical assistance** (☎ **787/754-3535**).

Health Care   Medical-care facilities on the island are on par with those in the United States, with excellent hospitals and clinics. Hotels can arrange for a doctor in case of an emergency. Most major U.S. health-insurance plans are recognized, but it's advisable to check with your carrier or insurance agent in advance of your trip, since medical attention is very expensive. See "Health & Insurance," earlier in this chapter.

Holidays   See "When to Go," earlier in this chapter.

Hospitals   In a medical emergency, call 911. The following facilities maintain 24-hour emergency rooms: **Ashford Presbyterian Community Hospital,** 1451 Ashford Ave. (☎ **787/721-2160**), and the **San Juan Health Center,** Avenida de Diego 150 (☎ **787/725-0202**).

Information   See "Visitor Information," earlier in this chapter.

Language   English is understood at the big resorts and in most of San Juan. Out in the island, Spanish is still *numero uno.* See the Appendix for basic English and Spanish words.

Liquor Laws   You must be 21 years of age to purchase liquor in stores or buy drinks in hotels, bars, and restaurants. If you are 21 or over but look younger, bring a photo identification such as a driver's license that gives your date of birth.

Maps   See "Getting Around," earlier in this chapter.

Marriage Requirements   There are no residency requirements for getting married in Puerto Rico. You'll need parental consent if either of you is under 18. Blood tests are required, although a test conducted within 10 days of the ceremony on the U.S. mainland will suffice. A doctor must sign the license after an examination of the bride and groom. For complete details, contact the **Commonwealth of Puerto Rico Health Department,** Demographic Register, 26 Fernandez Juncos (P.O. Box 9342), San Juan, PR 00917 (☎ **787/767-9120,** ext. 2302).

Newspapers/Magazines   *The San Juan Star,* a daily English-language newspaper, has been called the *"International Herald Tribune* of the Caribbean." It concentrates extensively on news from the United States. You can also pick up copies of *USA Today* at most news kiosks. If you read Spanish, you might enjoy *El Nuevo Dia,* the most popular local tabloid. Few significant magazines are published on Puerto Rico, but *Time* and *Newsweek* are available at most newsstands.

Passports   See "Visitor Information," earlier in this chapter.

Pets   To bring your pet in, you must produce a health certificate from a mainland veterinarian and show proof of vaccination against rabies. Very few hotels allow animals, so check in advance. Many veterinarians are listed in the yellow pages of the local telephone book.

Postal Services   Since the U.S. Postal Service is responsible for handling mail on the island, the regulations and tariffs are the same as on the mainland. Stamps may be purchased at any post office, each of which is open Monday through Friday from 8am to 5pm. Saturday hours are 8am to noon (closed Sunday). As on the mainland, one can purchase stamps at vending machines in airports, stores, and hotels. At press time, first-class letters to addresses within Puerto Rico, the United States, and its territories cost 32¢; postcards, 20¢. Letters and postcards to Canada both cost 46¢ for the first half-ounce. Letters and postcards to other countries cost 60¢ for the first half-ounce. But note: These rates will rise during the life of this edition.

Safety   Crime exists here as it does everywhere. Use common sense and take precautions. Muggings are commonplace on the Condado and Isla Verde beaches, so you might want to confine your moonlit beach nights to the fenced-in and guarded areas around some of the major hotels. The countryside of Puerto

Rico is safer than San Juan, but caution is always the rule. Avoid small and narrow country roads and isolated beaches, either night or day.

Taxes In addition to the government tax of 7% in regular hotels or 10% in hotels with casinos, some hotels add a 10% service charge to your bill. If they don't, you're expected to tip for services rendered. There is no airport departure tax.

Telephone, Telex, & Fax Coin-operated phones are found throughout the island, with a particularly dense concentration in San Juan. After depositing your coins, you can dial a seven-digit number at the sound of the dial tone. If you're calling long-distance within Puerto Rico, add a 1 before the numbers. When you're placing a call to the U.S. mainland or to anywhere else overseas, preface the number with 011. An operator (or a recorded voice) will tell you how much money to deposit, although you'll probably find it more practical to use a calling card issued by such long-distance carriers as Sprint, AT&T, or MCI. Public phones that allow credit cards such as American Express, Visa, or MasterCard to be inserted or "swiped" through a magnetic slot are rare on the island. Most of these are located at the San Juan airport. Most phone booths contain printed instructions for dialing. Local calls are 10¢. Most Puerto Ricans buy phone cards valid for between 15 and 100 units. The 15-unit card costs $6.75; the 30-unit card, $13.50. The card provides an even less expensive and usually more convenient way of calling within Puerto Rico or to the U.S. mainland. They are for sale in most pharmacies and gift shops on the island.

Most hotels will send a telex or fax for you and bill the costs to your room, and in some cases, they'll even send a fax for a nonguest if you agree to pay a charge. Barring that, several agencies in San Juan will send a fax anywhere you want for a fee. Many are associated with print shops/photocopy stands. **Eagle Print,** 1229 F.D. Roosevelt Blvd., Puerto Nuevo, San Juan, PR 00920 (☎ **787/782-7830**), charges $2 per page for faxes sent to the U.S. mainland.

Time Puerto Rico is on Atlantic standard time year-round, which is 1 hour later than eastern standard time. Puerto Rico does not go on daylight saving time, however, so the time here is the same year-round.

Tipping Tipping is expected here, so hand over the money as you would on the U.S. mainland. That usually means 15% in restaurants, except for fast-food places; 10% in bars; and 10% to 15% for taxi drivers, hairdressers, and other services, depending on the quality of the service rendered. Tip a porter, either at the airport or at your hotel, $1 per bag. Europeans and others may not like this method of compensation, but the U.S. government imposes income tax on wait staff and other service-industry workers whose income is tip-based according to the gross receipts of their employers; therefore, those workers could end up paying tax on a tip you didn't give them.

Visitor Information See "Visitor Information, Entry Requirements & Money," earlier in this chapter.

Weights & Measures There's a mixed bag of measurements in Puerto Rico. Because of its Spanish tradition, most weights (meat and poultry) and measures (gasoline and road distances) are metric. But because of the American presence, speed limits appear in miles per hour, and liquids such as beer are sold by the ounce.

Getting to Know San Juan **4**

San Juan, the capital city, will introduce you to the commonwealth. All but a handful of visitors arrive here. This is the political base, economic powerhouse, and cultural center of the island, and home to about one-third of all Puerto Ricans.

The second-oldest city in the Americas (behind Santo Domingo in the Dominican Republic), this metropolis presents two completely different faces to the world. On one hand, the charming historic district, Old San Juan, is strongly reminiscent of the Spanish Empire. On the other, modern expressways outside the historic district cut through its urban sprawl to link towering concrete buildings and beachfront hotels resembling those of Miami Beach.

Old San Juan is a 7-square-block area that was once completely enclosed by a wall erected by the Spanish with slave labor. This most powerful fortress in the Caribbean repeatedly was able to hold off would-be attackers. By the 19th century, however, the old city had become one of the most charming residential and commercial areas of the Caribbean. Today it's a setting for restaurants and shops. Most of the major resort hotels are located nearby, along the Condado beachfront and at Isla Verde (see chapter 5).

1 Orientation

ARRIVING BY PLANE
Visitors from overseas arrive at **Luis Muñoz Marín International Airport** (☎ 787/791-1014), the major transportation center of the Caribbean. The airport is on the easternmost side of the city, rather inconvenient to nearly all hotels except the resorts and small inns at Isla Verde.

The airport offers an array of services including a tourist information center, fast-food restaurants, barbershops and hairdressers, coin lockers to store luggage (particularly useful if you're visiting one of the smaller islands on a shuttle plane), bookstores, banks, money-exchange kiosks, and even a bar (open daily from noon to 4pm) offering a sampling of the best Puerto Rican rums in all their many hues and flavors.

GETTING FROM THE AIRPORT INTO THE CITY
BY TAXI Dozens of taxis line up outside the airport to meet arriving flights, so you rarely have to wait. Fares can vary widely,

ic conditions. If you're staying at one of the beachfront hotels
o, the average fare from the airport is $13.

nically cab drivers should turn on their meters, more often than
a flat rate before starting out.

BY ... OR LIMOUSINE   Be aware that a wide variety of vehicles at the San Juan airport call themselves *limosinas* (their Spanish name). One outfit whose sign-up desk is in the arrivals hall of the international airport, near American Airlines, is the **Airport Limousine Service** (☎ 787/791-4745). They offer minivan service from the airport to various San Juan neighborhoods for prices that are lower than what a taxi would charge. Whenever 8 to 10 passengers can be accumulated, the fare for transport, with luggage, to any hotel in Isla Verde is $2.50 per person; to the Condado, $3 per person; and to Old San Juan, $3.50 per person.

For conventional limousine service, **Bracero Limousine** (☎ 787/253-5466) offers upholstered cars with drivers to meet you and your entourage at the arrivals terminal of the airport for luxurious and strictly private transportation to your hotel. Transport to virtually anywhere in San Juan ranges from $85 to $100, whereas transport to points throughout the island varies from $125 to $275, depending on the time and distance. Ideally, transport should be arranged in advance of your arrival, in which event a car and driver will be waiting for you near the arrivals terminal.

BY CAR   All the major car-rental companies have kiosks at the airport. Although it's possible to rent a car once you arrive, your best bet is to reserve one before you leave home. See the "Getting Around" section of chapter 3 for details.

To drive into the city, head west along Route 26, which becomes Route 25 as it enters Old San Juan. If you stay on Route 25 (also called Avenida Muñoz Rivera), you'll have the best view of the ocean and the monumental city walls.

Just before reaching the Capitol building, turn left between the Natural Resources Department and the modern House of Representatives office building. Go 2 blocks until you reach the intersection of Paseo de Covadonga, then take a right past the Treasury Building and park your car in the Covadonga Parking Garage on the left. This garage is open 24 hours. A free shuttle-bus service loops the old town from here on two different routes.

BY BUS   Those with little luggage can take the T1 bus, which runs to the center of the city.

VISITOR INFORMATION

Tourist information is available at the **Luis Muñoz Marín Airport** (☎ 787/ 791-1014), daily from 9am to 5:30pm. Another office is at **La Casita,** Pier 1, Old San Juan (☎ 787/722-1709).

CITY LAYOUT

Metropolitan San Juan includes the old walled city on San Juan Island; the city center on San Juan Island, containing the Capitol building; Santurce, on a larger peninsula, which is reached by causeway bridges from San Juan Island (the lagoon-front section here is called Miramar); Condado, the narrow peninsula that stretches from San Juan Island to Santurce; Hato Rey, the business center; Río Piedras, site of the University of Puerto Rico; and Bayamón, an industrial and residential quarter.

The Condado strip of beachfront hotels, restaurants, casinos, and nightclubs is separated from Miramar by a lagoon. Isla Verde, another resort area, is near the airport, which is separated from the rest of San Juan by an isthmus.

FINDING AN ADDRESS   Finding an address in San Juan isn't always easy. You'll have to contend not only with missing street signs and numbers but also with street addresses that appear sometimes in English and at other times in Spanish. The most common Spanish terms for thoroughfares are *calle* (street) and *avenida* (avenue). When they are used, the street number will follow them; for example, the Gran Hotel El Convento is located at Calle del Cristo 100, in Old San Juan. Locating a building in Old San Juan is relatively easy, with the odd numbers on one side of the street and the even numbers on the other. The area is only 7 square blocks, so by walking around it's possible to locate most addresses.

STREET MAPS   *Qué Pasa?,* the monthly tourist magazine distributed free by the tourist office, contains accurate, easy-to-read maps of San Juan and the Condado, pinpointing the major attractions.

NEIGHBORHOODS IN BRIEF

OLD SAN JUAN   This 7-square-block area is the most historic in the West Indies. Filled with Spanish colonial architecture and under constant restoration, it lies on the western end of an islet. It's encircled by water; on the north is the Atlantic Ocean, and on the south and west is the tranquil San Juan Bay. Ponte San Antonio bridge connects the old town with "mainland" Puerto Rico. Ramparts and old Spanish fortresses form its outer walls.

PUERTA DE TIERRA   Translated as "gateway to the land" or "gateway to the island," Puerta de Tierra lies just east of the old city walls of San Juan. This section of metropolitan San Juan is split by Avenida Ponce de León and interconnects the historic peninsula of Old San Juan with the Puerto Rican "mainland." The settlement, founded by freed black slaves, today functions as the island's administrative center and is the site of many military and government buildings, including the Capitol building and various U.S. naval reserves.

MIRAMAR   This is an upscale residential neighborhood, across the bridge from Puerto de Tierra. Many yachts anchor in its waters on the bay side of Ponte Isla Grande, and some of the finest homes on Puerto Rico are found here. It's also the site of Isla Grande Airport, where you can board flights to the offshore islands of Vieques and Culebra.

CONDADO/SANTURCE   The Condado is the glittering beachfront strip of San Juan—site of most of the major hotels. It's linked to Puerto de Tierra and Old San Juan by a bridge built in 1910. The greater neighborhood of Santurce, adjoining the Condado, was once the most exclusive in San Juan. However, now it's in sad decline.

HATO REY   Santurce's loss was Hato Rey's gain. Situated to the south of the Martín Peña canal, this area today is the Wall Street of the West Indies, filled with many high-rises, a large federal complex, and many business and banking offices. Actually, it was once a marsh until landfill and concrete changed it forever.

RIO PIEDRAS   South of both Hato Rey and Santurce, this is the site of the University of Puerto Rico and its student population. It's dominated by the landmark Roosevelt Bell Tower, named for Theodore Roosevelt, who donated the money for its construction. The main thoroughfare is Paseo de Diego, site of a popular local market where produce is sold. The Agricultural Experimental Station of Puerto Rico maintains a Botanical Garden; there are many tropical plants here, including 125 species of palms.

San Juan Orientation

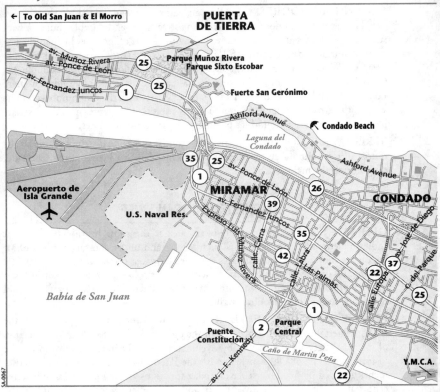

← To Old San Juan & El Morro

PUERTA DE TIERRA

av. Muñoz Rivera
av. Ponce de León
av. Fernandez Juncos

25
25
1
25

**Parque Muñoz Rivera
Parque Sixto Escobar**

⚓ **Fuerte San Gerónimo**

Ashford Avenue
↖ **Condado Beach**

Laguna del Condado

Ashford Avenue

35
25
1
av. Ponce de León
26
CONDADO

MIRAMAR

Aeropuerto de Isla Grande
✈

av. Fernandez Juncos
39

U.S. Naval Res.

Espreso Luis Muñoz Rivera
calle Cerra
35

42
calle Labra
calle Las Palmas
22
37

calle Europa
av. José de Diego
c. del Parque
25

Bahía de San Juan

1

2
Parque Central

Puente Constitución

Caño de Martín Peña

av. J.F. Kennedy

22

Y.M.C.A.

SA-0067

BAYAMÓN   The San Juan sprawl has reached this once-distant southwestern suburb, which had been farmland before industry moved in and took over. Some 200,000 people and nearly 200 factories are now located in this geographically large district. Bus no. 46 from the center of San Juan runs out here. At Route 2, kilometer 6.4, in Guayanobo are the ruins of Caparra, the first colonial settlement on the island.

2 Getting Around

BY TAXI   Except for a handful of important, high-profile tourist routes, public taxis are metered within San Juan, or should be. The island's **Public Service Commission**, or PSC (☎ 787/756-1919), establishes flat rates between the Luis Muñoz Marín airport and major tourist zones as listed here: From the airport to any hotel in Isla Verde, the fee is $8; to any hotel in the Condado district, the charge is $12, and to any hotel in Old San Juan, the cost is $16. Normal tipping supplements of between 10% and 15% of that fare are appreciated.

Away from those routes, passengers traveling between most other destinations within greater San Juan are charged by meter readings. The initial charge is $1, plus 10¢ for each one-tenth mile and 50¢ for every suitcase, with a minimum fare of $3. These rates apply to conventional *taxis turísticos,* which are usually white-painted vehicles with official logos on their doors. Owned by a medley of individual outfitters within San Juan, they maintain standards that are higher than those for

the cheaper but more erratic and inconvenient *publicos,* which are described in chapter 3. Call the PSC to request information or to report any irregularities.

Taxis are invariably lined up outside the entrance to most of the island's hotels, and if not, a staff member can almost always call one for you. But if you want to arrange a taxi on your own, call the **Rochdale Cab Company** (☎ 787/721-1900) or the **Mejor Cab Company** (☎ 787/723-2460).

You'll have to negotiate a fare with the driver, usually at a flat rate, for trips to far-flung destinations within Puerto Rico.

BY BUS   The **Metropolitan Bus Authority** (☎ 787/250-6064 for route information) operates buses in the greater San Juan area. Bus stops are marked by upright metal signs or yellow posts reading PARADA. There's one bus terminal in the dock area and another at the Plaza de Colón. A typical fare is 25¢ to 50¢.

You can take an air-conditioned bus from the Condado or Isla Verde hotels to Old San Juan. You'll be deposited at the main bus terminal across the street from the Cataño ferry pier and the Plaza de Colón. This section of San Juan is the starting point for many metropolitan bus routes.

For example, bus no. 2 goes from the Plaza de Colón along the Condado, eventually reaching the commercial section of San Juan, Hato Rey. Bus no. A7 also passes from Old San Juan to the Condado and goes on to Avenida Isla Verde, and no. T1 heads for Avenida de Diego in the Condado district, then makes a long run to Isla Verde and the airport.

BY TROLLEY When you tire of walking around Old San Juan, you can board one of the free trolleys that run through the historic area. Departure points are the Marina and La Puntilla, but you can get on anyplace along the route. Relax and enjoy the sights as the trolleys rumble through the old and narrow streets.

ON FOOT This is the only way to explore Old San Juan. All the major attractions can easily be covered in a day. If you're going from Old San Juan to Isla Verde, however, you'll need to rely on public transportation.

BY RENTAL CAR See "Getting Around," in chapter 3 for details—including some reasons why you *shouldn't* plan to drive in Puerto Rico.

BY FERRY The *Agua* **Expreso** (☎ 787/751-7055) connects Old San Juan with the industrial and residential communities of Hato Rey and Cataño, across the bay. Ferries depart daily every 30 minutes from 6am to 9pm. The one-way fare to Hato Rey is 75¢, and the one-way fare to Cataño is 50¢. Departures are from the San Juan Terminal at the pier in Old San Juan. However, it's best to avoid rush hours since hundreds of locals who work in town use this ferry. Each ride lasts about 20 minutes.

FAST FACTS: San Juan

American Express The agency is represented in San Juan by **Travel Network,** 1035 Ashford Ave., Condado (☎ 787/725-0950). The office is open Monday through Friday from 9am to 1pm and 2 to 5pm, on Saturday from 9am to noon.

Bookstores The **Book Store,** at Calle San José 255 (☎ 787/724-1815), in Old San Juan, has one of Puerto Rico's best selections of English-language titles. Hours are Monday through Saturday from 9am to 7pm.

Camera & Film Both **Cinefoto** (☎ 787/753-7238) and **Rabola** (☎ 787/753-8778), located in the Plaza Las Americas Shopping Mall in Hato Rey, offer a wide variety of photographic supplies. Cinefoto is open Monday through Saturday from 9am to 10pm. Rabola is open Monday through Saturday from 9am to 9pm, Sunday from 11am to 5pm.

Car Rentals See "Getting Around," in chapter 3. If you want to reserve after you've arrived in Puerto Rico, call **Avis** (☎ 787/791-2500), **Budget** (☎ 787/791-3685), or **Hertz** (☎ 787/791-0840).

Currency Exchange The unit of currency is the U.S. dollar, so American travelers will not need this service. But for British and Canadian travelers, most banks will provide this service. You can also exchange money at the **Luis Muñoz Marín International Airport.** Otherwise, in Old San Juan, go to **Thomas Cook,** Calle Tetuan 201B (☎ 787/791-6015). Hours are Monday through Friday from 9am to 4:30pm and Saturday noon to 4pm. Also see "Visitor Information, Entry Requirements & Money," in chapter 3.

Drugstores One of the most centrally located pharmacies is the **Puerto Rican Drug Co.,** Calle San Francisco 157 (☎ 787/725-2202), in Old San Juan. It's open Monday through Saturday from 7:30am to 9:30pm and on Sunday from 8am to 7:30pm. **Walgreen's,** 1130 Ashford Ave., Condado (☎ 787/725-1510), is open 24 hours a day.

Emergencies In an emergency, dial 911. Or call the local **police** (☎ 787/343-2020), **fire department** (☎ 787/343-2330), **ambulance** (☎ 787/343-2550), or **medical assistance** (☎ 787/754-3535). Dental emergencies are handled at the **San Juan Health Center** at Avenida de Diego 150 in Santurce (☎ **787/725-0202**).

Eyeglasses Services are available at **Pearle Vision Express,** Plaza Las Americas Shopping Mall (☎ **787/753-1033**). Hours are Monday through Saturday from 9am to 9pm and Sunday from 11am to 5pm.

Hospitals **Ashford Presbyterian Community Hospital,** 1451 Ashford Ave. (☎ **787/721-2160**), and the **San Juan Health Center,** Avenida de Diego 150 (☎ **787/725-0202**), both maintain 24-hour emergency rooms.

Information See "Visitor Information," earlier in this chapter.

Post Office In San Juan, the General Post Office is at 585 Roosevelt Ave. (☎ **787/767-3604**). If you don't know your address in San Juan, you can ask that your mail be sent here "c/o General Delivery." This main branch is open Monday through Friday from 6am to midnight, Saturday from 8am to 2pm. A letter from Puerto Rico to the U.S. mainland will arrive in about 4 days. See "Fast Facts: Puerto Rico," in chapter 3, for more information.

Safety At night exercise extreme caution when walking along the back streets of San Juan, and don't venture onto the unguarded public stretches of the Condado and Isla Verde beaches at night. All these areas are favorite targets for muggings.

Telephone, Telex, & Fax Many public telephones are available at **World Service Telephone (AT&T),** Pier 1, Old San Juan (☎ **787/721-2520**). To send a fax or telex, go to **Eagle Print,** 1229 F. D. Roosevelt Blvd., Puerto Nuevo (☎ **787/782-7830**). For more information, see also "Fast Facts: Puerto Rico," in chapter 3.

Tourist Offices See "Visitor Information," earlier in this chapter.

Transit Information For information about bus routes in San Juan, call ☎ **787/250-6064**.

5

Where to Stay in San Juan

Whatever your preferences in accommodations—a beachfront resort or a place in the midst of historic Old San Juan, sumptuous luxury or an austere, inexpensive base from which to see the sights—you can find a perfect fit in San Juan.

In addition to checking the recommendations listed here, you may want to confer with a travel agent; there are package deals galore that can save you money and match you with an establishment that meets your requirements. See "Package Tours," in chapter 3.

Before even talking to a travel agent, refer to our comments about how to select a room in Puerto Rico. See "Hotels & Resorts" under "Tips on Choosing Your Accommodations," in chapter 3. You might also refer to comments under "Package Tours" in the same chapter, particularly if you're planning to book in on a deal with all your meals included.

Not all hotels here have air-conditioned rooms. We've pointed them out in the recommendations below. If air-conditioning is important to you, make sure "A/C" appears right after the number of units near the top of the listings.

In general, hotels charging more than $250 a night for a double room are **very expensive;** those asking $180 to $250 for a double are **expensive;** and those costing $100 to $180 are **moderate.** Anything under $100 is **inexpensive.** All rooms have private bathrooms unless otherwise noted.

TAXES & SERVICE CHARGES

All hotel rooms in Puerto Rico are subject to a 7% to 9% tax, which is *not* included in the rates given here. Most hotels also add a 10% service charge. When you're booking a room, it's always best to inquire about these added charges.

MAKING RESERVATIONS

You may make your reservations by telephone, mail, fax, and, in some cases, the Internet. If you're booking into a chain hotel, such as a Hilton, you can easily make your reservations by calling their toll-free phone numbers in many countries. We give the North American toll-free numbers in this book.

You can usually cancel a room reservation 1 week ahead of time and get a full refund. A few hoteliers will return your money on cancellations up to 3 days before the reservation date; others won't

Old San Juan Accommodations

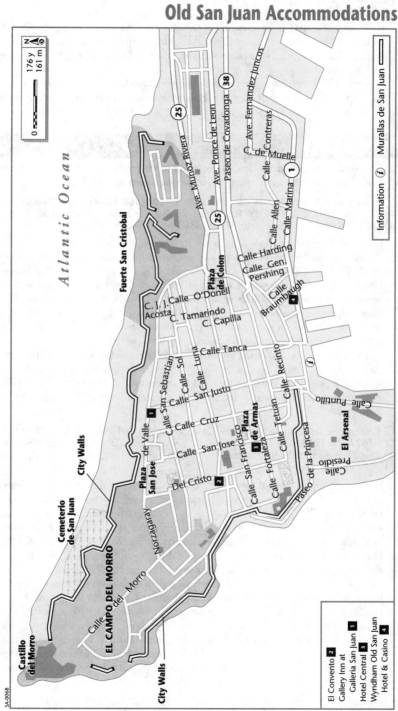

Atlantic Ocean

Castillo del Morro

Cemeterio de San Juan

City Walls

EL CAMPO DEL MORRO

Calle del Morro

Norzagaray

Plaza San Jose

Del Cristo

Calle de Valle

Calle San Sebastián

Calle Sol

Calle Luna

Calle Cruz

Calle San Justo

Calle San Jose

Calle San Francisco

Plaza de Armas

Calle Fortaleza

Calle San

Calle Tetuan

Paseo de la Princesa

Calle Presidio

El Arsenal

Calle Puntillo

Calle Recinto

Calle Tanca

C. J. J. Acosta

Calle O'Donell

C. Tamarindo

C. Capilla

Plaza de Colon

Calle Harding

Calle Gen. Pershing

Calle Braumbaugh

Fuerte San Cristobal

Ave. Muñoz Rivera

Ave. Ponce de Leon

Paseo de Covadonga

Ave. Fernandez Juncos

C. de Muelle

Calle de Contreras

Calle Allen

Calle Marina

25

25

38

1

4

1

2

3

N

176 y
161 m

0

SA-0068

El Convento 2

Gallery Inn at Galleria San Juan 1

Hotel Central 3

Wyndham Old San Juan Hotel & Casino 4

Information ⓘ   Murallas de San Juan

return any of your deposit, even if you cancel far in advance. It's best to clarify this issue when you make your reservation. If booking by mail, include a stamped, self-addressed envelope with your payment so that the hotel can easily send you a receipt and confirmation.

If you arrive without a reservation, begin your search for a room as early in the day as possible. If you arrive late at night and without a reservation, you may have to take what you can get, often in a price range much higher than you'd like to pay.

1 Old San Juan

Choose a hotel in Old San Juan if you're more interested in shopping and attractions than you are in water sports (it's a long way from the beach).

El Convento. 100 Cristo St., San Juan, PR 00901. ☎ **800/468-2779** or 787/723-9020. Fax 787/721-2877. 61 units. A/C TV TEL. Winter $315–$375 double; off-season $220–$280 double. Suite from $500 year-round. AE, DC, DISC, MC, V. Bus: A7, T1, or 21.

Puerto Rico's most famous—though not its best—hotel had been allowed to deteriorate to a shabby version of its former self before being restored and reopened in 1997. Built in 1651 in the heart of the old city, it was the New World's first Carmelite convent, but over the years it played many roles, from dance hall to flophouse. With some $275,000 spent to refurbish each room, El Convento now offers commodious accommodations on its third to fifth floors, with a concierge-style reception and check-in and a club lounge. The rooms have mahogany beams, handmade tile floors, and Spanish-style furnishings handcrafted in Spain.

The lower two floors feature artists and artisans in residence, with galleries, specialty shops, restaurants, and cafes. The interior courtyard is again open to the sky, as it was in the 1600s. Breakfast is served in an outdoor garden terrace. There's also a swimming pool, a Jacuzzi, an indoor fitness center, massage facilities, and an intimate casino.

✪ **Gallery Inn at Galería San Juan.** Calle Norzagaray 204-206, San Juan, PR 00901. ☎ **787/722-1808.** Fax 787/724-7360. 22 units. A/C TEL. Year-round $95–$150 double; $175–$350 suite. Rates include continental breakfast. AE, MC, V. Bus: A7, T1, or 21.

Set on a hilltop in the old town, with a sweeping view of the sea, Old San Juan's only bed-and-breakfast occupies a house built around a maze of verdant courtyards in the 1700s by an aristocratic Spanish family. Today it's one of the most whimsically bohemian hotels in the Caribbean, a sort of holdover from the 1940s or 1950s. There is no more offbeat place to stay in all of San Juan. Locals call it Jan D'Esopa's—for its owner, Connecticut-born duenna Jan D'Esopa, a noted painter, sculptor, and silk screen artist. She is assisted by her husband, Manuco Gandía. All courtyards and rooms are adorned with hundreds of sculptures, silk screens, or original paintings, usually for sale. The Library Room and the Stevy Room have no air-conditioning. There are three free parking spaces; other parking is available on street. There's no swimming pool on the premises, but no one here seems to mind because of the unusual presence of an artist's studio and iron foundry, where castings of sculpture by artists from throughout the island are transformed from models into durable art objects. Two of the units don't have air-conditioning but do have ceiling fans.

Hotel Central. Calle San José 202, San Juan, PR 00901. ☎ **787/722-2751.** 34 units (12 with bathroom). Year-round $35 double without bathroom, $45 double with bathroom. AE, MC, V. Bus: A7.

This is one of the most unusual hotels in the historic heart of Old San Juan, but it's definitely not for everyone. Its fans compare it to the kind of weather-beaten, run-down hotel that has staggered through revolutions, civil wars, and the changing tides of fashion. In fact, few other hotels on Puerto Rico will give you such a strong sense of nostalgia as will this battered remnant of another time. Originally built in the 1930s, it lies adjacent to the Old Town's plaza de Armas. Although the pleasures and distractions of the city's historic core lie all around, don't expect amenities of any kind in the rooms, which have ceiling fans and minimalist (and rather old) furnishings. Many also have creaky bathrooms. Local office workers partake of simple lunch platters in the somewhat dingy cafeteria, which also serves dinner. The nearest beach is a 20-minute ride away.

Wyndham Old San Juan Hotel & Casino. 100 Brumbaugh St., San Juan, PR 00901. ☎ **800/996-3426** or 787/721-5100. Fax 787/721-1111. 240 units. A/C TV TEL. Winter $315 double, from $475 suite; off-season $225 double, from $300 suite. AE, CB, DC, DISC, MC, V. Free self-parking, valet parking $15. Bus: A7.

Opened in 1997, this nine-story waterfront hotel in the historic core of San Juan is part of a $100 million renovation of the city's cruise-port facilities. Its position between buildings erected by the Spanish monarchs in the 19th century and the modern cruise-ship terminals is one of the most unusual in Puerto Rico. It's especially convenient if you plan to spend a few days in San Juan before boarding a ship. Although Floridians and New Yorkers predominate, the Wyndham gets one of the most widely diversified range of guests in San Juan.

Although the pastel-colored building is modern, iron railings and exterior detailing convey a sense of colonial San Juan, as does mahogany trim inside. Its triangular floor plan encloses an inner courtyard. Light floods into the tasteful and comfortable bedrooms, each of which has two phone lines and a modem connection for laptop computers.

Dining/Diversions: About 80% of the lobby level is devoted to a 10,000-square-foot casino with five-card stud poker, 240 slot machines, and roulette tables. The hotel has one restaurant, an upscale, fine dining emporium serving an international cuisine with some Puerto Rican regional specialties (Old San Juan's many restaurants are nearby, so dining in-house is not reason alone to stay here). Two bar/lounges, one with live music, round out the entertainment venue.

Amenities: 24-hour room service, concierge, conference center within an early-20th-century historic building (known as *Isla Bonita*) connected to the hotel by an aerial catwalk, rooftop swimming pool, fully equipped health club, Jacuzzi on the ninth floor overlooking the harbor and cruise-ship docks.

2 Puerta de Tierra

Stay in Puerta de Tierra only if you have a desire to be at either the Caribe Hilton or the Radisson Normandie (both of which are excellent choices), because when you stay there, you're sandwiched halfway between Old San Juan and the Condado, but you're not getting the advantages of staying right in the heart of either.

Caribe Hilton. Calle Los Rosales, San Juan, PR 00902. ☎ **800/HILTONS** or 787/721-0303. Fax 787/725-8849. 670 units. A/C MINIBAR TV TEL. Winter $340–$430 double; off-season $215–$340 double; year-round $500–$1,300 suite. Children 16 and under stay free in parents' room (maximum 4 people per room). AE, CB, DC, DISC, MC, V. Self-parking $7; valet parking $14. Bus: A7.

The Hilton, with the only private beach on the island, stands near the old Fort San Jerónimo, which has been incorporated into its complex. If there is one "party" hotel along the San Juan beachfront, this is it, often attracting conventions and tour groups. Only the Condado Beach and the Hotel El San Juan rival it for virtual non-stop activity. Set on San Juan Bay, it's also convenient to the walled city of San Juan. You can walk to the 16th-century fort or spend the day on a tour of Old San Juan, then come back and enjoy the beach and swimming cove. Built in 1949 in a 17-acre tropical park, the Hilton recently underwent a major $40 million renovation. The large, comfortable bedrooms have been given fresh, modern styling and pastel-colored shades.

Dining/Diversions: Although dining here is not as exciting as at El San Juan Hotel, the Hilton hires some of the most imaginative chefs on the island. They use some of the best ingredients, and their constantly changing international menus appeal to the widest possible number of palates. Venues include the Caribe Terrace restaurant complex, featuring an international cuisine with a different menu each night; El Batey del Pescador, a fish restaurant; La Rôtisserie Il Giardino, devoted to northern Italian cuisine; the Peacock Paradise Chinese Restaurant; and the Caribe Terrace Bar, with huge windows and a celebrated piña colada once enjoyed by the likes of movie legends Joan Crawford and Errol Flynn. The 12,400-square-foot casino, adjacent to the lobby atrium area, is open daily from noon to 4am, featuring blackjack, craps, baccarat, roulette, and slot machines.

Amenities: Room service (6am to 1am), laundry/valet, baby-sitting, Spa Caribe, two freshwater swimming pools, health club, aerobics, beach activities, children's playground, playroom, six lighted tennis courts, business center.

Radisson Normandie. Av. Muñoz-Rivera (at the corner of Calle Los Rosales), San Juan, PR 00902. ☎ **800/333-3333** or 787/729-2929. Fax 787/729-3083. 180 units. A/C MINIBAR TV TEL. Winter $220–$250 double, $490 suite; off-season $175–$205 double, $410 suite. Rates include full American breakfast. AE, DC, DISC, MC, V. Outdoor parking $5. Bus: A7.

Geared to the upscale business traveler, but also a haven for independently minded vacationers, the Normandie first opened in 1939 but was renovated and recon-structed to the tune of $20 million in 1989. Shaped like the famous French ocean liner the *Normandie,* it was originally built for a Parisian cancan dancer who was married to a building tycoon. It's a monument to art deco, with columns, cornices, and countless decorations. Next door to the Caribe Hilton and adjoining the noted Sixto Escobar Stadium, its beachside setting is only 5 minutes from Old San Juan. The elegant and elaborate rooms are spacious and well furnished with all the ameni-ties. The more expensive units are executive rooms.

Dining/Diversions: Although the continental menu with tableside cookery in the elegant Normandie Restaurant has a strong reliance on fresh ingredients and often is artistically presented, it cannot compete with the international culinary razzle-dazzle of the nearby Hilton. Accordingly, Radisson guests often head to the Hilton for dining and entertainment. For those who stay home, the Atrium Lounge is set in a swirl of greenery.

Amenities: Room service (to 11pm), laundry, concierge desk, baby-sitting, fresh-water swimming pool with a bar, hair salon. An on-site water-sports program offers scuba diving, snorkeling, sailing—all the usual stuff.

3 Condado

This is where you'll find the city's best beaches. Once the Condado area was filled with the residences of the very wealthy, but all that changed with the construction of the Puerto Rico Convention Center. Private villas gave way to high-rise hotel

---

A Skinny-Dipping Scandal

Much San Juan legend and lore—and at least one scandal—has taken place at what is today the Radisson Normandie hotel. Designed to resemble the famous French ocean liner *Normandie*, it was built by prominent construction tycoon Benitez Rexach to honor his French-born wife, Moineau, a former cancan dancer.

Moineau was a liberated woman well before her time. She wore pants, smoked cigarettes and drank in public, and was always surrounded by men. It is said that "she did everything a lady was not supposed to do at that time" in conservative Old San Juan.

On the night of the hotel's inaugural party in 1942, Moineau and some French friends dived stark naked into the swimming pool. Word of their scandalous skinny-dip quickly spread across San Juan, and some conservatives claim it led to the eventual downfall of the hotel (it has since been restored to its former luster). At any rate, many local society matrons boycotted social events at the hotel because of Moineau Rexach.

Benitez Rexach must not have been too upset with Moineau, for he gave her the largest yacht in the world—one equipped with a bed made of pure gold.

---

blocks, restaurants, and nightclubs. The Condado shopping area, along Ashford and Magdalena avenues, attracted an extraordinary number of boutiques. There are good bus connections into Old San Juan, or you can take a taxi.

VERY EXPENSIVE

✪ **Condado Plaza Hotel & Casino.** 999 Ashford Ave., San Juan, PR 00907. ☎ **800/468-8588** or 787/721-1000. Fax 787/253-0178. 555 units. A/C MINIBAR TV TEL. Winter $310–$470 double, $430–$1,500 suite; off-season $230–$370 double, $400–$1,400 suite. AE, CB, DC, DISC, MC, V. Valet parking $15. Bus: A7.

This is one of the busiest hotels on Puerto Rico, with enough facilities, restaurants, and distractions to keep a visitor busy for weeks. It is a favorite of business travelers, tour groups, and conventions, but it also attracts independent travelers because of its wide array of facilities, entertainment, and dining options. The Hilton is its major rival, but we prefer the Condado Plaza's style and flair, especially after its recent $6 million facelift. Although not the most intimate of San Juan's hotels, it is the most visible, set on a strip of beachfront at the beginning of the Condado. The original buff-colored structure is linked by an elevated passageway above Ashford Avenue to its annex, the Laguna Wing, which has its own lobby with direct access from the street.

All units have private terraces and are spacious, bright, and airy with good-size bathrooms. The complex's most deluxe section, the Plaza Club, contains 75 units, five duplex suites, a VIP lounge reserved exclusively for the use of its guests, and private check-in/check-out service.

The hotel is owned by the same consortium that owns the more upscale El San Juan Hotel & Casino. Use of the facilities at one hotel can be charged to a room at the other.

Dining/Diversions: Many local residents flock here at night to sample the hotel's culinary diversity. In fact, only the Hotel El San Juan has a more dazzling array of dining options. The latest additions are Mandalay, blending Chinese cuisine with a sushi bar and teppanyaki tables, and Cobia, a tapas bar and seafood grill specializing in American dishes along with Pacific Rim inspirations and Caribbean flavors. Ristorante Capriccio has northern Italian cuisine. La Posada, next to the casino and open 24 hours a day, is known for its deli food, including hot pastrami sandwiches that appeal to the most dedicated New Yorker. Las Palmas and Tony Roma's are other dining choices. For nighttime entertainment, La Fiesta offers live Latin music.

Amenities: 24-hour room service, fresh towels at beach and pools, laundry, five swimming pools, water sports, Plaza Spa, fitness center in the Laguna Wing, two lit Laykold tennis courts.

Radisson Ambassador Hotel & Casino. 1369 Ashford Ave., San Juan, PR 00907. ☎ **800/468-8512** or 787/721-7300. Fax 787/723-6151. 233 units. A/C TV TEL. Winter $245–$275 double, $275–$385 suite; off-season $220–$250 double, $250–$320 suite. AE, CB, DC, DISC, MC, V. Self-parking $6; valet parking $10. Bus: A7.

In the heart of the Condado but a short walk from the beach, the star-studded Ambassador offers theatrical drama and big-time pizzazz, with Czech and Murano chandeliers; hand-blown wall sconces; Turkish, Greek, and Italian marble; and yards of exotic hardwoods. What's missing (especially at these prices) are the resort amenities associated with the Hilton and the Condado Plaza.

Accommodations are in a pair of high-rise towers, one of which is devoted to suites. The decors are inspired variously by 18th-century Versailles, 19th-century London, imperial China, and art deco California. However, in spite of the gaudy, glitzy overlay, know that the hotel used to be a Howard Johnson and standard rooms reflect the size of those you might have encountered driving along America's roadside. Each unit has a balcony with outdoor furniture.

Dining/Diversions: If you like northern Italian cuisine or a perfectly done steak, you'll find them here at La Scala's, the hotel's culinary highlight, and Sweeney's, a "Scotch & Sirloin" grill. You also can strike out to the other rich dining offerings along the Condado. The casino (open noon to 4am) has more slot machines than any other on the Condado, and a singer/pianist performs from a quiet corner bar. There are four bar/lounges, one of which has live local dance music.

Amenities: Room service (6:30am to midnight), baby-sitting, laundry, 24-hour concierge, VIP floors with extra amenities and enhanced services, a social programmer offering a changing array of daily activities, penthouse-level fitness and health club, beauty salon, rooftop swimming pool, Jacuzzi, business center staffed with typists, translators, guides, and stenographers.

San Juan Marriott Resort & Stellaris Casino. 1309 Ashford Ave., San Juan, PR 00907. ☎ **800/981-8546** or 787/722-7000. Fax 787/722-6800. 538 units. A/C MINIBAR TV TEL. Winter $275–$380 double, from $550 suite; off-season $175–$310 double, from $550 suite. AE, DC, DISC, MC, V. Parking $8. Bus: A7.

It's the tallest building on the Condado, a 21-story landmark that Marriott spent staggering sums to renovate and enlarge after a tragic fire gutted the premises in 1989. The new entity packs lots of postmodern style, and one of the best beaches on the Condado lies right outside. Furnishings in the soaring lobby were inspired by the Chippendale salon of a high-style hotel. If there's a flaw, it's the decor of the comfortable, good-size but bland bedrooms whose pastel themes look washed out when compared to the rich mahoganies and jewel tones of those in the rival Condado Plaza Hotel. Nonetheless, the rooms boast one of the most advanced telephone networks on the island, carefully maintained security and fire-prevention systems, and safes. About half of them occupy a new nine-story, pink-and-turquoise wing that Marriott added during the rebuilding.

Eastern San Juan Accommodations

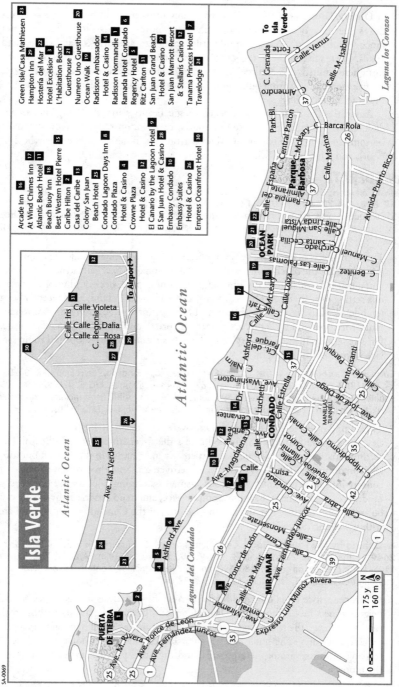

Green Isle/Casa Mathiesen [23]
Hampton Inn [29]
Hostería del Mar [22]
Hotel Excelsior [3]
L'Habitation Beach Guesthouse [21]
Numero Uno Guesthouse [20]
Ocean Walk [19]
Radisson Ambassador Hotel & Casino [14]
Radisson Normandie [1]
Ramada Hotel Condado [6]
Regency Hotel [5]
Ritz Carlton [31]
San Juan Grand Beach Hotel & Casino [27]
San Juan Marriott Resort & Stellaris Casino [12]
Tanama Princess Hotel [7]
Travelodge [24]

Arcade Inn [16]
At Wind Chimes Inn [17]
Atlantic Beach Hotel [11]
Beach Buoy Inn [18]
Best Western Hotel Pierre [15]
Caribe Hilton [2]
Casa del Caribe [13]
Colony San Juan Beach Hotel [25]
Condado Lagoon Days Inn [8]
Condado Plaza Hotel & Casino [4]
Crowne Plaza Hotel & Casino [32]
El Canario by the Lagoon Hotel [9]
El San Juan Hotel & Casino [28]
Embassy Condado [10]
Embassy Suites Hotel & Casino [26]
Empress Oceanfront Hotel [30]

Isla Verde

107

Dining/Diversions: We'd opt to have only one dinner in-house here—at Tuscany's (see "Best Bets" in chapter 6). Other options include La Vista, offering buffet lunches and dinners, and a poolside grill serving tropical drinks, sandwiches, and salads. There's live music in the lobby every evening from 6 to 9pm; two bands perform here Thursday to Saturday from 9pm to 3am. Stellaris Casino, which isn't as glitzy as some of its competitors, notably the casino at El San Juan Hotel, is next to the hotel's main lobby.

Amenities: 24-hour room service, concierge, beauty salon, shopping kiosks, tour desk, car-rental facilities, two tennis courts, two swimming pools (whose mosaic bottoms glow luminously when viewed from the hotel's observatory-style 21st floor), and a health club with many massage and spa treatments.

MODERATE

Best Western Hotel Pierre. Av. José de Diego 105, Condado, San Juan, PR 00914. ☎ **800/334-7234** or 787/721-1200. Fax 787/721-3118. 184 units. A/C TV TEL. Winter $136 double; off-season $119 double. Extra person $15. Children 11 and under stay free in parents' room. Rates include continental breakfast. AE, DC, DISC, MC, V. Free parking. Bus: 22.

The high-rise "Lucky Pierre" has long been one of the capital's major bargains. It's 4 blocks from the beach and an easy drive to most major San Juan attractions if you rent a car. It's a small resort, with a large swimming pool, deck, and poolside lanai, in a setting of palm trees. The bedrooms, although hardly grand, have recently been remodeled. Kids are welcomed here, and baby-sitting can be arranged. Two restaurants, Metropol and La Petite, are moderately priced and serve a respectable cuisine. On-site services include laundry and valet, a beauty and barber shop, and room service from 5pm to midnight.

Condado Lagoon Days Inn. Calle Clemenceau 6, Condado, San Juan, PR 00907. ☎ **800/858-7407** or 787/721-0171. Fax 787/723-4356. 50 units. A/C TV TEL. Winter $109 double, $159–$169 suite; off-season $89 double, $129–$139 suite. Rates include continental breakfast. Children 12 and under stay free in parents' room. AE, DC, MC, V. Bus: A5.

This family-oriented hotel, whose rooms were remodeled in 1996, rises seven stories above a residential neighborhood across the street from Condado Beach. The accommodations are small, and not particularly imaginative in their decor, but usually contain queen-size beds and a small refrigerator. Some rooms have sofas that convert into beds for children. There's a small swimming pool on the premises, a modest coffee shop near the lobby, room service, and maid service. Baby-sitting can be arranged. The bars, restaurants, and facilities of the Condado neighborhood are within walking distance.

El Canario by the Lagoon Hotel. Calle Clemenceau 4, San Juan, PR 00907. ☎ **800/533-2649** in the U.S. or 787/722-5058. Fax 787/723-8590. 40 units. A/C TV TEL. Winter $105–$115 double; off-season $80–$90 double. Rates include continental breakfast and morning newspaper. AE, DC, DISC, MC, V. Bus: A7 or 2.

A European-style hotel operated by the Olsons, El Canario is in a quiet residential neighborhood just a short block from Condado Beach. The attractive but small rooms all have their own balconies, rattan furniture, small refrigerators upon request, and safes. The hotel offers a guest laundry and an in-house tour desk. A relaxing, informal atmosphere prevails, and the hotel provides excellent value for the money.

Embassy Condado. 1126 Sea View, Condado, San Juan, PR 00907. ☎ **787/725-8284.** Fax 787/725-2400. 14 units. A/C TV. Winter $65–$115 double; $145 suite; off-season $45–$85 double, $100–$120 suite. Extra person $10–$15. AE, MC, V. Bus: A5.

Surrounded by a residential neighborhood, this two-story guesthouse sits on a quiet dead-end street about a block inland from the sands of Condado Beach. It offers a relaxed atmosphere—you could live in a swimsuit or shorts for your entire stay. The all-white bedrooms have rattan furniture and tropical accessories. Each has a kitchenette or access to one. The hotel features a rooftop sundeck with a view directly over the beach. Maid service is included, and baby-sitting can be arranged.

Ramada Hotel Condado. 1045 Ashford Ave., San Juan, PR 00907. ☎ **800/468-2040** or 787/723-8000. Fax 787/722-8230. 98 units. A/C MINIBAR TV TEL. Winter $170 double, $300 suite; off-season $140 double, $200 suite. AE, DC, DISC, MC, V. Parking $7. Bus: A7 or 21.

This standard hotel is right on the oceanfront in the heart of the Condado section. It lacks the style or facilities of some of its very expensive neighbors, but you can bask in the sun by the pool, have lunch or drinks on the sundeck, and dance the night away in the Polo Lounge to live music that alternates between Latin rhythms and soft romantic melodies. The on-site Restaurant Lelolai specializes in many Puerto Rican dishes, including *asopaos* (the local gumbo) often made with shrimp and lobster. A selection of seafood, including the fish of the day, is featured nightly. Shopping, sights, and island nightlife are within walking distance or just a short ride away. The rooms are classified as standard, superior, or deluxe. The price seems rather high for what you get here, but you must pay dearly for a beachfront Condado location, even though the shoreline adjacent to the hotel is rocky (head instead for the sandy beach at the Condado Plaza, a 5-minute walk away). Laundry service is available.

Regency Hotel. 1005 Ashford Ave., San Juan, PR 00907. ☎ **800/468-2823** in the U.S. or 787/721-0505. Fax 787/722-2909. 127 units. A/C TV TEL. Winter $175–$210 double, $280 suite; off-season $145–$170 double, $220 suite. Rates include continental breakfast. AE, DC, MC, V. Parking $5. Bus: A7.

This modest choice also occupies prime Condado real estate, although the beach here is approached through an underground parking garage. The generally spacious rooms aren't style-setters by any means, but most are comfortable and clean and are a good value for the tab-happy Condado district. Many of them are equipped with kitchenettes, and all of the suites contain fully equipped kitchens. Whether you like this hotel or not may depend on your room assignment: all rooms have balconies but not all open onto the seascape, and although the units are constantly being renovated, some are shabbier than others and of unequal quality. Discuss the rooms in detail with management before making reservations, and if possible, see the room before checking in. On the premises are a bar and the St. Moritz restaurant, a dining enclave with conservatively classic food. Although the hotel has its own small-scale freshwater pool, some guests prefer to do their swimming, gambling, dining, and drinking at the Condado Plaza next door.

GAY-FRIENDLY HOTELS

Atlantic Beach Hotel. 1 Vendig St., Condado, San Juan, PR 00907. ☎ **787/721-6900.** Fax 787/721-6917. 37 units. A/C TV TEL. Winter $117–$134 double; off-season $101–$111 double. Rates include continental breakfast. AE, DC, MC, V. Bus: A5.

The best-known gay-friendly hotel in Puerto Rico, this five-story building directly beside the sands of Condado Beach, near the San Juan Marriott, has styling that's vaguely art deco. It has appealed to a loyal clientele since it originally opened in the 1960s. Since taking over in 1977, owner William Cislak has offered a friendly refuge mostly for men but with an occasional smattering of women. Bedrooms are outfitted with tropical fabrics and accessories and rattan furnishings. There's a simple snack-style bar and restaurant on the premises. A Sunday afternoon tea and dance attracts many of the city's gay men.

Ocean Walk. 1 Atlantic Place, Condado, San Juan, PR 00911. ☎ **800/468-0615** or 787/728-0855. Fax 787/728-6434. 40 units, 5 apts with kitchenette. A/C TV TEL. Winter $75–$105 double; $120–$140 apartment; off-season $50–$70 double, $80–$95 apartment. Rates include continental breakfast. AE, DISC, MC, V. Free parking. Bus: A5.

Built in the 1950s, this hotel caters to a mostly gay male clientele from all over the world. The accommodations are in three low-rise Spanish colonial-style buildings that ring the edges of a sundeck and swimming pool. The beach is just outside the hotel gate, and on the premises are a bar and a simple restaurant that's open daily for breakfast and lunch. The accommodations are basic, not special in any way, but comfortable, summery, and airy. Some units are air-conditioned, but all have ceiling fans.

INEXPENSIVE

✪ **At Wind Chimes Inn.** Calle Taft 53, Condado, San Juan, PR 00911. ☎ **800/946-3244** or 787/727-4153. Fax 787/726-5321. 13 units. A/C TV TEL. Winter $65–$85 double; off-season $55–$75 double. Rates include continental breakfast. AE, DISC, MC, V. Bus: M8, A7, T1, 21, or 2.

This restored and renovated Spanish manor is one of the most appealing Puerto Rican–style guesthouses on the Condado, offering good value that's especially obvious when compared to the much higher rates for more plush accommodations at newer hotels closer to the beach. Five of the 13 rooms contain small kitchenettes, and management has acquired the house next door for the eventual installation of about a half-dozen new bedrooms sometime during the life of this edition. Upon entering a tropical patio, you'll find tile tables surrounded by palm trees and bougainvillea. There are plenty of space on the deck and a covered lounge for relaxing, socializing, and eating breakfast. Two dozen decorative wind chimes add melody to the daily breezes. The rooms offer a choice of size, beds, and kitchens; all contain ceiling fans and air-conditioning. The location is 1 short block from the beach and 3½ miles from the airport.

Casa del Caribe. Calle Caribe 57, San Juan, PR 00907. ☎ **787/722-7139**. Fax 787/725-3995. 9 units. A/C TV TEL. Winter $65–$85 double; off-season $55–$75 double. Rates include continental breakfast. AE, DISC, MC, V. Bus: A7, T1, or 2.

Formerly known as Casablanca, this renovated guesthouse on a shady side street just off Ashford Avenue in the heart of the Condado was built in the 1940s, later expanded, then totally refurbished with a tropical decor in 1995. A very Puerto Rican ambiance has been created, with emphasis on Latin hospitality and comfort. Behind a wall and garden, you'll discover Casa del Caribe's wraparound veranda. The front porch is a social center for guests. The cozy, often small guest rooms have both ceiling fans and air conditioners, and most of them feature original Puerto Rican art. This is a bargain on the Condado.

Tanama Princess Hotel. 1 Joffre St., Condado, San Juan, PR 00907. ☎ **800/228-5150** or 787/724-4160. Fax 787/724-4160 (same as phone). 113 units. A/C TV TEL. Winter $89 double; off-season $79 double. Children 12 and under stay free in parents' room. Rates include continental breakfast. AE, DC, DISC, MC, V. Bus: T1.

A seven-story white-painted structure, this recently expanded hotel has a desirable Condado location but without the towering prices of the grand resorts along the beach. Tanama is about a 2-minute walk from Condado Beach and is convenient to Old San Juan (a 15-minute drive) and the airport (a 20-minute drive). Most accommodations come with two double beds (ideal for families) and ceiling fans. Many open onto balconies with water views. It's about a 5-minute walk to such major casinos as the ones within the Condado Plaza and San Juan Marriott hotels (see above). A fairly good restaurant serves a nouvelle cuisine nightly, or you can walk to many nearby restaurants.

4 Miramar

Miramar, a residential neighborhood, is very much a part of metropolitan San Juan, and a brisk 30-minute walk will take you where the action is. Regrettably, the beach is at least half a mile away.

Hotel Excelsior. Av. Ponce de León 801, San Juan, PR 00907. ☎ **800/298-4274** or 787/721-7400. Fax 787/723-0068. 140 units. A/C TV TEL. Winter $134–$160 double, $175 suite; off-season $112–$138 double, $149 suite. Children under 10 stay free in parents' room; cribs free. AE, MC, V. Free parking. Bus: T1.

Handsome accommodations and good service are offered at this family-owned and -operated hotel. The bedrooms have been completely refurbished; many have fully equipped kitchenettes, and all have hair dryers, two phones (one in the bathroom), and marble vanities. Included in the rates are shoe shines and transportation to the nearby beach, as well as parking in the underground garage or the adjacent parking lot. This hotel is known for its excellent maintenance and meticulous housekeeping.

The award-winning Augusto's Restaurant is open for lunch Tuesday through Friday and for dinner Monday through Saturday; Café Miramar serves breakfast, lunch, and dinner, and is open 7am to 10pm. A cocktail lounge, an exercise room, and a beauty shop complete the hotel's facilities. Services include laundry and baby-sitting, plus limited room service.

5 Isla Verde

Beach-bordered Isla Verde is closer to the airport than the Condado and Old San Juan. The hotels here are farther from Old San Juan than those in Miramar, Condado, and Ocean Park. It's a good choice if you don't mind the isolation and want to be near fairly good beaches.

VERY EXPENSIVE

✪ **El San Juan Hotel & Casino.** 6063 Isla Verde Ave. Carolina, San Juan, PR 00902. ☎ **800/468-2818** or 787/791-1000. Fax 787/791-0390. 422 units. A/C MINIBAR TV TEL. Winter $330–$490 double, from $575 suite; off-season $250–$395 double, from $475 suite. AE, DC, DISC, MC, V. Self-parking $8; valet parking $13. Bus: A7, M7, or T1.

Dozens of reasons make this the best hotel on Puerto Rico—some say it's the best in the entire Caribbean basin. Built on a 700-yard-long sandy beach in the 1950s, and evoking Havana in its heyday, it was restored with an infusion of millions—some $80 million in 1997 and 1998 alone—each dollar directed to gilding the lily. The beachfront hotel is surrounded by 350 palms, century-old banyans, and gardens. The hotel's river pool, with its currents, cascades, and lagoons, evokes a jungle stream, and the lobby is the most opulent and memorable in the Caribbean. Entirely sheathed in red marble and hand-carved mahogany paneling, the public rooms stretch on almost endlessly.

The large, well-decorated guest units have intriguing touches of high-tech; each contains a dressing room and three phones. A few feature Jacuzzis. About 150 of the accommodations, designed as comfortable bungalows, are in the outer reaches of the garden. Known as *casitas,* they include Roman tubs, atrium showers, and access to the fern-lined paths of a tropical jungle a few steps away. A 17-story, $60 million wing with 120 suites, all oceanfront, was scheduled for completion in late 1998. These ultra-luxury accommodations will feature 103 one- or two-bedroom units, eight garden suites, five governor's suites, and four presidential suites. There will also be a three-floor underground parking garage and four new tennis courts and a pro shop. A complete spa facility is being added to the plush fitness center already on the 10th floor of the main hotel.

The resort is a great choice for families, with more activities for children than any other resort on Puerto Rico.

Dining/Diversions: Even if you're not a guest, consider at least one dinner at the El San Juan, for no other hotel in the entire Caribbean offers such a rich diversity of dining options and such high-quality food, often made with the finest and most expensive of ingredients. In fact, the dining options are a sightseeing attraction in their own right, with many different varieties making a trip here worth it. For example, you can promenade down a re-creation of a Hong Kong waterfront to a Chinese restaurant, Back Street Hong Kong. Take along a full wallet, however, especially at the 24-hour La Veranda Restaurant, near the beach, serving American and Caribbean food. Yamato, a Japanese restaurant, is one of the best at the hotel. Good Italian food is served for lunch and dinner at La Piccola Fontane. True excitement is generated by the Nuevo Latino cuisine at Aquarela, launched by Douglas Rodriguez of New York's much-lauded Patria restaurant. The Tequila Bar & Grill allows guests to sample Mexican dishes on the rooftop while admiring the San Juan beach coast. Finally, the main lobby now sports a trendy Cigar Bar. The in-house casino is open daily from noon to 4am.

Amenities: 24-hour room service, dry cleaning, baby-sitting, massage service, rooftop health club, Penthouse Spa, two swimming pools, water sports, steam room, sauna, tennis court, table tennis. The supervised Kids Klub has daily activities ranging from face painting to swimming lessons—all for children 5 to 12 years old.

The hotel fronts the best beach in Isla Verde. You can use the beach in front of the hotel without staying here. However, if you use the facilities of the hotel, including any water-sports equipment, you will have to pay extra for it.

✪ **The Ritz-Carlton.** 6961 State Rd., #187, Isla Verde, Carolina, PR 00979. ☎ **800/241-3333** or 787/253-1700. Fax 787/253-0700. 414 units. A/C MINIBAR TV TEL. Winter $400–$475 double, from $950 suite; off-season $300–$360 double, from $825 suite. AE, DC, MC, V. Valet parking $10. Bus: A7, M7, or T1.

Opened in late 1997, this beachfront trailblazer in tropical elegance is one of Puerto Rico's most spectacular deluxe hotels (the Hotel El San Juan has a slight edge). Only 15 minutes from the airport, it sits on 8 acres of prime ocean-view property. The decor reflects Caribbean flavor and the Hispanic culture of the island, with artwork from well-known local artists. Soft tones and pale colors are complemented by wrought-iron chandeliers and tropical plants, and beveled and leaded glass throughout the building captures ocean views.

The Ritz offers an array of beautifully furnished guest rooms and suites that open onto ocean or green mountain vistas. They are richly appointed in tropical green, coral, and gold, and complemented by rattan furniture and Latin contemporary artwork. Some meet the needs of guests with disabilities. The preferred accommodations are in the upper-floor Ritz-Carlton Club, accessed by a key-activated elevator; they have the added benefits of a private lounge and personal concierge staff. A total of 46 guest rooms and suites are in this private-seeming club.

Dining/Diversions: Like the hotel itself, the dining here is second only to the Hotel El San Juan. The premier dining venue, the Vineyard Room, rates a separate recommendation (see chapter 6). The Caribbean Grill offers alfresco dining and ocean views, with both Caribbean market buffets and an à la carte menu. The Ocean Bar and Grill is also an alfresco choice for lunches with panoramic views of the beach and ocean and often complemented by a steel band. Or you can retreat into "The Bar," as it's called; with its dark paneling and deep burgundy leather club chairs, it offers late-afternoon and evening drinks and a large selection of fine cigars and private humidors. The Lobby Lounge, also offering panoramic ocean views and live entertainment nightly, is especially noted for its afternoon tea. The hotel also offers the Caribbean's largest casino (see chapter 7).

Amenities: Twice-daily maid service, 24-hour room service, safe-deposit box, in-room dataport, honor bar in each guest room, laundry service, baby-sitting, beauty salon, programs for children, European-style spa featuring 11 treatments for body and beauty, aerobics, complete fitness cuisine, two lighted tennis curt, 7,200-square-foot outdoor pool overlooking the beach. Arrangements can be made for golf, snorkeling, fishing, waterskiing, sailing, and horseback riding.

San Juan Grand Beach Hotel & Casino. 187 Isla Verde Ave., Isla Verde, PR 00979. ☎ 800/443-2009 in the U.S. or 787/791-6100. Fax 787/791-8525. 420 units. A/C TV TEL. Winter $315–$465 double, from $525 suite; off-season $210–$310 double, from $380 suite. AE, DC, DISC, MC, V. Self-parking $5; valet parking $10. Bus: A7, M7, or T1.

This luxury beachfront resort reopened in 1997 on the site of the former Sands hotel, following an extensive $12 million restoration. It's outclassed by the far-swankier El San Juan Hotel next door, but it enjoys a high occupancy rate, with lots of guests on package tours. The comfortable, medium-size bedrooms have balconies and terraces. The most desirable are in the Plaza Club, a minihotel within the hotel that sports a private entrance, concierge service, complimentary food and beverage buffets, and suite/spa and beach facilities.

Dining/Diversions: Although this hotel's culinary status is not nearly the equal of the nearby El San Juan, it is a worthy choice for dining even for nonguests, because one of its restaurants, Giuseppe, offers some of the beachfront's best northern Italian food, and a branch of Ruth's Chris Steak House serves Puerto Rico's juiciest steaks. On the boardwalk, Ciao offers breakfast and light Mediterranean fare for lunch and dinner. In the lobby area is a teppanyaki and sushi bar. At the Grand Market, you can buy a picnic basket for a day out on the beach. The in-house night-club offers revue-style spoofs of Hollywood legends and glittery Vegas-inspired shows, depending on bookings. The in-house casino is also popular.

Amenities: Room service (6am to 2pm and 5pm to 2am), baby-sitting, laundry, limousine service, massage service, business center, scuba diving. The resort boasts the Caribbean's largest free-form swimming pool, complete with waterfalls, rockscapes, and a swim-up bar.

EXPENSIVE

Colony San Juan Beach Hotel. 2 Jose M. Tartak St., Isla Verde, Carolina, PR 00979. ☎ 800/777-1700 or 787/253-0100. Fax 787/253-0220. 83 units. A/C MINIBAR TV TEL. Winter $185–$265 double, $435 suite; off-season $140–$210 double, $325 suite. AE, MC, V. Self-parking free, valet parking $8. Bus: T1.

This well-designed branch of a Pittsburgh-based hotel chain opened in 1997, just across a quiet one-way street from the beach of Isla Verde and only about 2 blocks from the gambling and nightlife facilities of some of the most expensive hotels in Puerto Rico. In comparison, holidaymakers pay relatively reasonable rates here for

⊕ Family-Friendly Hotels

El San Juan Hotel & Casino *(see p. 111)*   This hotel, although expensive, offers more programs for children than any other hotel on Puerto Rico. Its supervised Kids Klub provides daily activities—ranging from face painting to swimming lessons—for children 5 to 12 years of age.

Empress Oceanfront Hotel *(see p. 115)*   Although this moderately priced hotel doesn't provide specific activities for children, all its units have two double beds. Thus, two children under 12 can stay here free.

Caribe Hilton *(see p. 103)*   Children under 16 stay free in their parents' room at this deluxe hotel, which has two swimming pools and is situated in a 17-acre tropical park.

comfortable, earth-toned accommodations. The Colony features its own outdoor swimming pool, snack bar, and health club on its uppermost (10th) floor, as well as a pizzeria and a more upscale Italian trattoria (Maxim's) adjacent to its lobby. Well-furnished, moderate-size bedrooms contain safes for valuables, and Nintendo games on their TVs. Some have balconies, and more than half enjoy sea views.

Crowne Plaza Hotel & Casino. Rte. 187, km 1.5, Isla Verde, San Juan, PR 00979. ☎ 800/2-CROWNE or 787/253-2929. Fax 787/253-0079. 276 units. A/C TV TEL. Winter $199–$279 double, $239–$369 suite; off-season $169–$209 double, $199–$269 suite. AE, DC, DISC, MC, V. Self-parking $6; valet parking $10. Bus: T1.

This easternmost of San Juan's grand modern hotels is the leading Caribbean showcase of the Holiday Inn chain. Rising 12 stories above a great beach, the resort has gathered a loyal clientele, both business and leisure travelers, from North America and the Caribbean since it opened in 1991. The setting is a landscaped plot of beachfront close to the airport. The decor incorporates tropical themes.

You register in a large but simple lobby sheathed in beige marble. Bedrooms are bright and inviting, though outfitted in a bland, modern style that might remind you of a roadside motel in Florida. Each has some kind of ocean view—some full-frontal, others set at an angle to the shoreline. The bathrooms are of modest style and done in either tile or marble. Each accommodation is double-insulated against noises from the nearby airport. Some floors have enhanced facilities and services, including a concierge staff providing free continental breakfasts and complimentary early evening hors d'oeuvres.

Dining/Diversions: The acceptable Italian cuisine offered at La Dolce Vita is not a major reason to stay here, but you can always take a taxi over to the El San Juan Hotel. There's also a large casino.

Amenities: Room service (6:30am to midnight), baby-sitting, laundry, large free-form swimming pool with swim-up bar, a sandy beachfront studded with palm trees and sea grapes, car-rental facilities, a tour desk, children's games room, children's pool, fitness center, an in-house gift shop, and both a sports club and a beach club devoted to land and water sports.

Embassy Suites Hotel & Casino. 8000 Jose M. Tartak St., Isla Verde, Carolina, San Juan, PR 00979. ☎ 800/362-2779 or 787/791-0505. Fax 787/791-0555. 300 suites. A/C MINIBAR TV TEL. Winter $265 1-bedroom suite, $550 2-bedroom suite, $750 presidential suite; off-season $150 1-bedroom suite, $320 2-bedroom suite, $500 presidential suite. Rates include breakfast. AE, DC, MC, V. Self-parking $6; valet parking $10. Bus: T1.

Inaugurated in 1997, this is the first venture of Memphis-based Embassy Suites into the Caribbean. Noted for its efficient and comfortably accessorized accommodations favored for medium-term stays by business travelers and others, it occupies an orange-colored, eight-story building across the busy avenue from such upscale beachfront hotels as the Colony Hotel.

There are a swimming pool and a fitness center here, and Playa Alambique, a public beach that's shared by several neighboring hotels, is a 10-minute walk away. Bedrooms contain cooking facilities with at least a refrigerator, microwave, and coffeemaker. You'll find a business center on the premises, and two restaurants, including the Wild Orchids Café, a low-key indoor/outdoor affair, and an independently managed Outback Steakhouse branch (see "Isla Verde" in chapter 6). There's also a small-scale casino on the property.

MODERATE

✪ **Empress Oceanfront Hotel.** 2 Amapola St., Isla Verde, PR 00979. ☎ **800/ 678-0757** or 787/791-3083. Fax 787/791-1423. 30 units. A/C TV TEL. Winter $168 double; off-season $108 double. AE, DC, MC, V. Bus: T1 and M8.

Set on 2½ acres of rocky headlands jutting out from the coastline, this four-story pink-sided hotel is efficiently run by an Anglo-Latino family originally from Brooklyn, New York. From its enclosed swimming-pool terrace, you'll enjoy sweeping views of the high-rise hotels and valuable real estate nearby.

On the premises is a popular bar, the Blue Dolphin, and the likable Sonny's Oceanfront Place for Ribs, with one of San Juan's best nighttime views and some of the island's best ribs (see chapter 6). A Jacuzzi is near the pool. The pleasantly airy decor is inspired by the tropics. Rooms are furnished in a standard motel-like format—nothing special, but they are clean and comfortable.

Hampton Inn. 6530 Isla Verde Ave., Isla Verde, Carolina, San Juan, PR 00979. ☎ **800/ 426-7866** or 787/426-8777. Fax 787/791-8575. 200 units. A/C TV TEL. Winter $129–$154 double, $149–$174 suite; off-season $99–$129 double, $129–$149 suite. AE, MC, V. Free parking. Bus: T1.

Inaugurated late in 1997, this chain hotel is set across the busy avenue from Isla Verde's sandy beachfront, far enough away to keep costs down but within a leisurely 10-minute walk to the casinos and nightlife. Two beige-painted towers, with four and five floors, hold the simple, clean, and comfortable bedrooms outfitted with whitewashed oak furniture, tiled bathrooms, and upholsteries in such jungle colors as green, red, and yellow. There's no restaurant on the premises, no real garden to speak of, and other than a swimming pool with its own swim-up bar and a Jacuzzi, very few facilities or amenities. Because of its reasonable prices and location, however, this Isla Verde newcomer could be a good choice.

Travelodge. Av. Isla Verde (P.O. Box 6007, Loiza Station), Santurce, PR 00914. ☎ **800/468-2028** or 787/728-1300. Fax 787/727-7150. 92 units. A/C TV TEL. Winter $137 double, $175 suite; off-season $91 double, $150 suite. AE, MC, V. Bus: T1.

Rising eight stories above the busy Isla Verde traffic, this chain hotel offers comfortable but small bedrooms furnished simply with bland modern furniture. Many guests carry a tote bag to the beach across the street, then patronize the bars, restaurants, and swimming facilities of the expensive hotels nearby. There's only one restaurant here (the Country Kitchen), one swimming pool, and one bar (the Escort Lounge), which features live dance music every Wednesday through Saturday night. About a third of the hotel's rooms were renovated in 1997. Despite a lack of personal service from staff, and the fact that it's far from being the best-equipped hotel at Isla Verde, this hotel is a viable cost-conscious choice. Look for its radical enlargement, thanks to the addition of a second tower, perhaps during the lifetime of this edition.

INEXPENSIVE

Green Isle/Casa Mathiesen. 36 Calle Uno, Villamar, Isla Verde, PR 00979. ☎ **800/ 677-8860** or 787/726-4330. Fax 787/268-2415. 45 units. A/C TV TEL. Winter $74 double; off-season $65 double. AE, MC, V. Bus: A5.

Small, unassuming, and subject to the roar of the nearby traffic, this hotel stands across the busy avenue from the larger and much-more-expensive San Juan Grand Beach Hotel & Casino. Each of the simple, low-slung accommodations contains its own kitchenette and simple, summery furniture. There's a small swimming pool on the premises, although most residents prefer to swim in the sea. Dozens of cheap fast-food joints are nearby.

6 Santurce & Ocean Park

Less fashionable (and a bit less expensive) than their nearest neighbors, Condado (to the west) and Isla Verde (to the east), Santurce and Ocean Park are wedged into a modern, not particularly beautiful neighborhood that's bisected with lots of roaring traffic arteries and commercial enterprises. Lots of San Juañeros come here to work in the district's many offices and to eat in its many restaurants. Of the two, the coastal subdivision of Ocean Park is a bit more fashionable than landlocked Santurce, but with the beach never more than a 20-minute walk away, few of Santurce's residents seem to mind.

Arcade Inn. 8 Taft St., Santurce, Condado, PR 00911. ☎ **787/725-0668.** Fax 787/ 728-7524. 19 units. A/C TV. Winter $65–$70 double, $90 suite; off-season $60–$65 double, $85 suite. DC, MC, V. Free parking. Bus: T1 or 2.

The Arcade Inn was originally built as a private home in 1943, and it was transformed into a simple hotel in 1948. But it didn't become well-known until the late 1960s, when its reasonable rates began to attract families with children and college students traveling in groups. It's a stucco-covered building with vaguely Spanish colonial detailing on a residential street lined with similar buildings. The accommodations each contain a small refrigerator and simple, slightly battered furniture. There's no swimming pool and few amenities on-site, but the beach is quite close.

Beach Buoy Inn. 1853 McLeary, Ocean Park, San Juan, PR 00911. ☎ **800/221-8119** or 787/728-8119. Fax 787/268-0037. 15 units. A/C TV. Winter $60–$70 double, $75 efficiency; off-season $50–$60 double, $60 efficiency. Children 11 and under stay free in parents' room. Rates include continental breakfast. AE, MC, V. Free parking. Bus: T1.

About a block from the beach, this B&B deserves to be better known. Its rooms are not decorated as nicely as those at the At Wind Chimes Inn (see above), but they're clean and decent, there's daily maid service, and on-premises parking is free. The efficiencies have two double beds or two twin beds. The units have color cable TVs, although many guests gather around the large TV in the lounge to watch basketball and football games. Some units have small refrigerators. This place is a comfortable, snug nest, and the staff is especially helpful and friendly. It has no restaurant, bar, or pool, but many of these features are available nearby. You can enjoy the complimentary breakfast outdoors on the patio if you wish.

✪ **Hosteria del Mar.** 1 Tapia St., Ocean Park, San Juan, PR 00911. ☎ **787/ 727-3302.** Fax 345/268-0772. 8 units, 4 apts. A/C TV TEL. Winter $141–$175 double,

$185 apartment; off-season $76–$109 double, $125 apartment. Children 11 and under stay free in parents' room. AE, MC, V. Bus: A5.

Lying a few blocks from the Condado casinos are the white walls of this distinctive landmark. It's located between Isla Verde and Condado in a residential seaside community that's popular with locals looking for beach action on weekends. The rates are a little high for this category, but ask for one of the least expensive units. The hotel boasts ocean-view rooms with balconies from its second floor. On the floor below, the units open onto patios. The bedroom style is invitingly tropical, with wicker furniture, pastel prints, and ceiling fans. There's no pool, but a full-service restaurant is known for its freshly made vegetarian, macrobiotic, and Puerto Rican plates. The apartments all come with kitchenette, in case you'd like to save on meals. And of the 12 units, all but four of the bedrooms have telephones. The place is simple, yet with its own elegance, and the hospitality is warm. Aficionados of small, select Caribbean inns would like to keep this one a secret.

GAY-FRIENDLY GUESTHOUSES

L'Habitation Beach Guesthouse. Calle Italia 1957, Ocean Park, San Juan, PR 00911. ☎ **787/727-2499.** Fax 787/727-2599. 10 units. A/C MINIBAR TV. Winter $66–$87 double; off-season $47–$69 double. Extra person $10. Rates include continental breakfast. AE, DISC, MC, V. Free parking. Bus: T1.

Formerly The Beach House, this gay-friendly hotel sits on a tranquil tree-lined street with a sandy beach right in its backyard. Located only a few blocks from the Condado, this inn is imbued with a laid-back French atmosphere (owner Alain Tasca is from Paris, having lived and worked in Guadeloupe and Key West before taking over this operation). Good-size and well-maintained bedrooms have ceiling fans, comfortable beds, and fairly simple furnishings. The most spacious are rooms 8 and 9, which also open onto ocean views. Chairs and beverage service are provided in a private beach area, and guests can enjoy breakfast alfresco. You can also eat or drink out in the breeze in the patio overlooking the sea. Ask for one of the bar's special margaritas—after two you will feel no pain; after a third, the night is yours.

Número Uno Guest House. Calle Santa Ana 1, Ocean Park, San Juan, PR 00911. ☎ **787/726-5010.** Fax 787/727-5482. 12 units. A/C. Winter $95–$165 double; off-season $75–$110 double. Rates include continental breakfast. AE, MC, V. Bus: T1.

In a prestigious residential neighborhood at the edge of the high-rise glitter of Isla Verde, this small and recently renovated hotel has a well-trained, English-speaking staff, which is gay friendly. There are a garden with palmettos and a swimming pool, easy access to a sandy beach, and all the distractions of several megaresorts relatively close at hand. The accommodations have wicker or rattan furniture. There are a bar and a very good restaurant on the premises, serving a Caribbean fusion cuisine. The owners can direct you to water-sports emporiums for scuba, waterskiing, sailing excursions, or whatever.

6 Where to Dine in San Juan

San Juan has the widest array of restaurants in the Caribbean. You can enjoy fine continental, American, Italian, Chinese, Mexican, and Japanese cuisines, to name a few. In recent years, many restaurants have shown a greater appreciation for traditional Puerto Rican cooking, and local specialties now appear on the menus of leading restaurants. Whenever possible, many chefs make use of local ingredients, which enhances all their dishes.

Before searching for a local restaurant, you should review "Puerto Rico's Exotic Bill of Fare" in chapter 2.

Many of San Juan's best restaurants are in the resort hotels along the Condado and at Isla Verde. There has been a restaurant explosion in San Juan in the past few years, but many of the newer ones are off-the-beaten tourist path, and some have not yet achieved the fine quality found at many of the older and more traditional restaurants.

Local seafood is generally in plentiful supply, but no restaurant guarantees that it will have fresh fish every night, especially during winter when the sea can be too turbulent for local fishermen to go out. In those cases the chef often has to rely on fish flown in either fresh or frozen from Miami. If you want local fish that's fresh and caught in Puerto Rican waters, ask your waiter to advise on the "catch of the day," and make your decision only after he or she has guaranteed that the fish was recently caught and sold to the restaurant and hasn't been resting for a while in the icebox.

In Puerto Rico, a **very expensive** restaurant is one charging more than $50 per person for a meal, excluding drinks and service. In restaurants classified as **expensive** or **moderate,** meals range from $30 to $50, and from $15 to $30, respectively. Any meal under $15 is definitely **inexpensive.**

GREAT PICNIC FARE

Puerto Rico is ideal for picnicking year-round. The best place to fill a picnic basket is the **Repostería Kassalta** (see "Ocean Park," below). Puerto Rican families often come to this cafeteria/bakery/deli to order delicacies for their Sunday outings.

The best places for a picnic are **Muñoz Marín Park,** along Las Américas Expressway, west of Avenida Piñero, and the **Botanical Gardens,** operated by the University of Puerto Rico in the Río Piedras section.

In case you want to be welcomed there.

We're here to see that you're always welcomed at establishments everywhere. That's why millions of people carry the American Express® Card – for peace of mind, confidence, and security, around the world or just around the corner.

do more®

AMERICAN
EXPRESS

Cards

In case you're running low.

We're here to help with more than 118,000 Express Cash

locations around the world. In order to enroll, just call

American Express before you start your vacation.

do more

And just in case.

We're here with American Express® Travelers Cheques
and Cheques *for Two*.® They're the safest way to carry
money on your vacation and the surest way to get a
refund, practically anywhere, anytime.
Another way we help you...

do more

AMERICAN
EXPRESS

**Travelers
Cheques**

1 Best Bets

- **Best All Around:** One of Puerto Rico's most celebrated chefs, Douglas Rodriguez of **Aquarela,** in El San Juan Hotel & Casino, 6063 Isla Verde Ave. (☎ 787/253-5566), is the culinary talk of the town with his innovative contemporary Latin cuisine. Award-winning and avant-garde, Rodriguez draws upon culinary references from around the world to turn out such dishes as grilled Chilean sea bass with yucca and a succulent version of paella that includes one of the most diverse collections of shellfish in Puerto Rico.
- **Best Newcomer:** The luxurious **Vineyard Room** in the dazzling new Ritz-Carlton, 6961 State Road #187, Isla Verde (☎ 787/253-1700), holds forth with a refined California/Mediterranean cuisine. Some of its recipes have never been seen in Puerto Rico before. Begin perhaps with cream of frog's leg soup flavored with sweet garlic petals, and go on to slow-roasted veal cheek with two types of beans. Desserts are as sumptuous as the setting. The Vineyard Room offers one of the island's finest wine lists.
- **Best Innovative Chef:** Acclaimed as one of Puerto Rico's finest chefs, Marisoll Hernández presides over **Chef Marisoll,** Calle del Cristo 202 (☎ 787/725-7475). *Gourmet* magazine plus some of the most savvy foodies in San Juan's Old Town love her imaginative dishes. She even makes soup aficionados out of those who normally aren't. Try her cream of exotic wild mushroom soup with an essence of black truffles or her butternut-squash soup with crisp ginger.
- **Best Classic French Cuisine:** If you like your French food classical, then head to **La Chaumière,** Calle Tetuán 367 (☎ 787/722-3330), in the Old Town San Juan. In back of the Tapía Theater, this two-story restaurant is intimate and inviting. The cuisine follows time-tested recipes of which Escoffier might have approved: onion soup, oysters Rockefeller, scallops Provençale, and a perfectly prepared rack of baby lamb Provençale.
- **Best Nuevo Latino Cuisine:** The **Parrot Club,** Calle Fortaleza 363 (☎ 787/725-7370), wows Old Town taste buds with its modern interpretation of Puerto Rican specialties. Even San Juan's mayor and the governor have made it their favorite. A married team, Emilio Figueroa and Gigi Zafero, borrow not only from a Puerto Rican and Spanish repertoire of recipes but even use Taíno and African influences in their cuisine. Their ceviche is the best in town, and their Créole-style flank steak is worth the trek in from Condado Beach.
- **Best Japanese & Best Sushi Restaurant:** In San Juan's Old Town, **Yukiyú,** Calle Recinto Sur 311 (☎ 787/721-0653), pioneered a style of Japanese and Asian cookery unfamiliar here. Some locals learned to eat raw fish (sushi) for the first time, and a few have become addicted to it. Other than its sushi bar—acclaimed as the best in the Caribbean—a wide array of other Japanese- and Asian-inspired dishes is available, especially a delectable yellowfin tuna with teriyaki.
- **Best Burgers:** Patrons freely admit that **El Patio de Sam,** Calle San Sebastián 102 (☎ 787/723-1149), is not always on target with all of its main dishes every night. But on one thing they do agree: its hamburgers are the juiciest and most delectable in San Juan. The Old Town atmosphere is also intriguing: you almost expect to encounter Bogie and Bacall munching as Sydney Greenstreet sits leering in the background. Sam's black-bean soup isn't bad either.
- **Best Asopao:** Soul food to Puerto Ricans, *asopao* is the regional gumbo made in as many different ways as there are chefs on island. Some versions are too thick to be called a soup, such as the seafood variety served at **La Bombonera,** Calle

San Francisco 259 (☎ **787/722-0658**), in San Juan's Old Town. It's more like a stew. Other favorite varieties of asopao include one made with pigeon peas, although the offering with chicken is better known.

- **Best Creole Cuisine:** You'd have to go all the way to Madrid to find Spanish food prepared as well as it is at **Ramiro's,** Av. Magdalena 1106 (☎ **787/721-9049**). The cuisine isn't classical, but innovative. The chefs take full advantage of fresh island produce. In fact, their cookery is New Créole, although its roots are firmly planted in Spain. Their fresh fish and char-grilled meats are succulent, and any dessert they drizzle freshly made strawberry-and-guava sauce over is a sure palate pleaser.

- **Best Local Cuisine:** Devoted to *la cocina criolla,* as the often starchy local cuisine is known, **Ajili Mójili,** 1052 Ashford Ave. (☎ **787/725-9195**), features food that locals might have enjoyed as prepared by their mamas. Try such specialties as *mofongos* (green plantains stuffed with veal, chicken, shrimp, or pork) or the most classic *arroz con pollo* (stewed chicken with saffron rice) in town.

- **Best Hotel Restaurant:** We concur with *San Juan City Magazine,* which hailed **Ristorante Tuscany** in the San Juan Marriott Resort, 1309 Ashford Ave. (☎ **787/722-7000**), as the best hotel restaurant of 1997. Its standards continued to be maintained in 1998. The chef searches the markets for some of the best and freshest ingredients to whip into a succulent northern Italian cuisine that is smooth and refined to the palate. Some diners even visit just to sample the gourmet pizzas from a wood-burning oven.

- **Best Italian Restaurant:** In El San Juan Hotel & Casino, **La Piccola Fontana,** Isla Verde Ave. (☎ **787/791-1000,** ext. 1271), takes you on a culinary tour of sunny Italy and does so exceedingly well. Plate after plate of delectable northern Italian food is presented nightly—everything from grilled fillets of fresh fish to succulent pastas. Service is first-rate, the welcome warm.

- **Best View, Best Alfresco & Best Ribs:** It may seem like a lot of bests, but **Sonny's Oceanfront Place for Ribs,** in the Empress Oceanfront Hotel, 2 Amapola St., Isla Verde (☎ **787/791-3083**), delivers on all counts. Its ribs are always tender and cooked to perfection and flavored with savory sauces. The alfresco dining terrace opens onto the twinkling lights along the Isla Verde and Condado coastlines.

- **Best Late-Night Dining:** If you have hunger pangs late at night, forget the fast-food joints and head to **Amadeus,** Calle San Sebastián 106 in Old San Juan (☎ **787/722-8635**). It offers Caribbean ingredients deftly handled with a nouvelle twist. And it does so Tuesday through Sunday until 2am. An attractive, trendy, most often young crowd shows up late to feast off the refined cuisine, enjoying such delights as Cajun-grilled mahimahi.

- **Best Family Meals:** Although some adults might find dining in a setting of mounted butterflies (for sale) a bit odd, kids generally enjoy the **Butterfly People Café,** Calle Fortaleza 152 (☎ **787/723-2432**). Here in the world's largest gallery devoted to mounted butterflies, you can enjoy light continental and American cuisine, all at reasonable prices. Food is made with fresh ingredients and includes one of the town's best quiches. Desserts tempt all members of the family, especially the tantalizing raspberry chiffon pie. The fruit drinks at the bar feature everything from freshly squeezed Puerto Rican orange juice to a frappé of seven fruit fruits.

- **Best Pizza:** You'll think you're back in Italy at **Via Appia,** 1350 Ashford Ave. (☎ **787/725-8711**), on the Condado. Try the special: it's delectable, made with sausages, onions, mushrooms, pepperoni, green pepper, and bubbling cheese. There's even a pizza with meatballs, and one for vegetarians as well.

- **Best Sunday Brunch:** Both locals and American visitors flock to the **Caribe Hilton,** Calle Los Rosales (☎ **787/721-0303**), for its delectable all-you-can-eat Sunday brunch. Good food, glamour, and live music are combined here. The freshly prepared seafood alone is worth the set price, which includes champagne.
- **Best Breakfast & Best Ice Cream:** A winner on both counts, **Café Ventana,** in the Radisson Ambassador Plaza Hotel & Casino, 1369 Ashford Ave. (☎ **787/721-7300**), long ago became locally famous for serving the best breakfasts on the Condado, usually less expensive than those at the fancy hotel dining rooms. A favorite with Puerto Rican politicians, the cafe is busy all morning turning out everything from omelettes and pancakes to hash-brown potatoes and sausages. The cafe was once a Howard Johnson's and still sells all the ice cream flavors purveyed in its former incarnation, many made with fresh berries and all rich and creamy.
- **Best Drinks:** Even when we're in San Juan waiting for plane connections and have time available, we take a taxi to **Maria's,** Calle del Cristo 204 (no phone) in Old San Juan, for the coolest and most refreshingly original drinks in the city. More fresh fruit is consumed here in blending machines every 5 minutes or so than Carmen Miranda ever had on one of her hats. On a hot day, there is no finer place to enjoy a mixed-fruit frappé; a banana, pineapple, or chocolate frost; or an orange, papaya, or lime freeze.

2 Old San Juan

EXPENSIVE

✪ **Chef Marisoll.** Calle del Cristo 202. ☎ **787/725-7454.** Reservations required. Main courses $24–$30. AE, MC, V. Tues–Sat noon–2:30pm and 7–10:30pm, Sun 7–10:30pm. Bus: A7, T1, or 2. INTERNATIONAL.

Marisoll Hernández is one of the top chefs of Puerto Rico. Trained in Hilton properties, including one in London, she broke away to become an independent restaurateur in the Old Town of San Juan. In a Spanish colonial building, with a courtyard patio for dining, her eight-table restaurant is warm and intimate. Service is low-key, a bit distracted, and slightly formal. You could have a sandwich for lunch, but few would want to settle for that when they can sample one of the chef's imaginative dishes. Two of her soups have appeared in *Gourmet* magazine: a cream of exotic wild mushrooms with an essence of black truffles and her butternut-squash soup with crisp ginger. Caesar salads might appear garnished with duck or lobster. There's usually a catch of the day, such as dorado with a medley of sauces—whatever strikes the chef's fancy. You can also sample her risotto with shrimp, lobster, and scallops in a saffron sauce. A truly elegant and beautifully flavored tenderloin with foie gras is another specialty.

Il Perugino. Calle del Cristo 105. ☎ **787/722-5481.** Reservations required. Main courses $18–$31. AE, MC, V. Daily 6:30–11pm. Bus: A7, T1, or 2. TUSCAN/UMBRIAN.

This is one of the most elegant Italian restaurants in San Juan, with a courtyard containing covered tables. It's located in a 200-year-old town house, a short walk uphill from the town's cathedral. The entire setting is painted in shades of ochre and umber reminiscent of Perugia, the homeland of owner/chef Franco Seccarelli. Dishes and flavors are perfectly balanced. Examples include shrimp salad (usually a mundane dish, but quite special here), a carpaccio of scallops, a perfectly marinated fresh salmon, veal entrecôte with mushrooms, and medaillons of beef flavored with balsamic vinegar. Want something more adventurous? Try the "black pasta" with crayfish and baby eels. Daily specials add variety to the menu.

⭐ **La Chaumière.** Calle Tetuán 367. ☎ **787/722-3330.** Reservations recommended. Main courses $21.50–$32.50. AE, DC, MC, V. Mon–Sat 6pm–midnight. Closed July–Aug. Bus: A7, T1, or 2. CLASSICAL FRENCH.

Behind the famous Tapía Theater, this restaurant with a cafe-like decor has a loyal following of foodies drawn to its classic cuisine—the kind of dishes that you might find in a first-class hotel somewhere deep in France. The setting is appropriate, a bit flowery like a greenhouse. You might begin with a rather heartily flavored country pâté, then follow with a rack of baby lamb Provençale. A tender chateaubriand is served only for two. Those old standbys, veal Oscar and oysters Rockefeller, also regularly appear.

⭐ **Parrot Club.** Calle Fortaleza 363. ☎ **787/725-7370.** Reservations not accepted. Main courses $8.50–$13 at lunch, $13.50–$17 at brunch, $12–$21 at dinner. MC, V. Tues–Sat 11:30am–3pm, Sun noon–4pm, Tues–Wed 6–11pm, Thurs–Sat 6pm–midnight, Sun 6:30–10pm. Closed 2 weeks in July. MODERN PUERTO RICAN.

The hot, hot restaurant in Old San Juan is this bistro and bar serving a Nuevo Latino cuisine blending traditional Puerto Rican cookery with its Spanish, Taíno, and African influences and heightened by rich, contemporary touches. In a neighborhood known as SOFO (South of Fortaleza Street), it occupies a stately looking building constructed in 1902 as a hair tonic factory. Today you might spot Gloria Vanderbilt, San Juan's mayor, and the governor of Puerto Rico in the cheerful dining room or a verdantly landscaped courtyard where tables for at least 200 diners are scattered amid potted ferns, palms, and orchids. Live music—Brazilian, salsa, or Latino jazz—is the norm every night of the week and during the popular Sunday brunches. Menu items are updated interpretations of old-fashioned Puerto Rican specialties. They include ceviche derived from the succulent flesh of halibut, salmon, tuna, or mahimahi marinated in lime juice and seasonings; smoked and pickled conch served with a breadfruit mofongo; a delicious version of crab cakes; criolla-style flank steak, and pan-seared tuna served with a sauce made from dark rum and essence of oranges. Everybody's favorite drink is a "parrot passion" made from lemon-flavored rum, triple sec, oranges, and passion fruit. The owners of this place, Emilio Figueroa and his wife, Gigi Zafero, learned their restaurant-keeping craft well, thanks to work stints in places as diverse as Spain, Key West, Miami, and New Orleans.

⭐ **Yukiyú.** Calle Recinto Sur 311. ☎ **787/721-0653.** Reservations recommended. Main courses $19–$26; fixed-price teppanyaki dinners $19.50–$36; sushi $2.75–$10.50 per piece. AE, DISC, MC, V. Mon–Fri noon–2:20pm and 5–11pm, Sat noon–2:20pm and 7–11pm; Sun 3:30–9pm. Bus: A7, T1, or 2. JAPANESE.

Traditional Japanese and other Asian cooking techniques are combined in this restaurant in Old Town. Tabs can mount quickly at the sushi bar, acclaimed as the best in the Caribbean. Sushi is available at both lunch and dinner, but the teppanyaki grill at the front, where your own personal chef cooks your meal, is open only at dinner. The dining room itself is postmodern and monochromatic.

Against this backdrop, the various chefs tempt you with hibachi chicken or chicken with scallops and sesame seeds. You might begin with miso soup or steamed pork dumplings, then go on to a shrimp-and-vegetable tempura, or perhaps fillet of sole with capers. Fresh yellowfin tuna with teriyaki is a favorite, as is the chicken

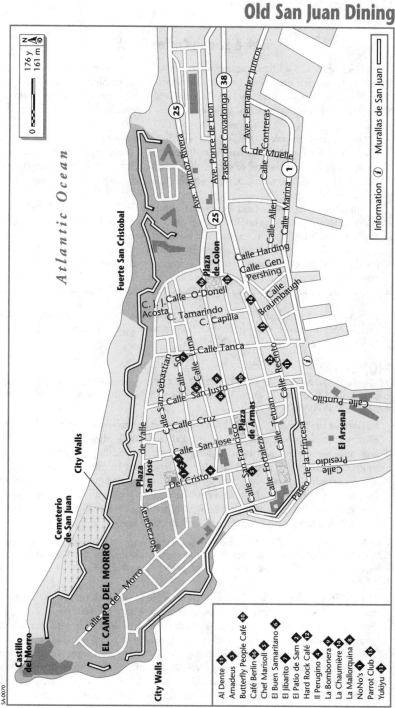

Old San Juan Dining

Atlantic Ocean

Fuerte San Cristobal

Castillo del Morro

Cemeterio de San Juan

EL CAMPO DEL MORRO

City Walls

City Walls

Plaza San Jose

Del Cristo

Plaza de Armas

Plaza de Colon

El Arsenal

Calle del Morro
Calle Norzagaray
Calle de Valle
Calle San Sebastian
Calle Sol
Calle Luna
Calle San Justo
Calle Cruz
Calle San Jose
Calle San Francisco
Calle Fortaleza
Calle Tetuan
Calle Recinto
Calle Tanca
C. Capilla
C. Tamarindo
C. J. J. Acosta
Calle O'Donell
Calle Harding
Calle Gen. Pershing
Calle Braumbaugh
Ave. Muñoz Rivera
Ave. Ponce de Leon
Paseo de Covadonga
Ave. Fernandez Juncos
C. de Muelle
Calle de Contreras
Calle Allen
Calle Marina
Calle Puntillo
Paseo de la Princesa
Calle Presidio

25 38 25 1

Information (i)   Murallas de San Juan

SA-0070

Al Dente 11
Amadeus 3
Butterfly People Café 10
Café Berlin 16
Chef Marisoll 5
El Buen Samaritano 6
El Jibarito 7
El Patio de Sam 2
Hard Rock Café 12
Il Perugino 4
La Bombonera 9
La Chaumière 14
La Mallorquina 8
NoNo's 1
Parrot Club 15
Yukiyu 13

0   176 y
     161 m
N

123

Take a Strong Coffee Break

A coffee break in Old San Juan might last an afternoon. *Taza* (cup) after taza of Puerto Rico's rich brew might make you desert Jamaican Blue Mountain coffee or Hawaiian Kona forever. By law, Puerto Rican coffeehouses must serve coffee made from homegrown beans, most often from the mountains in the center of the island.

For years we've taken our espresso—from early morning until our final "nightcap"—at **Cuatro Estaciones** (no phone) at a rather ugly and completely nondescript kiosk at the end of the bustling Plaza de Armas (see the walking tour in chapter 7). You'll get a quick jolt from this tasty brew, which attracts local java heads day and night.

Another choice spot is **Casa Papyrus**, Calle Tetuán 357 (☎ 787/724-6105), which is an unpretentious bookstore cum cafe. In a setting of tranquil little nooks and crannies, filled with magazines and books in both English and Spanish, you can enjoy Old Town's best cappuccino. If you're lucky enough to snare a seat out on the wrought-iron balcony, you can enjoy not only your taza but a book or most definitely the view of the port across the way.

---

teriyaki. If you order sushi and a lot of extras, this restaurant can become very expensive; however, if you opt for the fixed-price teppanyaki dinner at $19.50, it becomes one of the bargains of Old Town.

MODERATE

Al Dente. Calle Recinto Sur 309. ☎ 787/723-7303. Reservations recommended. Main courses $10–$17. AE, MC, V. Mon–Fri noon–2pm and 5:30–10pm; Sat noon–10:30pm. Bus: A7, T1, or 2. SICILIAN.

Located in the heart of Old San Juan, this unpretentious restaurant has a decor that evokes some trattoria you enjoyed in Palermo. Both the dress code and the ambiance are relaxed and casual. You might sample the scallops on a bed of spinach sautéed in cream, or gnocchi with pesto, fettuccine maestro, ravioli (cheese or shrimp versions), or well-seasoned calamari. The chef also makes his own desserts, including cheesecake, tiramisu, and chocolate tortes. Nearly all dishes are genuinely satisfying, and the restaurant delivers quality food at a reasonable price. Brochettes of fresh tuna laced with pepper and Mediterranean herbs is an excellent choice.

✪ **Amadeus.** Calle San Sebastián 106 (across from the Iglesia de San José). ☎ 787/722-8635. Reservations recommended. Main courses $7–$22. AE, MC, V. Tues–Sun noon–2am (kitchen closes at 12:30am). Bus: M2, M3, or T1. NOUVELLE/ CARIBBEAN.

Housed in a brick-and-stone building constructed in the 18th century by a wealthy merchant, Amadeus offers Caribbean ingredients with a nouvelle twist. The appetizers alone are worth the trip here, especially Amadeus dumpling with guava sauce and arrowroot fritters. The chef will even prepare a smoked salmon and caviar pizza. While receiving a cordial welcome, you can enjoy dishes *de la tierra* (from the land) or *del mar* (from the sea), including a fresh catch of the day. One zesty specialty is pork scaloppini with sweet-and-sour sauce. More recent and rather delectable additions to the menu include chicken breast with escargots and mushrooms, linguini with shrimp in an Alfredo sauce, along with an array of freshly made sandwiches and salads available at lunch.

A Toothpick on Your Table

When you've had too many hotel meals or patronized too many first-class restaurants and want something authentic, head for **El Jibarito,** Calle Sol 280 (☎ **787/725-8375**), where locals flock for food like the type their mamas used to make.

Don't be put off by the setting. We're not talking luxe here. Established in the mid-1970s by Pedro and his wife, Aïda, two self-professed *jibaros* (peasants), the restaurant is a dive complete with the mandatory fluorescent lighting, vinyl tablecloths, and even blinking Christmas bulbs (at any time of the year). The waiter, as one diner recently observed, is likely to take out his toothpick and lay it on your table as he scribbles down your menu selections for the evening. Even Sifredo, the restaurant's most visible assistant, claims to be a jibaro; he's both proud and amused by the word's hillbilly implications.

Stick to the simple dishes and you'll rarely go wrong here. We sampled the lamb stew on a recent occasion and found it perfectly seasoned and tender. Other specialties that have endured over time are the yellow rice with green beans and shredded pork, shrimp with garlic sauce, and several kinds of mofongo. The nicest part for last: your final tab, which is invariably inexpensive. Main courses range from $7 to $12.50, and American Express, Diners Club, MasterCard, and Visa are accepted. El Jibarito is open Monday to Thursday from 7am to 7pm, and Friday to Saturday from 8:30am to 9pm.

✪ **El Patio de Sam.** Calle San Sebastián 102 (across from the Iglesia de San José). ☎ **787/723-1149.** Main courses $17.50–$22; sandwiches, burgers, salads $7.50–$12. AE, DC, DISC, MC, V. Sun–Thurs 11am–midnight, Fri–Sat 11am–1:30am. Bus: A7, T1, or 2. AMERICAN/PUERTO RICAN.

This popular gathering spot for American expatriates, journalists, and shopkeepers is known for having the best burgers in San Juan. Even though the dining room is indoors, you'll swear you're dining alfresco: every table is placed near a cluster of potted plants, and canvas panels and awnings cover the skylight. The burgers are your best bet here, since some visitors have written us that the food was overpriced and the service confused. Nevertheless, it remains Old Town's most popular dining room. They have live entertainment Monday through Saturday, with a guitarist playing Spanish music some nights, a classical pianist on other nights. The prices appear steep here, but the burger plates with a lot of extras are filling meals for under $20.

INEXPENSIVE

Butterfly People Café. Calle Fortaleza 152. ☎ **787/723-2432.** Main courses $4.50–$10. AE, DC, MC, V. Mon–Sat 10am–6pm. Bus: A7, T1, or 2. CONTINENTAL/AMERICAN.

This restaurant is on the second floor of a restored mansion next to the world's largest gallery devoted to butterflies. Wherever you look, thousands of framed butterflies will delight or horrify you (depending on how you feel about these beautiful insects). You can dine at one of the 15 tables inside the cafe, which overlooks a courtyard. The cuisine is tropical and light European fare made with fresh ingredients. You might begin with gazpacho or vichyssoise, follow with quiche or one of the daily specials, and finish with chocolate mousse or the tantalizing raspberry chiffon pie with fresh raspberry sauce. A full bar offers tropical specialties such as piña coladas, fresh-squeezed Puerto Rican orange juice, and Fantasias, a frappé of seven fresh fruits.

Café Berlin. Calle San Francisco 407. ☎ **787/722-5205.** Main courses $3.75–$16.95. AE, MC, V. Mon–Fri 10am–11pm, Sat–Sun 9am–11pm. Bus: A5. INTERNATIONAL/VEGETARIAN.

This indoor-outdoor cafe-style restaurant overlooking plaza de Colón is a beloved favorite of locals. No one is quite sure how it got its name because this cafe is not German; instead, it's known for its vegetarian dishes, including a special eggplant tofu sandwich with the works. You can also order chicken and turkey dishes, along with a delectable mahimahi. Salmon, shrimp, and most definitely quiche appear on the menu. You can make up various combinations of dishes. The cafe specializes in fresh bread, used in its tasty lunch sandwiches. You can also drop in for breakfast to sample homemade pastries.

El Buen Samaritano. Calle Luna 255 (near San Justo St.). ☎ **787/721-6184.** Reservations not accepted. Platters and main courses $4–$8. No credit cards. Daily 7am–6pm. Bus: A5. PUERTO RICAN.

Only the most experimental foreign tourists would venture in here, despite the fact that its format provides lots of insights into the subculture of this thriving inner-city neighborhood. In fact, we have included this authentic little eatery to answer the often-posed question "Where do the locals dine?" It stands adjacent to the back door of city hall, near the corner of San Justo Street, on one of our favorite "back-water" streets of the historic Old Town. Almost no English is spoken, it's as Creole and ethnic as anything on the island, and it contains no more than four well-scrubbed tables in a setting Hemingway would have praised. Everything is predictably filling and starchy, including roast pork with yellow rice and beans or a fillet of red snapper in pungent tomato sauce. The menu, which depends largely on whatever was available in the marketplace that morning, will be recited lethargically by a member of the family who owns this tiny hole-in-the-wall. Except during the midday crush, no one will mind if you opt for just a cup of thick Puerto Rican coffee, a beer, or a soda, which you'll consume beneath the high rafters of a building from the Old Town's dimly remembered colonial past.

Hard Rock Café. Calle Recinto Sur 253. ☎ **787/724-7625.** Main courses $7–$17. AE, MC, V. Daily 11:30am–midnight. (Bar, daily 11am–2am.) Bus: A7, T1, or 2. AMERICAN.

Serving a "classic" American cuisine against a backdrop of loud rock music, this member of the American chain packs in the crowds for drinks, burgers, and T-shirts. Check out the chain's trademark rock 'n' roll memorabilia ranging from a wig worn by Elton John to a jacket that once encased the torso of John Lennon. There's also a Pink Floyd guitar and Phil Collins' drumsticks, plus artifacts from Elvis Presley, Jimi Hendrix, and the Beatles. Well-stuffed sandwiches and juicy burgers are served throughout the day, although many prefer to head here for dinner, filling up on fajitas, barbecued chicken, pork ribs, or even the catch of the day. The chili will set you ablaze.

✪ La Bombonera. Calle San Francisco 259. ☎ **787/722-0658.** Reservations recommended. Main courses $6.45–$17.75; American breakfast $5. AE, DISC, MC, V. Daily 7:30am–8pm. Bus: M2, M3, or T1. PUERTO RICAN.

This favorite, which offers exceptional value at affordable prices, was established in 1902 and has been offering homemade pastries and endless cups of coffee amid traditional colonial decor ever since. Its sandwiches are the most well-stuffed in town. For decades it was a rendezvous for the island's literati and for Old San Juan families, but now it has been discovered by foreign visitors. Its atmosphere evokes

turn-of-the-century Castile transplanted to the New World. The food is authentically homemade Puerto Rican, including rice with squid, roast leg of pork, and
seafood asopao. For dessert, you might select an apple, pineapple, or prune pie, or
one of many types of flan. Service is polite, if a bit rushed, and the place fills up
quickly at lunchtime.

La Mallorquina. Calle San Justo 207. ☎ **787/722-3261.** Reservations not accepted at
lunch, recommended at dinner. Main courses $13.95–$23.95 at dinner. AE, MC, V. Mon–Sat
11:30am–10pm. Bus: A7, T1, or 2. PUERTO RICAN.

San Juan's oldest restaurant was founded in 1848. It's in a three-story, glassed-in
courtyard with arches and antique wall clocks. The food seems little changed over
the decades; visit here for tradition and exceptional value rather than innovation.
The chef specializes in asopao, the most typical Puerto Rican rice dish. You can have
it with chicken, shrimp, or lobster and shrimp. Arroz con pollo is almost as popular. Begin with garlic soup or gazpacho. Other worthy main dishes are grilled pork
chop with fried plantain, beef tenderloin Puerto Rican style, and assorted seafood
stewed in wine. Paella is an enduring favorite. Lunch is busy; dinners are sometimes
quiet. Most of the main courses are priced at the lower end of the scale, and main
dishes come with a lot of extras, including rice and beans, so a filling feast can cost
less than $15. Appetizers aren't really needed except for gargantuan appetites. Even
if you've already eaten elsewhere, you might want to stop by for a drink at the old-
fashioned wooden bar.

NoNo's. Calle San Sebastián 100 (at Calle Cristo). ☎ **787/725-7819.** Hamburgers and main
courses $3.95–$12.95. AE, MC, V. Daily 11am–7:30pm. (Bar, daily 11am–4am.) Bus: A7, T1,
or 2. AMERICAN/FAST FOOD.

In the heart of Old San Juan in a 2-century-old building, NoNo's brings Stateside
food to those eager for a taste of the salads, mozzarella sticks, three-decker sandwiches, chicken-fried steaks, hamburgers (here called NoNo burgers), and onion
rings. You'll sit beneath a beamed ceiling, near a large and accommodating bar
where folks seem only peripherally interested in the food.

3 Puerta de Tierra

Caribe Hilton. Calle Los Rosales. ☎ **787/721-0303.** Reservations recommended. All-you-
can-eat buffet brunch $38.50 for adults, $18.50 for children under 10. AE, DC, MC, V. Sun
only 12:30–4pm. Bus: A7. INTERNATIONAL.

Every Sunday the Hilton's brunch captivates the imagination of island residents and
U.S. visitors with its combination of excellently prepared food, glamour, and entertainment. There's a clown to keep the children amused, as well as live music on the
bandstand for anyone who cares to dance. Champagne is included in the price.
Food is arranged at several different stations: Puerto Rican food, seafood, paella,
ribs, cold cuts, steaks, pastas, and salads. Afterward, you might like to stroll amid
the boutiques and seafront facilities of this famous hotel.

4 Condado

VERY EXPENSIVE

La Scala. In the Radisson Ambassador Plaza Hotel & Casino, 1369 Ashford Ave. ☎ **787/
721-7300.** Reservations recommended. Main courses $16.95–$36. AE, MC, V. Tues–Fri
noon–3pm and daily 5:30–11:30pm. Bus: A7. NORTHERN ITALIAN.

One of the most sophisticated Italian restaurants in San Juan caters to discerning
diners who appreciate the nuances of fine cuisine and service. The decor includes

neutral colors, stucco arches, and murals. The menu lists just about the entire repertoire of northern Italian cuisine. You'll find a specialty version of Caesar salad, fresh
mushrooms in garlic sauce, and a succulent half-melted version of fresh mozzarella
in carozza. The fresh fish and seafood are flown in from New York and Boston. Specialties include fresh halibut cooked in parchment, rigatoni with shiitake mushrooms and ricotta, and rack of lamb in a red wine sauce. Most meals here are
memorable, and the cookery, for the most part, is creative and delicate. Service is
attentive.

✪ **Ramiro's.** Av. Magdalena 1106. ☎ **787/721-9049.** Reservations recommended
off-season, required in winter. Main courses $23–$35; 5-course fixed-price
meal $59.95. AE, DC, MC, V. Mon–Thurs noon–3pm and 6:30–10:30pm, Fri noon–3pm
and 6:30–11pm, Sat 6:30–11pm, Sun noon–3pm and 6–10pm. Bus: A7, T1, or 2.
SPANISH/CREOLE/INTERNATIONAL.

In a half-century-old building near the Marriott Hotel, you'll find a refined cuisine
and a touch of Old Spain. The menu is the most imaginative on the Condado and
features "New Creole" cooking, a style pioneered by owner and chef Jesús Ramiro.
You might begin with breadfruit mille-feuille with local crabmeat and avocado. For
your main course, any fresh fish or meat can be charcoal-grilled for you on request.
Some of the specialties include paillard of lamb with spiced root vegetables and
guava sauce, char-grilled black Angus steak with shiitake mushrooms, or grilled
striped sea bass with a citrus sauce. Among the many homemade desserts are
caramelized mango on puff pastry with strawberry-and-guava sauce and "four seasons" chocolate.

Ristorante Capriccio. On the mezzanine level of the Condado Plaza Resort, 999 Ashford
Ave. ☎ **787/721-1000.** Reservations recommended. Main courses $14–$40. AE, DC, DISC,
MC, V. Daily noon–10pm. Bus: A7. ITALIAN.

Despite the superb service of an international staff, this restaurant is surprisingly
unpretentious. Much of this is because of the tact and charm of its Provence-born
director, Roger Duperray, whose Italian cuisine is refined and superbly prepared.
This is the kind of place where big business deals are clinched. On the mezzanine
level, tables overlook an ocean view that seems to stretch all the way to Spain. Soft
lighting, stiff drinks, and well-chosen wines add to the ambiance. The menu pro-
poses a half-dozen kinds of pasta, including *linguine Redina* enriched with seafood
and cream sauce; medaillons of veal with porcini mushrooms and marsala sauce;
medaillons of filet mignon "Cavour," layered with prosciutto, eggplant, and mozzarella; breast of chicken Boscaiolo, served with chestnuts, mushrooms, and
asparagus; lobster Fra Diavola; a roster of grilled fish prepared the way you like it;
and a succulent version of *cioppino*, a fish stew made in the style of Genoa with lots
of shellfish and spices. This restaurant reduces the price of everything on the menu
(except fish, shellfish, and both alcoholic and non-alcoholic drinks) by 50% every
day between noon and 6:30pm. That basically creates a "sunset special" every day
for folks looking for a bargain. Accordingly, the texture of the restaurant is radically
different between the day and night shifts.

EXPENSIVE

The Chart House. 1214 Ashford Ave. ☎ **787/724-0110.** Reservations recommended
Mon–Fri, required Sat–Sun. Main courses $16.50–$40. AE, DC, DISC, MC, V. Sun–Thurs
5–11:30pm, Fri–Sat 5pm–12:15am. Bus: A7, T1, or 2. STEAK/SEAFOOD.

This member of the restaurant chain based in California attracts hundreds of locals
on any night. It's housed in a lattice-trimmed villa built in 1910. Today the heavy
ceiling beams have been exposed, track lighting has been installed, and paintings

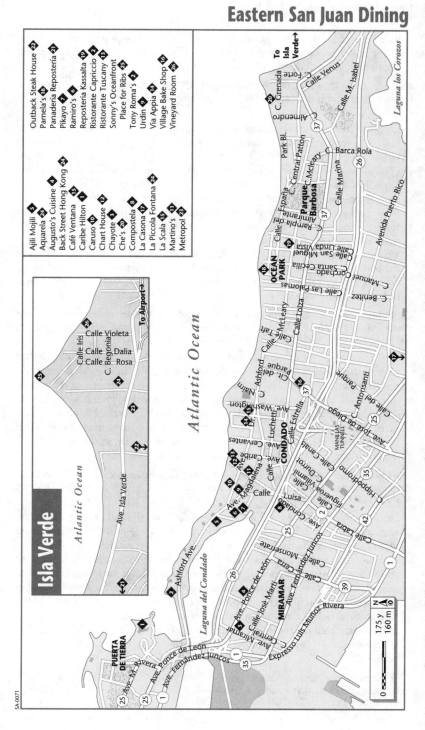

Outback Steak House 22
Pamela's 18
Panadería Repostería 21
Pikayo 7
Ramiro's 6
Repostería Kassalta 19
Ristorante Capriccio 2
Ristorante Tuscany 13
Sonny's Oceanfront
Place for Ribs 25
Tony Roma's 2
Urdin 9
Via Appia 14
Village Bake Shop 5
Vineyard Room 28

Ajili Mojili 5
Aquarela 24
Augusto's Cuisine 4
Back Street Hong Kong 22
Café Ventana 15
Caribe Hilton 1
Caruso 10
Chart House 12
Chayote 3
Che's 20
Compostela 8
La Casona 17
La Piccola Fontana 24
La Scala 15
Martino's 17
Metropol 23

Isla Verde

Atlantic Ocean

Calle Violeta
Calle Iris
Calle Begonia
Calle · Dalia
Calle · Rosa
C. Begonia

To Airport→

Ave. Isla Verde

Atlantic Ocean

Laguna del Condado

Ashford Ave.

Laguna del Condado

PUERTA DE TIERRA

Ave. Ponce de León
Ave. M. Rivera
Ave. Fernández Juncos

Ave. Miramar
Ave. Central
Calle José Martí

MIRAMAR

Calle Cerra
Ave. Ponce de León
Calle Fernández Vilamil

Expresso Luis Muñoz Rivera

Ave. Fernández Juncos

CONDADO

Ave. Ashford
Calle del Parque
Ave. Washington
Calle McLeary
Calle Loíza
Calle Taft

OCEAN PARK

Calle Las Palomas
Calle Santa Cecilia
C. Manuel Corchado
C. Benítez
Calle Cervantes
Luchetti
Calle Caribe
Ave. Magdalena
Calle Luisa
Ave. Condado
Calle Canals
Calle Estrella
Calle Cervantes
Calle Vendig
Calle Durtot
Calle Higuero Vilamil

Parque Barbosa
Ave. José de Diego
Calle C. Antonsanti
Parque del Parque
Ave. José de Diego

Calle San Miguel
Calle Linda Vista
Rampla del Almirante
Ampla del Almirante
Calle España

C. Central-Patton
C. McLeary
C. Barca Rola
Calle Marina

C. Grenada
C. Forte
Calle Venus
Calle M. Isabel

Laguna los Corozos

Avenida Puerto Rico

To Isla Verde→

Almendro
Park Bl.

MANILLAS TUNNEL

Hippódromo

Calle Labra

N

0   175 y
         160 m

SA-0071

have been added to create a warm ambiance. The food is well prepared. Prime rib is a specialty here. You can also order tuna fillet, seafood pasta, top sirloin, live Nicaraguan lobster, Alaskan king crab, and a copious salad.

Chayote. In the Olimpo Hotel, Av. Miramar 603. ☎ **787/722-9385.** Reservations recommended. Main courses $16–$21. AE, MC, V. Mon–Sat 7–10:30pm. Bus: 5. PUERTO RICAN/INTERNATIONAL.

Chayote's cuisine is among the most innovative in San Juan. It draws local business leaders, government officials, and film stars such as Sylvester Stallone and Melanie Griffith. The setting is a modern, basement-level, peach-colored enclave in the Olimpo, an obscure hotel. Some aspects of the place might remind you of an artsy bistro in New York City or Washington, D.C. The restaurant changes its menu every 3 months. Chances are you'll find such appetizers as a yucca turnover stuffed with crabmeat and served with a mango and papaya chutney, corn tamales with shrimp in a coconut sauce, or ripe plantain stuffed with chicken and served with a fresh tomato sauce. For a main dish, you might try a red snapper fillet with a citrus vinaigrette made of passion fruit, orange, and lemon. An exotic touch appears in the pork fillet seasoned with dried fruits and spices in a tamarind sauce and served with a green banana and taro root timbale. There's nothing better than the mango flan served with macerates strawberries to finish off the meal.

✪ Compostela. Av. Condado 106. ☎ **787/724-6088.** Reservations required. Main courses $19–$32.95. AE, DC, MC, V. Mon–Fri noon–3pm and 6:30–10:30pm, Sat 6–11pm. Bus: 2. SPANISH/PUERTO RICAN.

This restaurant's formality is largely derived from the battalion of well-dressed waiters whose manners evoke Old Spain. Established by a Galician-born family, the pine-trimmed restaurant has gained a reputation as one of the best in the capital. The chef made his name on his roast peppers stuffed with salmon mousse. Equally delectable is duck with orange and ginger sauce or baby rack of lamb with fresh herbs. Any shellfish grilled in a brandy sauce is a sure winner, and the chef makes two different versions of paella, both savory. The wine cellar, storing some 10,000 bottles, is one of the most impressive in San Juan.

Martino's. In the Diamond Palace Hotel & Casino, Av. Condado 55. ☎ **787/722-5256.** Reservations recommended. Main courses $18–$38. AE, DC, MC, V. Daily 5:30–11:30pm. Bus: A7. NORTHERN ITALIAN.

Martino's offers some of the finest service on the Condado and a classic Italian cuisine, centered primarily in the north of Italy, especially Lombardy. It's the domain of chef and owner Martin Acosta. His restaurant's picture windows open onto views of the Atlantic and the night lights of the Condado. Appetizers include hot seafood antipasti and Caesar and spinach salads. The Caesar salad is made at tableside with real panache. You can order one of the homemade pasta dishes for a main course or else roam the menu, finding such appetizing dishes as seafood suprême, vitello Martino (with shrimp), gnocchi with cream sauce and Parmesan, and filet mignon Monnalisa, which is flambéed at your table. In fact, almost any dish can receive a tableside flambé if you want. Good and reasonably priced wines add to the dining pleasure.

✪ Pikayo. In the Tanama Princess Hotel, 1 Calle Joffre. ☎ **787/721-6194.** Reservations recommended. Main courses $25–$36. AE, MC, V. Mon–Sat 6–10:30pm. Closed 2 weeks in Dec–Jan. Bus: T1. PUERTO RICAN/CAJUN.

This is an ideal place to go for the new generation of Puerto Rican cookery, with a touch of Cajun thrown in for spice and zest. This place not only keeps up with the latest culinary trends, but often sets them. On the lobby level of the Tanama Princess Hotel on the Condado, the dining room is lined with mahogany, varnished cherry, and light pastel shades of turquoise and green. Formal but not stuffy, Pikayo is a specialist in the criolla cuisine of colonial Puerto Rico, emphasizing the Spanish, Indian, and African elements in its unusual recipes. A staff member, perhaps chef Wilo Benet or his wife, Lorraine, will advise you on such traditional dishes as mofongo (plantains layered with shrimp and served with saffron-flavored broth), *viandas* (mashed tropical tubers), *tostones* (fritters made from green plantains) stuffed with codfish or cheese, or crabmeat stew. One innovative main course is fresh red snapper with a plantain crust flavored with a white wine reduction. Most main courses are accompanied with the staff of life in the criolla world: *arroz y habichuelas coloradas* (white rice and beans). Especially delicious is seared yellowfin tuna with fresh onions.

✪ **Ristorante Tuscany.** In the San Juan Marriott Resort, 1309 Ashford Ave. ☎ **787/722-7000.** Reservations recommended. Main courses $12.50–$28. AE, DC, DISC, MC, V. Daily 6–11pm. Bus: A7. NORTHERN ITALIAN.

Richly accessorized with mahogany and granite, this is the showcase restaurant of one of the most elaborate hotel reconstructions in Puerto Rico's history. In 1995, its team of chefs swept most of the first prizes at the annual Culinary Exposition, a contest held by the Puerto Rico Tourism Association, and *San Juan City Magazine* voted it the city's best hotel restaurant in 1997. You'll have lots of choices here, including a range of gourmet pizzas prepared in a wood-burning oven tucked into one corner.

The chef doesn't skimp on ingredients, and he prepares such elegant selections as a veal chop with a Brunnelo Tuscan red wine sauce, or seafood casserole with shrimp, scallops, and prawns with tomato sauce. There are several appealing pastas, such as ravioli filled with lobster and herbs (served with a leek and saffron sauce), or a trio of risottos that can be ordered as an appetizer or a main course. Sirloin steak Florentine style arrives perfectly cooked.

MODERATE

✪ **Ajili Mójili.** 1052 Ashford Ave. (at the corner of Calle Joffre). ☎ **787/725-9195.** Reservations recommended. Main courses $16–$34. AE, MC, V. Mon–Thurs 6–10pm, Fri–Sat 6–11pm, Sun 5–10pm. Bus: A7. PUERTO RICAN/CRÉOLE.

Set in the heart of the Condado, across from the Convention Center, this is the only restaurant in San Juan's tourist zone devoted exclusively to la cocina criolla, the starchy, sometimes greasy cuisine that developed on the island a century ago. Despite the relative modernity of the building, look for artfully battered replicas of the kind of crumbling brick walls you'd expect in Old San Juan, and a bar that evokes something you'd have found in a Spanish colony a century ago. The staff will willingly describe menu items in colloquial English. Locals come here for a taste of the food they enjoyed at their mother's knee, and a meal here might afford insights into the island's culture. Examples include mofongos (green plantains stuffed with veal, chicken, shrimp, or pork), arroz con pollo (stewed chicken with saffron rice), *medallones de cerdo encebollado* (pork loin sautéed with onions), *carne mechada* (beef rib eye stuffed with ham), and *lechon asado con maposteado* (roast pork with rice and beans), the last of which is offered only during the cooler months from December through April. The preferred accompaniment for this hearty island fare? Ice-cold bottles of local beer, such as Medalla. Most dishes are priced at the lower end of the scale, and portions are so large you can skip the appetizers.

⚐ Family-Friendly Restaurants

Caribe Hilton *(see p. 127)*   The Sunday brunch here—which is half price for children—is an all-you-can-eat buffet. There's even a clown on hand to keep the kids entertained.

Hard Rock Café *(see p. 126)*   The local branch of this international chain is a sure-fire hit with kids (and despite the hype, the burgers are pretty good).

Butterfly People Café *(see p. 125)*   Children love eating lunch in this fantasy world of mounted butterflies. A favorite drink is Fantasia—a frappé made from seven fresh fruits.

Urdin. Av. Magdalena 1105. ☎ **787/724-0420.** Reservations recommended. Main courses $14.95–$33.95. AE, MC, V. Daily noon–midnight. Bus: A7. PUERTO RICAN/ INTERNATIONAL.

Urdin is proud of the reputation it has built as one of the capital's bright young restaurants. It occupies a low-slung, stucco-covered house set near a slew of competitors near the Condado. Inside, a fanciful decor of postmodern, Caribbean-inspired accents and cut-out metal sculpture brings a touch of Latino New York. Filled with authentic Spanish flavor that's not necessarily geared to the palates of timid diners, the food is innovative, flavorful, strong, opinionated, and earthy. For starters, there are baby eels Bilbaina style or a Castilian lentil soup. Main courses include fresh fillet of salmon in a mustard sauce, fillet of fish "Hollywood style" (with onions, raisins, and mango slices served in a white wine sauce), ostrich in a red wine sauce (opinion at our table was divided over this choice), and rack of lamb with an orange sauce. One always-pleasing dish is piquillo peppers stuffed with a seafood mousse and black-olive sauce. Savvy locals finish their meal with a slice of sweet-potato cheesecake. The staff can diminish (if they're sulky) or enhance (if they're welcoming) a meal here.

INEXPENSIVE

Café Ventana. In the Radisson Ambassador Plaza Hotel & Casino, 1369 Ashford Ave. ☎ **787/721-7300.** Main courses $5–$19; full American breakfast $6–$12. AE, DC, MC, V. Daily 6:30am–11pm. Bus: A7. INTERNATIONAL.

On the lobby level of one of the best hotels of the Condado, this comfortable and cozy eatery for many years was the most famous Howard Johnson's in the Caribbean. It attracts some of the most prestigious politicians and financiers in Puerto Rico to its booths and tables (many luminaries live nearby and consider it their neighborhood diner). Depending on the time of day, you can be served pancakes, omelettes, muffins, hash-brown potatoes, and sausages; or you can order lunch and dinner foods such as fish fries, teriyaki steaks, clam platters, and an array of sandwiches and burgers, as well as typical Puerto Rican dishes. Although Howard Johnson's is long gone, the cafe still retains its many flavors of ice cream—in fact, the best selection on the Condado.

Caruso. 1104 Ashford Ave. ☎ **787/723-6876.** Main courses $7–$33; lunch platters $5–$10. AE, DC, MC, V. Daily noon–11pm. Bus: A5. ITALIAN.

Its decor and the brisk efficiency of its staff might remind you of a neighborhood trattoria in New York City, and in fact it's become the preferred neighborhood restaurant of many Condado residents who hail from New York. It's one of the most popular places around for pasta, partly because of its low prices and partly because of its simple but down-to-earth food. Menu items include shrimp scampi, filet mignon, veal piccata, veal marsala, and grilled fish of the day. If featured, the antipasti is a good bet, as is the carpaccio of salmon.

Tony Roma's. In the Condado Plaza Hotel, 999 Ashford Ave. ☎ **787/721-1000,** ext. 2123. Reservations not accepted. Main courses $7.85–$19.85. AE, DC, DISC, MC, V. Daily noon–midnight. Bus: A7. BARBECUE.

Efficient and unpretentious, this is Puerto Rico's busiest branch of the international chain and one of the least expensive restaurants in the Condado. It's well appreciated for its spicy barbecued food (the honey barbecue is not as fiery). Menu items include a wide range of barbecued dishes, such as chicken and several varieties of ribs, as well as hamburgers and the famous Tony Roma onion ring loaf. The most expensive item in the house, reasonably priced at less than $20, is a combination platter containing several kinds of ribs with all the fixings—a meal in itself that's a particularly good value in this high-price neighborhood.

Via Appia. 1350 Ashford Ave. ☎ **787/725-8711.** Pizza $8.95–$14.95; main courses $8.95–$14.95. AE, MC, V. Mon–Fri 11am–11pm, Sat–Sun 11am–midnight. Bus: A5. ITALIAN.

A favorite of *sanjuaneros* visiting Condado for the day, Via Appia offers food that's sometimes praiseworthy. Its pizzas are the best in the neighborhood. The chef's signature pizza Via Appia is a savory pie made with sausages, onions, mushrooms, pepperoni, green peppers, cheese, and spices. Vegetarians also have a pizza to call their own (made with whole-wheat dough, eggplant, mushrooms, green peppers, onions, tomatoes, and cheese). There's even a pizza with meatballs. Savory pasta dishes, including baked ziti, lasagne, and spaghetti with several of your favorite sauces, are also prepared. All of this can be washed down with sangría. During the day, freshly made salads or sandwiches are also available.

5 Santurce

✪ La Casona. Calle San Jorge 609 (at the corner of Av. Fernández Juncos). ☎ **787/727-2717.** Reservations required. Main courses $24–$45. AE, DC, MC, V. Mon–Fri noon–3pm and 6–11pm, Sat 6–11pm. Bus: 1. SPANISH/INTERNATIONAL.

La Casona offers the kind of dining usually found in Madrid, complete with a strolling guitarist. Since 1972, the chefs here have dispensed their special dishes in a turn-of-the-century mansion surrounded by gardens. The much-renovated but still-charming place draws some of the most fashionable diners on Puerto Rico. Paella marinara, prepared for two or more, is a specialty, as is *zarzuela de mariscos* (seafood medley). Or you might select fillet of grouper in Basque sauce, octopus vinaigrette, rabbit stew, or a rack of lamb. Grilled red snapper is a specialty, and you can order it with almost any sauce you want, although the chef recommends one made from olive oil, herbs, lemon, and pulverized toasted garlic. The cuisine has flair and flavor and is served with much effort and expense.

6 Miramar

✪ Augusto's Cuisine. In the Hotel Excelsior. 101 Av. Ponce de León, Miramar. ☎ **787/725-7700.** Reservations recommended. Main courses $25–$32; set menu $65–$80. AE, MC, V. Tues–Fri noon–3pm, Tues–Sat 7–9:30pm. Bus: 1. FRENCH/INTERNATIONAL.

This restaurant is firmly within the upper tier of the commonwealth's most elegant and glamorous restaurants, with a decidedly European texture that's hard to reproduce within larger, more anonymous restaurants. Austrian-born owner and chef Augusto Schreiner, assisted by a partly French-born staff, operates from a gray-and-green dining room set on the lobby level of a 15-story hotel in Miramar, the suburb near the island's main airport. Menu items, concocted from strictly fresh ingredients, include such dishes as lobster Rockefeller (cooked au gratin with spinach, bacon, and Parmesan cheese); rack of lamb with aromatic herbs and fresh garlic; an oft-changing cream-based soup of the day (one of the best is corn and fresh oyster soup); and a succulent version of medaillons of veal Rossini-style, prepared with foie gras and Madeira sauce. The wine list is as extensive as you'll find here.

7 Isla Verde

EXPENSIVE

✪ **Aquarela.** In the El San Juan Hotel & Casino, 6063 Isla Verde Ave. ☎ **787/253-5566.** Reservations recommended. Main courses $23–$36. AE, MC, V. Daily 6–11pm. Bus: A7, M7, or T1. NUEVA LATINA.

The cuisine at this restaurant, which has won several awards from the prestigious James Beard Foundation, is so avant-garde and unusual that tables are reserved several days in advance by sophisticated gastronomes. You could be utterly baffled by the combination of references and culinary techniques from around the world, but fortunately the staff is adept at describing the various offerings. The establishment's creator is Douglas Rodriguez, one of Puerto Rico's most celebrated chefs, whose earlier successes included the Restaurant Patria in New York City. You'll dine overlooking a view of the hotel's swimming pool and the sea, amid marble floors and a pastel-colored rendering of the underwater life of a teeming reef. A particularly succulent beginning for any meal here involves sampling the restaurant's two kinds of ceviche, the succulent citrus-and-ginger–infused portions of raw fish that taste so delicious in hot climates. One version is made solely from scallops and salmon; the other, from a medley of mixed fish and shellfish. Other menu items change with the seasons and the chef's inspiration, but they are likely to include such dishes as lobster enchiladas, grilled Chilean sea bass with yucca, sweet corn relish, and spinach; plantain-encrusted dorado with marinated cabbage, smoked shrimp, and tamarind-flavored tartar sauce; a succulent version of paella that includes *chorizo* sausage and one of the most diverse collections of shellfish in Puerto Rico; and a "twisted" version of skirt steak served with mashed root vegetables and black-bean broth. Dessert might include a "smokeless cigar," a torpedo-shaped specialty made from chocolate truffles, white chocolate, and mocha-flavored ice cream, and "edible" matches.

Back Street Hong Kong. In El San Juan Hotel & Casino, Isla Verde Ave. ☎ **787/791-1000,** ext. 1758. Reservations recommended. Main courses $16.50–$31.50. AE, MC, V. Daily 6pm–midnight. Bus: A7, M7, or T1. MANDARIN/SZECHUAN/HUNAN.

To reach this restaurant, head down a re-creation of a backwater street in Hong Kong—disassembled from its original home at the 1964 New York World's Fair. It was rebuilt here with its original design intact. A few steps later you enter one of the best Chinese restaurants in the Caribbean, serving consistently good food, filled with fragrance and flavor. Beneath a soaring redwood ceiling, you can enjoy pineapple fried rice served in a real pineapple, a version of scallops with orange sauce, Szechuan beef with chicken, or a Dragon and Phoenix (lobster mixed with shrimp).

✪ **La Piccola Fontana.** In El San Juan Hotel & Casino, 6063 Isla Verde Ave.
☎ **787/791-1000,** ext. 1271. Reservations required. Main courses $17–$35. AE, MC, V. Daily 6pm–midnight. Bus: A7, M7, or T1. NORTHERN ITALIAN.

Right off the luxurious Palm Court in El San Juan Hotel, this restaurant delivers plate after plate of delectable and extremely well-prepared northern Italian cuisine nightly. You'll dine in one of two neo-Palladian dining rooms whose wall frescoes, painted by a visiting French artist a few years ago, depict Italy's ruins and landscapes at their most appealing. Menu items range from the appealingly straightforward and simple (grilled fillets of fish or grilled veal chops) to more elaborate dishes such as tortellini San Daniele, made with veal, prosciutto, cream, and sage; or linguine scogliere, with shrimps, clams, and seafood. Scallopine of veal is delicious with lemon and white wine sauce, and grilled medaillons of filet mignon are served with braised arugula, Parmesan cheese, and balsamic vinegar.

✪ **Vineyard Room.** The Ritz-Carlton, 6961 State Rd. #187, Isla Verde, Carolina. ☎ **787/253-1700.** Reservations required. Main courses $30–$45. AE, DC, MC, V. Daily 7pm–midnight. Bus: A7, M7, or T1. CALIFORNIAN/MEDITERRANEAN.

The Ritz's fine restaurant offers dinner in a charming setting reminiscent of a Napa Valley winery. The room's decor features rich red and gold fabrics, Frette linens, and dark etimoe-wood paneling. The Californian-Mediterranean cuisine is complemented by an extensive selection of California, French, German, South American, and additional Stateside wines. The menu is forever refreshing and will excite you with its possibilities. Each dish seems to be more agreeable than the next, and the staff is the best trained on island.

We have made an entire menu from the cold and hot appetizers. Launch yourself into the repast with Bacardi-marinated salmon in a cucumber dill salad, which manages to wed Puerto Rican and Scandinavian culinary traditions. The salad of sesame, seaweed, and seared scallops is surpassed only by the black truffle and sweetbread medaillons. Always count on two tempting soups a night, perhaps cream of frog's legs with sweet garlic petals. Main dishes are wisely limited, but quite exquisite, going from a braised leg of rabbit with wild mushrooms and sultanas to fillet of turbot with a saffron cracked wheat crush and crayfish. Slow-roasted veal cheek appears with two types of beans, and mild-fed lamb rack is served with a spice rub, ravioli, and French beans. Save room for dessert, which might be a trio of crème brûlée or else green lime sabayon with a light tuile and berries. You'll feel like Dolores Del Rio ordering the roast pineapple with coconut ice cream and rum sauce. The best of Puerto Rican coffee finishes off many a meal.

MODERATE

Outback Steak House. In the Embassy Suites Hotel & Casino, 8000 José M. Tartak St. ☎ **787/791-4679.** Reservations not accepted. Main courses $11–$23. AE, MC, V. Mon–Thurs 5:30–10:30pm, Fri–Sat 5:30pm–midnight; Sun 2–10pm. Bus: T1. STEAKS.

This Puerto Rican branch of the two-fisted, Australian-themed restaurant chain occupies a dark-paneled room with booths positioned around a prominent bar area. Here you can study memorabilia devoted to the Land Down Under while ordering such drinks as a genuinely delicious Wallabee Darn. There's a simple steak-and-potato-with-salad special priced at $11, a cost-conscious meal in itself. But more appealing are some of the chain's signature dishes, such as a Blooming Onion (a batter-dipped deep-fried onion that fans out from its platter like a demented lotus and tastes delicious with beer); at least four kinds of steaks, including filet mignon; fish, including mahimahi and salmon; and our favorite of the lot, Alice

Springs chicken, a breast of chicken layered with bacon, mushrooms, and cheese, and served with honey-mustard sauce and french fries.

INEXPENSIVE

Metropol. Av. Isla Verde. ☎ **787/791-4046.** Main courses $7.95–$28.95. AE, DC, DISC, MC, V. Daily 11am–7pm. BUS: 1. CUBAN/PUERTO RICAN/INTERNATIONAL.

Part of a restaurant chain known for serving the island's best Cuban food, Metropol is the happiest blend of Cuban and Puerto Rican cuisines we've ever discovered. The black-bean soup is among the island's finest, served in the classic Havana style with a side dish of rice and chopped onions. Main courses are likely to include Cornish game hen stuffed with Cuban rice and beans, or perhaps marinated steak topped with a fried egg (reportedly Castro's favorite). Smoked chicken or chicken fried steak are also heartily recommended. Endless garlic bread accompanies most dinners, portions are huge, and plantains, yucca, and other good stuff accompany most dishes. Finish with a choice of thin or firm custard.

Panadería Repostería. Centro Villamar. ☎ **787/727-3860.** Reservations not accepted. Sandwiches $3.50–$6. AE, DISC, MC, V. Daily 6am–10pm. Bus: A5 or T1. SANDWICHES/COFFEES.

We believe that whenever a restaurant becomes famous for one item, it's worth walking across town just to sample it. That's the case with the Panadería Repostería, which is said to make the Puerto Rican capital's definitive Cuban sandwich—a cheap meal in itself for budget travelers. Consisting of sliced, baked pork packed in crusty bread, it's about the only thing offered except for drinks and coffee dispensed from behind a much-used bar. There's also an assortment of gourmet items from Spain, which are arranged as punctuation marks on shelves set against an otherwise all-white decor. The place has been serving simple breakfasts, drinks, coffee, and Cuban sandwiches virtually every day, in very much the same format, since it opened around 1970.

✪ Sonny's Oceanfront Place for Ribs. In the Empress Oceanfront Hotel, 2 Amapola St. ☎ **787/791-3083.** Main courses $7.95–$29.95. AE, DC, DISC, MC, V. Daily 8am–11pm. Bus: T1 or M8. AMERICAN.

This restaurant overlooks the sea and the hotel's terraced swimming pool, opening onto one of San Juan's best nighttime views, made more glamorous by the glittering lights from all the resorts. The cuisine is unpretentious and guaranteed to satisfy hunger pangs for American-style burgers. Several types of barbecued ribs are among the island's most flavorful, always cooked to perfection and seasoned with the most savory of sauces. You can also order pastas and barbecued chicken. More formal dishes include surf and turf, catch of the day, or lobster. Most items are served with the house version of cole slaw and beans.

Village Bake Shop. 105 Jose de Diego Ave. ☎ **787/724-8566.** Pastas $12.95–$15.95; sandwiches $7.95–$8.95. AE, MC, V. Wed–Sat 7:30am–6pm, Sun 7:30am–5pm. Bus: 1. INTERNATIONAL.

At first glance the prices here seem a bit high, but one plate of pasta is a meal unto itself. The bake shop also features the area's most well-stuffed sandwiches. Incidentally, you might want to stock up on some of its excellent and freshly baked pastries to take back to your room.

8 Ocean Park

✪ **Pamela's.** In the Número Uno Guest House, Calle Santa Ana 1, Ocean Park.
☎ **787/726-5010.** Reservations required. Main courses $14–$20. AE, MC, V. Daily
noon–3:30pm and 7–10:30pm. Bus: T1. CARIBBEAN FUSION.

You would hardly expect this inexpensive guesthouse (see chapter 5) to be the venue
for some of San Juan's finest cuisine prepared by one of the best chefs in the
Caribbean, Pamela Hope Yahn, previously of the famous Ottley's Plantation on the
island of St. Kitts. For starters, we recommend her stuffed shrimp with a ginger
mousse or one of her delectable and original soups—perhaps spiced South American turkey, corn, and potato, served with an aji sauce, avocado, and sour cream.
For a main dish, her red snapper with baked stuffed mango, hearts of palm, and
both portabello and button mushrooms represents Caribbean dining at its finest.
You might also opt for the Jamaican-style roast loin of pork with candied ginger,
dark rum, cloves, lime, and garlic, accompanied by nutmeg-scented sweet potatoes.
The desserts are equally yummy.

Repostería Kassalta. Calle McLeary 1966. ☎ **787/727-7340.** Reservations not accepted.
Full American breakfast $3.50; soups $4; sandwiches $3.35–$4.35; pastries 75¢–$1.25 each.
AE, MC, V. Daily 6am–10pm. Bus: T1. SPANISH/PUERTO RICAN.

This is the most widely known of San Juan's cafeteria/bakery/delicatessens. You'll
enter a cavernous room flanked with modern sun-flooded windows and endless
ranks of glass-fronted display cases filled with meats, sausages, and pastries appropriate to Christmas, Easter, Thanksgiving, or whatever the forthcoming holiday.
Patrons line up at one end of the room to place their order at a cash register, then
carry their selections, cafeteria style, to one of the establishment's many tables. A
knowledge of Spanish is helpful but not essential. Among the selections offered are
steaming bowls of the best *caldo gallego* in Puerto Rico. Laden with collard greens,
potatoes, and sausage slices, accompanied by hunks of bread, and served in thick
earthenware bowls, this soup makes a meal in itself. Also popular are Cuban sandwiches (sliced pork, cheese, and fried bread), steak sandwiches, a savory octopus
salad, and an assortment of perfectly cooked omelettes. Paella Valenciano is a
Sunday favorite.

9 Punta Las Marias

Che's. Calle Caoba 35. ☎ **787/726-7202.** Reservations recommended for lunch, required
for dinner. Main courses $13–$25. AE, DC, MC, V. Sun–Thurs noon–midnight, Fri–Sat
noon–1am. Bus: T1. ARGENTINE/ITALIAN/INTERNATIONAL.

Named after the Latino revolutionary Che Guevara, this place re-creates some of
the color and drama of the Argentine pampas. It's about 2 miles east of Condado's
resorts. Many of the specialties are grilled in the style preferred by cowherding gau-
chos. If you're not in the mood for highly seasoned flank steak or any of the grilled
meats, you can choose a variety of pastas and veal dishes. Meats are very tender here
and well flavored.

7

Exploring San Juan

The Spanish began to settle in the area now known as Old San Juan around 1521. At the outset, the city was called Puerto Rico ("Rich Port"), and the whole island was known as San Juan.

The streets are narrow and teeming with traffic, but a walk through Old San Juan—in Spanish, *El Viejo San Juan*—is like a stroll through 5 centuries of history. You can do it in less than a day (see "Walking Tour: Old San Juan," below). In this historic 7-square-block area of the western side of the city, you can see many of Puerto Rico's chief sightseeing attractions and do some shopping along the way.

On the other hand, you may want to just plop yourself down on the sand with a tropical drink, or get outside and play. See section 3 of this chapter for details on all the beaches and active sports in the San Juan area.

MUSEUM HOURS

Many of the museums in Old San Juan close for lunch between 11:45am and 2pm, so schedule your activities accordingly if you intend to museum-hop.

SUGGESTED ITINERARIES

In case you would like to drag yourself away from the beach, here are some suggestions about how to see San Juan.

If You Have 1 Day

To make the most of a short stay, head immediately for Old San Juan for an afternoon of sightseeing and shopping. You should definitely schedule a visit inside El Morro Fortress. Try to spend 2 hours at Condado Beach. Enjoy a Puerto Rican dinner at a local restaurant, listen to some salsa music, and enjoy a rum punch before retiring for the night.

If You Have 2 Days

The first day spend the morning shopping and sightseeing in Old San Juan. Schedule interior visits to El Morro Fortress and San Juan Cathedral, then relax on Condado Beach for the rest of the day. Enjoy a Puerto Rican dinner and some local music before retiring.

On your second day spend the morning exploring El Yunque rain forest, a lush 28,000-acre site east of San Juan (see chapter 10). Schedule 2 or 3 hours at nearby Luquillo Beach, the finest on Puerto Rico. Buy lunch from one of the open-air kiosks. Return to San Juan for the evening, attending either a folk-culture show (if available) or a Las Vegas–style revue. Visit the casinos for some action before retiring.

1 Seeing the Sights

Although we have outlined a walking tour of Old San Juan later in this chapter, here is an introduction to some of the sights mentioned there, as well as others you may want to seek out yourself.

FORTS

✪ **Castillo San Felipe del Morro.** At the end of Calle Norzagaray. ☎ **787/729-6960.** Free admission. Daily 9am–5pm. Bus: T1 or M3.

Called "El Morro," this fort stands on a rocky promontory dominating the entrance to San Juan Bay. El Morro in time became the envy of both Europe and the Caribbean; it was known for its rich treasury and strategic position. Here Spanish Puerto Rico struggled to defend itself against the navies of Great Britain, France, and Holland, as well as hundreds of pirate ships that wreaked havoc throughout the colonial Caribbean. The fortress walls were designed as part of a network of defenses that made San Juan *La Ciudad Murada* (the Walled City).

The fortifications were financed by the Treasury of Mexico on orders from the King of Spain, beginning in 1539. Its design inspired by the French military strategist Vauban, El Morro repulsed attackers such as English privateer Sir Francis Drake, who bombarded it in 1595, and a much larger English armada in 1797. The American navy finally took El Morro during the Spanish-American War of 1898.

The original fort was a round tower, which can still be seen deep inside the lower levels of the castle. More walls and cannon-firing positions were added, and by 1787 the fortification attained the complex design you see today.

The National Park Service protects the fortifications of Old San Juan, which have been declared a World Heritage Site by the United Nations. Not only does it enjoy some of the most dramatic views in the Caribbean, but El Morro also is an intriguing labyrinth of dungeons, barracks, vaults, lookouts, and ramps. Historical and background information is provided in a video in English and Spanish shown to fort visitors. Sometimes park rangers lead hour-long tours free, although you can visit on your own. The nearest parking is the underground facility beneath the Quincentennial Plaza at the Ballajá barracks (Cuartel de Ballajá) on Calle Norzagaray.

✪ **Fort San Cristóbal.** In the northeast corner of Old San Juan (uphill from Plaza de Colón on Calle Norzagaray). ☎ **787/729-6960.** Free admission. Daily 9am–5pm. Bus: T1, M3, or A7; then the free trolley from Covadonga station to the top of the hill.

This huge fortress, begun in 1634 and reengineered in the 1770s, is one of the largest ever built in the Americas by Spain. A marvel of military engineering, its walls rise more than 150 feet above the sea. San Cristóbal protected San Juan against attackers coming by land as a partner to El Morro, to which it is linked by a half mile of monumental walls and bastions filled with cannon-firing positions. A complex system of tunnels and dry moats connects the center of San Cristóbal to its "outworks," defensive elements arranged layer after layer over a 27-acre site. You'll get the idea if you look at the scale model on display. Be sure to see the Garita del Diablo, or the Devil's Sentry Box, one of the oldest parts of San Cristóbal's defenses, and famous in Puerto Rican legend. The devil himself, it is said, would snatch away sentinels at this lonely post at the edge of the sea. In 1898, the first shots of the Spanish-American War in Puerto Rico were fired by cannons on top of San Cristóbal during an artillery duel with a U.S. Navy fleet. Check at the guard house at the entrance for the schedule of special activities. Sometimes park rangers lead hour-long tours free, although you can visit on your own. Like El Morro, the fort is administered and maintained by the National Park Service.

Fort San Jerónimo. Calle Rosales, east of the Caribe Hilton, at the entrance to Condado Bay. ☎ **787/724-1844.** Free admission. Wed–Sat 9am–3pm. Bus: T1.

Completed in 1608, this fort was damaged in the English assault of 1797. Reconstructed in the closing year of the 18th century, it is now operated by the Institute of Puerto Rican Culture. Anyone wanting to see the view from the inside must call the Caribe Hilton; security here will open the gate to let you inside, but a special request has to be made.

CHURCHES

Capilla de Cristo. Calle del Cristo (directly west of Paseo de la Princesa). Free admission. Tues 10am–2pm. Bus: T1.

Cristo Chapel was built to commemorate what legend says was a miracle. In 1753, a young rider lost control of his horse in a race down this very street during the fiesta of St. John's Day and plunged over the precipice. Moved by the accident, the secretary of the city, Don Mateo Pratts, invoked Christ to save the youth, and he had the chapel built when his prayers were answered. Today it's a landmark in the old city and one of its best-known historical monuments. The chapel's gold and silver altar can be seen through its glass doors. Since the chapel is open only 1 day a week, most visitors have to settle for a view of its exterior.

Catedral de San Juan. Calle del Cristo 153 (at Caleta San Juan). ☎ **787/722-0861.** Free admission. Daily 8:30am–4pm. Bus: T1.

San Juan Cathedral was begun in 1540 and has had a rough life. Restoration has been extensive, so it hardly resembles the thatch-roofed structure that stood here until 1529, when it was wiped out by a hurricane. Hampered by lack of funds, the cathedral slowly added a circular staircase and two adjoining vaulted Gothic chambers. But then in 1598, along came the Earl of Cumberland, to loot it, and a hurricane in 1615, to blow off its roof. In 1908, the body of Ponce de León was disinterred from the nearby Iglesia de San José and placed in a marble tomb near the transept, where it remains today (see the box in chapter 2 for more about Ponce de León). The cathedral also contains the wax-covered mummy of St. Pio, a Roman martyr persecuted and killed for his Christian faith. The mummy has been encased in a glass box ever since it was placed here in 1862. To the right of the mummy is a bizarre wooden replica of Mary with four swords stuck in her bosom. After all the looting and destruction over the centuries, the cathedral's great treasures, including gold and silver, are long gone, although many beautiful stained-glass windows remain. The cathedral faces Plaza de las Monjas (the Nuns' Square), a shady spot where you can rest and cool off.

Iglesia de San José. Plaza de San José, Calle del Cristo. ☎ **787/725-7501.** Free admission. Church and Chapel of Belém, Mon–Wed and Fri 7am–3pm, Sat 8am–1pm. Bus: T1.

Old San Juan Attractions

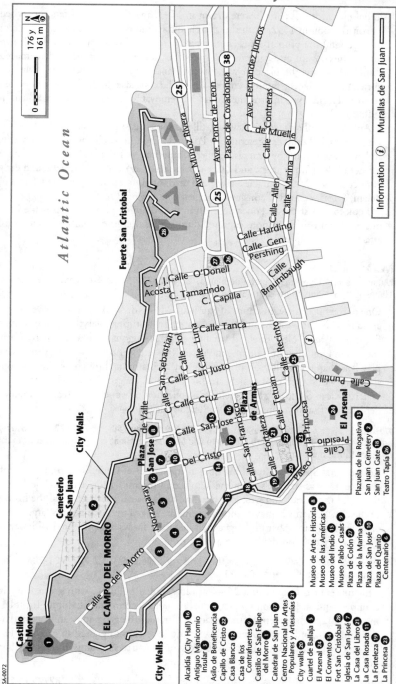

SA-0072

Atlantic Ocean

Castillo del Morro

Cemeterio de San Juan

City Walls

City Walls

EL CAMPO DEL MORRO

Calle del Morro

Calle Campo del Morro

Norzagaray

Plaza San José

Del Cristo

Fuerte San Cristóbal

Ave. Muñoz Rivera

Ave. Ponce de León

Paseo de Covadonga

Ave. Fernández Juncos

C. de Muelle

Calle Contreras

Calle Marina

Calle Allen

Calle Harding

Calle Gen. Pershing

Calle Braumbaugh

C. J. J. Acosta

Calle O'Donell

C. Tamarindo

C. Capilla

Calle Tanca

Calle San Sebastián

Calle Sol

Calle Luna

Calle San Justo

Calle Cruz

Calle San José

Calle San Francisco

Plaza de Armas

Calle Tetuán

Calle Fortaleza

Calle Recinto

Calle Puntillo

Calle Presidio

Paseo de la Princesa

El Arsenal

Plaza de la Rogativa

Plazuela de la Rogativa

City Walls
Alcaldía (City Hall) 16
Antiguo Manicomio Insular 3
Asilo de Beneficencia 4
Casa Blanca 12
Casa de los Contrafuertes 9
Castillo de San Felipe del Morro 1
Catedral de San Juan 17
Centro Nacional de Artes Populares y Artesanías 21
City walls 20
Cuartel de Ballajá 5
El Arsenal 24
El Convento 14
Fort San Cristóbal 28
Iglesia de San José 7
La Casa del Libro 21
La Casa Rosada 11
La Fortaleza 19
La Princesa 23

Museo de Arte e Historia 48
Museo de las Américas 5
Museo del Indio 15
Museo Pablo Casals 9
Plaza de Colón 27
Plaza de la Marina 25
Plaza de San José 10
Plaza del Quinto Centenario 6
Plazuela de la Rogativa 13
San Juan Cemetery 2
San Juan Gate 18
Teatro Tapia 26

Information ⓘ   Murallas de San Juan ▭

141

Initial plans for this church were drawn in 1523, and Dominican friars supervised its construction in 1532. Both the church and its monastery were closed by decree in 1838, and the property was confiscated by the royal treasury. Later, the Crown turned the convent into a military barracks. The Jesuits restored the badly damaged church. This was the place of worship for Ponce de León's descendants, who are buried here under the family's coat of arms. The conquistador, killed by a poisoned arrow in Florida, was interred here until his removal to the Catedral de San Juan in 1908.

Although badly looted, the church still has some treasures, including *Christ of the Ponces*, a carved crucifix presented to Ponce de León, four oils by José Campéche, and two large works by Francisco Oller. Campeche was the leading Puerto Rican painter of the 18th century, and Oller was its stellar artist of the late 19th and early 20th centuries. Many miracles have been attributed to a painting in the Chapel of Belém, a 15th-century Flemish work called *The Virgin of Bethlehem*.

Look for the statue of Ponce de León in the adjoining plaza—it was made from melted-down British cannons captured during Sir Ralph Abercromby's unsuccessful attack on San Juan in 1797.

MUSEUMS

Museo de las Americas. Cuartel de Ballajá. ☎ **787/724-5052.** Free admission. Tues–Fri 10am–4pm, Sat–Sun 11am–5pm. Bus: A7.

One of the major new museums of San Juan, Museo de las Americas, showcases the artisans of North, South, and Central America, featuring everything from carved figureheads from New England whaling ships to dugout canoes carved by Carib Indians in Dominica. It is unique in Puerto Rico and well worth a visit. Also on display is a changing collection of paintings by artists from throughout the Spanish-speaking world, some of which are for sale, and a permanent collection called "Puerto Rican Santos," which includes a collection of wood saints (carved wooden depictions of saints) donated by Dr. Ricardo Alegría.

Museo de Arte e Historia de San Juan. Calle Norzagaray 150. ☎ **787/724-1875.** Free admission. Wed–Sun 10am–5pm. Bus: T1 to Old San Juan terminal; then a trolley car from the terminal to the museum.

Located in a Spanish colonial building at the corner of Calle MacArthur, this cultural center was the city's main marketplace in the mid-19th century. Local art is displayed in the east and west galleries, and audiovisual materials reveal the history of the city. Sometimes major cultural events are staged in the museum's large courtyard. English- and Spanish-language audiovisual shows are presented Monday to Friday every hour on the hour from 9am to 4pm.

Museo del Indio. Calle San José (at the corner of Calle Luna). ☎ **787/721-2864.** Free admission. Tues–Sat 8am–4pm. Bus: T1.

This museum is housed in a 250-year-old colonial building, with green trim. Its cramped and airless rooms open onto a colonial courtyard. Exhibits include a modest collection of petroglyphs, maps celebrating the geography and diversity of the Americas, and a not particularly exciting collection of glassed-in exhibits. This is not a major museum, but a possible detour if you're shopping in the neighborhood.

Museo Pablo Casals. Plaza de San José, Calle San Sebastián 101. ☎ **787/723-9185.** Admission $1 adults, 50¢ children. Tues–Sat 9:30am–5:30pm. Bus: T1.

Adjacent to Iglesia de San José, this museum is devoted to the memorabilia left to the people of Puerto Rico by the musician Pablo Casals. The maestro's cello is here, along with a library of videotapes (played upon request) of some of his festival concerts. This small 18th-century house also contains manuscripts and photographs of Casals. The annual Casals Festival draws worldwide interest and attracts some of the greatest performing artists; it's still held during the first 2 weeks of June.

Museum of History, Anthropology and Art. Av. Ponce de León, Río Piedras Campus. ☎ **787/764-0000,** ext. 2452. Free admission. Mon–Fri 9am–4:15pm, Sat–Sun 9am–3:15pm. Closed holidays. Take the bus marked RÍO PIEDRAS from Plaza de Colón in Old San Juan to stop 36.

Here you'll find good collections of paintings by Puerto Rican artists, including Francisco Oller (late 19th and early 20th century) and José Campéche, the first important artist of the country (18th century). There's also a large collection of pre-Columbian Puerto Rican native artifacts from the Ingeri, sub-Taíno, and Taíno civilizations.

HISTORIC SIGHTS

In addition to the forts and churches listed above, you may want to see the following:

San Juan Gate, Calle San Francisco and Calle Recinto Oeste, built around 1635, just north of La Fortaleza, several blocks downhill from the cathedral, was the main point of entry into San Juan if you arrived by ship in the 17th and 18th centuries. The gate is the only one remaining of the several that once pierced the fortifications of the old walled city. The San Juan Gate was one of six heavy wooden doors cut into the walls. For centuries it was closed at sundown to cut off access to the historic old town. Bus: T1.

Plazuela de la Rogativa, Caleta de las Monjas, is a little plaza with a statue of a bishop and three women commemorating one of Puerto Rico's most famous legends. In 1797, the British across San Juan Bay at Santurce held the Old Town under siege. However, that same year they mysteriously sailed away. Later, the commander claimed he feared that the enemy was well prepared behind those walls—he apparently saw many lights and believed them to be reinforcements. Some people believe that those lights were torches carried by women in a *rogativa,* or religious procession, as they followed their bishop. An artfully stylized bronze statue of a bishop, trailed by a trio of torch-bearing women, was donated to the city on its 450th anniversary. Bus: T1.

The **city walls** around San Juan were built in 1630 to protect the town against both European invaders and Caribbean pirates. The city walls that remain today were once part of one of the most impregnable fortresses in the New World and even today are an engineering marvel. Their thickness averages 20 feet at the base and 12 feet at the top, with an average height of 40 feet. At their top, notice the balconied buildings that served for centuries as hospitals and also residences of the island's various governors. Between Fort San Cristóbal and El Morro, bastions were erected at frequent intervals. The walls come into view as you approach from San Cristóbal on your way to El Morro. Bus: T1.

San Juan Cemetery, Calle Norzagaray, officially opened in 1814 and has since been the final resting place for many prominent Puerto Rican families. The circular chapel, dedicated to Saint Magdalene of Pazzis, was built in the 1860s. Aficionados of old graveyards can wander among marble monuments, mausoleums, and statues, marvelous examples of Victorian funereal statuary. However, since there are no trees or any form of shade here, it would be best not to go exploring in the noonday sun. In any case, be careful here—the cemetery is often a venue for illegal drug deals and can be dangerous. Bus: T1.

Alcaldía (City Hall). Calle San Francisco. ☎ **787/724-7171,** ext. 3070. Free admission. Mon–Fri 8am–5pm, Sat 9am–5pm. Closed holidays. Bus: T1.

The City Hall, with its double arcade flanked by two towers resembling Madrid's City Hall, was constructed in stages from 1604 to 1789. Still in use, this building today contains a tourist information center downstairs plus a small art gallery on the first floor.

Casa Blanca. Calle San Sebastián 1. ☎ **787/724-4102.** Admission $2. Tues–Sat 9am–noon and 1–4:30pm. Bus: T1.

Ponce de León never lived here, although construction of the house—built in 1521, 2 years after his death—is sometimes attributed to him. The work was ordered by his son-in-law, Juan García Troche. The parcel of land was given to Ponce de León as a reward for services rendered to the Crown. Descendants of the explorer lived in the house for about 2½ centuries until the Spanish government took it over in 1779 for use as a residence for military commanders. The U.S. government also used it as a home for army commanders. On the first floor, the **Juan Ponce de León Museum** is furnished with antiques, paintings, and artifacts from the 16th through the 18th centuries. In back is a garden with spraying fountains, offering an intimate and verdant respite from the monumental buildings of Old San Juan.

Casa de los Contrafuertes (House of the Buttresses). Plaza de San José, Calle San Sebastián 101. ☎ **787/724-5477.** Free admission. Tues–Sat 8:30am–4:30pm. Bus: T1.

Adjacent to the Museo de Pablo Casals, this thickly buttressed building is believed to be the oldest residence remaining in El Viejo San Juan. The complex also contains a **pharmacy museum,** which documents the history of a 19th-century pharmacy in the town of Cayey. Even if you're not a specialist, this museum is fascinating and fun if only to see what was acceptable as cures for what ailed you back in those days. Upstairs you'll find a **graphic arts museum,** displaying prints and paintings by local artists.

El Arsenal. La Puntilla. ☎ **787/724-0700.** Free admission. Wed–Sun 8:30am–4:30pm. Bus: T1.

The Spaniards used a shallow craft to patrol the lagoons and mangroves in and around San Juan. Needing a base for these vessels, they constructed El Arsenal in the 19th century. It was at this base that they staged their last stand, flying the Spanish colors until the final Spaniard was removed in 1898, at the end of the Spanish-American War. Changing art exhibitions are held in the building's three galleries.

La Casa del Libro. Calle del Cristo 255. ☎ **787/723-0354.** Free admission. Tues–Sat 11am–4:30pm. Bus: T1.

This restored 19th-century house shelters a library and museum devoted to the arts of printing and bookmaking, with examples of fine printing dating back 5 centuries, as well as some illuminated medieval manuscripts.

La Fortaleza. Calle Fortaleza, overlooking San Juan Harbor. ☎ **787/721-7000,** ext. 2211. Free admission. 30-minute tours of the gardens and building (conducted in English and Spanish) given Mon–Fri, every hour 9am–4pm. Bus: T1.

The office and residence of the governor of Puerto Rico is the oldest executive mansion in continuous use in the western hemisphere, and it has served as the island's seat of government for more than 3 centuries. Yet its history goes back further, to 1533, when construction began on a fortress to protect San Juan's Spanish settlers during raids by Carib tribesmen and pirates. The original medieval towers remain, but as the edifice was subsequently enlarged into a palace, other modes of architecture and ornamentation were also incorporated, including baroque, Gothic, neoclassical, and Arabian. La Fortaleza has been designated a national historic site by the U.S. government. Informal but proper attire is required.

Teatro Tapía. Av. Ponce de León. ☎ **787/722-0407.** Viewed only by ticket holders at performances (see "San Juan After Dark").

Standing across from the Plaza de Colón, it's one of the oldest theaters in the western hemisphere, built about 1832. In 1976, a restoration returned the theater to its original appearance. Much of Puerto Rican theater history is connected with the Tapía, named after the island's first prominent playwright, Alejandro Tapía y Rivera (1826 to 1882). Various productions—some musical—are staged here throughout the year, representing a repertoire of drama, dance, and cultural events.

HISTORIC SQUARES

In Old San Juan, **Plaza del Quinto Centenario** (or Quincentennial Plaza, in English) overlooks the Atlantic from atop the highest point in the city.

A striking and symbolic feature of the plaza, which was constructed as part of the 1992 through 1993 celebration of the 500th anniversary of the discovery of the New World, is a sculpture that rises 40 feet from the plaza's top level. The monumental totemic sculpture in black granite and ceramics symbolizes the earthen and clay roots of American history and is the work of Jaime Suarez, one of Puerto Rico's foremost artists. From its southern end, two needle-shaped columns point skyward to the North Star, the guiding light of explorers. Placed around the plaza are fountains, other columns, and sculpted steps that represent various historic periods in Puerto Rico's 500-year heritage.

Quincentennial Plaza is at the hub of a group of some of the most significant and impressive structures dating from Colonial times. Clear and sweeping views extend from the plaza to El Morro Fortress at the headland of San Juan Bay and to the Dominican Convent and San José Church, a rare New World example of true Gothic architecture. Asilo de Beneficencia, dating from 1832 as an indigents' hospital, occupies a corner of El Morro's entrance and is now the new home of the Institute of Puerto Rican Culture. Adjacent to the plaza stands the Cuartel de Ballajá, built in the mid-19th century as Spanish army headquarters and still the largest edifice in the Americas constructed by Spanish engineers. It houses the Museum of the Americas.

Centrally located, Quincentennial Plaza is one of modern Puerto Rico's respectful gestures to its colorful and lively history. It is a perfect introduction for visitors seeking to discover the many rich links with the past in Old San Juan.

Once named St. James Square or Plaza Santiago, **Plaza del Colón** in the heart of San Juan's Old Town is bustling and busy, reached along the pedestrian mall of Calle Fortaleza. The square was renamed Plaza de Colón to honor the 400th anniversary of the explorer's so-called "discovery" of Puerto Rico. Of course, it is more politically correct today to say that Columbus explored or came upon an already inhabited island. He certainly didn't discover it. But when a statue here, perhaps the most famous on the island, was erected atop a high pedestal, it was clearly to honor Columbus, not to decry his legacy.

PARKS & GARDENS

Administered by the University of Puerto Rico, the Botanical Garden, Barrio Venezuela at the intersection of routes 1 and 847 in Río Piedras (☎ 787/ 767-1710), is a lush tropical garden with some 200 species of vegetation. You can pack a picnic lunch and bring it here if you choose. The orchid garden is exceptional, and the palm garden is said to contain some 125 species. Footpaths blaze a trail through heavy forests opening onto a lotus lagoon. Admission is free. It's open daily from 8am to 4:30pm. Take bus 19 to reach it.

Muñoz Rivera Park, Avenida Ponce de León (☎ 787/724-4430), is affiliated with Luis Muñoz Marín Park (see below), with which it is frequently confused. This green space is administered by the Park Trust of Puerto Rico (☎ 787/763-0613). More closely linked to central San Juan than to the suburbs, it's a rectangular, seaward-facing park that was built about 50 years ago to honor Luis Muñoz Rivera, the Puerto Rican statesman, journalist, and poet. It's filled with picnic areas, wide walks, shady trees, landscaped grounds, and recreational areas. Its centerpiece (El Pabellon de la Paz) is sometimes used for cultural events and expositions of handcrafts. Admission is free, and the park is open 24 hours. Take the Los Américas Expressway to Avenida Piñero, then head west until you reach the entrance.

Luis Muñoz Marín Park, Avenida Piñero, at Alto Rey (☎ 787/763-0787), also is administered by the Park Trust of Puerto Rico, and it is the best known, most frequently visited children's playground in Puerto Rico, although it is of equal appeal to adults, even those without kids. It has an incomparable view of San Juan. Conceived as a verdant oasis in an otherwise crowded urban neighborhood, it's a fenced-in repository of swings, jungle gyms, and slides set amid several small lakes. A small-scale cable car carries passengers aloft at 10-minute intervals for panoramic views of the surrounding landscape ($1.25 per person). Entrance for pedestrians is free, although parking costs $4 per vehicle. Open Wednesday through Sunday from 8:30am to 5pm.

Parque Central de San Juan, Calle Cerra (☎ 787/722-1646), was inaugurated in 1979 for the Pan-American Games. This mangrove-bordered park covers 35 acres and lies southwest of Miramar. Joggers appreciate its labyrinth of trails, tennis players come to use the courts, and all kinds of city dwellers stroll to relieve the pressures of urban life. Admission for pedestrians is free, although parking costs 75¢. Open Monday through Thursday from 6am to 10pm, Friday from 6am to 9pm, and Saturday and Sunday from 6am to 6pm.

SIGHTSEEING TOURS

If you want to see more of the island but you don't want to rent a car or manage the inconveniences of public transportation, perhaps an organized tour is for you.

Castillo Sightseeing Tours & Travel Services, 2413 Calle Laurel, Punta La Marias, Santurce (☎ 787/791-6195), maintains offices at some of the capital's best-known hotels, including the Caribe Hilton, San Juan Marriott Resort, El San Juan Grand, the El San Juan Towers, Embassy Suites, and Crowne Plaza Holiday Inn. Using six of their own air-conditioned buses, with access to others if demand warrants it, the company's tours include pickups and drop-offs at hotels as an added convenience.

One of the most popular half-day tours departs most days of the week between 8:30 and 9am, lasts 4 to 5 hours, and costs $30 per person. Leaving from San Juan, it tours along the northeastern part of the island to El Yunque Rain Forest.

The company also offers a city tour of San Juan that departs daily at 1 or 1:30pm. The 4-hour trip costs $30 per person and includes a stopover at the Bacardi Rum

Factory, where you're treated to a complimentary rum drink. The company also operates full-day snorkeling tours to the reefs near the coast of a deserted island off Puerto Rico's eastern edge aboard one of two sail and motor-driven catamarans. With lunch, snorkeling gear, and piña coladas included, the full-day (7:45am to 5pm) excursion goes for $69 per person.

Few cities of the Caribbean lend themselves so gracefully to walking tours. You can always embark on these on your own, stopping and shopping en route (see "Walking Tour: Old San Juan," below). You can also go on an organized walking excursion with **Colonial Adventures,** 201 Calle Recinto Sur, in Old San Juan (☎ **787/729-0114**). Participation in these tours requires an advance reservation. Tours are conducted Monday through Saturday at 10am, 2pm, and 4pm, last for 2 hours, and begin and end at Pier 1, near the Plaza Darsena, in Old San Juan. The price is $20 per person for a 2-hour tour.

ESPECIALLY FOR KIDS

Puerto Rico is one of the most family-friendly islands in the Caribbean, and many hotels offer family discounts. Programs for children are also offered at a number of hotels, including day and night camp activities and baby-sitting services. Trained counselors at these camps supervise children as young as 3 in activities ranging from nature hikes to tennis lessons, coconut carving, and sand-sculpture contests.

Teenagers can learn to hip-hop dance Latino style with special salsa and merengue lessons, learn conversational Spanish, indulge in water sports, take jeep excursions, or scuba dive in some of the best diving locations in the world.

The best kiddies program is offered at **El San Juan Hotel & Casino** (see chapter 5), where camp activities are presented to children between the ages of 5 and 12. Counselors design activities according to the interests of groups of up to 10 children. Kids Klub members receive a T-shirt membership card and three "Sand Dollars" for use in the game room or at a poolside restaurant. The daily fee of $28 includes lunch.

Another worthy choice is the **Condado Plaza Hotel & Casino** (see chapter 5), where the daily Camp Taíno offers a regular program of activities and special events for children ages 5 to 12. The $25-per-child fee includes lunch. The hotel also has a toddlers' pool, and the kids' water slide in its main pool starts in a Spanish-style castle turret. For teenagers the hotel has a video game room, a tennis court, several putting greens, and various organized activities.

San Juan even has its own **Museo del Niño,** or Children's Museum, at Calle del Cristo 150 (☎ 787/722-3791) in Old Town. If your child is young and small, he or she can enter the museum through the legs of a large wooden figure. Inside exhibits are educational and definitely hands-on. These displays include a village of playhouses, and even a "Visit the Dentist" section where children can play dentist with their parents in the patient's chair. There are three floors of exhibits and activities here. Open Tuesday through Thursday 9am to 3:30pm, Friday 9am to 5pm, and Saturday and Sunday from 12:30 to 5pm. Admission is $2 for all.

In addition to the places listed below, children should love **El Morro Fortress** (see "Forts," above), since it looks just like the castles they have seen on TV and at the movies. On a rocky promontory, El Morro is filled with dungeons and dank places and also has lofty lookout points for viewing San Juan Harbor.

Luis Muñoz Marín Park (see "Parks & Gardens," above) is one of the best places to take your children for a picnic. It has the most popular children's playground in Puerto Rico. It's filled with landscaped grounds and recreational areas—lots of room for fun in the sun.

Plaza Acuatica. Las Américas Expressway, opposite Plaza de las Américas, Hato Rey. ☎ **787/754-9800.** Admission $12.95, $8.95 for children under 11 (activities are extra). Feb–May, Sat–Sun 10am–6pm; June–Aug, daily 10am–6pm; Sept Sat–Sun 10am–6pm. Closed Oct–Jan.

This water park is an outdoor amusement area that the whole family can enjoy. Activities range from water slides and "rapids" to miniature golf. There are also dining facilities.

Time Out Family Amusement Center. Plaza de las Américas, Las Américas Expressway at Roosevelt Ave., Hato Rey. ☎ **787/753-0606.** Free admission (activities are extra). Sun–Thurs 9:30am–10pm, Fri–Sat 9:30am–11pm.

This is the most popular venue for family outings on Puerto Rico. On weekends, seemingly half of the families in the city show up. It has a large variety of electronic games for children and adults alike, but there are no rides.

WALKING TOUR:
OLD SAN JUAN

Start: Plaza de la Marina.
Finish: Fort San Cristóbal.
Time: 2 hours (not counting stops).
Best times: Any sunny day between 7am and 6pm.
Worst times: When several cruise ships are in port simultaneously.

The streets are narrow and teeming with traffic, but a walk through Old San Juan (in Spanish, *El Viejo San Juan*) is like a stroll through 5 centuries of history. Beneficiary of millions of dollars' worth of restoration since the early 1970s, Old San Juan is one of the world's most potent reminders of the power and grandeur of the Spanish Empire. This tour follows an itinerary that begins at a point just to the west of San Juan's cruise piers and then encircles the perimeter of some of the best-preserved of the fortifications built by the Spaniards during the 16th and 17th centuries. En route, it will pass beneath the governor's historic mansion, La Fortaleza, and encircle the Casa Blanca—ancestral home of the Ponce de León family—before ending at a point beyond the entrance of one of the most fiercely guarded fortresses of the colonial age, Fort San Cristóbal.

Begin your walking tour near the post office, amid the taxis, buses, and urban congestion of:

1. Plaza de la Marina, a sloping, many-angled plaza situated at the eastern edge of one of San Juan's showcase promenades—Paseo de la Princesa. This 19th-century paseo was an esplanade where the Spanish colonial gentry once strolled while enjoying the balmy Caribbean air.

Towering royal palms shade the broad esplanade, now paved with brick. On the paseo's west side overlooking the sea, a large bronze fountain, *Raíces* (Roots), sculpted in 1992 by the Spanish artist Luís Sanguino, depicts the Amerindian, African, and Spanish origins of Puerto Rico as human figures with dolphins cavorting at their feet. Viewed from afar, the entire ensemble looks like a caravel being steered out to sea by dolphins, setting its course for the 21st century. On the paseo's east side stand five allegorical pieces on the island's heritage sculpted by José Buscaglia at the same time as Señor Sanguino did the fountain. This work is said to symbolize the various epochs that Puerto Rico has undergone in the

Walking Tour—Old San Juan

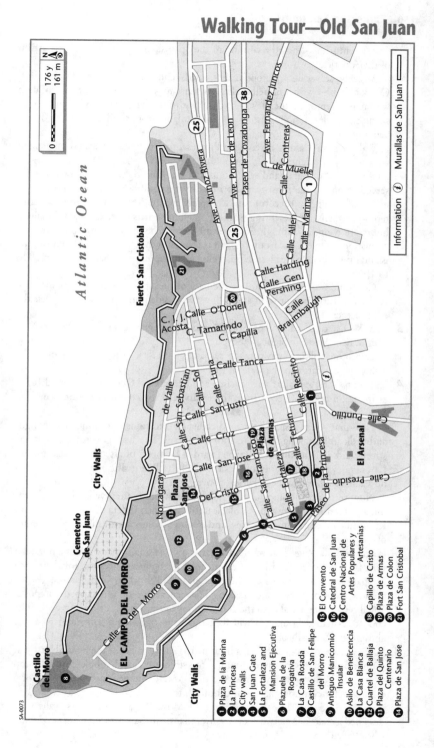

Atlantic Ocean

Castillo del Morro

Cemeterio de San Juan

EL CAMPO DEL MORRO

Calle del Morro

Fuerte San Cristobal

City Walls

City Walls

N

176 y
161 m
0

1 Plaza de la Marina
2 La Princesa
3 City walls
4 San Juan Gate
5 La Fortaleza and
   Mansion Ejecutiva
6 Plazuela de la
   Rogativa
7 La Casa Rosada
8 Castillo de San Felipe
   del Morro
9 Antiguo Manicomio
   Insular
10 Asilo de Beneficencia
11 La Casa Blanca
12 Cuartel de Ballaja
13 Plaza del Quinto
   Centenario
14 Plaza de San Jose

15 El Convento
16 Catedral de San Juan
17 Centro Nacional de
   Artes Populares y
   Artesanias
18 Capillo de Cristo
19 Plaza de Armas
20 Plaza de Colon
21 Fort San Cristobal

Information (i)   Murallas de San Juan

Ave. Muñoz Rivera
Ave. Ponce de Leon
Paseo de Covadonga
Ave. Fernandez Juncos
C. de Muelle
Calle Contreras
Calle Marina
Calle Allen
Calle Harding
Calle Gen. Pershing
Calle Braumbaugh
Calle O'Donell
C. Tamarindo
C. Capilla
C. J. J. Acosta
Calle Tanca
Calle Recinto
Calle Luna
Calle Sol
Calle San Sebastian
de Valle
Norzagaray
Calle San Justo
Calle Cruz
Calle San Jose
Del Cristo
Plaza San Jose
Plaza de Armas
Calle San Francisco
Calle Fortaleza
Calle Tetuan
Calle de la Princesa
Paseo de la Princesa
El Arsenal
Calle Presidio
Calle Puntillo

25
38
25
1
1

SA-0073

149

past 5 centuries—from the coming of the Spanish conquistadores to the arrival of the Americans.

A gazebo serves light seafood dishes, salads, and the island's famed rich coffee. Outdoor tables with umbrellas allow parents to keep an eye on their children who may be enjoying the playground nearby. More than 20 trees were planted to shade the tables. Criollo dishes are also available from food carts with colored awnings.

Walk westward along Paseo de la Princesa, past heroic statues and manicured trees until you reach:

2. **La Princesa,** the gray-and-white building on your right, which for centuries served as one of the most-feared prisons in the Caribbean. Today it houses the offices of the Puerto Rico Tourism Company and an exhibit of Puerto Rican contemporary artists representing works by regional artists since the 1950s. Gallery hours are Monday through Friday from 9am to noon and 1 to 4pm, with no admission charged. In front of La Princesa stands a sculpture of one of the island's most beloved leaders, Doña Felisa Gautier, mayor of San Juan from 1946 to 1968.

Continue walking westward to the base of the heroic fountain near the edge of the sea. Turn to your right and follow the seaside promenade as it parallels the edge of the:

3. **City Walls,** once part of one of the most impregnable fortresses in the New World. See "Historic Sights," above.

Continue walking between the sea and the base of the city walls until the walkway goes through the walls at the:

4. **San Juan Gate,** at Calle San Francisco and Recinto del Oeste, built around 1635, as the main point of access from the wharves to the colony's interior. See "Historic Sights," above.

Now that you're inside the once-dreaded fortifications, turn immediately right and walk uphill along Calle Recinto del Oeste. The wrought-iron gates at the street's end, which will probably be guarded by a pair of attendants, lead to:

5. **La Fortaleza,** the centuries-old residence of the Puerto Rican governor, located on Calle La Fortaleza. See "Forts," above).

Now retrace your steps along Calle Recinto del Oeste, walking first downhill and then uphill for about a block until you reach Caleta de las Monjas. Fork left until you see a panoramic view and a contemporary statue marking the center of:

6. **Plazuela de la Rogativa,** where the statue on this small square commemorates a time in 1797 when British soldiers mistook a religious procession for the arrival of Spanish reinforcements and fled. See page 143 for more information.

Now, continue westward, passing between a pair of urn-capped gateposts. You'll be walking parallel to the crenellations of the 17th-century city walls. The cool, tree-shaded boulevard will fork (take the right-hand fork) and pass just above the pink walls of:

7. **La Casa Rosada,** a graceful villa built in 1812 for leaders of the Spanish army. It cannot be visited. Continue climbing the steeply inclined cobble-covered ramp to its top. Walk westward across the field toward the neoclassical gateway of a fortress believed impregnable for centuries, the:

8. **Castillo de San Felipe del Morro** ("El Morro"), whose fortress walls were designed as part of a network of defenses that made San Juan *La Ciudad Murada* (the Walled City). See "Forts," above.

AT&T Direct℠ Service

Steps to follow for easy calling worldwide:

1. Just dial the AT&T Access Number for the country you are calling from.

2. Dial the phone number you're calling.

3. Dial your card number.

AT&T Access Numbers

Anguilla✦	1-800-872-2881	Brit. Vir. Isl ✦	1-800-872-2881
Antigua✦	1-800-872-2881	**Canada**	**1 800 CALL ATT**
Argentina	0-800-54-288	Cayman Isl ✦	1-800-872-2881
Aruba	800-8000	**Chile**	**800-800-311**
Bahamas	1-800-872-2881	**Colombia**	**980-11-0010**
Barbados✦	1-800-872-2881	Costa Rica	0-800-0-114-114
Belize ▲	811	Dominica✦	1-800-872-2881
Belize ✝	555	Dom. Rep. ★□	1-800-872-2881
Bermuda✦	1-800-872-2881	**Ecuador ▲**	**999-119**
Bolivia ●	**0-800-1112**	**El Salvador○**	**800-1785**
Brazil	**000-8010**	Grenada✦	1-800-872-2881

AT&T Direct℠ Service

Steps to follow for easy calling worldwide:

1. Just dial the AT&T Access Number for the country you are calling from.

2. Dial the phone number you're calling.

3. Dial your card number.

AT&T Access Numbers

Anguilla✦	1-800-872-2881	Brit. Vir. Isl ✦	1-800-872-2881
Antigua✦	1-800-872-2881	**Canada**	**1 800 CALL ATT**
Argentina	0-800-54-288	Cayman Isl ✦	1-800-872-2881
Aruba	800-8000	**Chile**	**800-800-311**
Bahamas	1-800-872-2881	**Colombia**	**980-11-0010**
Barbados✦	1-800-872-2881	Costa Rica	0-800-0-114-114
Belize ▲	811	Dominica✦	1-800-872-2881
Belize ✝	555	Dom. Rep. ★□	1-800-872-2881
Bermuda✦	1-800-872-2881	**Ecuador ▲**	**999-119**
Bolivia ●	**0-800-1112**	**El Salvador○**	**800-1785**
Brazil	**000-8010**	Grenada✦	1-800-872-2881

AT&T Access Numbers

Guatemala ○▲×	99-99-190	Paraguay ▲[2]	008-11-800
Guyana*	165	Perú △	0-800-50000
Haiti	183	Puerto Rico	1 800 CALL ATT
Honduras	800-0-123	St. Kitts/Nevis ◆	1-800-872-2881
Jamaica □	872	St. Vincent △	1-800-872-2881
Mexico ▽[1]	01-800-288-2872	Suriname △	156
Montserrat	1-800-872-2881	Turks & Caicos ◆	01-800-872-2881
Neth. Ant. ◉×	001-800-872-2881	Uruguay	000-410
Nicaragua	174	U.S. Virgin Isl.	1 800 CALL ATT
Panama	109	Venezuela	800-11-120

Bold-faced countries permit country-to-country calling outside the U.S.

+ Public phones and select hotels.
● + Public phones require coin or card deposit.
✦ May not be available from every phone/public phone
→ Collect calling only.
◉ Available from select hotels.
◉ × From St. Maarten or phones at Bobby's Marina, use 1-800-872-2881.
⊕ ● Public phones require local coin payment during call.
△ When calling from public phones, use phones marked "Ladatel."
▽ Available from public phones only.
□ Calling card calls available from select hotels.
1 If call does not complete, use 001-800-462-4240.
2 From Asuncion only.

Visit our Web site at: www.att.com/traveler

For access numbers not listed ask any operator for AT&T Direct℠ Service. In the U.S., call 1-800-331-1140 for a wallet card listing all worldwide AT&T Access Numbers.

When placing an international call *from* the U.S., dial 1 800 CALL ATT.

© 5/98 AT&T

AT&T Access Numbers

Guatemala ○▲×	99-99-190	Paraguay ▲[2]	008-11-800
Guyana*	165	Perú △	0-800-50000
Haiti	183	Puerto Rico	1 800 CALL ATT
Honduras	800-0-123	St. Kitts/Nevis ◆	1-800-872-2881
Jamaica □	872	St. Vincent △	1-800-872-2881
Mexico ▽[1]	01-800-288-2872	Suriname △	156
Montserrat	1-800-872-2881	Turks & Caicos ◆	01-800-872-2881
Neth. Ant. ◉×	001-800-872-2881	Uruguay	000-410
Nicaragua	174	U.S. Virgin Isl.	1 800 CALL ATT
Panama	109	Venezuela	800-11-120

Bold-faced countries permit country-to-country calling outside the U.S.

+ Public phones and select hotels.
● + Public phones require coin or card deposit.
✦ May not be available from every phone/public phone
→ Collect calling only.
◉ Available from select hotels.
◉ × From St. Maarten or phones at Bobby's Marina, use 1-800-872-2881.
⊕ ● Public phones require local coin payment during call.
△ When calling from public phones, use phones marked "Ladatel."
▽ Available from public phones only.
□ Calling card calls available from select hotels.
1 If call does not complete, use 001-800-462-4240.
2 From Asuncion only.

Visit our Web site at: www.att.com/traveler

For access numbers not listed ask any operator for AT&T Direct℠ Service. In the U.S., call 1-800-331-1140 for a wallet card listing all worldwide AT&T Access Numbers.

When placing an international call *from* the U.S., dial 1 800 CALL ATT.

© 5/98 AT&T

(put on a happy face)

ping someplace festive? Bring along an **AT&T Direct**® Service wallet guide. It's a list of access numbers you need to call

ome fast and clear from around the world, using an AT&T Calling Card or credit card. And that's something to smile about.

For a list of **AT&T Access Numbers,** take the attached wallet guide.

It's all within your reach. **AT&T**

For Travelers
who want more than
the Official Line

After your visit, with El Morro behind you, retrace your steps through the sunlit, treeless field to the point you stood at when you first sighted the fortress. Walk down the Calle del Morro past the:

9. **Antiguo Manicomio Insular,** whose construction was decreed by the Spanish king in 1854 as an insane asylum. Converted to a U.S. army barracks after the Spanish-American War, it has functioned since 1965 as the Puerto Rican Academy of Fine Arts. Iron fences of grace and elegance protect a pair of court-yards centered around splashing fountains. Walk parallel to the facade of this former asylum, turning right at an unmarked street that passersby might tell you is the Calle de Beneficias. Futher on, notice the stately neoclassical building (painted buff with fern-green trim) on your right. It's the:

10. **Asilo de Beneficencia ("Home for the Poor"),** which dates from the 1840s. It has two attractive interior patios, an austere dignity, and usually an echoing silence. Today, it houses the administrative offices of the Institute of Puerto Rican Culture, with several changing exhibition galleries, plus an interesting room filled with pre-Columbian artifacts. The galleries are open Wednesday to Friday from 9am to 4:30pm and on Saturday and Sunday from 11am to 6pm. The little museum of pre-Columbian artifacts can be visited Tuesday from 9am to 7pm and Wednesday through Sunday from 9am to 5pm. For more information, call ☎ **787/724-0700.**

Continue walking uphill to the small, formal, and sloping plaza at the street's top. On the right-hand side, within a trio of buildings is:

11. **La Casa Blanca,** which was built by the son-in-law of Juan Ponce de León as the great conquistador's island home (he never actually lived here). See "Historic Sights," above.

After your visit, exit by the compound's front entrance and walk downhill, retracing your steps for a half-block, heading toward the massive and monu-mental tangerine-colored building on your right, the:

12. **Cuartel de Ballajá,** the 19th-century military barracks of Ballajá, which once housed troops from Spain along with their wives and children, in a setting evoca-tive of the most austere and massive monasteries of Old Spain. It is still the largest edifice in the Americas constructed by Spanish engineers. It was declared a National Historic Monument in 1954. On the building's second floor is the **Museo de las Americas** (see "Museums," above).

After your visit, exit through the barrack's extremely narrow eastern door, where you'll immediately spot one of the most dramatic modern plazas in Puerto Rico, the:

13. **Plaza del Quinto Centenario,** a terraced tribute to the European colonization of the New World, and one of the most elaborate and formal piazzas in Puerto Rico.

Now, walk a short block to the southeast to reach the ancient borders of the:

14. **Plaza de San José,** whose center is dominated by a heroic statue of Juan Ponce de León, which was cast from an English cannon captured during a naval battle in 1797. Around the periphery of the square, notice three important sites: the Museo de Pablo Casals, whose exhibits honor the life and work of the Spanish-born cellist who adopted Puerto Rico as his final home (see "Museums," above); the Casa de los Contrafuertes (House of the Buttresses), which is adjacent to the Museo de Pablo Casals (see "Historic Sights," above); and the Iglesia de San José, where the conquistador's coat of arms hangs above the altar (see "Churches," above). Established by the Dominicans in 1523, this church is one of the oldest places of Christian worship in the New World.

⚈ **TAKE A BREAK** Plaza de San José is home to at least three prominent bars and restaurants, all of which serve beer, coffee, or a simple meal. They include **El Patio de Sam** and a supremely informal tavern, **NoNo's,** where local night owls occupy virtually every nook and barstool, especially after sundown (see chapter 6). Also appealing is **El Boquerón,** operating out of a narrow store-front midway between the two.

Now exit from the plaza's southwestern corner and walk downhill along one of the capital's oldest and best-known streets, Calle del Cristo (also known as Calle Cristo). Two blocks later, at the corner of Calle las Monjas, you'll find the venerable walls of:

15. **El Convento,** which originally was conceived as a convent in the 17th century but functioned for many decades as one of the few hotels within the old city (see the recommendation in chapter 5). Across the street from El Convento lies the island's most famous church and spiritual centerpiece, the:

16. **Catedral de San Juan,** a distinguished landmark that in recent years has been restored to its original Spanish beauty. See "Churches," above.

Now walk 2 more blocks southward along Calle del Cristo, through one of the most attractive shopping districts in the Caribbean. After passing Calle Fortaleza, look on your left for the:

17. **Centro Nacional de Artes Populares y Artesanias,** a popular arts and crafts center that belongs to the Institute of Puerto Rican Culture. See "Shopping," below.

After your visit, continue to the southernmost tip of Calle del Cristo (just a few steps away) to the wrought-iron gates that surround a chapel no bigger than an oversized newspaper kiosk, the:

18. **Capilla de Cristo,** its altar dedicated to the "Christ of Miracles." See "Churches," above.

Now retrace your steps about a block along the Calle del Cristo, walking north. Turn right along Calle Fortaleza. One block later, turn left onto Calle de San José, which leads to the site of the capital's most symmetrical and beautiful square:

19. **Plaza de Armas,** a broad and open Spanish-style plaza that was the original main square of Old San Juan and the very hub of the city. It has a lovely fountain with 19th-century statues representing the four seasons. In times gone by, families with unmarried daughters would parade around the square. It was a proper way for fully chaperoned young women to catch the eye of young, available men. The plaza is bordered by the Calles San Francisco, Fortaleza, San José, and Cruz. Two important buildings flanking this square are the neoclassic Intendencia (which houses certain offices of the U.S. State Department) and San Juan's City Hall, or Alcaldía. Relax on one of the benches if you choose, before leaving the square eastword along Calle San Francisco.

⚈ **TAKE A BREAK La Bombonera,** Calle San Francisco 259 (☎ 787/722-0658), offers take-away baked goods, as well as sandwiches, spicy platters of Puerto Rican food, and endless cups of richly scented coffee. No one will mind if you just order something to drink, but if you want lunch, the portions are copious and inexpensive. It's rather informal; the place bustles, but no one goes away hungry.

After your pick-me-up, continue your promenade eastward along the length of Calle San Francisco. It will eventually deposit you beside the traffic, parked cars, and open-air conviviality of the very large:

20. **Plaza de Colón,** with its stone column topped with a statue of Christopher Columbus. See "Historic Squares," above. To the side of the square is the Tapía Theater, which has been restored to its original 19th-century elegance (see "Historic Sights," above).

Continue along Calle San Francisco to the intersection with Calle de Valle, and follow the signs to:

21. **Fort San Cristóbal,** built as part of the string of fortifications guarding one of Spain's then-most-valuable colonies. Today, like its twin, El Morro, it is maintained by the National Park Service and can be visited throughout the day. See "Forts," above.

2 Nearby Attractions

Called "the Cathedral of Rum," the **Bacardi Distillery** at Route 888, kilometer 2.6 at Cataño (☎ **787/788-1500**), is the largest of its kind in the world. Reached by taking a ferry across San Juan Bay (50¢ each way), the distillery produces 100,000 gallons of rum daily. Free 45-minute guided tours take place Monday through Saturday from 9:30am to 3:30pm. Complimentary rum drinks are offered at the beginning of tour, and a well-stocked gift shop sells a wide assortment of handsome items, from T-shirts to duffel bags. Naturally, you can purchase Bacardi rums here at prices that are slightly more reasonable than those at home. Some rums available here are not sold on the U.S. mainland and make unusual gifts.

Upon entering the first floor, you'll get a glimpse of what rum production was like a century ago, including oak barrels used in the aging process and an old sugarcane wagon. On the fifth floor you'll enter the Hall of Rum with a collection of beverages made by the corporation over a period of years. You'll then witness "the birth of rum"—the fermentation processes of molasses (it takes 100 gallons of molasses to produce one barrel of rum).

At the end of the tour you'll visit the Bacardi Family Museum, documenting the family's history, and you can watch a short video about the bottling process. Afterward, you can stroll through the beautiful grounds overlooking Old San Juan.

3 Diving, Fishing, Tennis & Other Outdoor Pursuits

Active vacationers will have a wide choice of things to do in San Juan, from beaching to windsurfing. The beachside hotels, of course, offer lots of water-sports activities (see chapter 5).

THE BEACHES

With their big resorts and some of the Caribbean's finest white sand, the ✪ **Condado** and **Isla Verde** beaches are the most frequented in town. In our view, the best and most beautiful Condado beach is the one that fronts the Marriott, and the finest and loveliest beach at Isla Verde is at the Hotel El San Juan. All beaches on Puerto Rico, even those fronting the top hotels, are open to the public, although you will be charged for parking and for use of balneario facilities, such as lockers and showers. Good snorkeling is possible at both beaches, and both have rental equipment for water sports. However, don't walk along these beaches at night.

The public beaches on the north shore of San Juan at **Ocean Park** and **Park Barbosa** are not quite as beautiful as Condado and Isla Verde, but they also have white sand, offer good snorkeling, and are likely to be less crowded—which makes them worth the trouble to reach. Both are accessible by bus route T1. Each beach has changing rooms and showers, but you won't have the other facilities here that you'll find on Condado and Isla Verde.

If you are willing to go some 30 miles east of San Juan on the north coast, ☼ **Luquillo** is even better, with wider white sands than either Ocean Park or Park Barbosa. Luquillo has changing rooms, showers, and picnic tables.

Public beaches are closed on Monday unless it's a holiday, when they are open but close the next day, Tuesday. Beach hours are 9am to 5pm in winter, to 6pm off-season.

BIKE RENTALS

Much favored by the dozens of holidaymakers pedaling up and down the Condado, **Hot Dog Bicycles,** 1024 Ashford Ave. (☎ 787/721-0623), rents big-geared mountain bikes for $15 a day. Fortunately for the neighborhood's noise pollution, they don't rent mopeds or motor scooters. The best places to bike are along Ashford Avenue (in Condado), Calle Loiza (between Condado and Ocean Park), and Avenida Baldorioty de Castro (in Santurce). Other streets in this area may be too congested. Similarly, because of the traffic, biking in Old San Juan is not recommended.

DEEP-SEA FISHING

Capt. Mike Benitez of **Benitez Fishing Charters,** P.O. Box 9066541, Puerto de Tierra, San Juan, PR 00906 (☎ **787/723-2292** until 9pm), has chartered out of San Juan for more than 40 years and has been listed by the *Sports Fishing Tournament Guide* as one of the 15 most qualified sport-fishing captains in the world. Past clients have included ex-President Carter. The captain offers a 45-foot air-conditioned deluxe Hatteras, the *Sea Born.* Fishing tours for parties of up to six cost $450 for a half day, $750 for a full day, with beverages and all equipment included.

Two deep-sea fishing boats, each with space for up to six passengers, are based at the **San Juan Bay Marina,** Avenida Fernández Juncos, Stop 10, Santurce (☎ **787/796-4645** or 787/721-8062), a 10-minute drive from Old San Juan. Their fees also start at $450.

GOLF

A 45-minute drive east from San Juan on the northeast coast takes you to Palmer and its 6,145-yard ☼ **Rio Mar Golf Course** (☎ 787/888-8811). Inexperienced golfers prefer this course to the more challenging and more famous courses at Dorado (see chapter 8), even though trade winds can influence your game along the holes bordering the water, and occasional fairway flooding can present some unwanted obstacles. Greens fees are $140 before 2pm, $90 after 2pm. A gallery of 100 iguanas also adds spice to your game at Rio Mar.

HORSE RACING

Great thoroughbreds and outstanding jockeys compete all year at **El Comandante,** Av. 65 de Infantería, Route 3, kilometer 15.3, at Canovanas (☎ 787/724-6060), Puerto Rico's only racetrack, a 20-minute drive east of the center of San Juan. Post time varies from 2:15 to 2:45pm on Monday, Wednesday, Thursday, Friday, and Sunday. A restaurant is open on race days from 12:30 to 4:30pm. Entrance to the

clubhouse costs $3 per person, but no admission is charged for the
ahead for luncheon reservations; most credit and charge cards are

JOGGING

The cool, quiet, early morning hours before 8am are a good time to jog through the
streets of Old San Juan. Head for the wide, sweeping thoroughfares adjacent to the
fortress of San Felipe del Morro and then the fortress of San Cristóbal, whose walls
jut upward from flat areas around them. You might join Puerto Rico's governor, a
dedicated jogger, in making several laps around the seafront Paseo de la Princesa at
the base of his home, La Fortaleza.

Finally, if you don't mind heading out into the island a bit from your base in Old
San Juan, you might opt for a jog through the palm trees of the Parque Central,
near Calle Cerra and Route 2, in Santurce. Condado's Ashford Avenue is a busy site
for morning joggers as well.

SCUBA DIVING

Based at the Radisson Normandie Hotel, **Caribe Aquatic Adventures,** P.O. Box
9024278, San Juan Station, San Juan, PR 00902 (☎ **787/724-1882**), offers diving
certification from both PADI and NAUI as part of 40-hour courses priced at $465
each. A resort course for first-time divers costs $97. Also offered are local daily dives
in San Juan or windsurfing (see below), and a choice of full-day diving expeditions
to various reefs off the east coast of Puerto Rico. Bay cruises start at $29.95 per
person, with a maximum boat capacity of 35 people on a 60-foot motor yacht, *San
Antonio.* If you have limited time, this outfitter will take you to nearby sites, but
since the best diving is out on the island's coasts, allow a full day if you can.

SNORKELING

The best snorkeling is out on the island. In the San Juan area, one of the best places
is the San Juan Bay marina near the Caribe Hilton. Most water-sports desks at the
big hotels at Isla Verde and Condado can make arrangements for instruction, equipment rental, and excursions to the best places. If your hotel doesn't have such services, you can hook up directly with **Caribe Aquatic Adventures** (see "Scuba
Diving," above), which caters to both snorkelers and scuba divers. Other possibilities for equipment rental are **Caribbean School of Aquatics,** Taft No. 1, Suite 10F,
in San Juan (☎ **787/728-6606**); and **Mundo Submarino,** Laguna Gardens Shopping Center, Isla Verde (☎ **787/791-5764**).

SPAS & FITNESS CENTERS

Except the fitness center at Palmas del Mar, which charges nonguests $7 per day,
the fitness centers at the following hotels are open only to hotel guests. On the other
hand, spa treatments are open to all, and prices are standardized. See chapter 5 for
details about the hotels and resorts.

Massages may vary from $65 to $80 per hour, with another $15 for aro-
matherapy. Facials range from $55 to $100, depending on how deep and how thor-
ough you want the treatment. Special clay and seaweed beauty masks range from
$80 to $100, with body scrubs costing from $60 to $100. Standard manicures are
$18, with pedicures costing $30.

The grandest and largest spa in Puerto Rico is at the Ritz-Carlton (☎ **800/
241-3333** or 787/253-1700). This 12,000-square-foot elegant marble and stone
bi-level building offers panoramic ocean views to accompany self-improvement
therapies such as yoga, fitness activities, aerobics, and aqua-aerobics in the pool.

Upstairs, there are 11 treatment rooms, offering facials, massages, manicures, pedicures, hydrotherapy, and body wraps, among other treatments.

The Spa at the **Caribe Hilton & Casino** (☎ **800/HILTONS** or 787/721-0303) offers Universal and Nautilus weight machines, aerobics and yoga classes, treadmills, aerobicycles, massages, herbal wraps, loofah body polishes, and facials.

The Plaza Spa at the **Condado Plaza Hotel & Casino** (☎ **800/468-8588** or 787/721-1000) features Universal weight training machines, video exercycles, sauna, whirlpools, facials and massages.

The Penthouse Spa at the **El San Juan Hotel & Casino** (☎ **800/468-2818** or 787/791-1000) offers fitness evaluations, supervised weight-loss program, aerobics classes, sauna, steam room, and massage.

The Spa Caribe at the **Hyatt Regency Cerromar Beach** (☎ **800/233-1234** or 787/796-1234) offers shape-up programs including aerobics and "talking" Powercise machines and health evaluations, plus skin-and-body-care treatments such as massage, facials, and loofah polish.

TENNIS

If nonguests make reservations, they can use the courts at the **Caribe Hilton & Casino** (☎ **787/721-0303**) and the **Condado Plaza Hotel & Casino** (☎ **787/721-1000**). Also, there's a **public court** at the old navy base, Isla Grande, Miramar, which operates on a first-come, first-served basis. The entrance is from Avenida Fernández Juncos at Stop 11.

WINDSURFING

The sheltered water of the Condado Lagoon in San Juan is a favorite spot. Throughout the island, many of the companies featuring snorkeling and scuba diving also offer windsurfing equipment and instruction, and dozens of hotels offer facilities on their own premises. One of the best places in San Juan to go windsurfing is at **Caribe Aquatic Adventures,** with its main branch at the Radisson Normandie Hotel (☎ **787/724-1882**). Rentals cost $25 per hour, with a lesson costing $45.

4 Shopping

Because Puerto Rico is a U.S. commonwealth, American citizens don't pay duty on items brought back to the mainland. And you can still find great bargains on Puerto Rico, where the competition among shopkeepers is fierce. Even though the U.S. Virgin Islands are duty free, you can often find far lower prices on many items in San Juan than on St. Thomas.

The streets of Old Town, such as Calle San Francisco and Calle del Cristo, are the major venues for shopping. Note, however, that most stores in Old San Juan are closed on Sunday.

Native handcrafts can be good buys, including needlework, straw work, ceramics, hammocks, and papier-mâché fruits and vegetables, as well as paintings and sculptures by Puerto Rican artists (see "Puerto Rican Handcrafts" in chapter 2). Among these, the carved wooden religious idols known as santos (saints) have been called Puerto Rico's greatest contribution to the plastic arts and are sought by collectors. For the best selection of santos, head for Galeria Botello, Olé, or Puerto Rican Arts & Crafts (see "Gifts & Handcrafts," below).

Puerto Rico's biggest and most up-to-date shopping mall is **Plaza Las Americas,** in the financial district of Hato Rey, right off the Las Americas Expressway. This complex, with its fountains and advanced architecture, has more upscale shops. The variety of goods and prices is about comparab Stateside malls.

ANTIQUES

El Alcazar. Calle San José 103. ☎ **787/723-1229.**

Established in 1986 by retired career officers with the U.S. Army and the U.S. State Department, this is the largest emporium of antique furniture, silver, and art objects in the Caribbean. The best way to sift through the massive inventory is to begin at the address listed above, on Calle San José between Calle Luna and Calle Sol, and ask the owners, Sharon and Robert Bartos, to guide you to the other three buildings that are, literally, stuffed with important art and antiques. Each shop lies within a half-block of the organization's headquarters, and each is within a historic building of architectural or historic importance (public areas of several large hotels here contain furnishings acquired here). Hint: For antique silver, crystal, delicate porcelain, glittering chandeliers, Russian icons, and objects of religious devotion such as santos, look first at the organization's above-mentioned headquarters. Some of the objects, especially the 1930s-era dining-room sets, whose backs are composed of wood medallions held in place by woven canes or wicker, derive from Puerto Rico. The majority of the objects, however, are culled from estates and galleries throughout Europe.

José E. Alegria & Associates. Calle del Cristo 152-154. ☎ **787/721-8091.**

For generations, this shop reigned as the most stylish and prestigious repository of 19th-century art and antiques in San Juan, with an inventory of stately furniture that often evoked the grandest days of the Spanish colonial empire. You'll find these in La Arcada, an old-fashioned arcade lined with gift shops and boutiques. The remaining space is devoted to modern inventories of leather goods, Mexican artifacts, and gift items that include Caribbean herbs and spices.

ART

Galería Botello. Calle del Cristo 208. ☎ **787/723-2879.**

A contemporary Latin American art gallery, Galería Botello is a living tribute to the late Angel Botello, one of Puerto Rico's most outstanding artists. Born after the Spanish Civil War in a small village in Galicia, Spain, he fled to the Caribbean and spent 12 years in Haiti. His paintings and bronze sculptures, evocative of his colorful background, are done in a style uniquely his own. This galería is his former colonial mansion home, which he restored himself. Today it displays his paintings and sculptures, showcases the works of many outstanding local artists, and offers a large collection of Puerto Rican antique santos.

Galería Palomas. Calle del Cristo 207. ☎ **787/725-2660.**

This and the also-recommended Galería Botello are the two leading art galleries of Puerto Rico. Works range from $75 to $35,000, include some of the leading painters of the Latin American world, and are rotated every 2 to 3 weeks. The setting is a 17th-century colonial house. Of special note are works by such local artists as Homer, Moya, and Alicea.

Haitian Souvenirs. Calle San Francisco 206. ☎ **787/723-0959.**

In spite of its name, this is the best store in San Juan specializing in Haitian art and artifacts. Its walls are covered with framed versions of primitive Haitian landscapes, portraits, crowd scenes, and whimsical visions of jungles where lions, tigers, parrots, and herons take on quasi-human personalities and forms. Most paintings range from $35 to $350, although you can usually bargain them down a bit. Look for the brightly painted wall hangings crafted from sheets of metal (priced at around $120 each). Also look for satirical metal wall hangings, brightly painted, representing the *tap-taps* (battered public minivans and buses) of Port-au-Prince. Selling for around $45 each, they make amusing and whimsical souvenirs of a trip to the Caribbean.

BUTTERFLIES (MOUNTED)

Butterfly People. Calle Fortaleza 152. ☎ **787/723-2432.**

Butterfly People is a gallery and cafe (see chapter 6) in a handsomely restored building in Old San Juan. Butterflies, sold here in artfully arranged boxes, range from $20 for a single mounting to thousands of dollars for whole-wall murals. The butterflies are preserved and will last forever. The dimensional artwork is sold in limited editions and can be shipped worldwide. Most of these butterflies come from farms around the world, some of the most beautiful hailing from Indonesia, Malaysia, and New Guinea. Tucked away within the same premises, with ownership by the daughter of the owner of the cafe, is **Malula Antiques.** Specializing in tribal art from the Moroccan sub-Sahara and Syria, it contains a sometimes-startling collection of primitive and timeless crafts and accessories.

CLOTHING & BEACH WEAR

Lindissima Shop. Calle Fortaleza 300. ☎ **787/721-0550.**

This outlet offers a collection for women of contemporary sportswear and dresses for both daytime and evening. If you lack an outfit for a formal evening aboard ship, you are likely to find it here. Garments generally range from $59 to $700.

London Fog. Calle del Cristo 156. ☎ **787/722-4334.**

The last thing you need in steamy San Juan is a winter overcoat or parka, but the prices at this factory outlet of London Fog are usually so low that a purchase is often well worth it. Prices are often between 30% and 35% less than those at many retail stores on the U.S. mainland. Men's, women's, and children's garments are displayed on two floors of a colonial house.

Nono Maldonado. 1051 Ashford Ave. ☎ **787/721-0456.**

Named after its owner, a Puerto Rico–born designer who worked for many years as the fashion editor of *Esquire* magazine, this is one of the most fashionable and upscale haberdashers in the Caribbean. Selling both men's and women's clothing, it contains everything from socks to dinner jackets, as well as ready-to-wear versions of Maldonado's twice-a-year collections. Both ready-to-wear and couture are available here. Although this is the designer's main store (midway between the Condado Plaza and the Ramada Hotel), there is also a Maldonado boutique in El San Juan Hotel in Isla Verde.

Polo Ralph Lauren Factory Store. Calle del Cristo 201. ☎ **787/722-2136.**

It's as stylish and carefully orchestrated as anything you'd expect from one of North America's leading clothiers. Even better, its prices are often 35% to 40% less than the cost in retail stores on the U.S. mainland. You can find even greater discounts on irregular or slightly damaged garments, but inspect them carefully before buying. The store occupies two floors of a pair of colonial buildings, with one upstairs room devoted to home furnishings. Men's sizes larger than a 42 waist are almost never in stock.

W. H. Smith. In the Condado Plaza Hotel, 999 Ashford Ave. ☎ **787/721-1000,** ext. 2094.

This outlet sells mostly women's clothing, everything from bathing suits and beach attire to jogging suits. For men, there are shorts, bathing suits, and jogging suits. There's also a good selection of books and maps.

GIFTS & HANDCRAFTS
Anaiboa. Calle San Francisco 100. ☎ **787/724-8017.**

Anaiboa occupies a cubbyhole that opens onto a pedestrians-only stretch adjacent to Calle del Cristo. Run by a married team of artists (Edgard Rodriguez and Mari-anne Ramirez), it sells one-of-a-kind artifacts, including ceramic boxes, hat racks, mirrors, serving trays, and small-scale furniture accented with whimsical drawings of faces, plants, and animals. Many objects sell for as little as $15. Recently, the owners diversified into a greater emphasis on stained glass and mosaics.

Bared & Sons. Calle Fortaleza 65 (at the corner of Calle San Justo). ☎ **787/724-4811.**

Now in its fourth decade, this is the main outlet of a chain of at least 20 upper-bracket jewelry stores on Puerto Rico. There's a worthy inventory of gemstones, gold, diamonds, and wristwatches on the street level that does a thriving business with cruise-ship passengers. But the real value of this store lies one floor up, where a monumental collection of porcelain and crystal is packed, in claustrophobic prox-imity, for display. It's a great source for hard-to-get and discontinued patterns (priced at around 20% less than at equivalent outlets Stateside) from Christofle, Royal Doulton, Wedgwood, Limoges, Royal Copenhagen, Lalique, Lladró, Herend, Baccarat, and Daum.

Centro Nacional de Artes Populares y Artesanias. Calle Cristo 253. ☎ **787/722-0621.**

Many stores in San Juan sell tourist junk passed off as handcrafts. But at this center, run by the Institute of Puerto Rican Culture, the quality of craft work is high. It is a superb repository of native crafts, many of which are for display only but others of which are for sale. Housed in a colonial building, this shop scans the island for artisans still practicing time-treasured crafts and doing so with considerable skill. The prices aren't always cheap but the quality is high.

El Artesano. Calle Fortaleza 314. ☎ **787/721-6483.**

If your budget doesn't allow for an excursion to the Andes, head for this shop. You'll find Mexican and Peruvian icons of the Virgin Mary; charming depictions of fish and Latin American birds in terra-cotta and brass; all kinds of woven goods; painted cupboards, chests, and boxes; and mirrors and Latin dolls.

Galería Bóveda. Calle del Cristo 209. ☎ **787/725-0263.**

This long, narrow space is crammed with exotic jewelry, clothing, greeting cards with images of life in Puerto Rico, some 100 handmade lamps, antiques, Mexican punched tin and glass, and art nouveau reproductions, among other items.

Olé. Calle Fortaleza 105. ☎ **787/724-2445.**

Browsing this store is a learning experience. Practically everything comes from Puerto Rico or Latin America. If you want a straw hat from Ecuador, hand-beaten Chilean silver, Christmas ornaments, or Puerto Rican *santos,* this is the place.

Puerto Rican Arts & Crafts. Calle Fortaleza 204. ☎ **787/725-5596.**

Set in a 200-year-old colonial building, this unique store is one of the premier outlets on the island for authentic artifacts. Of particular interest are papier-mâché carnival masks from Ponce, whose grotesque and colorful features were originally conceived to chase away evil spirits. Taíno designs inspired by ancient petroglyphs are incorporated into most of the sterling-silver jewelry sold here. There's an art gallery in back, with silk-screened serigraphs by local artists. The outlet has a gourmet Puerto Rican food section with items like coffee, rum, and hot sauces for sale. A related specialty of this well-respected store involves the exhibition and sale of modern replicas of the Spanish colonial tradition of *santos,* which are carved and sometimes polychromed representations of the Catholic saints and the infant Jesus. Priced from $44 to $225 each, and laboriously carved by artisans in private studios around the island, they're easy to pack in a suitcase because the largest one measures only 12 inches from halo to toe.

JEWELRY

Barrachina's. Calle Fortaleza 104 (between Calle del Cristo and Calle San José). ☎ **787/725-7912.**

The birthplace, in 1963, of the piña colada, Barrachina's is a favorite of cruise-ship passengers. It offers one of the largest selections of jewelry, perfume, cigars, and gifts in San Juan. There's a patio for drinks where you can order (what else?) a piña colada. There are also a Bacardi rum outlet (bottles cost less than Stateside but the same as at the Bacardi distillery), a costume-jewelry department, a gift shop, and a section for authentic silver jewelry, plus a restaurant.

The Gold Ounce. Plaza los Muchachos, Calle Fortaleza 201. ☎ **787/724-3102.**

This is the direct factory outlet for the oldest jewelry factory on Puerto Rico, the Kury Company. Most of the output is shipped Stateside. Don't expect a top-notch jeweler here: many of the pieces are replicated in endless repetition. But don't overlook the place for 14-karat-gold ornaments. Some of the designs are charming, and prices are about 20% less than those at retail stores on the North American mainland. In addition, the outlet has opened an art store, called **Arts and More,** featuring regional works, plus a cigar store called **The Cigar Shop.**

Joyería Riviera. Calle La Cruz 205. ☎ **787/725-4000.**

This emporium of 18-karat gold and diamonds is the island's leading jeweler. Adjacent to Plaza de Armas, the shop has an impeccable reputation. Its owner, Julio Abislaiman, stocks his store at such diamond centers as Antwerp, Tel Aviv, and New York. This is the major distributor of Rolex watches on Puerto Rico. Prices range from $150 into the tens of thousands of dollars—at these prices, it's a good thing you can get "whatever you want," according to the owner.

200 Fortaleza. Calle Fortaleza 200 (at the corner of Calle La Cruz). ☎ **787/723-1989.**

Known as a leading cost-conscious place to buy fine jewelry in Old San Juan, this shop has 14-karat Italian gold chains and bracelets that are measured, fitted, and sold by weight. You can purchase watches or beautiful gems in modern settings in both 14- and 18-karat gold. The store recently expanded its collection to include 18-karat, emerald, ruby, diamond, and pearl jewelry, along with platinum bridal jewelry.

Vergina Gallery. Calle del Cristo 202. ☎ **787/721-0592.**

San Juan's most exotic jewelry emporium, this is the only outlet in the Caribbean showcasing the neo-Byzantine and ancient Greek designs of Zolotos, one of Greece's most spectacular jewelers. Most of the pieces are made of hammered 18- and 22-karat gold, inset with colorful glittering gemstones. There's also an inventory of streamlined platinum jewelry from Germany and worthy reproductions of medieval Greek and Russian icons, priced from $10 to $3,000.

Yas Mar. Calle Fortaleza 205. ☎ **787/724-1377.**

This shop sells convincing, glittering fake diamonds for those who don't want to wear the real thing. It also stocks real diamond chips, emeralds, sapphires, and rubies.

LACE & LINENS

There are no major stores in San Juan that specialize exclusively in lace, a collector's item here (see "Puerto Rican Handcrafts" in chapter 2). You can find it at The Linen House (see below). Serious collectors head for the hamlet of Moca, near Aquadilla, the island's headquarters for lace making. Moca's best artisans are **Nelly Vera** (☎ 787/877-0387) and **Jolanda Romero** (☎ 787/877-2971). They do not publish their addresses because they don't want customers showing up without calling first, so phone ahead for an appointment. If you don't speak Spanish, ask the staff at your hotel to call and make arrangements for a personal shopping visit.

You can also attend the Puerto Rican Weaving Festival, held annually at the end of April in the town of Isabela.

The Linen House. Calle Fortaleza 250. ☎ **787/721-4219.**

This unpretentious store specializes in napery, bed linens, and lace and has the island's best selection. Some of the more delicate pieces are expensive, but most are moderate in price. Inventories include embroidered shower curtains selling for around $35 each, and lace doilies, bun warmers, place mats, and tablecloths that seamstresses took weeks to complete. Some astonishingly lovely items are available for as little as $30. The aluminum/pewter serving dishes have strikingly beautiful Spanish-colonial designs. Prices here are sometimes 40% lower than those on the North American mainland.

LEATHER

Leather & Pearls. Calle Tanca 252 (at the corner of Calle Tetuán). ☎ **787/724-8185.**

Majorca pearls and fine leather garments (bags, shoes, suitcases, briefcases, and accessories) are sold here from manufacturers that include Gucci and Fendi. Also look for leather goods from the same Iberian enterprise that brings you Lladro porcelain. A relative newcomer to the field of leather goods, they've impressed consumers with their quality and pizzazz.

5 San Juan After Dark

San Juan nightlife comes in all varieties. From the vibrant performing-arts scene to street-level salsa or the casinos, discos, and bars, there's plenty of entertainment available almost any evening.

Qué Pasa, the official visitor's guide to Puerto Rico, lists cultural events, including music, dance, theater, film, and art exhibits. It's distributed free by the tourist office.

THE PERFORMING ARTS

Centro de Bellas Artes. Av. Ponce de León 22. ☎ **787/724-4747,** or 787/725-7334 for the ticket agent. Tickets $13–$65; 50% discounts for seniors. Bus: 1.

In the heart of Santurce, the Performing Arts Center is a 6-minute taxi ride from most of the Condado hotels. It contains the Festival Hall, Drama Hall, and the Experimental Theater. Some of the events here will be of interest only to Spanish speakers; others attract an international audience.

Teatro Tapía. Av. Ponce de León. ☎ **787/723-2079.** Tickets $15–$38, depending on the show.

Standing across from Plaza de Colón and built about 1832, this is one of the oldest theaters in the western hemisphere (see "Historic Sights," earlier in this chapter). Productions, some musical, are staged here throughout the year and include drama, dances, and cultural events. You'll have to call the box office (open Monday to Friday from 9am to 6pm) for specific information.

THE CLUB & MUSIC SCENE

Babylon. In El San Juan Hotel & Casino, 6063 Isla Verde Ave., Isla Verde. ☎ **787/791-1000.** Cover $10, free for residents of the El San Juan Hotel. Wed–Sat 9:30pm–3am. Bus: A7, T1, or 2.

Modeled after an artist's rendition of the once-notorious city of Mesopotamia, this nightclub is designed in the form of a circle, with a central dance floor and a wrap-around balcony where onlookers and voyeurs—a 25 to 45 age group—can observe the activities on the floor below. Accessorized with one of the best sound systems in the Caribbean, its location within the most exciting hotel in San Juan allows guests the chance to visit the hotel's bars, its intricately decorated lobby, and its casino en route.

Café Don Rafael. Plazoleta Rafael, Calle Tetuán 206. ☎ **787/724-9827.**

During the daylight hours, this place in Old San Juan functions as an unpretentious but well-orchestrated luncheonette, where salads, sandwiches (especially stuffed baguettes), and hearty soups combine to nourish office workers and ship employees for the continuation of their afternoons. Expect to spend about $14 per person for a full meal. The heart and soul of the place, however, begins to expand after 4pm and continues throughout the evening. Then, lots of 30-something folk interested in art, photography, painting, and music congregate over cups of coffee, glasses of beer, margaritas, rum-and-cokes, and vodkas with 7UP to gossip, flirt, dream, or dialogue. The week's highlight occurs every Thursday, when live Latino jazz is performed from any of several well-respected local bands. Open Sunday to Wednesday from 11am to 10pm, and Thursday to Saturday from 11am to 2am.

Café Matisse. Ashford Ave. ☎ **787/723-7910.** Cover (Fri–Sat only) $7.

Although it serves platters of food, and defines part of its venue as a restaurant, this establishment is best known as a bar where live music—often salsa—is usually part of the ambiance. Overall, the site is best known for its conviviality, sense of Big Apple cool, and hot music that makes every red-blooded *Latino* inside want to dance, dance, dance. It's open Tuesday to Saturday from 5pm till around 2am or later, depending on the crowd.

Egipto. Av. Roberto H. Todd 1. ☎ **787/725-4664.** Cover (including 1 or 2 drinks) $5 Sun, $7 Wed, $10 Thurs–Sat.

This busy nightclub attracts young, upwardly mobile singles. There's a dance floor well worn by years of boogying, although many visitors just come for drinks at the long and very accommodating bar. The decor is inspired by ancient Egypt and includes sphinxes and hieroglyphs, which help reverberate the music from a sound system worthy of the most popular clubs of New York. There's live music Thursday and Friday. Its transformation from a bar to a crowded disco usually begins around 10 or 11pm. It seems that every upwardly mobile yuppie under 35 in San Juan has probably been to Egipto at least once, and many of them are regulars. You'll find the place in the Condado district, about 3 blocks south of Ashford Avenue. Closing time depends on the amount of business and could be anywhere from 2 to 6am. The club opens at 8pm on Wednesday and Sunday, at 5pm on Thursday and Friday, and at 9pm Saturday. It is closed Monday and Tuesday. The cover charge isn't imposed until after 8:30pm.

Laser. Calle del Cruz 251. ☎ **787/725-7581.** Cover $6–$10.

Set in the heart of the old town near the corner of Calle Fortaleza, this disco is especially crowded when cruise ships pull into town. Once inside, you can wander over the three floors of its historic premises, listening to whatever music happens to be hot in New York at the time of your visit, with lots of additional Latino merengue and salsa thrown in as well. Depending on the night, the age of the crowd varies, but in general it's the 20s, 30s, and even 40s set. Usually, it's open daily from 8pm to 4am. Women enter free after midnight on Saturday.

Millennium. In the Condado Plaza Hotel, 999 Ashford Ave. ☎ **787/722-1900.** Entrance $20 after 9pm.

It isn't the largest disco in San Juan, but it's one of the favorites of many Condado-watchers. The entry lies adjacent to the main entrance ramp of the Condado Plaza Hotel. Amid a modern, mostly blue background, you'll find a pleasant and highly accommodating cigar bar and a sound system that knows how to project the ongoing roster of techno music, Latino merengues, and disco classics from the 1970s. Most clients here are in their late 20s and early 30s, but in the animated setting, folks in their 40s and 50s don't feel out of place. The club is open Monday through Wednesday from 5pm to 2am, Thursday through Saturday from 9pm to 2am. Mixed drinks cost $5.50 each.

THE BAR SCENE

Unless otherwise stated, there is no cover charge at the following bars.

Cigar Bar. El San Juan Hotel & Casino, 6063 Isla Verde Ave., Carolina. ☎ **787/791-1000.**

The Palm Court Lobby at this elegant hotel boasts an impressive cigar bar, with a magnificent repository of the finest stogies in the world. Although the bar is generally filled with visitors, some of San Juan's most fashionable men—and women too—can be seen puffing away in this chic rendezvous while sipping a cognac.

Fiesta Bar. In the Condado Plaza Hotel & Casino, 999 Ashford Ave. ☎ **787/721-1000.**

This bar lures in a healthy mixture of local residents and hotel guests, usually the post-35 set. The margaritas are appropriately salty, the rhythms are hot and Latin, and the free admission usually helps you forget any losses you might have suffered in the nearby casinos.

Palm Court. In El San Juan Hotel & Casino, 6063 Isla Verde Ave., Isla Verde. ☎ **787/ 791-1000.**

Birth of the Piña Colada

When actress Joan Crawford tasted the piña colada at what was then the Beach-combers Bar in the **Caribe Hilton,** Calle Los Rosales (☎ **787/721-0303),** she claimed it was "better than slapping Bette Davis in the face."

This famous drink is the creation of bartender Ramon "Monchito" Marrero, now retired, who was hired by the Hilton in 1954. He spent 3 months mixing, tasting, and discarding hundreds of combinations until he felt he had the right blend. Thus the frothy piña colada was born. It's been estimated that some 100 million of them have been sipped around the world since that fateful time.

Monchito never patented his formula and doesn't mind sharing it with the world. Still served at the Hilton, here is his not-so-secret recipe:

2 ounces light rum
1 ounce coconut cream
1 ounce heavy cream
6 ounces fresh pineapple
1/2 cup crushed ice
Pineapple wedge and maraschino cherry for garnish

Pour rum, coconut cream, cream, and pineapple juice in blender. Add ice. Blend for 15 seconds. Pour into a 12-ounce glass. Add garnishes.

This is the most beautiful bar on the island—perhaps in the entire Caribbean. Most of the patrons are hotel guests, but rich-heeled locals make up at least a quarter of the business at this fashionable rendezvous. Set in an oval wrapped around a sunken bar area, amid marble and burnished mahogany, it offers a view of one of the world's largest chandeliers. After 9pm Monday to Saturday, live music, often salsa and merengue, emanates from an adjoining room (El Chico Bar).

Shannon's Irish Pub. Calle Bori 496, Río Piedras. ☎ **787/281-8466.**

Ireland and its ales meet the tropics at this pub with a Latin accent. A sports bar, it's the regular watering hole of many university students, a constant supplier of high-energy rock 'n' roll and 10 TV monitors. There's live music Wednesday through Sunday—everything from rock to jazz to Latin. There are pool tables, and a simple cafe serves inexpensive lunches Monday through Friday. A $3 cover charge is sometimes imposed for a special live performance.

Violeta's. Calle Fortaleza 56 (2 blocks from the Gran Hotel Convento). ☎ **787/723-6804.**

Stylish and comfortable, Violeta's occupies the ground floor of a 200-year-old beamed house. Because of its location in the old town, the bar draws an equal mix-ture of visitors and locals, usually in their 20s and 30s. Sometimes a pianist per-forms at the oversize grand piano. An open courtyard out back provides additional seating for sipping margaritas or other drinks.

HOT NIGHTS IN GAY SAN JUAN

Straight folks are generally welcome in each of these gay venues, and many local couples show up for the hot music and dancing. Local straight boys who show up to cause trouble are generally ushered out quickly. Unless otherwise stated, there is no cover.

The Barefoot Bar. 2 Calle Vendig. ☎ **787/724-7230.**

Along with the bar at the Atlantic Beach Hotel just across the street, this is the most tuned-in gay bar in Puerto Rico. It occupies a blue building whose terrace extends out over the sands of the same beach shared by the Marriott Hotel, almost next door. At least 98% of the clientele is gay and male, and includes goodly numbers of crew from the local airlines and whatever cruise ships happen to be in port. Simple lunches, consisting mostly of sandwiches and salads, are served from noon till around 4pm; after that the food service ends in favor of drinking and dialogue.

The Beach Bar. In the Atlantic Beach Hotel, 1 Calle Vendig. ☎ **787/721-6900.**

Its indoor/outdoor format and its position adjacent to a terrace extending out over the beach are roughly equivalent to the facilities at the Barefoot Bar, which is just across the street. Together, they form a complex of bars and terraces that appeal to a clientele that's mostly male and mostly gay. A restaurant within the hotel serves breakfast and lunch, but not dinner, to a clientele that shows up between 11am and 1am every day of the week.

Cups. 1708 Calle San Mateo, Santurce. ☎ **787/268-3570.**

Its venue is that of a Latino tavern, and its premises are valued as the only place in San Juan that caters almost exclusively to lesbians. Men of any sexual persuasion aren't particularly welcome. The scene reminds many lesbians of a tropical version of one of the bars they left behind at home. Although the club is open Wednesday through Sunday from 7pm to 4am, entertainment such as live music or cabaret is presented only on Wednesday night at 9pm, Friday night at 10pm, and Sunday at 8pm.

Eros. 1257 Ponce de León, Santurce. ☎ **787/722-1131.** Cover $10 Fri–Sat, includes 2 free drinks; otherwise, free.

Any gay male employed by any of the cruise lines that dock in San Juan's harbor overnight will almost invariably head for the flashing lights and up-to-date music of Puerto Rico's largest and busiest gay disco. Occupying two levels of a building in an urban neighborhood in the Santurce district, it sports an ancient Greek/Egyptian motif. The average age of clients is around 28. Rum-based drinks, merengue, and whatever music is favored in gay clubs around the U.S. are popular. Most of the male/male flirting, dancing, and conversations here begin after around 10:30pm. Open Wednesday through Sunday from 9pm to 5am.

CASINOS

Experienced gamblers claim you get better odds in Las Vegas or Atlantic City, but casinos remain one of the allures of Puerto Rico. In fact, many visitors come here on package deals just to gamble at one of the posh hotels at the Condado or Isla Verde.

The casino generating the most excitement today is the 18,500-square-foot **Casino at The Ritz-Carlton,** the largest facility of its kind in Puerto Rico. It combines the elegant decor of a bygone era (the 1940s) with tropical fabrics and patterns. This is one of the plushest and most exclusive entertainment complexes in the Caribbean. You expect to see Joan Crawford arrive beautifully gowned and on the arm of Clark Gable. It features traditional games such as blackjack, roulette, baccarat, craps, and slot machines.

One of the splashiest of San Juan's casinos is at the **Wyndham Old San Juan Hotel & Casino,** which turns some 80% of its lobby over to casino action. Five-card stud poker competes with some 240 slot machines and roulette tables. You can also try your luck at the **Caribe Hilton** (one of the better ones), **El San Juan Hotel**

& Casino on Isla Verde Avenue in Isla Verde, and the **Condado Plaza Hotel & Casino.** There are no passports to flash or admissions to pay, as in European casinos. The **Radisson Ambassador Plaza Hotel and Casino** is another deluxe hotel noted for its casino action. The **Diamond Palace Hotel & Casino,** Av. Condado 55, also has a gambling emporium. The Stellaris Casino at the **San Juan Marriott Resort** is one of the island's newest, as is El Tropical Casino at **Crowne Plaza Hotel & Casino.** El Tropical is open 24 hours a day and is the only theme casino in San Juan, re-creating El Yunque Tropical Rain Forest.

San Juan Grand Beach Hotel & Casino, 187 Isla Verde Ave. in Isla Verde, is open from noon to 4am daily. This 10,000-square-foot gaming facility is an elegant rendezvous. One of its Murano chandeliers is longer than a bowling alley. The casino offers 207 slot machines, 16 blackjack tables, 3 dice tables, 4 roulette wheels, and a minibaccarat table.

The best casinos "out in the island" are those at the **Hyatt Regency Cerromar Beach** and **Hyatt Dorado Beach.** In fact, you can drive to either of these from San Juan to enjoy their nighttime diversions. There are also casinos at **Wyndham Palmas del Mar Resort & Villas** and at **Westin Rio Mar at Palmer** and yet another at the **Mayagüez Hilton** in western Puerto Rico. Puerto Rico's "second city," Ponce, now has a major casino following the opening of the **Ponce Hilton and Casino.**

Most casinos are open daily from noon to 4pm and again from 8pm to 4am. Jackets for men are requested after 6pm.

MOVIES

Movie theaters in San Juan showing films in English include **Metro 1, 2, 3,** Av. Ponce de León 1255, Santurce (☎ **787/722-0465**); and **Fine Arts Cinema,** Av. Ponce de León 654, Miramar, Santurce (☎ **787/721-4288**).

COCKFIGHTS

A brutal sport and not to everyone's taste, cockfights are legal in Puerto Rico. The most authentic are in Salinas, a town on the southern coast with a southwestern ethos, which has *galleras,* or rings, for cockfighting. But you don't have to go all the way there to see these matches. About three fights per week take place at the **Coliseo Gallistico,** Route 37, kilometer 1.5, Isla Verde. Call ☎ **787/791-6005** for the schedule and to order tickets, which cost $8, $10, $15, or $25, depending on your seat.

Dorado, the North Coast & Palmas del Mar

Often people who book into one of five of the Caribbean's premier resorts—Westin Rio Mar Beach Resort & Casino at Rio Grande, Palmas del Mar, and El Conquistador on Puerto Rico's east coast, and the Hyatt Cerromar Beach and Hyatt Dorado Beach to the west of the capital—see San Juan only on their way to or from the airport. If you're going to Puerto Rico for the first time and will stay at one of these resorts, you may want to spend a day or so sightseeing and shopping in San Juan first. Once you've settled into your resort, you may not want to leave the grounds, since these properties are self-contained, with beach, swimming, golf, tennis, dining, and nightlife all on premises.

In this chapter we will take a look at Dorado, home of the Hyatt resorts; Rio Grande with its Westin Rio Mar Beach Resort & Casino; Las Croabas and its El Conquistador; Ceiba, whose little inns cater to those heading to El Yunque; and the huge Palmas del Mar resort near Humacao. The big resorts also make good short trips for anyone who doesn't want to pay for their luxury accommodations but would like to visit them for lunch and an afternoon on their splendid beaches.

Note that visitor information and rental cars must be acquired in San Juan before you head to the resorts (see chapter 3).

1 Dorado: The Hyatt Resorts

18 miles W of San Juan

The name Dorado itself evokes a kind of magic, as a world of luxury resorts and villas unfolds along the north shore of Puerto Rico. The elegant ✪ **Hyatt Dorado Beach Hotel** and the newer, larger ✪ **Hyatt Regency Cerromar Beach Hotel** sit on the choice white-sand beaches here.

The site was originally purchased in 1905 by Dr. Alfred T. Livingston, a Jamestown, N.Y., physician, who developed it as a 1,000-acre grapefruit and coconut plantation. Dr. Livingston's daughter, Clara, widely known in aviation circles and a friend of Amelia Earhart, owned and operated the plantation after her father's death. It was she who built the airstrip here. The building that houses Su Casa Restaurant (see "Where to Dine," below) was for many years the Livingstons' plantation home.

ESSENTIALS

GETTING THERE   If you're driving from San Juan, take Highway 2 west to Route 693 north to Dorado (trip time: 40 min.). Otherwise, call **Dorado Transport Corp,** which occupies a premises on the site shared by the Hyatt hotels (☎ 787/796-1234). Using 18-passenger minibuses, they offer frequent shuttle service between the Hyatt Hotels and the San Juan airport. They operate at frequent intervals, daily between 11am and 10pm. The fare is $15 per person, but a minimum of three passengers must make the trip for the bus to operate.

GETTING AROUND   Once you're in Dorado, you can get around via the shuttle bus that travels between the two hotels every 30 minutes during the day.

OUTDOOR ACTIVITIES

If you feel like doing something more energetic than lounging on the beautiful beachfront here, the Hyatt resorts (see below) both offer their guests a wide array of beachside water-sports activities. In fact, the Hyatt Regency Cerromar Beach Hotel has the world's longest freshwater swimming pool. Nonguests cannot use the swimming pools here, though they can use the facilities of the Lisa Penfield Watersports Center, for which they have to pay (see below for details).

GOLF

The ✪ **Hyatt Resorts Puerto Rico** at Dorado (☎ 787/796-1234), with 72 holes of golf, offers the greatest number of options in the Caribbean. The 18-hole Robert Trent Jones Sr.–designed courses at the Hyatt Regency Cerromar and the Hyatt Dorado Beach match the finest anywhere. The courses were built between 1959 and 1970. The two original courses—east and west (☎ 787/796-8961), both of which are associated with the Hyatt Dorado Beach Resort—were carved out of a jungle and offer tight fairways bordered by trees and forests, with lots of ocean holes. The somewhat newer, and less frequently televised, north and south courses (☎ 787/796-8915), which fall under the jurisdiction of the Hyatt Regency Cerromar, feature wide fairways with well-bunkered greens and an assortment of lakes, water traps, and tricky wind factors. Each of the four has a 72 par. The longest is the south course at 7,047 yards. Scheduling of tee-off times is almost always easier if you're a resident of one of the Hyatt resorts. For the north and south courses, Hyatt residents pay $65 for greens fees, whereas nonresidents are charged $85. At the east and west courses, Hyatt residents are charged $85 for greens fees, rising to $120 for nonresidents. Golf carts at any of the courses rent for $20, a fee that applies whether you play 9 or 18 holes. The north-and-south-course duo and the east-and-west-course pair maintain separate pro shops, each with a bar and snack-style restaurant. Both are open daily from 7am to 5:30pm.

TENNIS

Again, the twin Hyatt resorts of **Dorado** and **Cerromar** (☎ 787/796-1234) have the monopoly, with a total of 17 courts between them. The charge is $15 an hour, rising to $18 from 6 to 10pm. Lessons are available for $60 per hour. Nonguests can't use the courts, however.

WATER SPORTS GALORE: WINDSURFING, SCUBA DIVING & SNORKELING

The best place for windsurfing on the island's north shore is along the well-maintained beachfront of the Hyatt Dorado Beach Hotel near the 10th hole of the hotel's famous east golf course. Here, **Penfield Island Adventures**

(☎ **787/796-1234,** ext. 3768, or 787/796-2188) offers 90-minute lessons for $60 each; board rentals cost $50 per half day. Well supplied with a wide array of Windsurfers, including some designed specifically for beginners and children, the school benefits from the almost uninterrupted flow of the north shore's strong, steady winds and an experienced crew of instructors. A kayaking/snorkeling trip, departing daily at 9:15 and 11:45am, and lasting 1½ hours, costs $45.

You can go snorkeling on your way along the beachfront strip in front of the two Hyatts, but the Atlantic here is often turbulent. Summer is better for this than January or February, when the choppy waters are more suited for windsurfing than snorkeling.

At this same outfit, scuba divers can book two-tank boat dives for $119 per person.

Waverunners can be rented for $55 per half hour for a single rider, and $70 for two riders. A Sunfish rents for $50 an hour. The owner and namesake of this establishment, incidentally, is a well-known professional athlete, and winner of a world-class windsurfing competition in Australia in 1981.

WHERE TO STAY

The two Hyatt hotels in Dorado sprawl across the former Livingston estate, which now bristles with palms, pine trees, and purple bougainvillea, all fronting a 2-mile stretch of sandy ocean beach. The two side-by-side 18-hole championship golf courses designed by Robert Trent Jones are their big draw.

✪ **Hyatt Dorado Beach Resort & Casino.** Dorado, PR 00646. ☎ **800/233-1234** or 787/796-1234. Fax 787/796-6560. 298 units, 17 casitas. A/C MINIBAR TV TEL. Winter $495–$655 double, $785 casita for 2; off-season $170–$325 double, $385–$450 casita for 2. MAP (mandatory in winter) $65 extra per day for adults, $35 extra per day for children. AE, DC, DISC, MC, V.

Whereas its twin, the Cerromar, evokes a conventional hotel (see below), the Dorado Beach is a low-rise, less striking physical plant whose fans appreciate the emphasis on the natural terrain around it. It's superior to its sibling, the Cerromar, and more tranquil. Families interested in massive facilities and the best sports-oriented program in Puerto Rico gravitate there, whereas couples seeking a more subdued and romantic ambiance cast their vote here. The Dorado sprawls across grounds containing palms, pine trees, and purple bougainvillea, all within a short walk of a 2-mile-long sandy beach. The present hotel, originally a Rockefeller playground, opened in 1958, and many repeat guests, including celebrities, have been coming back ever since.

The Hyatt Hotels Corporation has spent millions on improvements. The renovated bedrooms have marble bathrooms and terra-cotta flooring throughout. Rooms are available on the beach or in villas tucked in and around the lushly planted grounds. The casitas are a series of private beach or poolside houses.

Dining/Diversions: Breakfast can be taken on your private balcony and lunch on an outdoor ocean terrace. Dinner is served in a three-tiered main dining room, where you can watch the surf. Hyatt Dorado chefs have won many awards, and the food at the hotel restaurants is among the most appealing in the Caribbean. The resort's Su Casa Restaurant is worthy of a separate mention under "Where to Dine," below, but dining there is not included in the MAP. The Beach Grill and Pro Shop are for casual meals. And don't forget the casino.

Amenities: 24-hour room service, baby-sitting, laundry/dry cleaning, two 18-hole golf courses, seven all-weather tennis courts, full-service spa, two swimming pools, children's camp, one of the best windsurfing schools in Puerto Rico.

⊕ Family-Friendly Hotels

Hyatt's Resorts *(see p. 169–170)*   These hostelries offer family getaway pack- ages at Camp Hyatt, featuring professionally supervised day and evening pro- grams for children ages 3 to 12. Children also receive a 50% discount on meals.

El Conquistador *(see p. 172)*   There's a special activities area and game room just for kids. Camp Coquí (daily 9am to 3pm) for children ages 3 to 12 costs $38 per day. Activities may include arts and crafts, fishing, sailing, and cooking lessons. Children under 12 stay free in their parents' room, and baby-sitting ser- vices are available.

Palmas del Mar Resorts *(see p. 179)*   This resort complex features a supervised activities program for children ages 5 to 14 in June and July; offerings include swimming, volleyball, aerobics, handcrafts, bowling, table games, sack races, table tennis, bingo, aquatic polo, basketball, and ring toss. Kids also delight in the 3 miles of beaches.

✪ **Hyatt Regency Cerromar Beach Hotel.** Dorado, PR 00646. ☎ **800/233-1234** or 787/796-1234. Fax 787/796-4647. 526 units. A/C MINIBAR TV TEL. Winter $340–$480 double, from $770 suite. Spring and fall $235–$325 double, from $570 suite. Summer $185–$220 double, from $435 suite. MAP $65 extra for adults, $35 extra for children. AE, DC, DISC, MC, V.

Near the more elegant Hyatt Dorado Beach Hotel (see above), this Hyatt is a tra- ditional cement-and-glass high-rise whose lines are softened with masses of land- scaping. It stands on its own beach and boasts a wealth of sports facilities and resort amenities. The name Cerromar is a combination of two words—*cerro* (mountain) and *mar* (sea)—and true to its name, it's surrounded by mountains and ocean. Approximately 22 miles west of San Juan, it shares the 1,000-acre former Liv- ingston estate with the Dorado, so guests can enjoy the Robert Trent Jones Sr. golf courses as well as the other sports facilities at the next-door hotel. A shuttle bus runs back and forth between the two resorts every half hour. Offering everything from a casino to a supper club to a dance club, this property attracts a more action-oriented clientele than does Dorado Beach. This is also a favorite hotel for conventions. Go here if you like a "theme park" type hotel; check into the Dorado if you prefer more class and style, and fewer screaming kids running up and down the corridor.

All rooms and 20 suites have first-class appointments and are well maintained; the majority contain private balconies. The floors throughout are tile and the fur- nishings are casual tropical, in soft colors and pastels. All rooms have honor bars and in-room safes.

The water playground here has the world's longest freshwater swimming pool, a 1,776-foot-long fantasy with a river-like current in five connected free-form pools. It takes 15 minutes to float from one end of the pool to the other. There are also 14 waterfalls, tropical landscaping, a subterranean Jacuzzi, water slides, walks, bridges, and a children's pool. In addition, a full-service spa and health club provide services for both body and skin care, including Swedish massages and a Powercise machine that "talks" to you.

Dining/Diversions: The outdoor Swan Café has three levels connected by a dra- matic staircase; some tables overlook a lake populated by swans and flamingos. Other dining choices include Sushi Wong's and the hotel's pride and joy, Medici's (see "Where to Dine," below). The Flamingo bar offers a wide, open-air expanse overlooking the sea and the water playground. The resort also has a casino and dance club.

Amenities: 24-hour room service, laundry/dry cleaning, baby-sitting, 21 tennis courts, Camp Hyatt children's program for guests 3 to 12.

WHERE TO DINE

El Malecón. Rte. 693, km 8.2. ☎ **787/796-1645.** Main courses $8.95–$33. AE, MC, V. Daily 11am–11pm. PUERTO RICAN.

If you'd like to discover an unpretentious local place serving good Puerto Rican cuisine, head for El Malecón, a simple concrete structure 1 minute from a small shopping center. It has a cozy family ambiance and is especially popular on weekends. Some members of the staff speak English, and the chef is best with fresh seafood, which most diners order. The chef might also prepare a variety of items not listed on the menu.

✪ **Medici's.** In the Hyatt Regency Cerromar. ☎ **787/796-1234,** ext. 3240. Reservations required. Main courses $18–$37. AE, DC, DISC, MC, V. Daily 6:30–9:30pm. INTERNATIONAL/ITALIAN.

Medici's serves the best food of the trio of upscale restaurants in the side-by-side Hyatts. Frequented by an affluent, usually well-dressed clientele, it occupies a soaring, two-story room whose marble and Italian-tile floors can be observed from the lobby above through plate-glass windows. Diners enjoy views of venerable trees draped in Spanish moss, a landscaped pond, and a waterfall while dining on well-conceived cuisine that changes at frequent intervals according to the season. Examples include lobster with caviar, bound together with a sherry and white-wine sauce; sautéed spinach with calamari; herb-encrusted filet mignon served with a fontina cheese sauce; and sautéed stuffed veal chop with spinach and a demi-glacé sauce. Everybody's favorite dessert is a coconut-enriched crème brûlée.

Su Casa. In the Hyatt Dorado Beach Resort & Casino. ☎ **787/796-1234.** Reservations required. Main courses $24–$39. AE, MC, V. Daily 7–9pm. Closed Sun Apr–Dec. SPANISH/CARIBBEAN.

Inspired by an Argentinean hacienda, the venerable building containing this restaurant was originally constructed as a beach house during the late 19th century by members of the Livingston family. Wealthy industrialists with ties to the Rockefellers (who later bought the house and enlarged it), they infused it with all the grandeur and comforts of their era. Today, it contains a half-dozen dining rooms, each with views of the sea. A cooperative staff emulates the informal grandeur of holiday life of the gilt-edged 1940s and 1950s. Food is well-prepared and a bit less nuanced than what you'll find at Medici's (see above). Examples include lobster Thermidor with a cream sauce; shrimp and garlic with yellow rice; steamed filet of halibut with fresh tomato sauce; lamb, pork, and veal chops; and breast of chicken stuffed with fresh mushrooms and fontina cheese. Dessert might include a lemon tart or chocolate mousse.

2 Las Croabas & Luquillo Beach

31 miles E of San Juan

Overlooking both the Caribbean Sea and the Atlantic Ocean from atop a 300-foot cliff at the northeastern tip of Puerto Rico, El Conquistador was the acknowledged leader in luxury resorts in the Caribbean from the 1960s through the late 1970s. Celebrities Elaine May, Jack Gilford, Celeste Holm (with her husband and two poodles), Elaine Stritch (and her dog), Amy Vanderbilt, Jack Palance, Burt Bacharach, Angie Dickinson, Omar Shariff, Marc Connelly, Maureen O'Sullivan, and Xavier Cugat attended its grand inaugural in 1968. Later, its circular casino, in black and stainless steel, appeared in the last scene of the James Bond movie *Goldfinger.* The original hotel closed in 1980, however, but was reborn in 1993 as the distinctive, $250 million El Conquistador we have today. Former President George Bush was among its first guests.

You'll be near ✪ **Luquillo Beach,** one of the island's best and most popular public stretches of sand. Much closer to Luquillo Beach and a major challenger to El Conquistador is Westin Rio Mar Beach Resort & Casino (see below).

ESSENTIALS

GETTING THERE   Both El Conquistador and the Westin Rio Mar Beach Resort & Casino greet all guests personally at the San Juan airport and transport them to the resort; alert the hotels to the time of your arrival. Guests at these hotels can take a taxi or a hotel courtesy car, or drive their rental car to Luquillo Beach.

If you're driving from San Juan, head east on Route 3 toward Fajardo. At the intersection, cut northeast on Route 195 and continue to the intersection with Route 987, at which point you turn north.

OUTDOOR ACTIVITIES

In addition to the lovely beach and the many recreational facilities that are part of El Conquistador itself (see the review below), there are a couple of other notable places to play in the vicinity.

BOATING, SAILING & SNORKELING

Nearby in Fajardo, the Caribbean's largest and most modern marina, **Puerto del Rey** (☎ 787/860-1000), has facilities for 70 boats, including docking and fueling for yachts up to 200 feet in length, and haul-out and repair for yachts up to 90 feet. The marina resort now includes boat rentals, yacht charters, and water sports, in addition to several shops and a French restaurant.

For a day at sea spent exploring the best islands, beaches, reefs, and snorkeling in the area, contact **Capt. Jack Becker,** Villa Marina Yacht Harbor, also in Fajardo (☎ 787/860-0861, or 809/385-3509 for cell phone). Captain Jack, a native of Washington, D.C., and a longtime resident of Puerto Rico, takes two to six passengers at a time on his Pearson-27 sloop. Participants appreciate various islands, the reefs, and the marine life that can be seen on this tour. Before departure, guests are directed to a nearby delicatessen, where they can buy drinks and a package lunch. The price for a 6-hour trip is $50 per person, and it lasts from 10am to 3:30pm. Reservations can be made any hour.

WHERE TO STAY

✪ **El Conquistador Resort & Country Club.** Las Croabas (P.O. Box 70001), Fajardo, PR 00738. ☎ **800/468-5228** or 787/863-1000. Fax 787/253-0178. 908 units. A/C MINIBAR TV TEL. Winter $350–$545 double; $1,400–$1,950 suite for 1–4 occupants; $1,075–$2,095 casita for 1–6 occupants. Off-season $200–$350 double; $1,075–$1,600 suite for 1–4 occupants; $985–$1,600 casita for 1–6 occupants. Children 15 and under stay free in parents' room. Additional bed for 3rd or 4th occupant $40 extra. MAP $82 extra per adult per day, $42 extra per child 12 and under. AE, DC, DISC, MC, V. Parking $10 per day. Private limousine from the San Juan airport $255 per carload. Hotel buses make trips to and from the San Juan airport at 30-minute intervals throughout the day for $55 per person, round-trip for transport to El Conquistador.

One of the most impressive hostelries anywhere in the Caribbean, El Conquistador is a destination unto itself, with an incredible array of facilities. Rebuilt in 1993 at a cost of $250 million, it incorporates a million dollars' worth of art and five divisions of distinctly different clusters of accommodations into 500 acres of forested hills whose edges slope down to the sea. Throughout, gardens mingle with murals, paintings, and sculptures. The architecture drew its inspiration from the Mediterranean.

Hotel accommodations are divided into five separate sections that share a common theme of white walls, terra-cotta tiled roofs, and lush landscaping. Most of them lie several hundred feet above the sea, within two sections (Las Brisas and La Vista) of the bulky main building. At the same altitude, a bit off to the side, is a replica of an Andalusian hamlet, Las Casitas Village, complete with many of the architectural quirks you might have expected in the south of Spain. A short walk downhill is a circular cluster of tastefully modern accommodations, Las Olas Village. And at sea level, adjacent to an armada of pleasure craft bobbing at anchor, is La Marina Village, whose balconies seem to hang directly over the water. The accommodations are outfitted with comfortable and stylish furniture, soft tropical colors, and about half a dozen unexpected amenities, such as bathrobes and ironing boards.

The resort's far-flung elements are interconnected by serpentine, landscaped walkways and by a railroad-style funicular that makes frequent trips up and down the hillside.

This hotel attracts the same clientele as the Westin Rio Mar Beach Resort & Casino (see below) or the Hyatt properties at Dorado—that is, tour groups, conventions, romantic couples, the family trade and, increasingly, Europeans. In the winter you see fewer children and more older couples, with American guests predominating, although younger people and families, especially those from Florida and the Middle West, are more evident in summer. Stay here only if you don't mind lots of crowds. Those seeking a total romantic ambiance would prefer the Horned Dorset Primavera in Rincón (see chapter 9).

Dining/Diversions: The resort contains 16 restaurants and lounges, one of which is a tropical deli. Some are highlighted in "Where to Dine," below. A casino offers gambling as well as live music from a nearby piano bar. The array of bars and nightlife includes Drake's Library, outfitted with books, mahogany, and a billiards table, and the disco, Amigos Bar and Lounge, with live merengue and salsa.

Amenities: Room service (7am to 11:30pm), baby-sitting, men's and women's beauty salon, laundry/dry cleaning, massages, spa services. There's a special activities area and games room just for kids. Camp Coquí provides for children 3 to 12 daily for $38 per day (9am to 3:30pm). Activities may include fishing, sailing, arts and crafts, nature walks, or treasure hunts. The hotel is sole owner of a "fantasy island" (Palomino Island), with caverns, nature trails, horseback riding, and a wide choice of such water sports as scuba diving, windsurfing, and snorkeling. About half a mile offshore, the island is connected by private ferries to the main hotel at frequent intervals. There are also a 25-slip marina where some of the boats are for rent, six swimming pools, many different Jacuzzi tubs, a fitness center, and state-of-the-art conference facilities. Seven tennis courts are lit for night play, and there's an 18-hole championship golf course designed by Arthur Hills with "unbelievable views"; greens fees are $95 to $155 per person. Plus, there's an arcade of 22 retail shops.

✪ **Westin Rio Mar Beach Resort & Casino.** 6000 Rio Mar Blvd., Rio Grande, PR 00745. ☎ **800/4 RIOMAR** or 787/888-6000. Fax 787/888-6600. 600 units. A/C

MINIBAR TV TEL. Winter $400–$600 double, $600–$3,000 suite; off-season $350–$550 double, $550–$3,000 suite. AE, CB, DC, DISC, MC, V. Resort is 19 miles east of Luis Muñoz Marin International Airport (entrance off Puerto Rico Highway 3). Hotel's shuttle from airport costs $23; a private taxi, $70. If driving, go past San Juan airport, following signs to Carolina; then link with Route 3 going east. Resort is signposted at turnoff sign for El Yunque (rain forest).

Marking the Westin chain's debut in the Caribbean, this $180 million, 481-acre resort opened in 1996 on a relatively uncrowded neighbor (Rio Mar Beach) of the massively popular Luquillo Beach, a 5-minute drive away. One of the three largest hotels in Puerto Rico, it was designed to compete with the more deeply entrenched Hyatt hotels at Dorado and El Conquistador, with which it's frequently compared. The Westin's centerpiece, and site of all of its accommodations, is a seven-story Spanish/Caribbean-style ochre-colored building whose U-shaped floor plan opens onto views of the sea.

The jungle-inspired motifs throughout the hotel emphasize its proximity (within a 15-minute drive) of the El Yunque Rain Forest and National Park. Landscaping includes lots of Jacuzzis, grottoes, fountains, and tropical gardens. More than 60% of guest rooms look out over palm trees to the Atlantic. Other accommodations open onto gardens and forests. Throughout, the style is Spanish hacienda as interpreted by exposure to the jungle, incorporating massive murals of tropical vegetation, alternating with dark woods, deep colors, rounded archways, big windows, and tile floors. Each room has a balcony or terrace. Muted earth tones, wicker, rattan, and painted wood furniture add to the ambiance.

Dining/Diversions: You'll never go hungry here. The resort boasts 12 restaurants and lounges, everything from Marbella (a relatively casual indoor/outdoor all-day dining restaurant), to Palio, an upmarket Italian gourmet restaurant that serves the most elegant food in the most formal setting. There's also a beachfront pool grill and bar and a lobby bar featuring prolonged bouts of live merengue and salsa. In the evening, guests usually gather to enjoy the recorded music in an outdoor nightclub, or else they try their luck within the hotel's 6,500-square-foot casino. Here, amid the whir of gaming machines, ceilings are painted with a constellation of stars, and carpeting has colors and patterns that emulate the jungle's floor.

Amenities: 24-hour room service, laundry/dry cleaning, an activities staff who help arrange sports-related diversions and activities. The resort encompasses the Rio Mar Country Club, site of two important golf courses. The older of the two, the Ocean Course, was designed by George and Tom Fazio as part of the original resort. In 1997, Westin opened the property's second 18-holer, the slightly more challenging River Course, designed as the first Greg Norman–designed course in the Caribbean. Par for both courses is 72. There are also 13 tennis courts and a beach club with a kiosk loaded with rentable watercraft. Nearby concessionaires include an array of qualified entrepreneurs who offer options for horseback riding, hiking, deep-sea game fishing, sailing, and boating. There's also a gymnasium and health club that organizes aerobics and aqua-aerobics classes, and a spa that emphasizes massage and beautification techniques. The Iguana Kid's Club keeps children ages 4 to 12 amused during prolonged morning and evening sessions.

WHERE TO DINE

Blossoms. In El Conquistador Resort. ☎ **787/863-1000.** Reservations recommended. Main courses $14.50–$45. AE, CB, DC, MC, V. Mon–Sat 6–11pm; Sun 1pm–midnight. CHINESE/JAPANESE.

This restaurant on the Mirador level features three culinary styles, including a sushi bar, and boasts some of the freshest seafood in eastern Puerto Rico. Sizzling delights are prepared on teppanyaki tables, and there's a zesty selection of Hunan and Szechuan specialties. On the teppanyaki menu, you can choose dishes ranging from chicken to shrimp, from filet mignon to lobster. Sushi-bar selections range from eel to squid, from salmon roe to giant clams.

✪ **Cassava.** In El Conquistador Resort. ☎ **787/863-1000.** Reservations recommended. Main courses $22–$28. AE, DISC, MC, V. Daily 6–10pm. PUERTO RICAN/CARIBBEAN.

This is the newest, most experimental, and most unusual restaurant within the many associated with the El Conquistador Resort. You'll find it within earshot of the casino, in a location adjacent to the resort's lobby. The interior sports a super-colorful setting in which pinks, greens, and yellows explode in your eyes, as do the flavors in your palate. Appetizers get off to a dazzling start with fried curried calamari in a lemon grass vinaigrette or steamed garlic clams flavored with a cilantro lemon sauce. The tuna carpaccio is served on a seaweed salad with a *tamarindo* sauce (a legume with a sweet-and-sour flavor). The main courses also have some culinary pyrotechnics, as exemplified by the seafood mofongo, a medley of lobster, shrimp, octopus, and scallops, one of the most Puerto Rican–inspired dishes on the menu. Live Maine lobsters are flown in, or you might opt for a seared sea bass with grilled vegetables. Desserts, which change frequently, all taste homemade and are most satisfying if you have any room left.

✪ **Isabela's Grill.** In El Conquistador Resort. ☎ **787/863-1000.** Reservations recommended. Main courses $14–$36; Sun buffet lunch $39.50 per person. AE, DISC, MC, V. Mon–Sat 6–10pm, Sun 11:30am–3pm and 6pm–midnight. SPANISH/INTERNATIONAL.

Of all the restaurants in El Conquistador Resort, this is the most Stateside inspired. The severe Spanish baroque room may have been inspired by an aristocratic monastery in Spain, but if Jack Benny, Jackie Gleason, or even President Eisenhower were to miraculously return, they would feel right at home with this 1950s menu. The massive gates are among the most spectacular pieces of wrought iron on Puerto Rico. The service is impeccable, and the steaks are tender, the seafood fresh.

Appetizers range from black-bean soup to Cajun crab cakes. Special care is taken with the beef dishes, even though the meat has to be imported frozen. Treats range from an extra-thick cut of veal chop to a prime rack of lamb. Prime rib of beef is a feature, as are New York strip and porterhouse. You might opt for the seafood, everything from grilled filet of salmon in a pink peppercorn sauce to grilled tuna flavored with ginger and tomato salsa for some island zest.

Otello's. In El Conquistador Resort. ☎ **787/863-1000.** Reservations required in winter, recommended off-season. Main courses $19.95–$37.95. AE, DISC, MC, V. Daily 6pm–midnight. NORTHERN ITALIAN.

Here you can dine by candlelight in the old-world tradition, with a choice of both indoor and outdoor seating. The decor is neo-Palladian. You might begin with one of the soups, perhaps pasta fagioli, or select one of the zesty Italian appetizers, such as clams Posillipo. Pastas can be ordered as a half-portion appetizer or as a main dish, and they include the likes of homemade gnocchi or fettuccine with shrimp. The chef is known for veal dishes. A selection of poultry and vegetarian food is offered nightly, along with several shrimp and fish dishes. When we last dined here, the salmon filet in champagne sauce had beautiful accents, as did the veal chop in an aromatic herb sauce.

3 Ceiba & El Yunque

35 miles W of San Juan, 15 miles E of El Yunque, 7 miles S of Fajardo

The rain forest of El Yunque (see "The Natural Environment," in chapter 2, and "Driving Tour 1," in chapter 10) is such a major attraction of Puerto Rico that little inns and bed-and-breakfasts have opened to accommodate visitors wishing to find a nearby place from which to explore this tropical paradise. The inns are not luxurious in any way; however, eco-tourists gravitate to them.

Playa de Naguabo, one of the best beaches in the area, lies about a 20-minute drive from Ceiba.

GETTING THERE

From San Juan, head east on Route 3 toward Fajardo. Pass through Fajardo and continue directly south to Ceiba.

EXPLORING EL YUNQUE

Encompassing four distinct forest types, El Yunque is home to 240 species of tropical trees, flowers, and wildlife. More than 20 kinds of orchids and 50 varieties of ferns share this diverse habitat with millions of tiny tree frogs whose distinctive cry of *coquí* (pronounced ko-*kee*) has given them their name. Tropical birds include the lively, greenish blue, red-fronted Puerto Rican parrot, once nearly extinct and now making a comeback. Other rare animals include the Puerto Rican boa, which grows to 7 feet. However, it is highly unlikely you will encounter a boa. The few who have are still shouting about it!

El Yunque is the best of Puerto Rico's 20 forest preserves. It's great for hiking; for a description of our favorite trails, see "Hiking," in chapter 3. The forest is situated high above sea level, with the peak of El Toro rising to 3,532 feet. You can be fairly sure you'll be showered upon, since more than 100 billion gallons of rain fall here annually. However, the showers are brief and there are many shelters. Many visitors reserve only a half day for El Yunque on a quickie tour. But it's unique and deserves at least a daylong outing.

El Yunque is the most popular spot in Puerto Rico for hiking. The **Department of Natural Resources Forest Service** (☎ 787/724-8774) administers some aspects of the park, although for the ordinary hiker, more useful information may be available at **El Yunque Catalina Field Office,** near the village of Palma, beside the main highway at the forest's northern edge (☎ 787/888-5670). The staff can provide material about hiking routes and, with 10 days' notice, help you plan overnight tours in the forest. If you reserve in advance, the staff will also arrange for you to take part in 2-hour group tours, costing $35 per person.

El Portal Tropical Forest Center, Route 191, Rio Grande (☎ 787/888-1810), an $18 million exhibition and information center, has 10,000 square feet of exhibition space. Three pavilions offer exhibits and bilingual displays. The actor Jimmy Smits narrates a documentary called "Understanding the Forest." The center is open daily from 9am to 5pm, charging an admission of $3.

WHERE TO STAY

Ceiba Country Inn. Road no. 977, km 1.2 (P.O. Box 1067), Ceiba, PR 00735. ☎ **787/885-0471.** Fax 787/885-0471. 9 units. A/C TEL. Year-round $70 double; $5 extra per person in room. Rates include breakfast. AE, DISC, MC, V.

If you're looking for an escape from the hustle and bustle of everyday life, then this is the place for you. This small, well-maintained bed-and-breakfast is located on the easternmost part of Puerto Rico near the Roosevelt Roads U.S. naval base (you must rent a car to reach this little haven in the mountains). El Yunque is only 15 miles away, San Juan 35 miles to the west. The rooms are on the bottom floor of a large old family home. All have private bathrooms; two also have small refrigerators. They are decorated in a tropical motif with flowered murals on the walls painted by a local artist. For a quiet evening cocktail, you may want to visit the small lounge on the second floor.

✪ 4 Palmas del Mar

46 miles SE of San Juan

A 60-minute drive east of San Juan, this residential resort community lies on the island's southeastern shore. Once here, you'll find plenty to do, for one of the most action-packed sports programs in the Caribbean offers golf, tennis, scuba diving, sailing, deep-sea fishing, and horseback riding. There's even a casino.

Palmas del Mar's location on the southeastern shore of Puerto Rico is one of its greatest assets. The pleasing Caribbean trade winds steadily blow across this section of the island all year, stabilizing the weather and making Palmas del Mar ideal for a great many outdoor sports all year.

GETTING THERE

No airline has regularly scheduled flights to **Humacao Regional Airport,** 3 miles north of Palmas del Mar. The resort (☎ **787/852-6000**) will arrange minivan or bus transport from Luis Muñoz Marín International Airport in San Juan to Humacao. The fare is $16 to $25 each way.

If you're driving from downtown San Juan, take Highway 52 south to Caguas, then take Highway 30 east to Humacao (trip time: 1 hr.).

BEACHES & OUTDOOR ACTIVITIES

The Palmas del Mar resort offers a great variety of choices to keep active vacationers in shape (many are also open to the public with prior reservation). Following are details on some of the most popular, along with a few other offerings in the area that are not connected with the resort complex.

BEACHES

The resort has 3 exceptional miles of white-sand beaches (all open to the public). Nonguests will pay a $1 charge for parking and 25¢ for a changing room and a locker. The waters here are calm year-round, and there's a water-sports center and marina (see "Scuba Diving & Snorkeling," below).

FISHING

Some of the best year-round fishing in the Caribbean is found in the waters just off Palmas del Mar. **Capt. Bill Burleson,** based in Humacao (☎ **787/850-7442**), operates charters on his fully customized 46-foot sport-fisherman, *Karolette,* which is electronically equipped for successful fishing. Burleson prefers to take fishing groups to Grappler Banks, 18 nautical miles away. The banks are two sea mounts, rising to about 240 feet below the surface and surrounded by depths of 6,000 to 8,000 feet. They lie in the migratory paths of the wahoo, tuna, and marlin. A maximum of six people are taken out, costing $500 for 4 hours, $675 for 6 hours, and $900 for 9 hours. He also offers snorkeling expeditions to Vieques Island at $85 per person for up to 5 hours. Other snorkeling locations include half- and full-day trips.

Monkey Business

In 1938, a collection of rhesus monkeys was brought from India to Cayo Santiago, a 39-acre islet off eastern Puerto Rico, to be studied for scientific purposes. The ancestors of those early monkeys are going bananas here today.

The island is administered by the University of Puerto Rico. Scientists from its Caribbean Primate Research Center spend days and weeks studying the behavioral patterns of this colony of some 700 monkeys (at last count). They have learned many interesting things by observing this frisky bunch. For example, like humans, monkeys are capable of forming friendships that last a lifetime. Because the monkeys are all contained on this island, as opposed to living in the wild, scientists can trace their entire development over their life span. Monkeys are marked and numbered, although many of the scientists know the animals upon sight. Many breakthroughs in human medicine have resulted from close encounters with and observation of these monkeys.

The scientists won't let visitors come ashore because it will interfere in their research work. However, a boat named *Brie...Z* transports guests to the water just off the island, where they can go snorkeling and get a close-up look at these rambunctious residents. The *Brie...Z* sails daily if the weather allows from Palmas del Mar Resort's marina at Harbourside Dock (no. 135).

When the boat anchors, dozens of monkeys show up to see what all the excitement is about, no doubt thinking the humans looking at them are just as funny as people think the monkeys are. Some monkeys can be seen swinging through the trees, enjoying the good life. On rare occasions they have been known to board the *Brie...Z*.

Groups of up to six passengers are taken to this rare enclave, costing $65 for the 4-hour excursion. The price includes drinks, snacks, and snorkeling gear. The 50-foot boat is skippered by Robert Eastman, who has a vast knowledge of the monkeys. He takes trips daily at 8am and again at 1:30pm. For more information, call ☎ **787/850-5045** or 787/318-4496.

GOLF

Few other real-estate developments in the Caribbean devote as much attention and publicity to their golf facilities as ✪ **The Palmas del Mar Golf Club** (☎ **787/ 852-6000, ext. 54**). In 1997, the community's new owners, the Wyndham group, added a second golf course to the complex, thereby pumping new interest and energy into the resort's infrastructure. Today, both the older "Gary Player" course and the newer "Reese Jones" course have pars of 72 and layouts of around 6,800 feet each. Crack golfers consider holes 11 to 15 of the older course among the toughest five successive holes in the Caribbean. The pro shop that services players on both courses is open daily from 7am to 5pm. Greens fees for residents or hotel guests of Palmas del Mar range from $82 to $114, depending on the season, and from $90 to $130 for nonresidents. These rates include use of a golf cart and 18 holes of play.

HIKING

Hiking on the resort's grounds is another favorite activity here, for Palmas del Mar's land is an attraction in its own right. There are more than 6 miles of Caribbean ocean frontage, 3½ miles of which is sandy beach; the balance is rocky cliffs and promontories. Large tracts of the 2,700-acre property have harbored sugar and coconut plantations over the years, and a wet, tropical forest preserve with giant ferns, orchids, and hanging vines covers about 70 acres near the resort's geographic center.

SCUBA DIVING & SNORKELING

Coral Head Divers & Water Sports Center, P.O. Box 10246, Humacao, PR 00792 (☎ **800/635-4529** or 787/850-7208), operates out of a building on the harbor at the Palmas del Mar Resort. The dive center owns two fully equipped boats, measuring 26 and 48 feet. The center offers daily two-tank open-water dives for certified divers, plus snorkeling trips to Monkey Island and Vieques. The two-tank dive includes tanks, weights, and computer for $80. A snorkeling trip to Monkey Island includes use of equipment and a beverage for $45 per person; a scuba resort lesson costs $45.

TENNIS

The ✪ **Tennis Center** at Palmas del Mar (☎ **787/852-6000,** ext. 51), the largest on Puerto Rico, features 15 hard courts and 5 clay courts open to hotel residents and nonresidents. Court fees are $18 per hour during the day and $22 at night. Special tennis packages are available, including accommodations. Call for more information.

WHERE TO STAY

One of the largest and most ambitious real-estate projects in the Caribbean, **Palmas del Mar,** 170 Candelero Dr., Humacao, PR 00792 (☎ **800/725-6273** or 787/852-6000), consolidates 2,700 rolling acres of what used to be a coconut plantation with private homes, a hotel, and an impressive golf facility. In 1996, the sprawling complex was acquired by the Wyndham hotel group, which immediately poured $4 million into a much-needed improvement of the infrastructure. Improvements included the addition of more entranceways into the complex (including a system that helped to segregate homeowners within the project from short-term hotel guests) and a radical overhaul of some of the resort's hotel accommodations. Other improvements included the addition of a second golf course (see "Golf," above).

The resort attracts conventions and small groups, plus vacationers in search of horseback riding, tennis, golf, and R&R. It is more suited for tranquillity seekers than the sprawling resorts of El Conquistador and Westin Rio Mar Beach are. Because of the resort's sheer land mass, there are more places to retreat from the hordes.

Villas, each with a kitchen, are clustered into groupings set near a marina, a beach, or a complex of tennis courts. But wherever you opt to stay, chances are high that you'll be exposed to the priorities and concerns of private homeowners, whose units might be immediately adjacent to your own.

Once you arrive at Palmas del Mar, you can depend on the free shuttle-bus service that interconnects the far-flung aspects of this community at 20- to 30-minute intervals. The complex offers families an activities program year-round. Children between the ages of 3 and 13 are divided into compatible age groups and exposed to such organized activities as arts and crafts, tennis and swimming lessons, minigolf, and water polo.

Palmas Inn. 170 Candelero Dr., Wyndham Palmas del Mar, Humacao, PR 00792. ☎ **800/725-6273** or 787/852-6000. Fax 787/852-6295. 23 junior suites. A/C TV TEL. Winter $328 double; off-season $229 double. Rates include continental breakfast. MAP $34.50 per person extra year-round. AE, DC, MC, V.

Small scale, and subject to the individual tastes of each unit's owners, this complex is less affected by the Wyndham takeover of Palmas than virtually any other entity at the resort. Separated from the sea by a palm grove, whose trees partially block water views, they were designed in a style that imitates a Mediterranean villa. Throughout, there's a spacious, airy feeling and lots of emphasis on Old Spain. There's no restaurant on-site, and because of their role as private, somewhat secluded private residences, there's a bit less emphasis on personalized service than you're likely to get within the nearby Wyndham Hotel (see below). But if you're looking for a sense of isolation and privacy in a roomy setting, a short-term rental of one of the units might suit your needs.

Wyndham Hotel. 170 Candelero Dr., Wyndham Palmas del Mar (P.O. Box 2020), Humacao, PR 00792. ☎ **800/725-6273** in the U.S., or 787/852-6000. Fax 787/852-6320. 101 units. A/C TV TEL. Winter $230–$263 double; off-season $166–$191 double. MAP $34.50 per person extra year-round. AE, DC, MC, V.

Although the acreage within the Palmas del Mar development contains thousands of privately owned villas, many of which can be rented by short-term holiday-makers, this is its only conventional, full-service hotel. Originally built as the Candelero Hotel, it was acquired by Wyndham in 1996, who retained its ochre-colored exterior but radically renovated most of its interior in 1997. None of the well-furnished bedrooms overlooks the sea, but many have private patios or verandas, and most are roomier than you might have expected. The beach, tennis center, and golf courses are close at hand, and the staff is well equipped to describe the many diversions that are available within the Palmas del Mar compound.

Wyndham Villa Suites. 170 Candelero Dr., Wyndham Palmas del Mar, Humacao, PR 00792. ☎ **800/725-6273** in the U.S., or 787/852-6000. Fax 787/852-6320. 135 town house–style suites. A/C TV TEL. Winter $331–$495 1-bedroom suite; $482–$650 2-bedroom suite; $620–$817 3-bedroom suite. Off-season $221–$297 1-bedroom suite; $321–$390 two-bedroom suite; $413–$490 3-bedroom suite. MAP $34.50 extra per person year-round. Minimum bookings ranging from 3 to 7 nights required during some peak seasons, depending on the accommodation.

Set almost adjacent to the Wyndham Hotel, this complex of red-roofed, white-walled Iberian-inspired town houses would be a good choice for a family vacation. Divided into three separate clusters, and carefully landscaped with tropical plants, each unit is furnished and decorated according to the taste of its individual owner. Each contains a working kitchen, a sense of privacy, and views of either the ocean or the gardens. Rental fees depend on the unit's proximity to the beachfront or golf course; an additional handful of villas built against a steep hillside overlook the resort's 21 tennis courts.

WHERE TO DINE

Thanks to the kitchens that come built into virtually every unit here, many guests opt to prepare at least some of their meals "at home." This is made relatively feasible thanks to the on-site presence of a "General Store," within the Palmanova Plaza, selling everything from fresh lettuce and sundries to liquor and cigarettes. Barring a romantic (or at least cheap) meal you prepare yourself, you'll have at least eight other dining options within the Palmas del Mar complex.

Each option has its own form of appeal, but the one that's always cited as the most romantic and elaborate is the **Palm Terrace,** in the Wyndham Hotel. It, along with Toco Coco's, is reviewed separately under "Where to Dine," below. Three other options within the complex are all clustered in the Palmanova Plaza, adjacent to the casino. They include **La Brochette** (French), **Luigi's** (a sports bar serving pizzas and pastas), and its more formal Italian cousin, **Scarpatti's.** Beside the marina, near a condominium complex that Palmas refers to as the Anchors Villas, is **Chez Daniel,** which is separately recommended below. The final options include the **Golf Deli,** which serves salads and thick-stuffed sandwiches from a big-windowed site whose view over the golf course, particularly the eighth hole, is absolutely splendid, but which is open only for lunch. There's also **Casa Verde,** a middle-bracket Italian restaurant set adjacent to the tennis courts. And if you're interested in ordering take-out food that will be delivered, ready-to-eat, to your hotel room or rented villa/condo, call **Lagniappe.** The meals they prepare range from a simple club sandwich or pizza for 2 to surprisingly elaborate formal dinners for 12. Their golf carts, which roar around the complex carrying meals, cutlery, and dining accessories, have salvaged many a marriage when residents of one of the villas or condos are simply not interested in cooking. Calls to any of the above-mentioned restaurants are routed through the general Palmas del Mar switchboard (☎ **787/852-6000**).

Regardless of your specific location within the Palmas del Mar complex, if you opt for a half-board plan (and many occupants even of villas with full kitchens sometimes arrange them), the resort will steer you to Toco Coco's for breakfast, and your choice of either the Palm Terrace or Toco Coco's for dinner.

All the restaurants are open during the winter season; however, in summer only three or four may be fully functional.

Chez Daniel/Le Grill. Marina de Palmas del Mar. ☎ **787/850-3838.** Reservations required. Main courses $19.50–$29.50. AE, MC, V. Fri–Sun noon–3pm and daily 6:30–10pm. Closed June and Tues Apr–Dec. FRENCH.

It's French, it's nautical, it's fun, and it's the preferred venue for occupants of the yachts moored at the adjacent pier. Normandy-born Daniel Vasse, the owner, and his French Catalonian wife, Lucette, maintain twin dining rooms that in their way are the most appealing at Palmas del Mar. Le Grill is a steak house with a Gallic twist and lots of savory flavor in the form of Béarnaise, garlic, peppercorn sauce, or whatever else you specify. Chez Daniel shows a more faithful allegiance to the tenets of classical French cuisine, placing an emphasis on such dishes as the bouillabaisse (both the Catalonian and Marseillaise versions), onion soup, and snails, as well as lobster and chicken dishes. For dessert, consider a soufflé au Cointreau.

✪ **The Palm Terrace.** Adjacent to the Wyndham Hotel, Palmas del Mar. ☎ **787/852-6000.** Reservations recommended. Main courses $17.25–$29.50. AE, DC, MC, V. Wed–Sat 6–10pm. CARIBBEAN/INTERNATIONAL.

Palm Terrace is the culinary showplace of the Palmas del Mar complex, with a key location adjacent to both the casino and the Wyndham Hotel. Everything about the place seems conducive to long, leisurely dinners laden with romance. Illuminated by candles and staffed with uniformed waiters, the room's focal point is a panoramic view that sweeps out as far as the island of Vieques.

Menu items include an excellent version of ceviche with marinated shrimp, sea bass, and octopus; portobello mushrooms stuffed with local cheese and lime-marinated chicken; stuffed breast of chicken with aji papaya relish; and a succulent version of roasted rack of lamb with a pistachio-studded mustard sauce. A long list of grills is available, including catch of the day; New York char-broiled steak with burgundy and green peppercorn/garlic sauce; and grilled veal chops with marsala and mushroom-flavored reduction.

Toco Coco's. In the Wyndham Hotel. ☎ **787/852-6000,** ext. 50. Reservations accepted only for groups of 6 or more. Main courses $15–$30. AE, DISC, MC, V. Daily 6:30–11am, noon–2:30pm, and 6–10:30pm. INTERNATIONAL.

Cooled by trade winds, this restaurant overlooking a courtyard and swimming pool is an ideal choice for any casual meal. Lunch always includes sandwiches and burgers; if you want heartier fare, ask for the Puerto Rican specialty of the day, perhaps red snapper in garlic butter, preceded by black-bean soup. Dinner is more elaborate—begin with stuffed jalapeños or chicken tacos, followed by Caribbean lobster, New York sirloin, paella, or the catch of the day. The cooking, although of a high standard, is never quite gourmet—it's just good hearty food. Every night in winter is a virtual theme night here, ranging from an Italian festival on Monday to a Puerto Rican night on Saturday.

PALMAS DEL MAR AFTER DARK

The **casino** in the Palmas del Mar complex, near the Palmas Inn (☎ 787/ 852-6000, ext. 10142), is close to the reception area. It has 12 blackjack tables, two roulette wheels, a craps table, and dozens of slot machines. The casino is open daily year-round, Sunday through Thursday from 6pm to 2am and Friday and Saturday from 6pm to 3am. Under Puerto Rican law, drinks cannot be served in a casino.

Ponce, Mayagüez & Rincón 9

For those who want to see a less urban side of Puerto Rico, Ponce, on the south shore, and Mayagüez and Rincón, on the west coast, offer a variety of places to stay, and each also makes a good center for sightseeing. From either Mayagüez or Ponce you can take a side trip to historic San Germán, site of Puerto Rico's second-oldest city with the oldest church in the New World.

Founded in 1692, Ponce is Puerto Rico's second-largest city and has received much attention because of its inner-city restoration. It is home to the island's premier art gallery.

Puerto Rico's third-largest city, Mayagüez is a port located about halfway down the west coast. It may not be as architecturally remarkable as Ponce, but it's a fine base for exploring some sights and enjoying some very good beaches.

Rincón, to the north of Mayagüez, is even smaller, but it boasts the finest country hotel in Puerto Rico—the Horned Dorset Primavera—and has some world-class surfing beaches.

Not too far from all three towns is ✪ **Boquerón Beach,** a mile-long west-coast white-sand beach, one of the finest on the island (see "Driving Tour 2" in chapter 10). **Cabo Rojo Lighthouse,** at the southwesternmost corner, is another interesting place to visit (after leaving Boquerón, continue along Highway 301 until its end).

1 Ponce

75 miles SW of San Juan

"The Pearl of the South," Ponce was named after Loíza Ponce de León, great-grandson of Juan Ponce de León. Founded in 1692, it is today Puerto Rico's principal shipping port on the Caribbean. The city is well kept and attractive, as reflected by its many plazas, parks, and public buildings. A suggestion of a provincial Mediterranean town lingers in its air. Look for the *rejas,* or framed balconies, on the handsome colonial mansions.

Timed to coincide with 1992's 500th anniversary celebration of Christopher Columbus's voyage to the New World, a $440 million renovation began to bring new life to this once-decaying city. The streets are lit with gas lamps and lined with neoclassical buildings, just as they were a century ago. Horse-drawn carriages clop by, and strollers walk along sidewalks edged with pink marble. Thanks to the restoration, Ponce now recalls the turn of the century, when it rivaled San Juan as a wealthy business and cultural center.

ESSENTIALS

GETTING THERE   American Eagle (☎ 800/433-7300) offers two daily flights between San Juan and Ponce (flight time: 35 min.) for $95 to $136 round-trip, depending on the ticket. However, prices are known to fluctuate, so call for last-minute details.

If you're driving, take Route 1 south to Highway 52, then continue south and west to Ponce. Allow at least 1½ hours.

VISITOR INFORMATION   The Ponce Municipal Tourist Office has a kiosk inside the Parque de Bombas, on Plaza de Las Delicias (see below). If you find it temporarily unstaffed, go across the street to the second floor of the Citibank Building, where the administrative offices are located (☎ 787/841-8044).

SEEING THE SIGHTS

Most visitors go to Ponce to see the city's major architectural restoration. Calle Reina Isabel, one of the city's major residential streets, is a virtual textbook of the different Ponceño styles, ranging from European neoclassical to Spanish colonial. Neoclassical, a kind of Greek-revival style, is known around the world because it also swept across America, especially in public buildings such as post offices.

The difference in this style in Ponce is that local architects, as befits the warmer climate, often incorporated balconies. Pink marble was also used extensively on local buildings. Ponce Créole is really Spanish colonial. This style also contains out-side balconies. In this case, inside balconies with a wall of tiny windows often were included. These windows let sunlight into the patio.

With partial funding from the governments of Puerto Rico and Spain, Ponce has restored more than 600 of its 1,000 historic buildings. Many are on streets radiating from the stately Plaza Las Delicias (Plaza of Delights). On Isabel, Reina, Pabellones, and Lolita Tizol streets, electrical and telephone wires have been buried, replica 19th-century gas lamps installed, and sidewalks trimmed with the distinctive, locally quarried pink marble. Paseo Atocha, one of Ponce's main shopping streets, is now a delightful pedestrian mall with a lively street festival on the third Sunday of every month. Paseo Arias, or Callejon del Amor (Lover's Alley), is a charming pedestrian passage between two 1920s bank buildings, Banco Popular and Banco Santander, on Plaza Las Delicias, where outdoor cafe tables invite lingering. Two monumental bronze lions by Spanish sculptor Victor Ochoa guard the entrance to the old section of the city.

In addition to the attractions listed below, the weekday **marketplace** at calles Atocha and Castillo is colorful, and the historic **La Perla Theater** and the **Serrallés rum distillery** are worth visits. Perhaps you'll want to simply sit in the plaza, watching the Ponceños at one of their favorite pastimes—strolling about town.

Cathedral of Our Lady of Guadalupe. Calle Concordia/Calle Union. ☎ 787/842-0134. Free admission. Mon–Fri 6am–3:30pm, Sat–Sun 6am–noon and 3–8pm.

In 1660, a rustic chapel was built on this spot on the western edge of the Plaza de Las Delicias, and since then fires and earthquakes have razed the church repeatedly. In 1919, a team of priests collected funds from local parishioners to construct the Doric- and Gothic-inspired building that stands here today. Designed by architects Francisco Porrato Doría and Francisco Trublard in 1931 and featuring a pipe organ installed in 1934, it remains an important place for prayer for many of Ponce's citizens. The cathedral, named after a famous holy shrine in Mexico, is the best-known church in southern Puerto Rico.

✪ **Museo de Arte de Ponce.** Av. de Las Américas 25. ☎ **787/848-0505.** Admission $4 adults, $1 children under 12. Daily 10am–5pm. Follow Calle Concordia from Plaza de Las Delicias 1½ miles south to Av. de Las Américas.

Donated to the people of Puerto Rico by Luís A. Ferré, a former governor, this museum has the finest collection of European and Latin American art in the Caribbean. The building itself was designed by Edward Durell Stone (who also designed the John F. Kennedy Center for the Performing Arts in Washington, D.C.) and has been called the "Parthenon of the Caribbean." Its collection represents the principal schools of American and European art of the past 5 centuries. Among the nearly 400 works on display are exceptional pre-Raphaelite and Italian baroque paintings. Visitors will also see artworks by other European masters, as well as Puerto Rican and Latin American paintings, graphics, and sculptures. On display are some of the best works of the two "old masters" of Puerto Rico, Francisco Oller and José Campéche. The museum also contains a representative collection of the works of the old masters of Europe, including Gainsborough, Velázquez, Rubens, and van Dyck. The museum is best known for its pre-Raphaelite and baroque paintings and sculpture—not only from Spain, but from Italy and France as well. Both the Whitney in New York and the Louvre in Paris have borrowed from its collection. Temporary exhibitions are also mounted here.

✪ **Museo Castillo Serralles.** El Vigía 17. ☎ **787/259-1774.** Admission $3 adults, $2 senior citizens over 62, $1.50 children under 16. Tues–Sun 9:30am–5:30pm. The roads leading to the museum are a confusing labyrinth of run-down, unnamed residential streets, so it's best to take a taxi; the fare is about $4 each way from the center of town.

Two miles north of the center of town is the largest and most imposing building in Ponce, constructed during the 1930s high on El Vigía Hill (see below) by the Serralles family, owners of a local rum distillery. One of the architectural gems of Puerto Rico, it is the best evidence of the wealth produced by the turn-of-the-century sugar boom. Guides will escort you through the Spanish Revival house, where Moorish and Andalusian details include panoramic courtyards, a baronial dining room, a small cafe and souvenir shop, and a series of photographs showing the tons of earth that were brought in for the construction of the terraced gardens.

Museum of the History of Ponce (Casa Salazar). Calle Reina Isabel 51-53 (at Calle Mayor). ☎ **787/844-7071.** Admission $3 adults, $1.50 seniors, $1 children. Mon and Wed–Fri 10am–5pm; Sat–Sun 10am–6pm.

Opened in the Casa Salazar in 1992, this museum traces the history of the city from the time of the Taíno peoples to the present. Interactive displays help visitors orient themselves and locate other attractions. The museum has a conservation laboratory, library, souvenir and gift shop, cafeteria, and conference facilities.

Casa Salazar ranks close to the top of Ponce's architectural treasures. Built in 1911, it combines neoclassic with Moorish styles and displays much decorative detail typical of Ponce: stained-glass windows, mosaics, pressed-tin ceilings, fixed jalousies, wood or iron columns, porch balconies, interior patios, and the use of doors as windows.

Museum of Puerto Rico Music. Calle Isabel 50. ☎ **787/848-7016.** Free admission. Wed–Sun 9am–noon and 1–4pm.

This museum showcases the development of Puerto Rican music, with displays of Indian, Spanish, and African musical instruments that were played in the romantic danza, the favorite music of 19th-century Puerto Rican society, as well as the more African-inspired bomba and plena styles. Also on view are memorabilia of composers and performers.

Parque de Bombas. Plaza de Las Delicias. ☎ **787/284-4141.** Free admission. Wed–Mon 9:30am–6pm.

Constructed in 1882 as the centerpiece of a 12-day agricultural fair intended at the time to promote the civic charms of Ponce, this building was designated a year later as the island's first permanent headquarters for a volunteer fire-fighting brigade. It has an unusual appearance—it's painted black, red, green, and yellow. A tourist-information kiosk is situated inside the building (see "Visitor Information," above).

El Vigía Hill. At the north end of Ponce. Take a taxi; from the Plaza de Las Delicias, the ride will cost about $4.

The city's tallest geologic feature, El Vigía Hill dominates Ponce's northern skyline. Its base and steep slopes have been covered with a maze of 19th- and early 20th-century urban development. Once you reach the summit, you'll see the soaring Cruz del Vigía (Virgin's Cross). Built in 1984 of reinforced concrete to replace a 19th-century wooden cross in poor repair, this modern 100-foot structure bears lateral arms measuring 70 feet long and an observation tower (accessible by elevator), from which you can see all of the natural beauty that surrounds Ponce.

The cross commemorates Vigía Hill's colonial role as a deterrent to contraband smuggling. In 1801, on orders from Spain, a garrison was established atop the hill to detect any ships that might try to unload their cargoes tax-free along Puerto Rico's southern coastline.

☺ Teatro la Perla at Calle Mayor and Calle Christina. ☎ **787/843-4080.**

The theater is one of the earliest examples of Bertoli's neoclassical structures in Ponce, built in 1864. Destroyed by an earthquake in 1918, it was rebuilt in 1940 according to the original plans and opened to the public in 1941. It is noted for acoustics so clear that microphones are unnecessary. After a radical restoration completed in 1990, the theater is now the largest and most historic in the Spanish-speaking Caribbean. Everything from plays to concerts to beauty pageants takes place here.

NEARBY ATTRACTIONS

The oldest cemetery in the Antilles, the **Tibes Indian Ceremonial Center** is on Route 503 at kilometer 2.7 (☎ **787/840-2255**). Bordered by the Portugues River and excavated in 1975, it contains some 186 skeletons, dating from A.D. 300, as well as pre-Taíno plazas from A.D. 700. Shaded by such trees as the calabash, seven rectangular ball courts and two dance grounds can be viewed. The arrangement of stone points on the dance grounds, in line with the solstices and equinoxes, suggests a pre-Columbian Stonehenge. A re-created Taíno village includes not only the museum but also an exhibition hall that presents a documentary about Tibes, a cafeteria where you can find refreshments, and a souvenir shop. The museum is open Wednesday through Sunday from 9am to 4:30pm. Admission is $2 for adults, $1 for children. Guided tours in English and Spanish are conducted through the grounds.

Hacienda Buena Vista, Route 10, kilometer 16.8 (☎ **787/848-7020** or 787/722-5882, is a 30-minute drive north of Ponce. Built in 1833, it preserves an old way of life, with its whirring waterwheels and artifacts of 19th-century farm production. Once it was one of the most successful plantations on Puerto

Rico, producing coffee, corn, and citrus. It was a working coffee plantation until the 1950s, and 86 of the original 500 acres are still part of the estate. The rooms of the hacienda have been furnished with authentic pieces from the 1850s. Tours, lasting 2 hours, are conducted Wednesday to Sunday at 8:30am, 10:30am, 1:30pm, and 3:30pm (in English only at 1:30pm). Reservations are required. Tours cost $5 for adults, $2 for children. The hacienda lies in the small town of Barrio Magüeyes, on Route 10 between Ponce and Adjuntas.

HIKING & BIRD WATCHING IN GUÁNICA STATE FOREST

Heading directly west from Ponce, you reach ✪ **Guánica State Forest** (☎ 787/724-3724), a setting that evokes Arizona or New Mexico. Here you will find the best-preserved subtropical ecosystem on the planet. The Cordillera Central cuts off the rain coming in from the heavily showered northeast, making this a dry region of cacti and bedrock, a perfect film location for one of those old-fashioned western movies.

It's also ideal country for birders. Some 50% of all of the island's terrestrial bird species can be seen in this dry and dusty forest. You might even spot the Puerto Rican emerald-breasted hummingbird. A number of migratory birds often stop here. The most serious ornithologists seek out the Puerto Rican nightjar, a local bird that was believed to be extinct until one was sighted. Now it's estimated that there are nearly a thousand of them. UNESCO has named Guánica a World Biosphere Reserve. Some 750 plants and tree species grow in the area.

To reach the forest, take Route 334 northeast of Guánica to the heart of the forest. There's a ranger station here that will give you information about hiking trails. The booklet provided by the ranger station outlines 36 miles of trails through the four forest types. The most interesting is the mile-long **Cueva Trail,** which gives you the most scenic look at the various types of vegetation. You might even encounter the endangered bufo lemur toad, once declared extinct but found to still be jumping in this area.

WALKING TOUR:
PONCE

Start: Plaza de Las Delicias.
Finish: Plaza de Las Delicias.
Time: 90 minutes, excluding coffee breaks, museum visits, and shopping stops.
The downtown revitalization of Ponce has required more money and generated more publicity than that of any other city (after San Juan) on Puerto Rico. Your tour of this Caribbean showplace begins on the eastern edge of the town's main square, the Plaza de Las Delicias (also known as Plaza Muñoz Rivera). Within the symmetrical borders of this main square, you'll see the red-and-black-striped clap-board facade of the town's most frequently photographed building. (Red and black, incidentally, are the colors of the city's flag.)

Note the Victorian gingerbread and the deliberately garish colors of the:
1. **Parque de Bombas (Old Municipal Fire House),** which housed the fire department before it moved into more modern quarters in another part of the city. You can still see a handful of bright-red fire engines parked inside.
    On the plaza's opposite side, adjacent to Calle Concordia/Calle Union is the:
2. **Cathedral of Our Lady of Guadalupe,** the best-known church in southern Puerto Rico. Its alabaster altars were commissioned by an ex-governor of Puerto

Rico in the late 1960s in Burgos, Spain; there will almost certainly be parishioners at prayer inside.

As you leave the cathedral, notice the many impeccably clipped trees ringing the perimeter of the plaza. Identified as Indian laurels, they were planted between 1906 and 1908 and are one of the botanical triumphs of Ponce. Clipped with manually operated shears into their carefully groomed topiary forms at frequent intervals by a master gardener, they are well worth a second or third glance. Even the elaborate iron lampposts illuminating them date from 1916.

Across Calle Concordia from the main entrance to the cathedral is one of Ponce's most famous houses, the:

3. **Casa Armstrong-Poventud,** a paneled and ornately crafted building that was once the home of a wealthy Scottish-born banker. The Poventud family moved in after the Armstrongs. Today, it's a cultural center.

Note that at this western border of the Plaza de Las Delicias, street signs might identify it as Plaza de Getou. Regardless of what the plaza is called, turn right on exiting Casa Armstrong-Poventud and walk southward beneath the Indian laurels. On the square's southern edge, you'll see one of the most historic buildings of Ponce, restored to reflect its original function during Spanish colonial days, the:

4. **Casa Alcaldía (City Hall),** standing on the site of an 18th-century monastery. This building was erected in 1840 as a general assembly, and then it served as the civic jail until 1905. Speeches by Theodore Roosevelt (in 1906), Herbert Hoover (in 1931), and Franklin D. Roosevelt (in 1934) were delivered from its central second-floor balcony to crowds assembled below. George Bush visited the building in 1987. The clock set into the tower was imported from London in 1877, and a tour of the baronial street-level interior reveals a memorial plaque dedicated to the fallen American dead (Second Wisconsin Regiment) during the Spanish-American War. A few paces farther on you'll see a galleried courtyard that formerly served as prisoners' cells. The building's main courtyard was used for public executions. In City Hall, other plaques make clear that the city of Ponce was named not after Juan Ponce de León, but rather after de León's great-grandson, Loíza Ponce de León, one of the town's early civic leaders.

Note across from the entrance to City Hall (in the town's main square) one of the most beautiful fountains of Puerto Rico, the:

5. **Lion Fountain,** crafted from marble and bronze and modeled after a famous fountain in Barcelona, Spain. It was made for the 1939 New York World's Fair and later purchased and erected in Ponce by its mayor.

Continue your walk along the southern edge of the square. Note the way the plaza has "chopped corners" (broadly rounded 45-degree corners rather than 90-degree perpendicular corners). They were designed this way for increased visibility by the Spanish armies as a deterrent to civil unrest and the contraband trade that flourished here during their regime. Ponce is said to have the only large square on Puerto Rico equipped with this military-inspired feature.

As you cross Calle Marina/Calle Commercio, which borders the southeastern edge of the square, look to your right to the faraway beaux arts:

6. **Centro Historico,** painted a creamy shade of white. Originally built in 1922, this landmark served as the town's casino until it was closed in the mid-1960s. Today it houses government agencies and is not open to the public, although it can be admired from the outside. Nearer and more spectacular are two banks flanking the southeastern edge of the square, the:

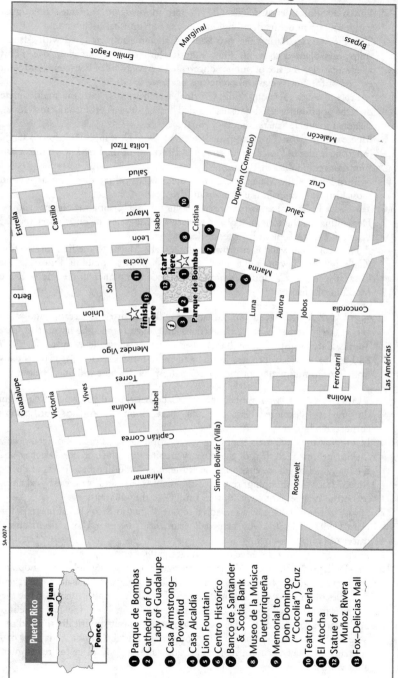

Walking Tour—Ponce

SA-0074

Puerto Rico

San Juan

Ponce

1. Parque de Bombas
2. Cathedral of Our Lady of Guadalupe
3. Casa Armstrong–Poventud
4. Casa Alcaldía
5. Lion Fountain
6. Centro Historíco
7. Banco de Santander & Scotia Bank
8. Museo de la Música Puertorriqueña
9. Memorial to Don Domingo ("Cocolia") Cruz
10. Teatro La Perla
11. El Atocha
12. Statue of Muñoz Rivera
13. Fox–Delicias Mall

7. **Banco de Santander and Scotia Bank,** both adorned with intricate stained-glass windows, art nouveau detailing, and dozens of unusual architectural features. The alleyway separating the two banks, Callejon Amor, is lined with African tulip trees planted to evoke the romantic spirit of any couple in love. (This alleyway is also the site of public concerts held every Sunday between 8 and 9pm by one of the town's classical orchestras or dance bands.)

   Proceed eastward along Calle Cristina, which funnels into the main square directly opposite the red-and-black-sided fire station. At the next cross street, diagonal to where you're standing, you'll see the:

9. **Memorial to Don Domingo,** dedicated to Don Domingo ("Cocolia") Cruz, longtime leader of Ponce's municipal band and one of the best-known musicians from Ponce. He died in 1934.

   Turn left at Calle Mayor and admire the neoclassical facade of the largest and most historic theater in the Caribbean, the:

10. **Teatro La Perla,** graced by six classical columns (see "Seeing the Sights," above). Depending on the time of day and the season, the lobby of this theater may be open for a quick look at its interior decoration.

    Now continue walking northward along Calle Mayor to the first intersection (Calle Isabel). To your right stands a Moorish-inspired building known as the Casa Salazar (Salazar House), which accommodates a branch of the Puerto Rican Museum of History.

    ⬤**TAKE A BREAK**   Copious cups of coffee, assorted ice creams, and sandwiches are offered to tired pedestrians and talkative neighbors at the **Café Tomas/Café Tompy,** Calle Isabel at the corner of Calle Mayor (☎ 787/840-1965). Divided into less-formal and more-formal sections, it is open daily from 7am to midnight. For more information, see "Where to Dine," below.

    After this break, walk westward along Calle Isabel until you reach the edge of the previously explored Plaza de Las Delicias. From the square's northeastern corner stretches:

11. **El Atocha,** the city's main shopping street. Stroll along its broad borders, noting the Spanish-inspired turn-of-the-century architecture, the cast-iron benches, and the many police guards ensuring one of the most tranquil urban streets of Puerto Rico. After your shopping, return to the main square and walk westward along its northern edge. Note, within the confines of the square is:

12. **Statue of Muñoz Rivera,** a memorial to one of Puerto Rico's best-known politicians (1898 to 1980), who helped Puerto Ricans become U.S. citizens after a career of political lobbying.

    Proceeding along the edge of the square, note the:

13. **Fox-Delicias Mall,** one of the city's most alluring watering holes and shopping enclaves. Originally built in 1931 as a movie theater, its pink walls are excellent examples of art deco architecture on Puerto Rico. In crumbling disrepair, the theater was transformed into a disco during the 1960s. In 1989, the government of Spain earmarked funds for the restoration of Ponce but specifically insisted that it be used to restore this building to its original celluloid glamour. Today this mall contains an array of shops, nightclubs, and cafes, a good place for refreshment after your stroll.

OUTDOOR ACTIVITIES

Ponce is a city—not a beach resort—and should be visited mainly for its sights. There is little in the way of organized sports, but a 10-minute drive west of Ponce will take you to ✪ **Playa de Ponce,** a long strip of white sand opening onto the tranquil waters of the Caribbean. This beach is usually better for swimming than the Condado in San Juan.

Scuba divers can go to the best dive sites along the southern coast with **Gregory's Dive Center** (☎ 787/840-6424). The center can also make arrangements for fishing and sailing in the Ponce area.

The city owns two **tennis complexes,** one at Poly Deportivos, with nine hard courts and another at Rambla, with six courts. Both are open from 9am to 10pm and are lighted for night play. You can play free but you must call to make a reservation. For information, including directions on how to get there, call the **Secretary of Sports** at ☎ 787/840-4400.

To play golf, you have to go to **Aquirre Golf Course,** Route 705, Aquirre (☎ 787/853-4052), 30 miles east of Ponce (take Highway 52). This nine-hole course, open from 7:30am to sunset daily, charges $8 greens fees Monday through Friday, going up to $15 on weekends and holidays. Another course, **Club Zeportivo,** Carretera 102, kilometer 15.4, Barrio Jogudas, Cabo Rojo (☎ 787/254-3748), lies 30 miles west of Ponce. This course is a nine-holer, open daily from 7am to 5pm. Greens fees are $30 daily.

CARITE FOREST PRESERVE

In southeastern Puerto Rico, lying off the Ponce Expressway near Cayey, **Carite** is a 6,000-acre reserve with a dwarf forest, which was produced by the region's high humidity and moist soil. From several peaks there are panoramic views of Ponce and the Caribbean Sea. On one peak is Nuestra Madre, a Catholic spiritual meditation center that permits visitors to stroll the grounds. Fifty species of birds live in the Carite Forest Reserve, which also has a large natural pool called Charco Azul. A picnic area and campgrounds are shaded by eucalyptus and royal palms. The forest borders a lake of the same name. Entrances to the forest are signposted from the town of Cayey, which itself is reached after an hour's drive from either Ponce or San Juan.

SHOPPING

If you feel a yen for shopping in Ponce, head for the **Fox-Delicias Mall,** at the intersection of Calle Reina Isabel and the Plaza de Las Delicias, the city's most innovative shopping center. Among the many interesting stores there is **Regalitos y Algo Mas,** located on the upper level. It specializes in unusual gift items from around Puerto Rico. Look especially for the Christmas tree ornaments, crafted from wood, metal, colored porcelain, or bread dough, and for the exotic dolls chosen and displayed by the owners. Purchases can be shipped anywhere in the world.

WHERE TO STAY

Days Inn. Rte. 1, km 123.5, Mercedita, Ponce, PR 00715. ☎ **800/329-7466** or 787/841-1000. Fax 787/841-2560. 122 units. A/C TV TEL. $105 double; $130 suite. Rates include continental breakfast. AE, DC, MC, V. Free parking.

A 15-minute drive east of Ponce on Highway 52, opposite the Interamerican University, this hotel opened in 1989. Its modest bedrooms are conservative and comfortable, equipped with contemporary furnishings. The prices appeal to families with children. Facilities include a courtyard swimming pool, a children's wading

---

Wet & Dry: A Hiking & Kayaking Tour

Southwestern Puerto Rico is the site of the world's largest remaining tract of tropical, dry, coast-forest, much of it preserved in Guánica State Forest. In contrast, this part of the island also features miles of mangrove channel systems. Visitors can visit this unusual terrain with **Tropix Wellness Tours** (☎ 787/268-2173; fax 787/268-1722), whose "Wet and Dry Tour" includes two expeditions: a "dry" forest hike in Guánica State Forest and "wet" paddles through the mangroves by kayak. Visits to secluded beaches at sunset are included.

The 4-day, 3-night tour costs $518 per person, double occupancy, including accommodations at the Copamarina Hotel, continental breakfast, and equipment for the escorted expeditions.

---

pool, a Jacuzzi, a coin-operated laundry, an international restaurant, a bar/disco, and ice and vending machines for sodas and snacks.

Hotel Meliá. Calle Cristina 2, Ponce, PR 00731. ☎ **787/842-0260.** Fax 787/841-3602. 78 units. A/C TV TEL. $76.30–$92.20 double. Rates include continental breakfast. AE, DC, MC, V. Parking $3.

A city hotel with southern hospitality, the Meliá, which has no connection with the international hotel chain, often attracts businesspeople. It's a few steps away from the Cathedral of Our Lady of Guadalupe and from the Parque de Bombas (the red-and-black firehouse). Although this old and somewhat tattered hotel was long ago outclassed by the Hilton, many of its admirers who could afford more upscale accommodations still prefer to stay here for its old-time atmosphere and aura. The lobby floor and all stairs are covered with Spanish tiles of Moorish design. The desk clerks speak English. The rooms are comfortably furnished and pleasant enough, and most have a balcony facing either busy Calle Cristina or the old plaza. Breakfast is served on a rooftop terrace with a good view of Ponce, and the Mark Restaurant plods along under separate management. You can park your car in the lot nearby.

✪ **Ponce Hilton and Casino.** Av. Caribe 1150 (P.O. Box 7419), Ponce, PR 00732. ☎ **800/HILTONS** in the U.S. and Canada, or 787/259-7676. Fax 787/259-7674. 153 units. A/C MINIBAR TV TEL. Year-round $200–$220 double; $420 suite. Additional person $45 extra. AE, CB, DC, DISC, MC, V. Self-parking $4.50; valet parking $10.

Opened in 1993 on an 80-acre tract right on the beach at the western end of Avenida Santiago de los Caballeros, about a 5-minute (7-mile) drive from the center of Ponce, this is the most glamorous hotel in southern Puerto Rico. Designed like a miniature village, with turquoise-blue roofs, white walls, and lots of tropical plants, ornamental waterfalls, and gardens, it welcomes conventioneers and individual tourists alike. Accommodations contain tropically inspired furnishings, ceiling fans, terraces or balconies, and several luxurious extra amenities.

Dining/Diversions: The food is the most sophisticated and refined on the south coast of Puerto Rico. Chefs use only the freshest ingredients available to them, which they whip into imaginative culinary taste treats. Everyone on the waitstaff seems to have an extensive knowledge of the menu and will aid and guide you through some exotic dishes—of course, you'll find familiar fare too. The more glamorous of the hotel's two restaurants is ✪ **La Cava,** whose cuisine is some of the most intricate and thoughtful in southern Puerto Rico. The less formal

La Terrazza, set nearby, specializes in well-organized and sometimes lavish buffets at both lunch and dinner. El Bohemio cocktail lounge offers sunset-colored drinks and live music every evening, and the hotel's casino, an appropriately glittery showcase, is open daily from noon to 4am.

Amenities: Room service (7am to midnight), laundry, baby-sitting (if arranged in advance), lagoon-shaped pool ringed with gardens, business center, fitness center, video arcade, bike rentals, playground, summer camp for children, water sports available.

NEARBY PLACES TO STAY ON THE BEACH

✪ **Copamarina Beach Resort.** Rte. 333, km 6.5, Caña Gorda (P.O. Box 805), Guánica, PR 00653. ☎ **800/468-4553** or 787/821-0505. Fax 787/821-0070. 106 units. A/C TV TEL. Winter $180 double; off-season $160 double; year-round $300 suite. AE, DC, DISC, MC, V. From Ponce, drive west along Rte. 2 to Rte. 116 and go south to Rte. 333, then head east.

Charming, low-key, and well maintained, this resort was originally built in the 1950s as the private vacation retreat of the de Castro family, Puerto Rico's cement barons. In 1991, it was enlarged and upgraded, and it now draws the European and North American tourist trade. It is situated beside a public beach, amid a landscaped palm grove.

The bedrooms are in wood-sided one- and two-story wings that radiate from the resort's central core. Each is decorated with lots of varnished pine (similar to what you might expect in the Adirondack Mountains) and is outfitted with rattan and pinewood furniture.

Dining: The resort houses two restaurants, Ballena's (an elegant indoor restaurant for dinner only) and Las Palmas, which is set in the open air beneath a heavily trussed canopy. Service is slow but the food is well prepared.

Amenities: Baby-sitting, laundry, swimming pool for adults, wading pool for children, two tennis courts, program of water sports (including snorkeling and scuba diving).

Mary Lee's by the Sea. Rte. 333, km 6.7 (P.O. Box 394), Guánica, PR 00653. ☎ **787/821-3600.** Fax 787/821-3600. 8 units. A/C. $70 double; $90 small suite with kitchenette; $110 suite with terrace and full kitchen; $150–$165 larger suites for up to 6 with full kitchen; $175–$200 3-bedroom unit for up to 6. No credit cards.

Owned and operated by Michigan-born Mary Lee Alvarez, a former resident of Cuba and a self-described "compulsive decorator," this is an informal collection of cottages, seafront houses, and apartments located beside the coastal highway, 4 miles east of Guánica. The five flat-roofed, California-style houses are subdivided into eight living units suitable for one to three couples. The entire compound is landscaped with flowering shrubs, trees, and vines.

There aren't any formally organized activities here, but the hotel sits next to sandy beaches and a handful of uninhabited offshore cays. The management maintains rental boats with putt-putt motors, two different waterside sundecks, and several kayaks for the benefit of its active guests. Hikers and bird-watchers can go north to the Guánica State Forest (see "Nearby Attractions," above).

Don't come here looking for nighttime activities or enforced conviviality. The place is quiet, secluded, and appropriate only for low-key vacationers looking for privacy and isolation with a companion and/or with nature. There isn't a bar or restaurant here, although each unit includes a modern kitchen and an outdoor barbecue pit. The rooms are serviced weekly, although for an extra fee guests can arrange to have a maid come in every day.

WHERE TO DINE
MODERATE

La Montserrate. Sector Las Cucharas, Rte. 2. ☎ **787/841-2740.** Main courses $15–$20. AE, DC, DISC, MC, V. Daily 11am–10pm. PUERTO RICAN/SEAFOOD.

Beside the seafront, about 4 miles west of the town center, this restaurant draws a loyal clientele from the surrounding residential neighborhood. A culinary institution in Ponce since it was established 20 years ago, it occupies a large, airy, modern building divided into two dining areas, one slightly more formal than the other. Most visitors, however, head for the large room in back, where windows on three sides encompass a view of some offshore islands. Specialties, concocted from the catch of the day, might include octopus salad, four kinds of asopao (the Puerto Rican gumbo), a whole red snapper in Créole sauce, or a selection of steaks and grills. Nothing is innovative or magical here; but the cuisine is typical of the south of Puerto Rico, and it's a family favorite. The fish dishes are better than the meat selections.

La Terraza. In the Ponce Hilton, Av. Caribe 1150. ☎ **787/259-7676.** Lunch buffet $16 per person; dinner buffets $18–$25 per person. AE, DC, DISC, MC, V. Daily 12:30–3pm and 6:30–10pm. INTERNATIONAL.

During the design phase of Ponce Hilton, a team of architects and restaurateurs devoted lots of attention to this restaurant's layout and traffic flows. The result is one of the most appealing ongoing rosters of buffets in Ponce. Featuring an impressive array of salads, soups, breads, meats, fish, and desserts, they're more formal and elaborate, and a bit more expensive, at dinner than at the self-service lunches, but overall, they represent one of the best restaurant values in Ponce. At dinner, a waitstaff will bring your main course to your table, although appetizers, salads, desserts, and garnishes are retrieved by clients at the buffet. A different theme is emphasized every night of the week, with Monday devoted to variations on traditional Puerto Rican mofongos (plantains layered with various combinations of meat or seafood), and Tuesday, Wednesday, and Thursday featuring Mexican fajitas, barbecued ribs, and lobster, respectively. Friday is fish night, Saturday is steak, and Sunday is most festive of all, devoted to Caribbean versions of paella.

INEXPENSIVE

Café Tomas/Café Tompy. Calle Isabel at Calle Mayor. ☎ **787/840-1965.** Lunch $6–$18; dinner $7–$20. AE, MC, V. Daily 11am–3pm and 6–11pm. Cafe daily 7am–midnight. PUERTO RICAN.

The more visible and busier section of this establishment functions as a simple cafe for neighbors and local merchants. On plastic tables often flooded with sunlight from the big windows, you can order coffee, sandwiches, or cold beer, perhaps while relaxing after a walking tour of the city.

The family-run restaurant is more formal. The discreet entrance is adjacent to the cafe on Calle Isabel. Here, amid a decor reminiscent of a Spanish *tasca* (tapas bar), you can enjoy such simply prepared dishes as salted fillet of beef, beefsteak with onions, four kinds of asopao, buttered eggs, octopus salads, and *yuca* (similar to cassava) croquettes.

Lupita's Mexican Restaurante. Calle Reina Isabel 60. ☎ **787/848-8808.** Reservations recommended. Main courses $7–$12; platters for 2, $12–$30. AE, DC, MC, V. Sun–Thurs 11am–11pm, Fri–Sat 11am–2am. MEXICAN.

Lending a note of lighthearted fun to the city, this is the only Mexican restaurant in Ponce. Set in a 19th-century building and its adjoining courtyard, a short walk from Ponce's main square, it's the creative statement of Hector de Castro, who traveled throughout Mexico to find the elaborate fountains and the dozens of chairs and decorative accessories that fill these premises. The trompe l'oeil murals on the inside (featuring desert scenes in an amusing surrealism) were painted by the owner's sister, Flor de Maria de Castro.

A well-trained staff serves blue and green margaritas (frozen or unfrozen) and a wide array of other tropical drinks. Any of these might be followed by Mexican dishes cooked in cholesterol-free vegetable oil. Specialties include tortilla soup, taco salads, grilled lobster tail with tostones, seafood fajitas, and burritos, tacos, and enchiladas with a wide choice of fillings. A mariachi band plays on Friday, and on Saturday either Puerto Rican or American bands entertain. Lupita is an affectionate nickname for Guadalupe, the patron saint of both Mexico and the city of Ponce.

AN EASY EXCURSION TO HISTORIC SAN GERMÁN

Only an hour's drive from Ponce or Mayagüez and the beaches of the southern coast, and just over 2 hours from San Juan, San Germán, Puerto Rico's second-oldest town, is a little museum piece. It was founded in 1512 and destroyed by the French in 1528. Rebuilt in 1570, it was named after Germain de Foix, the second wife of King Ferdinand of Spain. Once the rival of San Juan, San Germán harbored many inhabitants who were engaged in piracy, pillaging the ships that sailed off the nearby coastline. Indeed, many of today's residents are descended from the smugglers, poets, priests, and politicians who lived here.

Although the pirates and sugar plantations are long gone, the city retains many colorful reminders of those former days. Today it has settled into a slumber, albeit one that has preserved the feel of the Spanish colonial era. Flowers brighten the patios here as they do in Seville. Also as in a small Spanish town, many of the inhabitants stroll in the plaza in the early evening. Nicknamed "Ciudad de las Lomas," or City of the Hills, San Germán boasts scenery that provides a pleasant backdrop to a variety of architectural styles—Spanish colonial (1850s), criollo (1880s), neoclassical (1910s), art deco (1930s), and international (1960s)—depicted in the gracious old-world-style buildings that line its streets. So significant are these buildings that San Germán is only the second Puerto Rican city (the other is San Juan) to be included in the National Register of Historic Places.

The city's 249 noteworthy historical treasures are within easy walking distance of each other. Regrettably, you must view most of them from the outside. If some of them actually are open, count yourself fortunate because they have no phones, keep no regular hours, and are staffed by volunteers who rarely show up.

One building you can enter is ✪ **Iglesia Porta Coeli** (Gate of Heaven), on a knoll at one end of town. Dating from 1606, this is the oldest church in the New World. Restored by the Institute of Puerto Rican Culture, it contains a museum of religious art with a collection of ancient santos, the carved figures of saints that have long been a major branch of Puerto Rican folk art. Look for the 17th-century portrait of St. Nicholas de Bari, the French Santa Claus. Inside, the original palm-wood ceiling and tough, brown ausobo wood beams draw the eyes upward. Along the sides of the chapel are treasures gathered from all over the world, including early choral books from Santo Domingo, a primitive carving of Jesus, and 19th-century Señora de la Monserrate Black Madonna and Child statues. Further restoration work is now being done by Porta Coeli. Admission is $1. Open Tuesday through Sunday from 9am to 4:15pm. Call ☎ **787/264-4258** for more information.

Across the street, **The Tomás Vivoni House** is San Germán's most popular and widely recognized house. Named after the local architect who designed it, the home was built in 1913; it boasts a Queen Anne style, with a tower and gables that are key elements in the town's urban profile.

Next door is **Parque de Santo Domingo,** one of San Germán's two main plazas. Originally a marketplace, the plaza is now bordered with black iron and wooden park benches and features busts of some of the prominent figures in the town's history. The park also is the site of the Farmacia Martin, a Spanish colonial building converted to a pharmacy, which still operates today, and the Old City Hall.

San Germán de Auxerre Church is the centerpiece of Plaza Mariano Quiñones, the town's other main plaza. Built in the 19th century, its wooden vault features a beautiful trompe l'oeil painting in blue and gray. The original pattern on the ceiling was restored in 1993.

Acosta y Forés and Juán Ortiz Perichi houses, nearby, are recognized as being among the most beautiful homes in Puerto Rico. The Acosta y Forés House, a stunning example of criollo architecture, built in 1917, features traditional wood construction. Inside, the house has floor-to-ceiling stenciled designs painted over the walls of each room. Constructed in the 1920s and designed by Luis Pardo Fradera, the Juán Ortiz Perichi House is a fine example of Puerto Rican ornamental architecture. It features a multilevel design with a curved balcony and pitched roofs.

The Rafael Garcia Cabrera School, in the northwest corner of town, once served as the Casa del Rey or the Spanish Army Headquarters during colonial times. A nearby basketball court was once the Plaza de Armas in the 1700s. Also located in this area is Inter-American University. Founded in 1912 as the Instituto Politécnico, its name was changed in 1956. It was the first institution of higher education on the island to be accredited by the Middle States Association of Colleges in 1944.

Despite the city's richly historic origins, there are no recommendable hotels or guesthouses in town, and no restaurant that's formal enough to be even listed with the official literature of the Puerto Rican government. **Parador Oasis,** Calle Luna 72 (☎ 787/892-1175), has a restaurant, but it's the worst managed parador in the chain. At the very best, use it only as a refueling stop in a dire emergency. The other restaurants here are grimy cafes on streets radiating from the town's main plaza. Accordingly, we recommend that you stay in Mayagüez or Ponce and visit here briefly—and bring a picnic lunch with you. Park on the main square, near the Porta Coeli church.

2 Mayagüez

98 miles W of San Juan, 15 miles S of Aguadilla

The largest city on the island's west coast, Mayagüez is a port whose elegance and charm reached its zenith during the mercantile and agricultural prosperity of the 19th century. Most of the town's stately buildings were destroyed in a horrific earthquake in 1918, and today the town is noted more for its industry than its aesthetic appeal.

Mayagüez is a commercial city—not a tourist resort—but it's a convenient stopover for those exploring the west coast. (The Best Western Mayagüez Resort & Casino draws most tourists here.) If you want a windsurfing beach, you have to head north of Rincón, or if you want a more tranquil beach, you can drive south from Mayagüez along Route 102 to Boquerón.

Nevertheless, Mayagüez is still identified as the honeymoon capital of Puerto Rico, partly because of the lush and beautiful vegetation that grows here and partly because of a peculiarly romantic 16th-century legend. It is said that local farmers often kidnapped young Spanish sailors who had stopped at Mayagüez for provisions en route to South America. However, it's anyone's guess whether this was good or bad luck. There was a scarcity of eligible bachelors in Mayagüez, and the farmers kidnapped the young sailors in hopes of providing their daughters with husbands and their farms with overseers.

Although the town itself dates from the mid-18th century, the area around it has figured in European history since the time of Christopher Columbus, who landed nearby in 1493. Today a bronze statue of Columbus stands atop a metallic globe of the world. Both are poised above the gracious plaza in the center of Mayagüez.

Famed for the size and depth of its harbor (the second-largest on the island), Mayagüez was built to control the **Mona Passage,** a route essential to the Spanish Empire when Puerto Rico and the nearby Dominican Republic were vital trade and defensive jewels in the Spanish crown (today this waterway is notorious for the destructiveness of its currents, the ferocity of its sharks, and the thousands of boat people who arrive illegally from either Haiti or the Dominican Republic, both on the adjacent island of Hispaniola.

Queen Isabel II of Spain recognized Mayagüez's status as a town in 1836. Her son, Alfonso XII, granted it a city charter in 1877. Permanently isolated from the major commercial developments of San Juan, Mayagüez, like Ponce, has always retained its own distinct identity.

Today the town's major industry is tuna packing; in fact, 60% of the tuna consumed in the United States is packed here. It is also an important departure point for deep-sea fishing and is the bustling port for exporting the agricultural produce from the surrounding hillsides. Once the needlework capital of Puerto Rico, it still has women who create fine embroidery and drawn-thread work, industries that were brought to Puerto Rico centuries ago from Spain and Hapsburg-controlled Holland and Belgium.

ESSENTIALS

GETTING THERE **American Eagle** (☎ 800/433-7300) flies from San Juan to Mayagüez two times a day Monday through Friday, three times a day on weekends (flying time: 40 min.). Depending on restrictions, round-trip passage ranges from $95 to $136 per person.

Taxis meet arriving planes. If you take one, negotiate the fare with the driver first—cabs are unmetered here.

There are branches of **Avis** (☎ 787/833-7070), **Budget** (☎ 787/832-4570), and **Hertz** (☎ 787/832-3314) at the Mayagüez airport.

If you're driving from San Juan, head either west on Route 2 (trip time: 2½ hr.) or south from San Juan on the scenic Route 52 (trip time: 3 hr.). Route 52 offers easier travel.

VISITOR INFORMATION Mayagüez doesn't have a tourist information office. If you're starting out in San Juan, inquire there before you set out (see "Visitor Information" under "Orientation," in chapter 4).

EXPLORING THE AREA: SURFING BEACHES & TROPICAL GARDENS

Along the western coastal bends of Route 2, north of Mayagüez, lie the best surfing **beaches** in the Caribbean. Surfers from as far away as New Zealand come to ride the waves. You can also check out panoramic **Punta Higuero** beach, nearby on Route 413, near Rincón. For more information see "Rincón," below.

South of Mayagüez is ✪ **Boquerón Beach,** one of the island's best, with a wide strip of white sand and good snorkeling conditions.

Mona Island: The Galápagos of Puerto Rico

Off Mayagüez, the unique island of Mona teems with giant iguanas, three species of endangered sea turtles, red-footed boobies, and countless other sea birds. It features a tabletop plateau with mangrove forests and cacti, giving way to dramatic, 200-foot-high limestone cliffs that rise some 200 feet above the water and encircle much of Mona.

A bean-shaped pristine island with no hotels, Mona is a destination for the hardy pilgrim who seeks the road less traveled. A pup tent, backpack, and hiking boots will do fine if you plan to forego the comforts of civilization and immerse yourself in nature. Snorkelers, spelunkers, biologists, and eco-tourists find much to fascinate them in Mona's wildlife, mangrove forests, coral reefs, and complex honeycomb that is the largest marine-originated cave in the world. There also are miles of secluded white-sand beaches and palm trees.

Uninhabited today, Mona was for centuries the scene of considerable human activity. The pre-Columbian Taíno Indians were the first to establish themselves here. Later, pirates used it as a base for their raids, followed by guano miners who removed the rich crop fertilizer from Mona's caves. Columbus landed in Mona on his 1494 voyage, and Ponce de León spent several days here en route to becoming governor of Puerto Rico in 1508. The notorious pirate Captain Kidd used Mona as a temporary hideout.

Mona can be reached by organized tour from Mayagüez. Camping is available at $1 per night. Everything needed, including water, must be brought in, and everything, including garbage, must be taken out. For more information, call the Puerto Rico Department of Natural Resources at ☎ 787/724-3724.

Encantos Ecotours (☎ 787/272-0005) offers bare-boned but ecologically sensitive camping tours to Mona Island at sporadic intervals that vary according to the demand of clients who are interested. The experience includes ground transport to and from San Juan, sea transport departing from Cabo Rojo, use of camping and snorkeling gear, all meals (expect the equivalent of K rations cooked over a campfire), and fees. A package of 3 nights and 4 days of outdoor life, which comes with its share of discomforts and inconveniences, sells for around $600.

For golfers, the **Best Western Mayagüez Resort & Casino** at Mayagüez (☎ 787/832-3232) makes arrangements for guests to play at a nine-hole course at a nearby country club.

Mayagüez's chief attraction is the ✪ **Tropical Agriculture Research Station** (☎ 787/831-3435). It's located on Route 65, between Post Street and Route 108, adjacent to the University of Puerto Rico at Mayagüez campus and across the street from the **Parque de los Próceres** (Patriots' Park). At the administration office, ask for a free map of the tropical gardens, which have one of the largest collections of tropical plant species that are useful to people, including cacao, fruit trees, spices, timbers, and ornamentals. The grounds are open Monday through Friday from 7am to 5pm, charging no admission.

Mayagüez is the jumping-off point for visits to unique **Mona Island,** the "Galápagos of the Caribbean." See the box above for details.

Not far from Mayagüez is **Maricao.** You can reach it by taking Route 105 west and then driving north on Route 120. The town is colorful and rather small. On

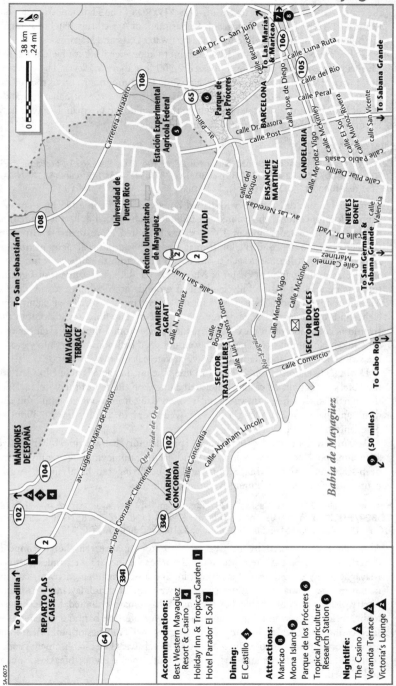

N

0   .38 km
     .24 mi

To Aguadilla↑

REPARTO LAS CAISEAS

102Z

104

102

2

341

64

341

102

MANSIONES DE ESPAÑA

2
3
4

av. José González Clemente

Quebrada de Oro

av. Eugenio María de Hostos

MARINA CONCORDIA

calle Concordia

MAYAGÜEZ TERRACE

To San Sebastián↑

108

108

Carretera Miradero

Universidad de Puerto Rico

Recinto Universitario de Mayagüez

RAMIREZ AGRAIT
calle N. Ramirez

calle San Juan

2

2

VIVALDI

SECTOR TRASTALLERES

Calle Bogata Torres

calle Luis Llorens

calle Abraham Lincoln

Río Yagüez

calle Comercio

Estación Experimental Agrícola Federal

5

av. París

65

Parque de Los Próceres

6

calle del Bosque

calle Dr. G. San Jurjo

calle Betances

To Las Marias & Maricao

7
8

106

106

calle Luna Ruta

105

calle del Rio

BARCELONA

calle Jose de Diego

calle Peral

calle Dr. Basora

calle Post

ENSANCHE MARTINEZ

av. Las Nereidas

CANDELARIA

calle Mendez Vigo

calle El Sol

calle Muñoz Rivera

calle Pablo Casals

calle San Vicente

To Sabana Grande→

calle Pilar Defillo

NIEVES BONET

calle Valencia

calle Dr. Vadi

calle Carmelo Martinez

To San Germán & Sabana Grande→

calle Mendez Vigo

calle McKinley

SECTOR DOLCES LABIOS

To Cabo Rojo→

Bahía de Mayagüez

9 (50 miles)↓

SA-0075

Accommodations:
Best Western Mayagüez Resort & Casino **4**
Holiday Inn & Tropical Garden **1**
Hotel Parador El Sol **7**

Dining:
El Castillo **3**

Attractions:
Maricao **8**
Mona Island **9**
Parque de los Próceres **6**
Tropical Agriculture Research Station **5**

Nightlife:
The Casino **2**
Veranda Terrace **2**
Victoria's Lounge **2**

199

the outskirts look for a sign that reads **LOS VIVEROS** (The Hatcheries); then take Route 410. Here, the Commonwealth Department of Agriculture hatches as many as 25,000 fish for stocking Puerto Rican freshwater lakes and streams.

Go back to Maricao to Route 120 south up to kilometer 13.8 until you reach the **Maricao State Forest** picnic area, located 2,900 feet above sea level. The observation tower provides a panoramic view across the green mountains up to the coastal plains. Continue on Route 120 across the forest to the town of Sabana Grande (Great Plain). Route 2 will then take you to the town of San Germán. (See "An Easy Excursion to Historic San Germán" from Ponce, above.)

WHERE TO STAY

Best Western Mayagüez Resort & Casino. Rte. 104 (P.O. Box 3629), Mayagüez, PR 00709. ☎ **800/528-1234** or 787/832-3030. Fax 787/834-3475. 148 units. A/C MINIBAR TV TEL. Year-round $145–$175 double; $250 suite. AE, MC, V. Parking $4.50.

A former Hilton, this five-story T-shaped hotel was bought in 1995 by a consortium of local investors, who poured 5.5 million much-needed dollars into a radical renovation. Since reopening in 1996, it has benefited more than ever from its redesigned casino, its country-club format, and its position on 20 acres of tropical gardens at the northern approach to the city, 3 miles from the airport. It functions as the major entertainment center of Mayagüez. The U.S. Department of Agriculture has designated its carefully landscaped grounds as an adjunct to the nearby Mayagüez Institute of Tropical Agriculture. There are five species of palm trees, eight kinds of bougainvillea, and numerous species of rare flora, set adjacent to the Institute's collection of tropical plants, which range from a pink torch ginger to a Sri Lankan cinnamon tree. The hotel's well-designed bedrooms open onto views of the swimming pool, and many units have private balconies.

Dining/Diversions: See "Where to Dine," below, for details about El Castillo, the hotel's restaurant. Its casino, renovated along with the rest of the hotel in 1995 through 1996, has free admission and is open daily from noon to 4am. You can drink and dance at the Victoria Lounge Wednesday to Sunday from 8:30pm to 3am; entrance is free.

Amenities: Room service (6:30am to 11pm), laundry, baby-sitting, Olympic-size swimming pool, children's pool, playground, Jacuzzi, minigym, three tennis courts, deep-sea fishing, skin diving; surfing and scuba diving can be arranged. A golf course lies within a 30-minute drive from the hotel.

Holiday Inn & Tropical Casino. 2701 Rte. 2, km 149.9, Mayagüez, PR 00680-6328. ☎ **800/HOLIDAY** in the U.S. and Canada, or 787/833-1100. Fax 787/833-1300. 152 units. A/C TV TEL. Year-round $109.50–$152 double; $210–$260 suite. AE, DC, MC, V.

Although it's outclassed by its rival, this six-story mainstream hotel competes directly with the Best Western Mayagüez Resort & Casino. It's set 2 miles north of Mayagüez's city center, behind a parking lot and a well-maintained lawn that's no match for the dramatically landscaped Best Western. The Holiday Inn is contemporary, clean, and comfortable, however, and it has a marble-floored, high-ceilinged lobby; an outdoor swimming pool with its own waterside bar; and a generously sized casino outfitted in glittering shades of green with touches of pink. Bedrooms are comfortably but functionally outfitted in motel style. The establishment's social center is Holly's Café, an airy, stylish eatery that's open daily for breakfast, lunch, and dinner.

Hotel Parador El Sol. Calle Santiago Riera Palmer, 9 Este, Mayagüez, PR 00680. ☎ **888/765-0303** or 787/834-0303. Fax 787/265-7567. 52 units. A/C TV TEL. Year-round $65–$82 double, $76–$92.50 triple. Rates include continental breakfast. AE, MC, V.

This circa-1970 hotel provides some of the most reasonable and hospitable accommodations in this part of Puerto Rico, although it's far more geared to the business traveler than to the tourist, with no-frills furnishings. Central to the shopping district and to all highways, 2 blocks from the landmark Plaza del Mercado in the heart of the city, the six-floor restored hotel offers up-to-date facilities that include cable TV, a standard restaurant, and a swimming pool.

NEARBY PLACES TO STAY

✪ **Hotal Paradores Joyuda Beach.** Rte. 102, km 11.7, Cabo Rojo, PR 00623. ☎ **787/851-5650.** Fax 787/265-6940. 41 units. A/C TV TEL. $80–$90 double. Two children under 12 stay free in parents' room. Rates include continental breakfast. AE, MC, V. Follow Rte. 102 south of Mayagüez to Joyuda.

Built on the beach in scenic Cabo Rojo in 1989, this is little more than an average motel with standard furnishings, but it's a convenient and reasonably priced stopover nevertheless. From here you can easily head to El Combate Beach and the Cabo Rojo Wildlife Refuge. Tennis and golf are just 5 minutes away, and sportfishing charters, as well as windsurfing and canoeing, can also be arranged. The hotel is often a favorite of Puerto Rican honeymooners.

Parador Hacienda Juanita. Rte. 105, km 23.5 (P.O. Box 777), Maricao, PR 00606. ☎ **800/443-0266** for reservations only, or 787/838-2550. Fax 787/838-2551. 21 units. TEL. $70–$75 double. Children under 12 stay free in parents' room. AE, MC, V. Free parking.

Named after one of its long-ago owners, a matriarch named Juanita, this pink stucco building was originally constructed in 1836 as part of a coffee plantation. Situated 2 miles west of the village of Maricao, beside Route 105 heading to Mayagüez, it has a long veranda and a living room furnished with a large-screen TV and decorated with the antique tools and artifacts of the coffee industry. Relatively isolated, it's surrounded by only a few neighboring buildings and the jungle. The Luis Rivera family welcomes visitors and serves drinks and meals in their restaurant. There are a swimming pool, billiards table, and Ping-Pong table on the premises. The bedrooms are simple and rural, with ceiling fans, rocking chairs, and rustic furniture. None of the rooms has TV or air-conditioning (ceiling fans suffice in the cool temperatures in this high-altitude place).

WHERE TO DINE

El Castillo. In the Best Western Mayagüez Resort & Casino, Rte. 104. ☎ **787/832-3232.** Breakfast buffet $12.25. Lunch buffet (Mon–Sat) $14.95, Sun brunch buffet $24.95. Main courses $12–$25. AE, MC, V. Daily 6:30am–11pm. INTERNATIONAL/PUERTO RICAN.

This hotel restaurant is the most professionally managed and large-scale dining room in western Puerto Rico. Ringed with paneling and known as the venue for copious lunchtime buffets, it serves only à la carte items at nighttime. These include such dishes as seafood stew served on beds of linguine with marinara sauce; grilled salmon with a mango-flavored Grand Marnier sauce; and fillets of sea bass with a cilantro, white wine, and butter sauce. Steak and lobster are served on the same platter, if you want them. The food has real flavor and flair and isn't the typical bland hotel fare so often dished up.

MAYAGÜEZ AFTER DARK

El Casino. At the Best Western Mayagüez Resort & Casino, Rte. 104. ☎ **787/832-3030.** No cover.

The completely remodeled casino with an adjoining Player's Bar is the only casino in Mayagüez. Try your luck at blackjack, dice, slot machines, roulette, and mini-baccarat. It's open daily from noon to 4am.

Victoria's Lounge. In the Best Western Mayagüez Resort & Casino, Rte. 104. ☎ **787/ 831-7575.**

The music's hot and it's most likely to be merengue or salsa. The music often originates in New York or Los Angeles, and even San Juan. Live music is presented at times during the opening hours of Thursday through Saturday from 8pm to 3:30am. There's no cover except on special occasions like Valentine's Day.

Veranda Terrace. In the Best Western Mayagüez Resort & Casino, Rte. 104. ☎ **787/ 831-7575.**

On a large and airy covered terrace that opens to a view of a manicured tropical garden, this is a relaxing and soothing place for a cocktail. The bartenders specialize in pastel-colored rum-based concoctions that seem to go well with the hibiscus-scented air. Daily from 10:30am to 1:30am.

3 Rincón

100 miles W of San Juan, 6 miles N of Mayagüez

North of Mayagüez and on the westernmost point of the island, the small fishing village of Rincón lies in the foothills of La Cadena mountains. It's not a sightseeing destination unto itself, but surfers from as far away as New Zealand say the area's half-dozen reef-lined beaches, off Route 2 between Mayagüez and Rincón, are the best spots in the Caribbean. Surfers are particularly attracted to the beach at **Punta Higuero,** on Route 413 near Rincón, which has been compared to the finest surfing spots in the world. During winter, uninterrupted swells from the North Atlantic form perfect waves averaging 5 to 6 feet in height, with ridable rollers sometimes reaching 15 to 25 feet.

Endangered humpback whales also winter here, attracting a growing number of whale watchers. The lighthouse at El Faro Park is a great place to spot these mammoth mammals.

And many nonsurfers visit Rincón for only one reason: the Horned Dorset Primavera Hotel, not only one of the finest hotels in Puerto Rico, but one of the best in the entire Caribbean.

ESSENTIALS

GETTING THERE **American Eagle** (☎ 800/433-7300) flies from San Juan to Mayagüez, the nearest airport, two times a day Monday to Friday, three times on Saturday and Sunday (flying time: 30 min.). Taxis meet planes arriving from San Juan, but they're unmetered—negotiate the fare at the outset with your driver. For car rentals, see "Essentials" in the Mayagüez section, above.

If you're driving from San Juan, travel either west on Route 2 (trip time: 2 hr.) or south from San Juan on scenic Route 52 (trip time: 3½ hr.). We recommend Route 52.

VISITOR INFORMATION There is no tourist information office in Rincón. Inquire in San Juan before heading to Rincón (see "Visitor Information" under "Orientation," in chapter 4).

GOLFING AT AN OLD U.S. AIR BASE

Punta Borinquén Golf Club, Route 107 (☎ 787/890-2987), 2 miles north of Aquadilla's center, across the highway from the city's airport, was originally built by the U.S. government as part of the Ramey Air Force base. Today, its 18 holes are a public golf course, open daily from 7am to 7pm. Greens fees cost $20 for an all-day pass, and a golf cart that can carry two passengers rents for $24 for 18 holes, or $12 for 9 holes. Clubs can be rented for $10 per set. The clubhouse contains a bar and a simple restaurant.

WHERE TO STAY

✪ **Horned Dorset Primavera Hotel.** Rte. 429 (P.O. Box 1132), Rincón, PR 00677. ☎ **800/633-1857** or 787/823-4030. Fax 787/823-5580. 31 units. A/C. Winter $380 double, $480–$800 suite for 2; off-season $280 double, $420–$650 suite for 2. MAP $71.25 per extra person. AE, MC, V. From the Mayagüez airport, take Rte. 2 north ½ mile to the Anasco intersection; turn left onto Rte. 115 toward Rincón for 4 miles; after El Coche Restaurant, take a sharp left onto Rte. 429 and go about 1 mile; the hotel is on the left, at distance marker km 3. For driving times from San Juan, see above. From Rincón, follow Rte. 115 south (signposted Mayagüez). When you approach El Coche Restaurant, take a sharp right onto Rte. 429 and go about 1 mile to distance marker km 3.

This is the most sophisticated hotel on Puerto Rico, and one of the most exclusive and elegant small hostelries anywhere in the Caribbean. Established in 1987, it was built on the massive breakwaters and seawalls erected by a local railroad many years ago, and it was named after a successful hotel (the Horned Dorset), which its owners still maintain in upstate New York.

The hacienda evokes an aristocratic Spanish villa, with wicker armchairs, hand-painted tiles, ceiling fans, seaside terraces, and cascades of flowers. Management does not allow children under 12, most pets, radios, or televisions—this is really a restful place. Accommodations are in a series of suites that ramble uphill amid lush gardens. The decor is tasteful, with four-poster beds and brass-footed tubs in marble-sheathed bathrooms.

In 1996, the hotel completed a $1.4 million addition, the eight-suite Casa Escondida villa. Set at the edge of the property, adjacent to the sea, it is decorated with an accent on teakwood and marble. Some of the units have private plunge pools; others offer private verandas or sundecks. Each contains high-quality repro-ductions of colonial furniture by Baker.

Dining/Diversions: The hotel's restaurant is one of the finest on Puerto Rico (see "Where to Dine," below). There's a bar open throughout the day that serves delectable rum punches. Guitarists and singers often perform during cocktail and dinner hours.

Amenities: Room service (at breakfast and lunch only), concierge, laundry, mas-sage, limousine and touring services, the best hotel library on Puerto Rico (books on art, music, comparative literature, and poetry), swimming pool, secluded semi-private beach, deep-sea fishing, gym, tennis courts, golf, and scuba diving available nearby.

The Lazy Parrot. P.O. Box 430, Rincón, PR 00677. ☎ **787/823-5654.** Fax 787/823-0224. 7 units. Year-round, $85 double. Extra person $10 each. AE, DISC, MC, V.

This is a simple, family-run inn set in a residential neighborhood. From here it's only a half-mile walk or drive to at least a half-dozen beaches. Its building was orig-inally a private home, converted into a guesthouse in 1989. The peach-colored accommodations are about as basic as we recommend, but if you're traveling with an extended group of family members or friends, the bunk-bed setup and the fact that each room can sleep up to five in any accommodation might make them appealing. (OK, it wouldn't be that comfortable if you packed in five people, but it's possible.) There are very few amenities in-house (no pool, tennis courts, or any other resort facilities), but there are a simple, somewhat sleepy bar and a restaurant serving inexpensive dinner platters.

Parador Villa Antonio. Rte. 115, km 12.3 (P.O. Box 68), Rincón, PR 00677. ☎ **800/443-0266** or 787/823-2645. Fax 787/823-3380. 55 apts. A/C TV TEL. Year-round $80.25–$107 double. AE, DISC, MC, V. From Mayagüez continue north 1½ miles to the Anasco intersection. Once here, turn left onto Rte. 115 signposted Rincón. Follow Rte. 115 until you reach the km 12.3 marker. From Rincón in the north follow Rte. 115 south until you see El Bambino Restaurant. After passing the restaurant, take a hard left, and in about 200 ft. make a right turn.

Ilia and Hector Ruíz offer apartments by the sea in their privately owned and run parador. The beach outside is a nice one—but we've seen litter here, it's not kept as clean as it should be, the air-conditioning doesn't work properly, and in general better maintenance is needed. Facilities include a children's playground, a game room, two tennis courts, and a swimming pool. Surfing and fishing can be enjoyed just outside your front door, and you can bring your catch right into your cottage and prepare a fresh seafood dinner in your own kitchenette. Room prices are based on the view, not the size.

A Nearby Place to Stay & Dine in Aguada

J.B. Hidden Village Hotel. Carretera 2, Intersection 4416, km 1, Punta Nueve, Barrio Piedras Blancas, Sector Villarrubia, Aguada, PR 00602. ☎ **787/868-8686.** Fax 787/868-8701. 40 units. A/C TV TEL. Year-round $74 double; $129 suite. AE, MC, V.

Named after the initials of its owners (Julio Bonilla, his wife, Jinnie, and their son, Julio, Jr.), this well-maintained and isolated hotel opened in 1990. Half a mile east of Aguada, on a side street running off Route 4414, it's nestled into a valley between three forested hillsides and almost invisible from the road outside, which makes it a quiet and simple refuge to vacationers who enjoy exploring the area's many beaches. There are two restaurants on the premises (one with a view looking out over a neighboring ravine), a small swimming pool, and a bar. Each comfortable bedroom is equipped with pastel-colored contemporary furniture and offers views of the pool.

WHERE TO DINE

The Black Eagle. Hwy. 413, km 1.0 interio, Barrio Ensenada. ☎ **787/823-3510.** Reservations recommended. Main courses $12–$21. AE, MC, V. Daily 11am–11pm. STEAKS/SEAFOOD.

This restaurant is one of the best in the neighborhood because of its inexpensive prices, its enormous portions, and its refusal to use any frozen ingredient in its well-recommended seafood. It occupies an isolated black-and-white house adjacent to the beach, about a quarter-mile north of the center of Rincón, close to the Black Eagle marina (with which it is not associated). Much of its clientele is made up of Europeans indulging in budget holidays at the nearby inns. In the dining room, you might begin your meal with a house-special drink, a deceptively potent pink-colored cocktail known appropriately as a Black Eagle. Menu items include lobster or shrimp cocktails, a 32-ounce porterhouse steak (the restaurant's trademark dish), grilled lobster, pan-fried conch, and an asopao (a gumbo) of lobster or shrimp. All the good-tasting main courses are accompanied with salad, bread, and vegetables, something that's bound to save you money on extras.

✪ **Horned Dorset Primavera.** Rte. 429. ☎ **787/823-4030.** Reservations recommended. Fixed-price dinners $56 for 5 courses, $88 for 11 courses. AE, MC, V. Daily noon–2:30pm and 7–9:30pm. For directions, see the hotel's entry, above. FRENCH/CARIBBEAN.

This place reigns without equal as the finest restaurant in western Puerto Rico, with a romance and an allure that are so pronounced that diners sometimes journey out from San Juan for an intimate dinner. It's the southern extension of an award-winning restaurant in Leonardsville, New York, the Horned Dorset, whose name derives from a species of sheep that's a lot more comfortable in chilly upstate New York than in the Caribbean tropics. A masonry staircase sweeps from the garden to reach the second-floor precincts, where soaring ceilings and an atmosphere similar to that within a private villa await you.

The menu, which changes virtually every night, based on the inspiration of the chef, is likely to include chilled parsnip soup, a fricassee of wahoo with wild mushrooms, grilled loin of beef with peppercorns, and medaillons of lobster in an orange-flavored beurre-blanc (white butter) sauce. The grilled breast of duckling with bay leaves and raspberry sauce is also delectable. On another occasion, dorado (mahimahi) was grilled and served with a ginger-cream sauce on a bed of braised Chinese cabbage. It was delicious, as was grilled squab with tarragon sauce. This restaurant serves people who dine at the best places in the world, and it pleases even their discriminating palates.

10

Exploring Puerto Rico off the Beaten Track: Island Drives & Paradores

Puerto Rico is a mere dot on most maps of the Caribbean. But the main island, about 100 miles long and 35 miles wide, is loaded with a wide variety of natural scenery. With your own wheels you can embark on an adventure that will take you up and down a tangled web of mountain roads to the El Yunque Rain Forest, to Luquillo Beach (the island's best and most popular), to an almost lunar subterranean landscape of caves, and through arid stretches where cacti grow along the south shore. You'll pass enormous boulders with mysterious petroglyphs carved by the ancient but vanished Taíno peoples, coffee and sugar plantations carved out of the landscape by Spanish colonists, and the very modern Arecibo Observatory, site of the world's largest radar/radio telescopes, where groundbreaking work is being conducted, including the search for extraterrestrial intelligence (E.T., give us a ring).

Seasonal changes transform the landscape here. In November the sugarcane fields are in bloom, and in January and February red and orange blossoms cover the flowering trees along the roads. Springtime brings delicate pink flowers to the Puerto Rican oak and deepred blossoms to the African tulip tree. Summer is a flamboyant time when the roadsides seem to be on fire with blooming flowers.

Following are two driving tours of the Puerto Rican countryside. The first will take you to the lush tropical forests and sandy beaches of eastern Puerto Rico; the second, to the subterranean sights of Karst Country and on to the west and south coasts. They are both extended tours—the first takes approximately 2 days to complete and the second approximately 6 days—but Puerto Rico's small size and many roads will give you many places to pick up or leave the tour. In fact, there are several points in the tours where we give you the opportunity to cut your tour short and head back to San Juan.

DRIVING IN PUERTO RICO

Renting a car is the way to go (see chapter 3 for rental information). It's conceivable that you could tour the island by *público* (public cars), but this will seem to take as long as trying to empty the Caribbean Sea with a cup.

Most of the major highways in Puerto Rico are broad, well-maintained boulevards. Once you veer off these prime arteries, however, be prepared in places for some often narrow and steep roads, especially if you venture into the mountains. Roads in many cases are just too narrow, especially if your car is wide and you meet an oncoming truck whose driver feels that the highway belongs to him. Do as the locals do: blow your horn around every narrow bend.

Be sure to take along a good map. Billboards and other commercial road signs are forbidden in Puerto Rico. Sometimes you'll wish the island had more of them.

Roadside markers note distances in kilometers (1km equals 0.62 mile). Remember that speed limits are given in miles per hour.

INNS & RESTAURANTS

Two programs that have helped the Puerto Rico Tourism Company successfully promote the commonwealth as "The Complete Island"—the *paradores puertorriqueños* and the *mesones gastronómicos*—will help make your travels even more enjoyable.

The paradores puertorriqueños are a chain of privately owned and operated country inns under the auspices and supervision of the Commonwealth Development Company. These hostelries are easily identified by the Taíno grass hut that appears in the signs and logos of each one. The Puerto Rico Tourism Company started the program in 1973, modeling it after Spain's parador system, although many of the paradores here are mere shanties when compared to some of the deluxe Spanish hostelries. Each parador is situated in a historic or particularly beautiful spot. They vary in size, but most share the virtues of affordability, hospitable staffs, and high standards of cleanliness. Most but not all of their rooms are air-conditioned; however, each contains a private bathroom.

For reservations or further information, contact the **Paradores Puertorriqueños Reservation Office,** P.O. Box 4435, Old San Juan Station, San Juan, PR 00905 (☎ **800/443-0266** in the U.S., 787/721-2884 within San Juan, or 800/981-7575 outside of San Juan but within Puerto Rico).

Except for those in major hotels, you'll find few well-known restaurants as you tour the island. However, there are plenty of roadside places and simple taverns. For authentic island cuisine, you can rely on the mesones gastronómicos ("gastronomic inns"). This established dining "network," sanctioned by the Puerto Rico Tourism Company, highlights restaurants recognized for excellence in preparing and serving Puerto Rican specialties at modest prices.

Mesón gastronómico status is limited to restaurants outside the San Juan area that are close to major island attractions. Membership in the program requires that restaurants have attractive surroundings and comply with strict standards of good service. Members must specialize in native foods, but if you ask for any fresh fish dish, chances are you'll be pleased.

Regrettably, there are no maps listing these myriad restaurants, but they are easy to spot as you drive around the island.

DRIVING TOUR 1:
Eastern Puerto Rico

Start: San Juan.
Finish: San Juan.
Time: Allow approximately 2 days, although you may wish to stay longer at places along the way.
Best Times: Any sunny days Monday through Friday.
Worst Times: Weekends, when the roads are often impossibly crowded.

This tour will take you through some of Puerto Rico's most stunning natural scenery, including El Yunque Rain Forest and Luquillo Beach. You will travel through the small towns of Trujillo Alto, Gurabo, Fajardo, Naguabo Beach, Humacao, Yabucoa, San Lorenzo, and Caguas before returning to San Juan.

From Condado, signs point the way southeast to Route 1. Near Rio Piedras on your right, Route 3 is the famous highway that most motorists take to visit Luquillo Beach and El Yunque Rain Forest (see below). Route 1 naturally blends into Route 3, which is sometimes called "Avenida 65 de Infantera" after the Puerto Rican regiment that fought in World War II and the Korean War.

At the intersection of Route 3 and Route 181, head south toward Trujillo Alto. South of Trujillo Alto connect with Route 851, which continues until it comes to an intersection with Route 941. At this point get on Route 941, which runs in a southwesterly direction. Along 941, and to your right, you'll come to the first worthy stopover:

1. **Lake of Loíza,** surrounded by mountains. You may see local farmers (jíbaros) riding horses laden with produce going to or from the marketplace. (Lake of Loíza is not to be confused with the northern coastal town of Loíza, which is known for its African heritage and its music.)

Leave the town by heading east along Route 30. Before you approach the town of Juncos, signs point the way to Route 185, which will lead you to the small town of Lomas. Continue north along Route 185, following the signs to the major artery of Route 3. Allow a leisurely hour of driving time for this trek after having left the lake.

Once you have connected with Route 3, take it east toward El Yunque and then turn right (south) onto Route 191, which climbs up into the forest surrounding El Yunque's peak and that of its taller sibling, El Toro. This is part of the Caribbean National Forest, and it is the most scenic, panoramic, and dramatic part of the eastern drive through Puerto Rico.

After viewing the lake, continue on Route 941, which now swings in a southeasterly direction through Puerto Rico's tobacco country to:

2. **Gurabo.** You'll know that you're nearing the town from the sweet aroma of drying tobacco leaves. Part of the town of Gurabo is set on the side of a mountain, and the streets consist of steps.

Leave Gurabo by heading east on Route 30. Near Juncos, turn left onto Route 185 north, follow it up through Lomas, and then get on Route 186 south. This road offers views of the ocean beyond the mountains and valleys. At this point you'll be driving through the lower section of the Caribbean National Forest; the vegetation is dense, and you'll be surrounded by giant ferns. The brooks descending from the mountains become waterfalls on both sides of the road. At about 25 miles east of San Juan is:

3. ✪ **El Yunque.** Consisting of about 28,000 acres, this rare natural treasure is the only tropical rain forest in the U.S. National Forest system. Its Spanish name derives from its distinctive anvil shape. It lies in the Luquillo Mountains, a name that harks back to the benign Indian god *Yuquiyú*, who, according to ancient legend, ruled from the forest's mighty peaks and protected the Taíno Indians, the island's original inhabitants. Today, El Yunque offers its visitors close encounters of the natural kind, from picnics amid rare flora and fauna to hikes along the panoramic trails. If the outdoors appeals, give yourself at least a day to explore this natural wonderland. See "The Natural Environment," in chapter 2, and section 3 on Ceiba and El Yunque in chapter 8 for details.

Driving Tour—Eastern Puerto Rico

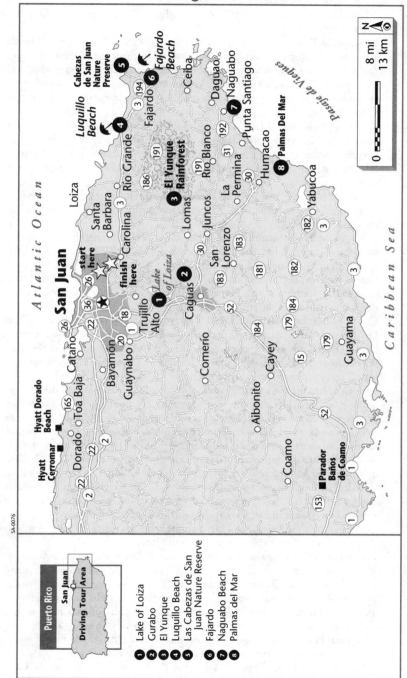

N

8 mi
13 km
0

Cabezas de San Juan Nature Preserve ⑤

Fajardo Beach

Luquillo Beach ④

Ceiba

Fajardo ⑥

Daguao

Naguabo ⑦

Punta Santiago

Pasaje de Vieques

194
3

191

El Yunque Rainforest ③

Río Blanco

192

Palmas Del Mar ⑧

Río Grande

186

191

La Permina

30

31

Humacao

Santa Barbara

Loiza

3

Lomas

Juncos

Yabucoa

Carolina

San Lorenzo

182

3

San Juan

start here

finish here

Lake of Loiza

Trujillo Alto

Caguas ②

①

183

183

181

182

3

Atlantic Ocean

26

36

22

1

18

Caribbean Sea

Bayamón

20

Guaynabo

52

184

Comerío

184

179

184

3

Cayey

15

179

Guayama

Cataño

Toa Baja

Dorado

22

2

Bayamón

Aibonito

52

165

Hyatt Dorado Beach

Hyatt Cerromar

22

2

Coamo

1

3

Parador Baños de Coamo

153

1

SA-0076

Puerto Rico

San Juan

Driving Tour Area

① Lake of Loiza
② Gurabo
③ El Yunque
④ Luquillo Beach
⑤ Las Cabezas de San Juan Nature Reserve
⑥ Fajardo
⑦ Naguabo Beach
⑧ Palmas del Mar

Backtrack on Route 191 until you reach Route 3. Five miles east from the intersection is:

4. ✪ **Luquillo Beach.** Edged by a vast coconut grove, this crescent-shaped beach is not only the best on Puerto Rico but also one of the finest in the Caribbean. You pay $1 to enter with your car, and you can rent a locker, take a shower, and use the changing rooms. Luquillo Beach becomes rather crowded on weekends, so if possible, go on a weekday when you'll have more sand to yourself. Picnic tables are available as well.

The beach is open Tuesday through Sunday from 9am to 5pm; it's closed Monday (if Monday is a holiday, the beach will be open Monday and closed Tuesday). Before entering the beach, you may want to stop at one of the road-side thatched huts that sell Puerto Rican snacks and pick up the makings for a picnic.

Not far from the beach is the **Parador Martorell,** where you can spend a restful night at the seaside (see "Where to Stay Along the Way in Luquillo," at the end of this tour).

From Luquillo, return to Route 3 east and continue for another 15 minutes until the first exit to Fajardo. Make a left onto Route 194, heading toward the eastern shore. At the traffic light at the corner of the Monte Brisas Shopping Center, turn left; stay on this road until the next traffic light, turn right, and continue to the intersection with Route 987. Turn left onto Route 987 and continue north until you reach the entrance to:

5. ✪ **Las Cabezas de San Juan Nature Reserve,** better known as *El Faro,* or "The Lighthouse," dating from 1882 and surrounded on three sides by the Atlantic Ocean. This northeast corner of Puerto Rico is one of the most beautiful and important areas of the island—unique because of the number of different eco-logical communities that flourishes here. The 316-acre El Faro site serves as a research center for the scientific community. It encompasses forests, mangroves, lagoons, beaches, cliffs, offshore cays, and coral reefs, and it's home to a vast array of terrestrial flora and fauna (such as sea turtles and other endangered species), as well as abundant and varied underwater life. It's an important spawning ground for fish, crustaceans, and shore and migratory birds. The nature reserve is open Wednesday through Sunday. Reservations are required, so call ☎ 787/722-5882 before going. Admission is $5 for adults, $2 for children under 12 (parking included). Guided tours, lasting 2 to 2½ hours, are scheduled Friday through Sunday at 9:30am, 10am, 10:30am, and 2pm. Of course, it isn't necessary to take a guided tour: you can hang out at the beach or simply visit on your own.

After visiting the reserve, you can take the same road back, heading south to Route 3. Then follow the highway signs south into:

6. **Fajardo,** a fishing port that was hotly contested during the Spanish-American War. Puerto Ricans are fond of giving nicknames to people and places—for many years, the residents of Fajardo have been called *cariduros* ("the hard-faced ones"). Don't let the label mislead you; local residents are very friendly. Sailors and fishers are attracted to the shores of Fajardo and nearby Las Croabas, which has several seafood restaurants. If you have time, you can take a very satisfying trip by ferry from Fajardo to either Vieques or Culebra, small islands off the Puerto Rican coast that make urban troubles seem far, far away (see chapter 11).

Continue south on Route 3, following the Caribbean coastline. At Cayo Lobos, just off the Fajardo port, the Atlantic meets the Caribbean. Here, the vivid colors of the Caribbean seem subdued compared to those of the deep blue ocean.

Go through the town of Ceiba, near the Roosevelt Navy Base, until you reach:

7. Naguabo Beach, a 30-minute drive from Fajardo. Here you can have coffee and *pastelillos de chapin,* pastry turnovers that were actually used as tax payments during Spanish colonial days. At kilometer 70.9 of Route 3, take a brief detour to the town of Naguabo, but only if you wish to enjoy the town plaza's scented, shady laurel trees, imported from India. There isn't much else to see.

Continue south along Route 3, going through Humacao and its sugarcane fields. When the cane blooms during November and December, the tops of the fields change colors according to the time of day. Humacao itself isn't of much interest, but it has a balneario-equipped beach with changing facilities, lockers, and showers. From here you can detour to:

8. Palmas del Mar, the sprawling resort covered in chapter 8. You can stop here or continue along Route 3 through Yabucoa, nestled amid some hills. The view along the road opens up at Cerro La Pandura, a mountain from which there's a panoramic outlook over giant boulders onto the Caribbean.

Directly to the west of Yabucoa you can connect to Route 182, heading west through some of the most dramatic scenery in Puerto Rico along the mountain chain of Cuchilla de Pandura. This road changes its number unexpectedly to Route 181 (but it's still the same road). After a sharp bend, it becomes Route 7740 (again the same road), and before it reaches the mountain station of Cerro la Santa, it becomes Route 184. Stay on Route 184, heading northwest and following the signs to Route 52, the major highway cutting across the heart of Puerto Rico. If you continue southwest on Route 52, you'll come to Ponce. But if you want to return to San Juan, where the driving tour began, go northeast, following the signs back into the heart of Puerto Rico's capital.

WHERE TO STAY ALONG THE WAY IN LUQUILLO

Parador Martorell. 6A Ocean Dr., Luquillo, PR 00773. ☎ **787/889-2710.** Fax 787/889-4520. 10 units (6 with bathroom). A/C TV TEL. $64.20 double without bathroom; $74.90 double with bathroom; $107 quad with bathroom. Rates include breakfast. MC, V. At km 36.2 along Rte. 3, turn toward the shore, then turn left and drive 4 short blocks.

Back in 1800, the Martorell family came to Puerto Rico from Spain and fell in love with the island. Today their descendants own and operate this Luquillo parador near the island's most impressive beach, only a half block away. When you arrive at the parador, you'll enter an open courtyard, which will have to suffice for your alfresco outings, because there are no grounds. Breakfast always features plenty of freshly picked fruit and homemade breads and compotes. The main reason for staying here is Luquillo Beach, which has shady palm groves, crescent beaches, coral reefs for snorkeling and scuba diving, and a surfing area. Be advised that this parador could be better maintained, and that the rather basic and simple rooms here have displeased many readers expecting more. All the rooms are small. Not all units are air-conditioned; insist on one of them if you book here.

DRIVING TOUR 2:
Western Puerto Rico & the Southwest Coast

Start: San Juan.
Finish: San Juan.
Time: Between 2 and 6 days, depending on how much of the itinerary you want to complete. The tour could run longer if you spend extra time at some of the stops along the way.

Best Times: Monday through Friday, any sunny day.
Worst Times: Weekends, when the roads are overcrowded with drivers from San Juan.

This tour begins with a foray into the famous Karst district of Puerto Rico. Along the way, you'll see the Taíno Indian Ceremonial Ball Park, Río Camuy Cave Park, and Arecibo Observatory. You will then emerge from the island's interior to begin a roundabout tour of the west and south coasts, taking in Guajataca Beach, Mayagüez, San Germán, Phosphorescent Bay, Ponce, Coamo, and numerous other towns and attractions.

A broad highway, Route 22 links San Juan with its western frontiers. The first major stopover is the city of Arecibo, directly north of Karst Country. However, there is an interesting detour along the way. Take Highway 22 west from San Juan until you reach the intersection with Route 140, at which point you head south (signposted to the town of Jayuya. Unless you're in a special hurry, you can allow a leisurely hour's drive from San Juan. But traffic is often heavy along Highway 22, since this is a major trucking route carrying supplies to and from the capital.

Route 140 will take you south through some of the most dramatic mountain scenery in Puerto Rico. At the intersection with Route 141, cut onto this highway and follow it south. It is signposted all the way to:

1. **Jayuya,** a village in the middle of the Cordillera Central and home to the **Parador Hacienda Gripinas,** a former coffee plantation where you can catch a very authentic and unique glimpse of the old days (see "The Paradores of Western Puerto Rico," at the end of this tour, for directions on how to reach the parador from Jayuya).

   If you decide to make this restful side trip, pick up the trail again by returning on Route 527 to Route 140; then travel west on Route 140 until you pass Lake Caonillas. Here, turn onto Route 111 west, and in 30 minutes you'll reach:

2. **Utuado,** a small mountain town boasting **Parador La Casa Grande,** with accommodations, a restaurant, and a swimming pool. It's a good place to stop after a day's touring in the area (see "The Paradores of Western Puerto Rico," at the end of the tour).

   From Utuado, continue west for 20 minutes on Route 111 to kilometer 12.3, where you'll find the:

3. ✪ **Taíno Indian Ceremonial Center.** Archaeologists have dated this site to approximately 2 centuries before Europe's discovery of the New World. It is believed that the Taíno chief Guarionex gathered his subjects on this site to celebrate rituals and practice sports. Set on a 13-acre field surrounded by trees, some 14 vertical monoliths with colorful petroglyphs are arranged around a central sacrificial stone monument. The ball complex also includes a museum, open daily from 9am to 5pm; admission is free. There is also a gallery, Herencia Indigena, where you can purchase Taíno relics at very reasonable prices, including the sought-after *Cemis* (Taíno idols) and figures of the famous little frog, the coquí. The Taínos have long gone, and much that was here is gone with them. The site is of special interest to those with academic pursuits, but of only passing interest to the lay visitor. However, it makes a good stopover along the route. You can get out, walk around, and stretch your legs before continuing with the tour. For more understanding of the site, see the box, "Life After Death, above."

   Continue west on Route 111 for another 20 minutes to the town of Lares, then turn onto Route 129 north. Drive about 3½ miles, then turn right onto Route 4456, and you'll soon reach the:

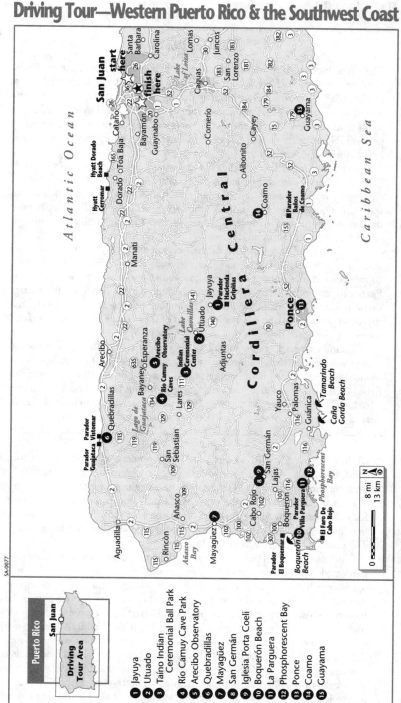

Puerto Rico

San Juan

Driving Tour Area

1 Jayuya
2 Utuado
3 Taíno Indian Ceremonial Ball Park
4 Río Camuy Cave Park
5 Arecibo Observatory
6 Quebradillas
7 Mayagüez
8 San Germán
9 Iglesia Porta Coeli
10 Boquerón Beach
11 La Parguera
12 Phosphorescent Bay
13 Ponce
14 Coamo
15 Guayama

SA-0077

Life After Death

The Taíno Indians who lived in Puerto Rico before Europeans came here were ruled by *Caciques,* or chiefs, who controlled their own villages and several others nearby. The Taínos believed in life after death, which led them to take extreme care in burying their dead. Personal belongings of the deceased were placed in the tomb with the newly dead, and bodies were carefully arranged in a squatting position. Near Ponce, visitors can see the oldest Indian burial ground uncovered in the Antilles (see chapter 9).

Even at the time of the arrival of Columbus and the conquistadores who followed, the Taínos were threatened by the warlike and cannibalistic Carib Indians coming up from the south. But though they feared the Caribs, they learned to fear the conquistadores even more. Within 50 years of the Spanish colonization, the Taíno culture had virtually disappeared, the Indians annihilated through either massacres or European diseases.

But Taíno blood and remnants of their culture live on. The Indians married with Spaniards and Africans, and their physical characteristics—straight hair, copper-colored skin, and prominent cheekbones—can still be seen in some Puerto Ricans today. Many Taíno words became part of the Spanish language that's spoken on the island even today. Hammocks, the weaving of baskets, and the use of gourds as eating receptacles are part of the heritage left by these ill-fated tribes.

Still standing near Utuado, a small mountain town, Taíno Indian Ceremonial Center was built by them for recreation and worship some 800 years ago. Stone monoliths, some etched with petroglyphs, rim several of the 10 *bateyes* (playing fields) used for a ceremonial game that some historians believe was a forerunner to soccer. The monoliths and petroglyphs, as well as the *dujos* (ceremonial chairs), are existing examples of the Taínos' skill in carving wood and stone.

4. ✪ Río Camuy Cave Park. The third-largest underground river in the world, Río Camuy runs through a network of caves, canyons, and sinkholes that have been cut through the island's limestone base over the course of millions of years. The caves, known to both the pre-Columbian Taíno peoples and local Puerto Rican farmers, came to the attention of speleologists in the 1950s. Developed by the Puerto Rico Land Administration, they were opened to the public in 1987. The cave lies 57 miles west of San Juan.

Gardens in the focal point of the park surround buildings where tickets can be purchased. Visitors first see a short film about the caves, then descend to where open-air trolleys carry them on the downward journey to the caves. The trip takes you through a 200-foot-deep sinkhole, a chasm where tropical trees, ferns, and flowers flourish, supporting many birds and butterflies. The trolley then goes to the entrance of Empalme Cave, one of the 16 in the Camuy Caves network, where visitors begin a 45-minute cave walk, viewing the majestic series of rooms rich in stalagmites, stalactites, and huge sculptures carved out and built up through the centuries. Tres Pueblos Sinkhole, measuring 650 feet in diameter with a depth of 400 feet, is big enough to accommodate all of San Juan's El Morro Fortress. Tres Pueblos lies on the boundaries of the Camuy, Hatillo, and Lares municipalities. In Tres Pueblos, visitors can walk along two platforms: one on the Lares side facing the town of Camuy and the other on the Hatillo side overlooking Tres Pueblos Cave and the Río Camuy.

Touring with the Cavemen

You don't have to take a driving tour to see the Río Camuy Cave Park. In fact, you don't even have to climb down into the caverns yourself. If you want the company of knowledgeable and environmentally sensitive guides, plus comfortable accommodations, **Tropix Wellness Tours** (☎ **787/268-2173**; fax 787/268-1722) conducts what it calls a "Camuy Caveman Tour" through this underground labyrinth.

The cost is $243 per person, including accommodations at the Parador el Guajataca at Quebradillas, where the tour begins. Rates are based on double occupancy for 3 days and 2 nights and include continental breakfast and equipment for the escorted tours.

The caves are open Tuesday through Sunday from 8am to 4pm. Tickets are $10 for adults ($5 for seniors), $7 for children 2 to 12, and free for children under 2. Parking is $1. For more information, phone the park at ☎ **787/898-3100.**

After your tour of the caves, follow the signs northeast (it's signposted) to the hamlet of Bayaney along Route 134. This takes only 10 minutes. Pass through the town and continue along Route 134 north until you reach the intersection with Route 635 heading east toward the small town of Esperanza. Before reaching the town, take a small road (Route 625) south for 10 minutes to:

5. ✪ **Arecibo Observatory,** officially the National Astronomy and Ionosphere Center of Cornell University. This observatory has the world's largest and most sensitive radar/radio-telescope, which you can observe. It features a 20-acre dish or radio mirror set in an ancient sinkhole. It's 1,000 feet in diameter and 167 feet deep, allowing scientists to examine the ionosphere, planets, and moon with powerful radar signals and to monitor natural radio emissions from distant galaxies, pulsars, and quasars. It has been used by scientists as part of the Search for Extraterrestrial Intelligence (SETI), a research effort based on the proposition that advanced civilizations elsewhere in the universe might communicate via radio waves; thus, Arecibo Observatory is called an "ear to the heavens." The location is 60 miles west of San Juan and 10 miles south of the town of Arecibo.

Unusually lush vegetation flourishes under the giant dish, benefiting from the filtered sunlight and rain. There are ferns, grasses, and other plants such as wild orchids and begonias. Creatures such as mongooses, lizards, frogs, dragonflies, and an occasional bird have taken refuge under the dish. Suspended in outlandish fashion above the dish is a 600-ton platform similar in design to a bridge. Hanging as it does in midair, it resembles a space station.

The observatory (☎ **787/878-2612**) is open for self-guided tours Tuesday through Friday from 2 to 3pm and on Sunday from 1 to 4:30pm. There's a souvenir shop on the grounds.

When you're ready to leave the observatory, follow Route 625 north until you reach the small town of Esperanza. From here, continue north on the same road (now called Route 635) toward the small city of Arecibo. Signs will point the way to Highway 22, the major traffic artery linking San Juan with the west. On the southern outskirts of Arecibo, you can either return east to San Juan if your time is limited or continue with the tour, this time heading west along Highway 22. This express highway from San Juan will come to an end on the western outskirts of Arecibo. At the point where Highway 22 terminates, pick up Route 2 and follow it west for about 30 minutes until you come to:

6. **Quebradillas.** Beautiful Guajataca Beach and two paradores are only a 15-mile trip from Arecibo along Route 2 in the vicinity of this small town near the sea. Guajataca is fine for sunning and collecting shells, but it's *playa peligrosa* (dangerous unless you're a strong swimmer). **Parador El Guajataca** and **Parador Vistamar** are located fairly close to each other (see "The Paradores of Western Puerto Rico," at the end of this tour, for full descriptions).

Instead of continuing west along Route 2 to the dull city of Aquadilla, you can cut south from Quebradillas along Route 113, which in 30 minutes will take you to Lago de Guajataca, one of the most beautiful lakes in Puerto Rico. After traversing its 2½-mile shoreline, you'll see signposts pointing the way to the town of San Sebastián, a 15-minute drive to the west along Route 119. As you travel this region, you'll be on the northern border of the richest coffee-growing district of Puerto Rico.

Once you reach San Sebastián, follow Route 109 southwest to the small town of La Parade, and continue westerly along this route until you reach the slightly larger town of Añasco. This is an area of many coffee plantations, although they are private and not open to visitors.

Once at Añasco, you will be but 30 minutes northeast of the city of Mayagüez. To reach it, continue along Route 109 for about 10 minutes until you get back on the previously traveled Route 2. This will lead directly into the heart of:

7. **Mayagüez,** the Commonwealth's western port city (see chapter 9).

When you're ready to leave Mayagüez, continue southeast along Route 2 for 45 minutes until you reach:

8. ✪ **San Germán,** Puerto Rico's second-oldest town and a little museum piece included in the National Register of Historic Places (see chapter 9). On a knoll at one end of town stands the chapel of:

9. ✪ **Iglesia Porta Coeli (Gate of Heaven),** one of the gems of the town's 249 noteworthy sites (see chapter 9).

After visits to San Germán, and if you're now ready for some beaches, allow 40 minutes to travel on Route 102 west to Cabo Rojo, from which you can make a connection onto Route 307 heading south to:

10. **Boquerón Beach,** one of Puerto Rico's best beaches for swimming. There's a comfortable parador with a good restaurant only 2 blocks away. The beach also has facilities, including lockers and changing places, plus kiosks that rent watersports equipment. For more information about **Parador Boquemar,** see "The Paradores of Western Puerto Rico," at the end of this tour.

After time at the beach at Boquerón, you can discover more beaches in the east. From Boquerón leave town along Route 101 heading east and following the signs to the town of Lajas. Once at Lajas, get on Route 116 heading directly south. Once you reach the intersection with 304, get on this road and drive directly south to:

11. **La Parguera,** a small fishing village with **Parador Villa Parguera** and the **Parador Posada Porlamar** (see "The Paradores of Western Puerto Rico," at the end of this tour). If you have the good fortune to find yourself in La Parguera on a moonless night, go to:

12. **Phosphorescent Bay.** A boat leaves Villa Parguera pier nightly from 7:30pm to 12:30am, depending on the demand, and heads for this small bay to the east of La Parguera. Here, a pitch-black night will facilitate a marvelous show, since you can see fish leave a luminous streak on the water's surface and watch the boat's

Puerto Rico's Secret Beaches

Some of Puerto Rico's most beautiful and isolated beaches lie on the island's southwestern coast, facing south toward the Caribbean Sea, far from major highways. Stretching between Ponce, in the east, and Cabo Rojo, on Puerto Rico's extreme southwestern tip, these beaches flank some of the least densely populated parts of the island. And because the boundaries between them are relatively fluid, only a local resident (or perhaps a professional geographer) could say for sure where one ends and the other begins.

If you consider yourself an aficionado of isolated beaches, it's worth it to rent a car and strike out for these remote locales. Drive westward from Ponce along Highway 2, branching south along Route 116 to **Guánica,** the self-anointed gateway and capital of this string of "secret beaches." Don't expect a lot—you're likely to see only a handful of simple bars, tacky luncheonettes, and gas stations peppering a verdant and perpetually sunbaked landscape.

By far the most accessible and appealing beach is **Caña Gorda.** Set about a quarter-mile south of Guánica, at the edge of a legally protected marsh that's known for its rich bird life and thick reeds, Caña Gorda is a sprawling expanse of pale beige sand that's dotted with ramshackle-looking *bohios* (huts) crafted from tree branches and palm fronds. Despite its rusticity, it's a site that's been improved and developed by the local authorities. The centerpiece here is a well-recommended hotel, the **Copamarina** (☎ **787/821-0505;** see review in chapter 9). Here you can check in for a night or two of sun-flooded R&R, along with the occasional beachgoer and honeymooner. Even if you're staying at the hotel, consider dropping in for a cuba libre, a margarita, or a meal. The Copamarina is about a 45-minute drive from Ponce.

Stray even farther west from Ponce, along coastal highways like 324, 304, and 323, and you'll pass beaches with such names as **Tamarindo, Manglillos, Rosado,** and **Playa Santa.** Most westerly of all is **Bahia Sucia** (whose name rather unappetizingly translates as "Dirty Beach"), 45 minutes west of Ponce, at the end of rutted and badly potholed roads. All of these beaches may be hard to reach, but persevere and you'll be met with warm water and long, uncrowded stretches of white sand, where towering king palms and salt-tolerant sea grapes provide an idyllic tropical backdrop for sun and surf. Keep in mind that besides Caña Gorda, the beaches mentioned above have virtually no services and public utilities. Pack what you'll need for the day—food, water, sunscreen, and so forth.

wake glimmer in the dark. This phenomenon is produced by a large colony of dinoflagellates, a microscopic form of marine life that produces sparks of chemical light when their nesting is disturbed.

To travel on, take Route 304 up to Route 116 and drive west through Ensenada. At Guánica, you can turn south and follow Route 333 out to Caña Gorda Beach for lunch or a swim. While here, look for the cacti that flourish in this unusually dry region. Back on Route 116, drive north to Palomas, where you can take Route 2 into:

13. Ponce, The old colonial city with many interesting restaurants, inns, and sights (see chapter 9).

When you're ready to leave Ponce, take Route 1 east toward Guayama. At the town of Santa Isabel, you may want to take an interesting detour north along Route 153 to:

14. Coamo. Along the way to this town, you'll see signs pointing to the Baños de Coamo. Legend has it that these hot springs were the Fountain of Youth sought by Ponce de León. It is believed that the Taíno peoples, during pre-Columbian times, held rituals and pilgrimages here as they sought health and well-being. For more than a century between 1847 and 1958, the site was a center for rest and relaxation for Puerto Ricans and others, some on their honeymoon, others in search of the curative powers of the geothermal springs, which lie about a 5-minute walk from **Parador Baños de Coamo** (see "The Paradores of Western Puerto Rico," at the end of this tour). Nonresidents can come here to use the baths, but the experience is hardly special today. The baths are in poor condition.

After a look at the baths, you can backtrack. Instead of going all the way back to Route 1, you can get on the expressway (no. 52), heading east for a 40-minute drive to:

15. Guayama, a green and beautiful small town with steepled churches and Casa Cautiño Museum, on the main plaza of town (☎ **787/864-0600**). It is open Tuesday through Sunday from 10am to 4pm. Admission is $1 for adults and 50¢ for seniors, students, and children 7 to 12 (free for 6 and under). This museum is in a turn-of-the-century mansion that once was occupied by the Cañuelo family. It contains all of their original belongings and is a showplace for fine turn-of-the-century furnishings and pictures of the prize horses for which Guayama is famous. Just minutes from town is Arroyo Beach, a tranquil place to spend an afternoon, but lacking facilities.

To begin the final leg back to San Juan, take Route 15 north. If you take this road in either spring or summer, you'll be surrounded by the brilliant colors of flowering trees. This route connects with express Highway 52 going north to San Juan, a trip of about an hour, depending on traffic.

THE PARADORES OF WESTERN PUERTO RICO

Listed below are the paradores referred to in Driving Tour 2.

El Yunque has become such a major attraction that little inns and bed-and-breakfasts have sprung up at Ceiba to cater to visitors heading to the forest. See chapter 8 for more information about these places.

AT JAYUYA

Parador Hacienda Gripiñas. Rte. 527, km 2.5 (P.O. Box 387), Jayuya, PR 00664. ☎ **787/828-1717.** Fax 787/828-1718. 20 units. A/C TV. Year-round $125 double. Rates include 2 meals a day. AE, MC, V. From Jayuya, head east via Rte. 144; at the junction with Rte. 527, go south 1½ miles.

A former coffee plantation about 2½ hours from San Juan, in the very heart of the Cordillera Central (Central Mountain Range), Hacienda Gripiñas is reached by a long, narrow, and curvy road. This home-turned-inn is a delightful blend of the hacienda of days gone by and the conveniences of today. The plantation ambiance is everywhere—created by ceiling fans, splendid gardens, hammocks on a porch gallery where you can sit and enjoy a piña colada, and more than 20 acres of coffee-bearing bushes. You'll taste the homegrown product when you order the inn's aromatic brew.

Most of the modest rooms come with ceiling fans, and, although the rooms vary in size, they are kept neat as a pin. For meals, stick to the restaurant's Puerto Rican dishes rather than going for its international cuisine. You can swim in the two chilly mountain pools (away from the main building), soak up the sun, or enjoy the nearby sights, such as the Taíno Indian Ceremonial Ball Park at Utuado. Boating and plenty of fishing are just 30 minutes away at Lake Caonillas. The parador is also near the Río Camuy Cave Park.

AT UTUADO

Parador La Casa Grande. P.O. Box 616, Caonillas, Utuado, PR 00641. ☎ **888/343-2272** or 787/894-3939. Fax same as phone. 20 units. Year-round $75–$85 double. AE, MC, V. From Arecibo take Rte. 10 south to Utuado; then head east on Rte. 111 to Rte. 140; head north on Rte. 140 to Rte. 612 for ¼ mile.

This parador, situated on 107 acres of a former coffee plantation in the Caonillas Barrios district, in the mountainous heartland of the island about 2½ hours from San Juan, has been vastly improved since its takeover by Steven Weingarten and his wife, Marlene, who is a gourmet cook. Steven is still a practicing attorney in New York City, commuting to Puerto Rico on a regular basis. All the comfortably but very simply furnished bedrooms have ceiling fans in lieu of air-conditioning, hardly needed during the cool nights up here. Each room has a balcony, hammock, and mountain view. There are a swimming pool and nature trails carved out of the jungle.

Marlene presides over Jungle Jane's Restaurant, which serves an array of delectably prepared international and Puerto Rican dishes. Even if you're not a guest, you can feast here daily from 7:30am to 9:30pm. It might make an ideal luncheon stopover if you're touring in the area.

AT QUEBRADILLAS

Parador El Guajataca. Rte. 2, km 103.8 (P.O. Box 1558), Quebradillas, PR 00678. ☎ **800/964-3065** or 787/895-3070. Fax 787/895-3589. 38 units. A/C TV TEL. Year-round $80–$90 double. AE, DC, MC, V. From Quebradillas, continue northwest on Rte. 2 for 1 mile (the parador is signposted).

You'll find this place on a rolling hillside reaching down to a surf-beaten beach along the north coast, 70 miles west of San Juan. Stay here for the stunning natural setting and don't expect too much, because the hotel itself is somewhat seedy. Each room is rather standard and has its own entrance and private balcony opening onto the turbulent Atlantic.

Served in a glassed-in dining room where all the windows face the sea, the cuisine isn't much more memorable than the accommodations, with little care going into the preparation or the often-canned ingredients. A local musical group plays for dining and dancing on Friday and Saturday evenings. The bar is open daily from 4 to 10pm (until 1 or 2am on Friday and Saturday). Room service is available from 7 to 8:30am. There are two swimming pools (one for adults, another for children), plus a playground for children.

Parador Vistamar. 6205 Rte. 113N (P.O. Box T-38), Quebradillas, PR 00678. ☎ **787/895-2065.** Fax 787/895-2294. 55 units. A/C TV TEL. Year-round $73.85–$96.30 double. Up to 2 children under 12 stay free in parents' room. AE, DC, MC, V. At Quebradillas, head northwest on Rte. 2, then go left at the junction with Rte. 113 for ½ mile.

In the Guajataca area, this parador, one of the largest on Puerto Rico, sits like a sentinel surveying the scene from high atop a mountain overlooking greenery and a seascape. There are gardens and intricate paths carved into the side of the mountain where you can stroll while enjoying the fragrance of the tropical flowers. Or you may choose to search for the calcified fossils that abound on the carved mountainside. For a unique experience, visitors can try their hand at freshwater fishing just down the hill from the hotel. Flocks of rare tropical birds are frequently seen in the nearby mangroves.

Bedrooms are comfortably furnished in a rather bland motel style. There's a dining room with an ocean view, where you can have a typical Puerto Rican dinner or choose from the international menu.

A short drive from the hotel will bring you to the Punta Borinquén Golf Course. Tennis courts are just down the hill from the inn itself. Sightseeing trips to the nearby Arecibo Observatory—the largest radar/radio-telescope in the world—and to Monte Calvario (a replica of Mount Calvary) are available. Another popular visit is to the plaza in the town of Quebradillas.

AT BOQUERÓN BEACH

Parador Boquemar. 101 Rte. 307, Boquerón, Cabo Rojo, PR 00622. ☎ **787/851-2158.** Fax 787/851-7600. 75 units. A/C TV. Year-round $65–$80 double. AE, DC, MC, V. From either Mayagüez or San Germán, take Rte. 102 into Cabo Rojo and then Rte. 100 south; turn right onto Rte. 101 and the hotel will be 2 blocks from the beach.

In the southwest corner of the island, between Mayagüez and Ponce, Parador Boquemar was built in the late 1980s a block or so from Boquerón Beach, one of the best bathing beaches on the island. Despite rooms that can tend to be too small for comfort, Puerto Rican families like this place a lot, causing readers to complain that children run up and down the corridors until late. The TVs often don't work, but the hotel does have one of the best restaurants in the area, Las Cascadas, offering typical dishes of the area, including lobster asopao, a seafood gumbo. Neighboring roosters will see that you don't sleep late in the morning. The place is a little too rustic and not well maintained enough for our tastes, but the beach somehow compensates. Check in only if you plan to spend most of your time exploring and don't plan to be hotel bound.

AT LA PARGUERA

Parador Posada Porlamar. Rte. 304 (P.O. Box 405), La Parguera, Lajas, PR 00667. ☎ **787/899-4015.** Fax 787/899-5558. 40 units. A/C TV. Year-round $80–$118 double. AE, MC, V. Drive west along Rte. 2 until you reach the junction of Rte. 116; then head south along Rte. 116 and Rte. 304.

Life in a simple fishing village plus modern conveniences are what you'll find at this "Guesthouse by the Sea" in the La Parguera section of Lajas, in the southwestern part of the island. The area is famous for its Phosphorescent Bay. Short on style, the guesthouse, built in 1960, is near several fishing villages and other points of interest. If you like to collect seashells, you can beachcomb. Other collectors' items found here are fossilized crustacea and marine plants. A scuba shop is on-site. Bedrooms are plain and, although neat, don't invite lingering. Some are better than others, containing in a few cases a balcony, a minibar, and a small sitting room. The best rooms are generally on the third floor. If possible, ask to look at a room before committing yourself, and try to get one with a sea view. Paradora Villa Parguera nearby has far more flair and style (see below).

Parador Villa Parguera. 304 Main St. (P.O. Box 273), La Parguera, Lajas, PR 00667. ☎ **787/899-7777.** Fax 787/899-6040. 70 units. A/C TV TEL. Sun–Fri $75 double; Sat $90 double (including 2 meals a day), $310 double-occupancy packages (for 2 days). Two children under 10 stay free in parents' room. AE, DC, DISC, MC, V. Drive west along Rte. 2 until you reach the junction with Rte. 116; then head south along Rte. 116 and Rte. 304.

Although the water in the nearby bay is too polluted for swimming, guests here can still enjoy a view of the water and take a dip in the swimming pool. Situated on the southwestern shore of Puerto Rico, this parador—a classic fishermen's inn—is known for its seafood dinners (the fish are not caught in the bay), its comfortable and colorfully decorated rooms, and its location next to the phosphorescent waters of one of the coast's best-known bays. Bedrooms have either a balcony or a terrace.

The spacious dining room offers daily specials, as well as such chef's favorites as fillet of fish stuffed with lobster and shrimp. Both international and Puerto Rican specialties are served. Open daily from noon to 5pm and 7:30 to 11pm. Nonresidents are welcome. There's a play area for children because this is a popular inn for Puerto Rican families, especially on crowded and often noisy weekends. We prefer to check in here during a weekday, when it's more tranquil.

Because the inn is popular with the residents of San Juan on weekends, there's a special weekend package for a 2-night minimum stay; $310 covers the price of the double room, welcome drinks, breakfasts, dinners, flowers, and dancing with a free show.

AT COAMO

Parador Baños de Coamo. P.O. Box 540, Coamo, PR 00769. ☎ **787/825-2186.** Fax 787/825-4739. 48 units. A/C TV TEL. Year-round $75 double. AE, DC, DISC, MC, V. From Rte. 1, turn onto Rte. 153 at Santa Isabel; then turn left onto Rte. 546 and drive west 1 mile.

Coamo is inland on the south coast, about a 2-hour drive from San Juan. The spa at Baños de Coamo features a parador offering hospitality in the traditional Puerto Rican style. The Baños has welcomed many notable visitors over the years, including Franklin D. Roosevelt, Frank Lloyd Wright, Alexander Graham Bell, and Thomas Edison, who came here to swim in the hot springs on-site, said to be the most radioactive in the world. (Locals sometimes purchase a day pass and use the pool, which leads to noise, confusion, and overcrowding on weekends.)

The buildings range from a lattice-adorned, two-story motel unit with wooden verandas to a Spanish colonial pink stucco building housing the restaurant. The bedrooms draw a mixed reaction from visitors, so ask to see your prospective room before deciding to stay here. Many of the often-dark rooms are not well maintained, and the bathrooms seem more appropriate for a campsite. Mildew is also evident. The cuisine here is both Créole and international, and the coffee Baños style is a special treat.

Swimming is limited to an angular pool, but you can easily drive to a nearby public beach. The staff here can arrange for you to ride the island's unique breed of show horse called *paso fino*.

11

Vieques & Culebra

They may be virtually unknown to many visitors, but the offshore islands of Vieques and Culebra are where Puerto Ricans go for their own vacations. Sandy beaches and low prices are a powerful attraction for both islands.

Vieques, with more tourist facilities than Culebra, lies 7 miles off the eastern coast of Puerto Rico. It is visited today mainly for its 40-odd white-sand beaches. The island had been occupied at various times by both the French and the British before Puerto Rico acquired it in 1854. The ruins of many sugar and pineapple plantations testify to its once-flourishing agricultural economy. The U.S. military, which took control of two-thirds of the island's 26,000 acres in 1941, has largely refrained from using this part as a bombing range, but it is still an important military training area. The fact that the island is a military base should not deter a visit. It is unlikely that you'll hear planes flying low overhead, and it's very rare to hear any test bombs exploding, as you might have a few years ago. It is also unlikely that you'll even be aware of any military equipment and personnel when you visit.

Culebra, 18 miles east of the Puerto Rican "mainland" and 14 miles west of St. Thomas in the U.S. Virgin Islands, is surrounded by coral reefs and edged with nearly deserted, powdery white-sand beaches. Much of the island has been designated a wildlife refuge by the U.S. Fish and Wildlife Service.

1 Vieques

41 miles E of San Juan, 7 miles SE of Fajardo

About 7 miles east of the big island of Puerto Rico lies Vieques (Bee-*ay*-kase), an island about twice as large as New York's Manhattan with about 8,000 inhabitants and some 40 palm-lined white-sand beaches. Since World War II, about two-thirds of the 21-mile-long island has been controlled by the U.S. military forces. Much of the government-owned land is now leased for cattle grazing, and when there are no military maneuvers, the public can visit the beaches, although you might be asked to produce some form of photo ID. Freedom to use the land has not, however, totally defused local discontent at the presence of Navy and Marine Corps personnel on the island.

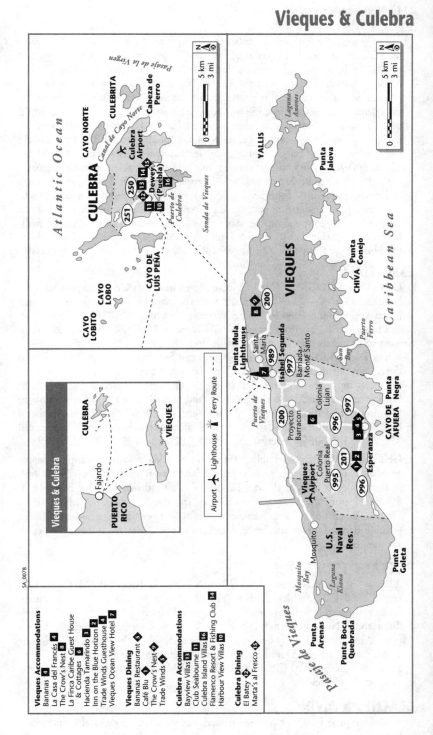

Vieques Accommodations
Bananas **4**
La Casa del Francés **8**
The Crow's Nest **8**
La Finca Caribe Guest House & Cottages **6**
Hacienda Tamarindo **3**
Inn on the Blue Horizon **2**
Trade Winds Guesthouse **4**
Vieques Ocean View Hotel **7**

Vieques Dining
Bananas Restaurant **5**
Café Blu **5**
The Crow's Nest **9**
Trade Winds **5**

Culebra Accommodations
Bayview Villas **13**
Club Seabourne **11**
Culebra Island Villas **16**
Flamenco Resort & Fishing Club **14**
Harbour View Villas **10**

Culebra Dining
El Batey **12**
Marta's al Fresco **15**

SA_0078

223

The Spanish conquistadores didn't think much of Vieques. They came here in the 16th century but didn't stay long, reporting that the island and neighboring bits of land held no gold and were therefore *las islas inutiles* (the useless islands). The name Vieques comes from a native Amerindian word for small island, *bieques.*

Later Spanish occupation is attested to by the main town, **Isabel Segunda,** on the northern shore. Construction on the last Spanish fort built in the New World began around 1843 during the reign of Queen Isabella II, for whom the town was named. The fort, never completed, is not of any special interest. **The Punta Mula lighthouse,** north of Isabel Segunda, provides panoramic views of the land and sea. The island's fishers and farmers conduct much of their business in Isabel Segunda.

On the south coast, **Esperanza,** once a center for the island's sugarcane industry and now a pretty little fishing village, lies near **Sun Bay (Sombe) public beach.** Sun Bay, a government-run, panoramic crescent of sand, is the beach to visit if you have only 1 day to spend on the island. The fenced area has picnic tables, a bathhouse, and a parking lot. A recently built resort, marina, and other facilities add to the allure of the many scalloped stretches of sandy waterfront along the south coast.

ESSENTIALS

GETTING THERE   Flights to Vieques leave from Isla Grand Airport near the heart of San Juan—not to be confused with the main Luis Muñoz Marín International Airport out beyond Isla Verde. **Vieques Air Link (☎ 787/741-3266)** operates four daily flights from San Juan. **Isla Nena (☎ 787/741-6362)** also flies to Vieques from San Juan three times daily. Both charge $45 one-way.

The Puerto Rico Port Authority operates two **ferryboats** a day to Vieques from the eastern port of Fajardo; the trip takes about an hour. The round-trip fare is $4 for adults and $2 for children. Tickets for the morning ferry leaving Saturday and Sunday sell out quickly, so passengers should be in line at the ticket window in Fajardo before 8am to be certain of a seat on the 9:30am boat. Otherwise, they'll have to wait until the 3pm ferry. For more information about these sea links, call **☎ 787/723-2260.** For reservations, call **☎ 787/863-0705** or 787/863-0852.

GETTING AROUND   Public cabs or vans called *públicos* transport people around the island. To rent a car, contact **Island Car Rental (☎ 787/741-1666),** in the hamlet of Florida, about a 12-minute ride southwest of Isabel Segunda, or 5 minutes from the airport. The office is next door to the Crow's Nest Guest House. The cost of the local vehicles begins at $40 per day, plus another $10 for collision damage-waiver insurance. American Express, MasterCard, and Visa cards are accepted.

PACKAGE TOURS

An easy way to visit Vieques is with **Tropix Wellness Tours (☎ 787/268-2173;** fax 787/268-1722), which offers a "Phosphorescent Bay Tour" from the Puerto Rican mainland. It includes a visit to Mosquito (Phosphorescent) Bay and an expedition to Isla Nena, home of one of Puerto Rico's most spectacular reefs, bird sanctuaries, and deserted sandy beaches. The tour costs $368.75 per person, including airfare from the Rivas Dominici Airport in Miramar to Vieques airport, 3 nights' accommodations at The Crow's Nest, continental breakfast, and equipment for the escorted expeditions.

BEACHES & DIVING

Few of Vieques's beaches have been named, but most have their loyal supporters—loyal, that is, until too many people learn about them, in which case the devotees can always find another good spot.

The U.S. Navy named some of the beaches, such as **Green Beach,** a beautiful clean stretch at the island's west end. **Red and Blue Beaches** are great jumping-off points for snorkelers. ✪ **Sun Bay (Sombe)** is also a very beautiful white-sand beach, and it offers picnic tables, a bathhouse, tent sites, and good snorkeling off-shore. Other popular beaches are **Navia, Half Moon, Orchid,** and **Silver,** but if you continue along the water, you may find your own nameless secluded cove with a fine strip of sand.

Outdoor activities, including scuba diving and deep-sea fishing, aren't well organized on Vieques. Sometimes outfitters will appear in the winter but disappear by summer. If you'd like to go snorkeling off the coast of Vieques, you can call **Erin Go Bragh/Tropic Charter** (☎ 787/860-4401) in Fajardo, on the Puerto Rican mainland. This outfitter offers day trips to Vieques at $75 per person. If a minimum of four people can be booked, a snorkeling trip with an overnight stop in Vieques can be arranged for $250 per person. The second day is spent on the boat with a return to Fajardo at 6pm.

THE LUMINOUS WATERS OF PHOSPHORESCENT BAY

One of the major attractions on the island is ✪ **Mosquito Bay,** also called Phosphorescent Bay, with its glowing waters produced by tiny bioluminescent organisms that live near the surface. These organisms dart away from boats, leaving eerie blue-white trails of phosphorescence. *The Vieques Times* wrote: "By any name the bay can be a magical, psychedelic experience and few places in the world can even come close to the intensity of concentration of the dinoflagellates called pyrodiniums (whirling fire). They are tiny ($\frac{1}{500}$ -inch) swimming creatures that light up like fireflies when disturbed but nowhere are there so many fireflies. Here a gallon of bay water may contain almost three-quarters of a million."

The ideal time to tour is on a cloudy, moonless night, and you should wear a bathing suit since it's possible to swim in these glowing waters.

Shannon Grasso (☎ 787/741-0717) operates trips aboard her *Luminosa* from La Casa del Francés (see "Where to Stay," below). These trips are not offered around the time of the full moon. The charge for these trips is $20, and most jaunts last about 90 minutes. A similar tour on a kayak and costing the same price is offered by **Blue Caribe Dive Center** (☎ 787/741-2522 for complete details).

SEEING THE SIGHTS

The Fort Conde de Mirasol Museum at Magnolia 471 (☎ 787/741-1717) is the major man-made attraction on the island.

In the 1840s, Count Mirasol convinced the Spanish government to build a defensive fortress here. Today the carefully restored fort houses a museum of art and history celebrating the story of Vieques. There are Indian relics, displays of the Spanish conquest, and old flags of the Danes, British, and French. The French sugarcane planters and their African slaves are depicted, and there's even a bust of Simón Bolivar based on a visit to Puerto Rico by the great liberator. A unique collection of maps shows how the world's cartographers envisioned Vieques. Since the U.S. Navy occupies more than two-thirds of the island, its presence and controversial role are chronicled. The museum and fort are open Wednesday through Sunday from 10am to 4pm, charging $1 for adults, 50¢ for children.

WHERE TO STAY

Bananas. Barrio Esperanza (P.O. Box 1300), Vieques, PR 00765. ☎ **787/741-8700.** Fax 787/741-0790. 8 units. $45–$55 double; $65 suite. AE, MC, V.

While filming *Heartbreak Ridge* here in 1986, the actors and crew transformed this establishment's windswept porch into their second home. Located on the south shore, east of the U.S. Naval Reservation, and best known for its bar and restaurant, this guesthouse also has seven simple, clean, and comfortable rooms, some recently renovated. Each has a ceiling fan; however, three rooms and the suite are air-conditioned, with their own screened-in porches.

There is a loud salsa bar several feet away from the rooms on the east side of Bananas. The music starts playing at 10 in the morning and lasts until around 2am. Should you decide to stay at Bananas, be sure to ask for a room on the west side of the hotel.

The Crow's Nest. Rte. 201, km 1.6, Box 1521, Vieques, PR 00765. ☎ **787/741-0033.** Fax 787/741-1294. 14 units. Year-round $55–$80 double. AE, MC, V.

Set high on 5 acres of forested hillside, about 1½ miles east of Isabela, this inn enjoys northward-facing views over the Atlantic, and a cozy, responsive setting that's favored by many repeat guests. Each of the units contains some kind of cooking facilities, and all but two offer air-conditioning. There are a rectangular swimming pool on the premises, a bar with a sweeping view, and a restaurant that's favored by nonresidents as something of an island staple for dine-arounds. Like most of the other hotels on the island, this one requires a car ride of around 10 minutes for access to the nearest worthwhile beach.

Hacienda Tamarindo. Rte. 996, P.O. Box 1569, Vieques, PR 00765. ☎ **787/741-8525.** Fax 787/741-3215. 16 units. A/C. $115–$140 double; $175 suite. Rates include breakfast. AE, MC, V.

Established in the late 1990s on the site of an older property, less than a mile west of Esperanza, this inn has lots of flair, style, and pizzazz, and easy access to a very appealing beach as well as a rectangular swimming pool. Its centerpiece is a massive, 200-year-old tamarind tree whose production of fruit (between February and March) is heralded with much excitement by Vermont-born owners Burr and Linda Vail. They have transformed a thick-walled, rather unimaginative-looking concrete building into a replica of a Spanish colonial hacienda, thanks to the application of skills that were developed by Linda during an earlier career as a decorator. Each accommodation contains an appealing mishmash of art and antiques, some of which they brought from Vermont. Breakfast is a generous continental one. There's no restaurant on the premises, but the Café Blu is a short walk away (see "Where to Dine," below).

✪ **Inn on the Blue Horizon.** Rte. 996, Box 1556, Vieques, PR 00765. ☎ **787/ 741-3318.** Fax 787/741-0052. 9 units. Winter $150–$200 double, $185 casita; off-season $125–$175 double, $160 casita. AE, MC, V.

Set on the southern coastal road, less than a mile west of Esperanza, this is one of the most charming hotels on Vieques. The airy seafront house was originally built as one of two Vieques homes by a prosperous Italian. It was transformed into an inn in the mid-1990s by a pair of refugees from New York, Bill Knight and James Weis. Three of the bedrooms are in the main house; a half-dozen others are in three small bungalows, each of which contains two units, each accommodation of which has a private balcony and sea view. The airy, clean, and comfortable bedrooms are out-fitted with antiques and eclectic art from a wide variety of on- and off-island artists. One of the most appealing spots in the hotel is the bar, which writers from *Newsweek* magazine defined as one of the best in the Caribbean during a recent visit (a plaque to that effect is proudly displayed inside). Set beneath a red-tin roof, it's a blue-colored circular arrangement nestled within an octagonal room that's partially open to the ocean breezes. Café Blu, the in-house restaurant, doesn't serve lunch (most clients are at the beach anyway), but dinners are island events and are reviewed separately in "Where to Dine," below.

✪ **La Casa del Francés.** Barrio Esperanza (P.O. Box 458), Vieques, PR 00765. ☎ **787/741-3751.** Fax 787/741-2330. 18 units. Winter (including breakfast and dinner) $177.50 double; off-season $98.10 double. AE, MC, V.

La Casa del Francés is about a 15-minute drive southeast of Isabel Segunda, just north of the center of Esperanza. Set in a field near the southern coastline, the hotel has an imposing, column-fronted facade that rises from the lush surrounding landscape. It was built in 1905 by a retired French general as the headquarters for his working sugar plantation. The present owner has installed a swimming pool and transformed the high-ceilinged bedrooms into old-fashioned hotel accommodations. Many units enjoy access to the sweeping two-story verandas ringing the white facade.

Scattered throughout the dozen acres surrounding the main house are century-old tropical trees. The estate's architectural highlight is the two-story interior courtyard, whose center is lush with bamboo, palms, philodendron, and well-chosen examples of Haitian art.

The fixed-price dinners attract many island residents who partake of Italian, barbecue, or Puerto Rican buffets, which the staff spreads out beneath a 200-year-old mahogany tree.

La Finca Caribe Guest House & Cottages. Rte. 995, km 1.2 (P.O. Box 1332), Vieques, PR 00765. ☎ **787/741-0495.** E-mail: lafinca@merwincreative.com. 6 units (none with bathroom), 2 cottages. Year-round $65 double; winter $650 cottage; off-season $375 cottage. MC, V.

Formerly known as New Dawn's Caribbean Retreat & Guest House, this bare-bones establishment, situated on a forested hillside 3 miles from Sun Bay in the center of the island north of Esperanza and southwest of Isabel Segunda, caters to budget-conscious travelers and youthful adventurers. The present owners, the Merwin family, have renamed it *finca,* which means a rustic estate in Spanish. The centerpiece of the property is a plywood-sided house originally built by a previous owner with student assistants in 1986. Today the guesthouse enjoys a spacious porch outfitted with hammocks and swinging chairs. A series of outbuildings contains a bathhouse and communal kitchen. On a hill, there's a family-style, two-story wooden cottage that sleeps three to four comfortably; it comes with a kitchen, a private bath, decks, and a living area. A casita, another cottage nestled in the garden, can accommodate three with its sleeping loft and queen bed. It has a private deck and its own kitchen. A new nonchlorinated pool has been installed, and bike rentals are available.

Trade Winds Guesthouse. 107C Flamboyan, Barrio Esperanza (P.O. Box 1012), Vieques, PR 00765. ☎ and fax **787/741-8666.** 14 units. $55–$70 double; $75–$85 studio. AE, MC, V.

Along the shore on the south side of the island, in the fishing village of Esperanza, this oceanside guesthouse offers 9 units, four of them air-conditioned and with terraces. The others have ceiling fans, and some also open onto terraces. It's well known for hospitable ambiance and its open-air restaurant overlooking the ocean (see "Where to Dine," below).

Vieques Ocean View Hotel. Isabel Segunda (P.O. Box 124), Vieques, PR 00765. ☎ **787/741-3696.** Fax 787/741-1793. 30 units. A/C TV. $55–$75 double. AE, MC, V.

Situated in the heart of Isabel Segunda, directly on the coast and a block from the wharf where the ferryboat lands, this three-story building is one of the tallest on Vieques. Built in the early 1980s, it offers simple rooms with uncomplicated furniture and balconies overlooking either the sea or the town. Twenty-five of the 30 rooms are air-conditioned. The hotel has a restaurant serving Chinese food, open daily from 11am to 11pm, and there's a swimming pool here.

WHERE TO DINE

Bananas Restaurant. In the Bananas, Barrio Esperanza. ☎ **787/741-8700.** Main courses $13–$15; sandwiches at lunch $4–$7.50. AE, MC, V (tab must exceed $15 to use a credit card). Daily noon–9:30pm. INTERNATIONAL.

Bananas has some of the best food on the island, including familiar fare such as charbroiled New York sirloin, barbecue back ribs, and marinated boneless breast of chicken. Slightly more exotic main dishes might include the grilled Jamaican-style jerk chicken or the lemon chicken sautéed in butter and wine. You might opt instead for the grilled fresh catch of the day served with lemon butter. The chef also makes pizzas with a wide choice of toppings. Baked potato in four different versions, including one with broccoli and chili, also appears on the menu. Sandwiches are available at lunch, including grilled chicken and fresh fish. You can also order a juicy half-pound burger with a number of toppings.

Café Blu. In the Inn on the Blue Horizon, Rte. 996. ☎ **787/741-3318.** In restaurant, main courses $17–$24; in bar, sandwiches and platters $6–$18. AE, MC, V. Thurs–Sun 6–10pm; bar, daily 4–11pm. INTERNATIONAL.

In the premises of the Inn on the Blue Horizon (see "Where to Stay," above), on the island's southern coastal road less than a mile west of Esperanza, this restaurant serves some of the best food on Vieques. Also on-site is a bar that a team of journalists recently declared as one of their favorites within the entire Caribbean, so consider starting your evening with a drink or two in the octagonal premises of the "Blu Bar." Meals are served either within the inn's main building or on a seafront terrace lined with plants. Menu items include pan-blackened tuna, tenderloin of black Angus beef, fresh fish prepared virtually any way you want, rack of lamb, and Mediterranean-style prawns ("camarones") wrapped in prosciutto and basil leaves and served with penne.

The Crow's Nest. Rte. 201, km 1.6. ☎ **787/741-0033.** Reservations recommended. Main courses $12.50–$18. AE, MC, V. Mon–Sat 6–9:30pm. INTERNATIONAL.

Come here as much for the view, which sweeps northward over the Atlantic, as for the food. The setting is a hillside aerie positioned on 5 acres of forested hillside, about 1½ miles east of Isabela. Cuisine is uncomplicated but well prepared, and it includes such dishes as pork tenderloin with apples and sweet potatoes; Angus sirloin of beef; honey chicken with sesame sauce resting on a bed of coconut-flavored rice; and fresh fish.

Trade Winds. In Trade Winds Guesthouse, Barrio Esperanza. ☎ **787/741-8666.** Reservations recommended. Main courses $10.50–$25. AE, MC, V. Daily 7:30–10:30am and 6–9pm; bar, daily 4–11pm. STEAK/SEAFOOD.

You'll find this guesthouse restaurant at the ocean esplanade in the fishing village of Esperanza, on the south side of the island (see "Where to Stay," above). It features the Topside Bar for relaxing drinks, with a view of the water, and the Upper Deck for open-air dining. The chef's specialty, with real island flavor, is *piñon*, made with layers of sweet plantains, tomato sauce, green beans, spiced beef, and mozzarella.

For many, this is an acquired taste; you may prefer the best steak on the island, a New York sirloin, 12 ounces, cooked just right over the charbroiler and served with a baked potato and a house or Caesar salad. The fresh fish special of the night varies with the catch of the day but is usually a good item to order, as is the jumbo shrimp sautéed with fresh garlic and lemon. Black-bean soup is a good opener.

2 Culebra

52 miles E of San Juan; 18 miles E of Fajardo

A tranquil, inviting little island, Culebra lies in a mini-archipelago of 24 chunks of land, rocks, and cays 18 miles east of Puerto Rico's main island, halfway to St. Thomas, U.S. Virgin Islands. It's just 7 miles long and 3 miles wide and has only 2,000 residents. The landscape is dotted with everything from scrub and cacti to poincianas, frangipanis, and coconut palms.

Today vacationers and boaters can explore the island's beauties, both on land and under water. Culebra's white-sand beaches (especially Flamenco Beach), its clear waters, and its long coral reefs invite swimmers, snorkelers, and scuba divers.

This little-known, year-round vacation spot in what was once called the Spanish Virgin Islands was settled as a Spanish colony in 1886, but like Puerto Rico and Vieques, it became part of the United States after the Spanish-American War in 1898. In fact, Culebra's only town, a fishing village called **Dewey,** was named for Admiral George Dewey, an American hero of that war, although the locals defiantly call it **Puebla.**

Both illustrious and notorious characters have visited Culebra in the past. It is believed that Columbus spotted the island on his second voyage to the New World in 1493. When the Spanish started colonizing Puerto Rico, many of the Taíno Indians fled to Culebra as a last refuge. It wasn't many decades later that the swashbuckling Sir Henry Morgan and other notorious pirates used Culebra as a hideout. The island supposedly still shelters their buried loot.

From 1909 until 1975, Culebra was used by the U.S. Navy as a gunnery range, even serving as a practice bomb site in World War II. Today the four tracts of the **Culebra Wildlife Refuge,** plus 23 other offshore islands, are managed by the U.S. Fish and Wildlife Service. The refuge is one of the most important turtle-nesting sites in the Caribbean, and it also houses large seabird colonies, notably terns and boobies.

Culebrita, a mile-long coral-isle satellite of Culebra, has a hilltop lighthouse and crescent beaches.

ESSENTIALS

GETTING THERE   **Flamenco Airways, Inc.** (☎ **787/725-7707** in San Juan), flies to Culebra five times daily from San Juan's Isla Grande Airport. A round-trip ticket costs $60 per person.

The Puerto Rico Port Authority operates one or two **ferryboats** a day (depending on the day of the week) from the mainland port of Fajardo to Culebra; the trip takes about an hour. The round-trip fare is $4.50 for adults, $2.25 for children 3 to 12 (free for 2 and under). For information and reservations, call ☎ **787/863-0705** or 787/863-0852.

PACKAGE TOURS

If you don't want to make your own arrangements, you can visit Culebra with **Tropix Wellness Tours** (☎ **787/268-2173;** fax 787/268-1722), whose "Happy

From Leathernecks to Leatherbacks

In one of his last executive orders before leaving the White House in 1909, President Theodore Roosevelt established Culebra as a national wildlife refuge. Today this pint-sized archipelago, one of the last frontier outposts of the Caribbean, is one of only two nesting sites in the United States for the leatherback sea turtle, one of the world's largest marine reptiles. It and three other endangered species of turtles—the loggerhead, green, and hawksbill—are protected by the wildlife refuge.

Although Culebra was a national wildlife refuge, the U.S. Navy and Marine Corps began to use it as a practice bombing range during World War II. Culebrans massively protested the decision, especially when word leaked out that the Navy planned to relocate them to Vieques.

Arguments between Culebrans and the U.S. government didn't end with the war. Molotov cocktail-throwing violence erupted in 1971, with several islanders imprisoned for their hostile acts of defiance. President Richard Nixon finally brought peace to Culebra by ending all weapons training on the island. By 1975, the Navy swabbies and Marine Corps leathernecks had ceased shelling the island. The leathernecks may be long gone, but the leatherbacks are still here. The **Culebra Leatherback Project,** P.O. Box 190, Culebra, PR 00775 (☎ **703/ 450-0339**), gathers statistics about the nesting sea turtles and takes applications on a first-come, first-served basis from eco-tourists who want to participate in its nightly patrols from April to June. Early reservations are advised, since many nature-minded travelers want to participate.

Turtle Tour" includes a half-day kayaking-and-snorkeling expedition and a visit to the sea turtles' nesting sites during the spring and summer. The tour costs $473 per person, including airfare from Rivas Dominici Airport in Miramar to Culebra Airport, 3 nights' accommodations, continental breakfast, and equipment for the escorted tours.

BEACHES & DIVING

The island's most popular beach is ✪ **Flamenco Beach,** a mile-long, horseshoe-shaped cove on the island's northwestern edge. It's popular partly because of its nearness to Dewey, partly because of its soft sands.

More isolated is **Zoni Beach,** a 1-mile strip of sand flanked on the landward side by large boulders and scrub. On the island's northeastern edge, about 7 miles from Dewey (Puebla) on the island's opposite side, it's one of the most beautiful on the island. Snorkelers, but not scuba divers, find it particularly intriguing, despite the surf that makes underwater visibility a bit murky during rough weather.

Known for its beautiful corals, unspoiled underwater vistas, and absence of other divers, Culebra is like the rest of the Caribbean used to be before the huge flood of divers began exploring the sea. At least 50 dive sites, on all sides of the island, are considered worthwhile.

Culebra Dive Shop, 138 Escobar St. (☎ **787/742-0566;** fax 787/742-1953), offers a resort course for novice divers, including training in a sheltered cove and a tank dive in 15 to 20 feet of water ($65). Full PADI certification costs $425 and requires 5 days of participation in both classroom and ocean experience. Certified divers pay $85 for a two-tank open-water dive. The outfitter provides all the equipment you'll need for any of the above-mentioned dive experiences. It's rare that more than six divers go out in one of his boats on any day.

WHERE TO STAY

Bayview Villas. Punta Aloe, Culebra, PR 00775 (mailing address: Parque de las Fuentes 2402, Hato Rey, PR 00918). ☎ **787/765-5711** or 787/742-3392. 2 villas. A/C TEL. Year-round $225–$250 double. No credit cards.

Located on a hillside above Ensenada Honda a mile east of Dewey, at the end of a privately maintained road, this compound consists of two separate villas, each of which overlooks the sea and has two floors and comfortably solid pinewood furniture. Each has a full kitchen and two bedrooms, suitable for housing four occupants—and under cramped conditions, up to six. Each unit has high peaked ceilings with fans, washing machines, and mahogany doors leading onto terraces. Although daily rentals are available, the villas are often taken by Puerto Rican "mainlanders" for periods of a week or more.

Club Seabourne. Fulladosa Rd. (P.O. Box 357), Culebra, PR 00775. ☎ **787/742-3169.** Fax 787/742-3176. 13 units. A/C. Year-round $95–$105 double in the clubhouse; $115–$125 double in a villa or the Crow's Nest. Rates include continental breakfast. AE, MC, V. From Dewey (Puebla), follow Fulladosa Rd. along the south side of the bay for 1½ miles.

Across the road from an inlet of the sea, about an 8-minute drive from the center of town, this concrete-and-wood structure is set in a garden of crotons and palms, lying at the mouth of one of the island's best harbors, Ensenada Honda. It offers scattered villas and four rooms inside the clubhouse. All units are equipped with small refrigerators and are air-conditioned. Dive packages and day sails can be arranged at the office.

Overlooking Fulladosa Bay, the club's dining room serves some of the best food on Culebra, with fresh lobster, shrimp, snapper, grouper, and conch, as well as steaks and other specialty dishes. The hotel also has a large patio bar with a nightly happy hour, plus the only freshwater swimming pool on the island.

Culebra Island Villas. Punta Aloe (P.O. Box 596), Culebra, PR 00775. ☎ or fax **787/742-0333.** Alternate fax 908/458-5591 for reservations. 10 units. Winter $695 per week studio or 1-bedroom suite; $950 per week 2-bedroom suite. Off-season $495 per week studio or 1-bedroom suite; $695 per week 2-bedroom suite. No credit cards.

Located south of Ensenada Honda, half a mile south of Dewey, and separated from the Culebran "mainland" by a canal with a drawbridge, lies Punta Aloe, whose forested hillsides shelter about 15 privately owned houses. Each floor in four of these houses, which were built by different owners between 1980 and around 1990, is available for weekly rental. Each offers a view of the bay, wood-sided construction, and a simple kitchen. The studios and one-bedroom suites can accommodate one to three guests; the two-bedroom suites can hold two to six occupants. None of the units has air-conditioning, although the building has direct access to the trade winds. No meals are available, nor is there maid service.

Flamenco Resort & Fishing Club. 10 Pedro Marquez, Flamenco Beach (P.O. Box 183), Culebra, PR 00775. ☎ **787/742-3144.** 32 units. A/C. Year-round $115 1-bedroom; $185 2-bedroom; $250 3-bedroom. MC, V.

This is the only guesthouse or hotel near the white sands of Flamenco Beach, one of the best in the region. Each unit has its own kitchen. This place would really be attractive to a group of friends or an extended family, since the accommodations are situated around spacious sitting rooms much like those in an informal beach house. The owner has studio apartments suitable for two, one-bedroom apartments suitable for four, two-bedroom bungalows suitable for six, and a three-bedroom unit that can house eight (it contains two bathrooms). All units are air-conditioned. Varied activities are available, including day trips on a sailboat to one of the nearby islands, snorkeling, and fishing expeditions. A small restaurant on-site, Coconut Beach Grill, serves food, often seafood, Thursday through Sunday nights.

Harbour View Villas. Melones Beach, west of Dewey (P.O. Box 216), Culebra, PR 00775. ☎ **800/440-0070** or 787/742-3855. 3 villas, 3 suites. A/C. Winter $75–$125 double, $175 triple or quad; off-season $75–$95 double, $145 triple or quad.

Set on a 5-acre estate and offering one of the best values on the island, these villas and suites are private but not isolated. They were designed for tropical living with 12-foot ceilings and big French doors opening onto the main balcony with its 180-degree view of the ocean. The bedrooms also have private balconies. From the rooms you'll have panoramic views of the ocean. The complex lies within walking distance of Melones Beach. Five of the units have a full kitchen, the other a smaller kitchenette. Each unit has a master bedroom with a queen-size bed, whereas two of the villas have a second bedroom for two more guests.

WHERE TO DINE

El Batey. 250 Carretera. ☎ **787/742-3828.** Sandwiches $2.50–$3.75. MC, V. Sun–Thurs 9am–2pm; Fri 9am–noon, Sat 9am–2am. DELI.

Across from the harbor, this large, clean establishment maintains a full bar and prepares an array of deli-style sandwiches. They'll hand you a cold beer when the afternoon sun is out, and the pool tables make the place lively, especially on weekends when many locals are there. Disco reigns on Saturday night. Weekdays, it's much calmer. The owners, Digna Feliciano and Tomás Ayala, have many fans on the island. Breezes from the harbor cool the place.

Marta's al Fresco. 10 Pedro Marquez. ☎ **787/742-3575.** Sandwiches $2.75–$3; main courses $3.50–$22. MC, V. Thurs–Sun 8–10pm. AMERICAN/PUERTO RICAN.

In a simple building near the wharf where the ferryboats from Puerto Rico's mainland arrive and depart, this restaurant is named after its owner's wife, Marta. The furniture is made of rattan, and big windows offer a view of the sea. In addition to the deli-style sandwiches, the menu lists a wide range of fresh seafood, as well as steaks, asopaos, burgers, and pork chops with rice and beans. Although hardly memorable, the cooking is home-style and satisfying.

A Side Trip to St. Thomas: Shopping Capital of the Caribbean

12

St. Thomas is the most popular excursion from Puerto Rico—it's just a short hop from San Juan. Although San Juan has bargains galore, the duty-free shopping of St. Thomas is extremely appealing. Thousands of visitors make a quick day trip to take advantage of the $1,200 duty-free shopping limit available to Americans.

This incentive, combined with the ease of getting here from San Juan, make this U.S. Virgin Island an interesting and fairly easy day trip. Some visitors spend just an afternoon, but we've included some restaurants where you can break your shopping foray with lunch or refreshment.

Sometimes a ticket to St. Thomas that takes you from the mainland United States to San Juan, where you change planes, is actually cheaper than the APEX nonstop fare to Puerto Rico. Therefore, you may want to include both Puerto Rico and the U.S. Virgin Islands in one vacation. See *Frommer's Virgin Islands* for more details, and also call **American Airlines** (☎ **800/433-7300**) to get the current fares for a combined Puerto Rico–St. Thomas trip.

1 St. Thomas Orientation

Boasting the busiest cruise-ship harbor in the West Indies, St. Thomas is the second largest of the U.S. Virgin Islands. It lies about 40 miles north of the larger U.S. Virgin Island of St. Croix. St. Thomas is about 12 miles long and 3 miles wide; its north shore faces the Atlantic Ocean, while the calmer Caribbean washes its south side. It's not unheard of to find the sun shining in the south while the north is experiencing showers.

The town of Charlotte Amalie is both the capital of the U.S. Virgin Islands and the shopping mecca of the Caribbean. The island is indeed a boon for cruise-ship shoppers, who frequently flood Main Street, where dozens of shops are located within a 3- or 4-block radius. This area can get very crowded; but it's away from the beaches, major hotels, most restaurants, and entertainment facilities, so the mobs don't have to interfere if you're here just to soak up the sun.

One important note: If you're visiting in the summer months, bring along some mosquito repellent.

VISITOR INFORMATION   On St. Thomas, the **Visitors Center** is at Emancipation Square (☎ **809/774-8784**). Much useful information is dispensed here, and you can pick up a copy of *St. Thomas This Week,* which includes maps of St. Thomas and nearby St. John, as well as descriptions of the vast array of shopping possibilities.

MAIN STREETS & ARTERIES   The capital, Charlotte Amalie, is the only town on St. Thomas. Bordering the waterfront, its seaside promenade is called **Waterfront Highway,** or just the Waterfront. Its old Danish name is Kyst Vejen. From the Waterfront, you can take any number of streets or alleyways leading back into town to the **Main Street,** or Dronningens Gade. Principal links between Main Street and the Waterfront include **Raadets Gade, Tolbod Gade, Storetvaer Gade,** and **Strand Gade.**

Main Street is aptly named, since it is the center of the capital and the site of the major shops. The western part of Main Street is **Market Square,** which was once the site of the biggest slave-market auctions in the Caribbean Basin. It lies near the intersection with Strand Gade. Today it's an open-air block of stalls where island gardeners sell their produce, particularly on Saturday. Go early in the morning to see the market at its best. It's closed Sunday.

Running parallel to Main Street and lying north of it is **Back Street,** or Vimmelskaft Gade, which has many stores, including some of the less expensive ones. Although quite dangerous to walk along at night, it's reasonably safe for daytime shopping.

In the eastern part of town, midway between Talbod Gade and Fort Pladsen, is **Emancipation Park,** northwest of Fort Christian, commemorating the liberation of the slaves in 1848. Most of the major historical buildings, including the Legislative Building, Fort Christian, and Government House, are within a short walk of this park.

Southeast of the park looms **Fort Christian,** crowned by a clock tower and painted a rusty red, constructed by the Danes in 1671. The **Legislative Building,** seat of the elected government of the U.S. Virgin Islands, is on the harbor side of the fort.

Kongens Gade (King's Street) leads to Government House on Government Hill, which overlooks the town and the harbor. Here stands a white-brick building, Government House, dating from 1867.

Between **Hotel 1829,** a former mansion constructed that year by a French sea captain, and Government House is a staircase known as the **Street of 99 Steps.** Actually, someone miscounted; it should be called the Street of 103 Steps. These steps lead to the summit of Government Hill.

Nearby are the remains of the 17th-century **Fort Skytsborg,** or Blackbeard's Tower, a reference to the notorious pirate Edward Teach, who is said to have spied on treasure galleons entering the harbor in the 1700s from here. Today an 11-room hotel, Blackbeard's Castle, stands here.

This should not be confused with **Bluebeard's Tower,** which crowns a 300-foot hill at the eastern edge of town. This is the site of what is the best-known (but not the best) hotel in the Virgin Islands—Bluebeard's Castle.

GETTING AROUND   Administered by the government, **Vitran buses** service Charlotte Amalie, its outlying neighborhoods, and the countryside as far away as Red Hook. Vitran stops are found at reasonable intervals beside each of the most important traffic arteries on St. Thomas. Among the most visible are those along the edges of Veterans Drive on Charlotte Amalie. Buses run daily between 6am and

9pm. A one-way ride costs 75¢ within Charlotte Amalie, $1 for rides from Charlotte Amalie into its outer neighborhoods, and $3 for rides from Charlotte Amalie to such other communities as Red Hook, site of ferryboat departures for St. John. For information about Vitran buses, their stops, and schedules, call ☎ **340/774-5678.**

2 Shopping

Shoppers have not only the benefits of St. Thomas's liberal duty-free allowances (a $1,200 limit before duty is imposed), but also the opportunity to buy well-known brand names that may be on sale at 40% below stateside prices. However, that doesn't happen every day. To find true value, you may have to plow through a lot of junk. Many items offered for sale—binoculars, stereos, watches, and cameras—can be matched in price at your hometown discount store. Therefore, you need to know the price back home to determine whether you are in fact saving money. Having sounded that warning, we'll survey some St. Thomas shops where we have personally found good buys. There are lots more you can discover on your own.

Most of the shops, some of which occupy former pirate warehouses, are open from 9am to 5pm, and some stay open later. Nearly all stores close on Sunday and major holidays—that is, unless a cruise ship is in port. Few shopkeepers can stand the prospect of hundreds of potential customers, their purses full, wandering by their padlocked doors. Therefore, those gates are likely to swing open, at least for half a day on Sunday. Try to avoid shopping on Friday, the biggest cruise-ship visiting day (we counted eight ships in port here one Friday).

Nearly all the major shopping in St. Thomas is concentrated along the harbor of Charlotte Amalie. Cruise-ship passengers mainly shop at the **Havensight Mall,** where they disembark at the eastern edge of Charlotte Amalie. The principal shopping street downtown is called **Main Street,** or Dronningens Gade (its old Danish name). North of this street is merchandise-loaded **Back Street,** or Vimmelskaft.

Many shops are also spread along the **Waterfront Highway** (also called Kyst Vejen). Between these major streets or boulevards is a series of side streets, walkways, and alleys, all filled with shops. Other major shopping streets are Tolbod Gade, Raadets Gade, Royal Dane Mall, Palm Passage, Storetvaer Gade, and Strand Gade.

All the major stores in St. Thomas are located by number on an excellent map in the center of the publication *St. Thomas This Week,* distributed free to all arriving plane and boat passengers.

If you want to combine a little history with shopping, you might go into the courtyard of the old **Pissarro Building,** entered through an archway off Main Street. The impressionist painter lived here as a child. The old apartments have been turned into a warren of interesting shops.

ANTIQUE FURNITURE REPRODUCTIONS
Mahogany Island Style. Al Cohen's Plaza, Raphune Hill, Rte. 38. ☎ **340/777-3060**.

St. Thomas locals sometimes regret that neighboring St. Croix has a better-developed sense of historic plantation life than bustling St. Thomas, so Jane Coombs created this store partly as a means of correcting that situation. It contains high-quality reproductions, crafted by Baker Furniture, of the antique furniture within St. Croix's Whim Plantation Museum. Examples include lavishly carved four-poster beds that are certain to become heirlooms in their own right, and wicker-and-mahogany planters chairs that look spectacular on a breezy veranda.

There's also a built-in humidor for the stockpiling of cigars; the store's owner spent an apprenticeship in Cuba learning the nuances of the cigar trade.

ART GALLERIES & FINE CRAFTS

Bernard K. Passman. 38A Main St. ☎ **340/777-4580.**

Bernard K. Passman is the world's leading sculptor of black coral art and jewelry, famous for his "Can Can Girl" and his four statues of Charlie Chaplin. On Grand Cayman he learned to fashion exquisite treasures from black coral found 200 feet under the sea. After being polished and embellished with gold and diamonds, some of Passman's work has been treasured by royalty. There are also simpler and more affordable pieces for sale.

Camille Pissarro Building Art Gallery. Caribbean Cultural Centre, 14 Dronningens Gade. ☎ **340/774-4621.**

In the house where Pissarro, dean of Impressionism, was born on July 10, 1830, this art gallery—reached by climbing a flight of stairs—honors the illustrious painter. In three high-ceilinged and airy rooms, you'll discover all the available Pissarro paintings relating to the islands that were created from 1852 to 1856. Many prints and note cards of local artists are also available, and the gallery also sells original batiks, alive in vibrant colors.

Mango Tango Art Gallery. Al Cohen's Plaza, Raphune Hill, Rte. 38. ☎ **340/777-3060.**

Associated with Mahogany Island Style, which sits next door (see below), this is one of the largest art galleries in St. Thomas, with close contacts with about a half-dozen internationally recognized artists. Except for less-expensive prints and posters, original artworks inside begin at $200, rising to a maximum of around $7,000. Represented are internationally reputed artists who spend at least part of their year in the Virgin Islands, many of them sailing during breaks from their studio time. Well-known examples include Don Dahlke, Max Johnson, Anne Miller, David Millard, Dana Wylder, and Shari Erickson.

Native Arts and Crafts Cooperative. Tarbor 1. ☎ **340/777-1153.**

The largest arts and crafts emporium in the U.S. Virgin Islands combines the output of 90 artisans into one sprawling shop. Contained within the former headquarters of the U.S. District Court, a 19th-century brick building adjacent to Charlotte Amalie's tourist information office, it specializes in items small enough to be packed into a suitcase or trunk, and which almost never need to be specially shipped. Examples include spice racks, paper towel racks, lamps crafted from conch shells, salad utensils and bowls, crocheted goods, and straw goods.

BAGS

Coki. Compass Point Marina. ☎ **340/775-6560.**

Coki of St. Thomas has a factory at Compass Point Marina amidst a little restaurant row, so you might want to combine a gastronomic tour with a shopping expedition. From the factory's expansive cutting board come some of the most popular varieties of shoulder tote bags in the Virgin Islands. These include pieces of canvas and elegant cotton prints converted to beach bags, zip-top bags, and draw-string bags. All Coki bags are 100% cotton stitched with polyester sailmaker's thread.

Shopping in Charlotte Amalie

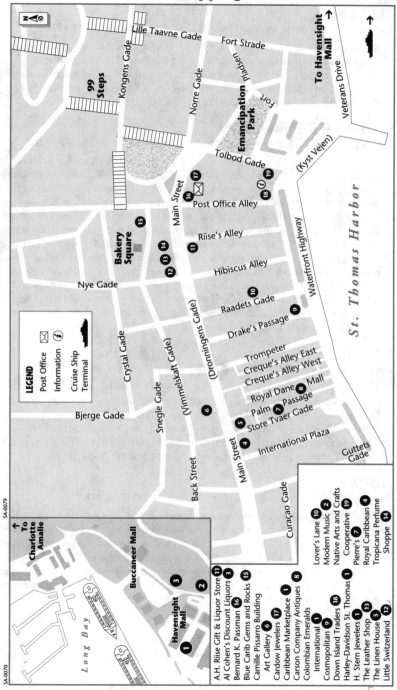

99 Steps

Lille Taavne Gade
Fort Strade
Kongens Gade
Norre Gade
Pladsen
Fort
Emancipation Park

To Havensight Mall →

Veterans Drive

St. Thomas Harbor

Tolbod Gade

Main Street
Post Office Alley

Bakery Square
Riise's Alley
Hibiscus Alley
Nye Gade
Raadets Gade
Drake's Passage
Trompeter
Creque's Alley East
Creque's Alley West
Royal Dane Mall
Palm Passage
Store Tvaer Gade
International Plaza

Crystal Gade
(Dronningens Gade)
(Vimmelskaft Gade)
Snegle Gade
Bjerge Gade

Main Street
Back Street
Guttets Gade
Curaçao Gade

Waterfront Highway
(Kyst Vejen)

LEGEND
Post Office
Information
Cruise Ship Terminal

← To Charlotte Amalie

Long Bay

Buccaneer Mall

Havensight Mall

A.H. Riise Gift & Liquor Store 11
Al Cohen's Discount Liquors 3
Bernard K. Passman 16
Blue Carib Gems and Rocks 15
Camille Pissarro Building 1
Art Gallery 6
Cardow Jewelers 17
Caribbean Marketplace 1
Carson Company Antiques 8
Colombian Emeralds International 1
Cosmopolitan 9
Down Island Traders 18
Harley-Davidson St. Thomas 1
H. Stern Jewelers 13
The Leather Shop 5
The Linen House 1
Little Switzerland 12

Lover's Lane 10
Modern Music 2
Native Arts and Crafts Cooperative 19
Pierre's 7
Royal Caribbean 4
Tropicana Perfume Shoppe 14

237

BRIC-A-BRAC

Carson Company Antiques. Royal Dane Mall, off Main St. ☎ **340/774-6175.**

Its clutter and eclecticism might appeal to you, especially if you appreciate small spaces loaded with merchandise, tasteless and otherwise, from virtually everywhere. Much of it is calibrated to appeal to the tastes of cruise-ship passengers looking for bric-a-brac that usually accumulates on shelves back home. Bakelite jewelry is cheap and cheerful, and the African artifacts are especially interesting.

CLOTHES & MEMORABILIA

Harley-Davidson St. Thomas. In the Havensight Mall, Bldg. 5. ☎ **340/776-7162.**

Gucci and Armani have their fans, and any emporium that stocks garments by Calvin Klein or Valentino is usually mobbed with fashionable international groupies. So it comes as no surprise that the rougher, more macho memorabilia associated with Harley-Davidson motorcycles has been elevated to new levels of either hipness or kitsch, depending on the way you interpret it. If you're interested in actually buying a motorcycle, you'll find models beginning at around $8,000 and going much higher, depending on the accessories. More feasible, however, especially in terms of transporting your purchase off-island, are any of the roster of sunglasses, pins, watches, "fanny packs," T-shirts, and leather belts, vests, and jackets designed by Harley for him and/or her. Cheerful and chipper, with a wholesomeness that's far removed from the image of Hell's Angels members roaring down the byways of California, this place is ready, willing, and eager to help transform even the most staid of tourists into Road Warriors.

ELECTRONICS

Royal Caribbean. 33 Main St. ☎ **340/776-4110.**

This largest camera and electronics store in the Caribbean carries Nikon, Minolta, Pentax, Canon, and Panasonic products. It's a good source for watches, including such brand names as Seiko, Movado, Corum, Fendi, and Zodiac. They also have a complete collection of Philippe Charriol watches, jewelry, and leather bags, and a wide selection of Mikimoto pearls, 14- and 18-karat jewelry, and Lladró figurines.

There's another branch at **Havensight Mall** (☎ **340/776-8890**).

FASHION

Cosmopolitan. Drakes Passage and the waterfront. ☎ **340/776-2040.**

Since 1973, this store has drawn a lot of repeat business. Its shoe salon features Bally of Switzerland, and Bally handbags are a popular addition. In swimwear, it offers one of the best selections of Gottex of Israel for women and Gottex, Hom, Lahco of Switzerland, and Fila for men. A menswear section offers Paul & Shark from Italy, and Burma Bibas sports shirts. The shop also features ties by Gianni Versace and Pancaldi of Italy (priced at least 30% less than on the U.S. mainland), and Nautica sportswear for men discounted at 10%.

FRAGRANCES

Tropicana Perfume Shoppe. 2 Main St. ☎ **800/233-7948** or 340/774-0010.

This store at the beginning of Main Street is billed as the largest perfumery in the world, and it offers all the famous names in perfumes, skin care, and cosmetics. They carry Lancôme and La Prairie, among other products, and men will also find Europe's best colognes and aftershave lotions here.

GIFTS & LIQUORS

Al Cohen's Discount Liquors. Long Bay Rd. ☎ **340/774-3690.**

In a big warehouse at Havensight, across from the West Indian Company docks where cruise-ship passengers disembark, you can make purchases from one of the island's biggest storehouses of liquor and wine. The wine department is especially impressive. The quarters have been recently expanded and remodeled, and there are now more brands and items on sale than ever before. You can also purchase fragrances, T-shirts, and souvenirs.

A. H. Riise Gift & Liquor Stores. 37 Main St. at A. H. Riise Gift & Liquor Mall (perfume and liquor branch stores at the Havensight Mall). ☎ **800/524-2037** or 304/776-2303.

St. Thomas's oldest outlet for luxury items such as jewelry, crystal, china, and perfumes is still the largest. It also offers the widest sampling of liquors and liqueurs on the island. Everything is displayed in a 19th-century Danish warehouse, extending from Main Street to the waterfront. The store boasts a collection of fine jewelry and watches from Europe's leading craftspeople, including Vacheron Constantin, Bulgari, Omega, and Gucci, as well as a wide selection of Greek gold, platinum, and precious gemstone jewelry.

Imported cigars are stored in a climate-controlled walk-in humidor. Delivery to cruise ships and the airport is free. A. H. Riise offers a vast selection of fragrances for both men and women, along with the world's best-known names in cosmetics and treatment products. Waterford, Lalique, Baccarat, and Rosenthal, among others, are featured in the china and crystal department. Specialty shops in the complex sell Caribbean gifts, books, clothing, food, art prints, note cards, and designer sunglasses.

Caribbean Marketplace. Havensight Mall (Bldg. III). ☎ **340/776-5400**.

The best selections of island handcrafts are found here, in addition to some distinctively Caribbean food items, including Sunny Caribbee's vast array of condiments (ranging from spicy peppercorns to nutmeg mustard). There's also a wide selection of Sunny Caribbee's botanical products. Other items range from steel-pan drums from Trinidad to wooden Jamaican jigsaw puzzles, from Indonesian batiks to bikinis from the Cayman Islands. Do not expect very attentive service.

Down Island Traders. Veterans Dr. ☎ **340/776-4641.**

The aroma of spices will lead you to these markets, which have Charlotte Amalie's most attractive array of spices, teas, seasoning, candies, jellies, jams, and condiments, most of which are packaged from natural Caribbean products. The owner carries a line of local cookbooks, as well as silk-screened T-shirts and bags, Haitian metal sculpture, handmade jewelry, Caribbean folk art, and children's gifts. Be sure to ask for their collection of tropical coconut-mango bath and body products and the Calypso Spa Sun Care line.

Little Switzerland. 5 Main St. ☎ **800/524-2010** or 340/776-2010.

A branch of this shop seems to appear on virtually every island in the Caribbean. Its concentration of watches, including Omega and Rolex, is topped by no one. Its china, especially the Rosenthal collection, is outstanding, as are its crystal and jewelry, including gorgeous South Seas pearls. The store also maintains the official outlets for Hummel, Lladró, and Swarovski figurines. There are several other branches of this store on the island, especially at the Havensight Mall, but the main store has the best selection.

JEWELRY

Blue Carib Gems and Rocks. 2 Back St. (behind Little Switzerland). ☎ **340/774-8525**.

For a decade, the owners of this shop scoured the Caribbean for gemstones, bringing them directly from the mines to you. The raw stones are cut, polished, and then fashioned into jewelry by the lost-wax process. On one side of the premises you can see the craftspeople at work, and on the other, view their finished products. A lifetime guarantee is given on all handcrafted jewelry. Since the items are locally made, they are duty-free and not included in the $1,200 customs exemption.

Cardow Jewelers. 39 Main St. ☎ **340/776-1140**.

Often called the Tiffany's of the Caribbean, Cardow Jewelers boasts the largest selection of fine jewelry in the world. This fabulous shop, where more than 20,000 rings are displayed, offers savings because of its worldwide direct buying, large turnover, and duty-free prices. Unusual and traditional designs are offered in diamonds, emeralds, rubies, sapphires, Brazilian stones, and pearls. Cardow has a whole wall of Italian gold chains and also features antique-coin jewelry. The Treasure Cove, a discount area within the store, has cases of fine gold jewelry all priced under $200.

Colombian Emeralds International. Havensight Mall. ☎ **340/774-2442**.

Colombian Emeralds stores are renowned throughout the Caribbean for offering the finest collection of Colombian emeralds, both set and unset. Here you buy direct from the source, cutting out the middleperson, which can mean significant savings for you. In addition to jewelry, the shop stocks fine watches. There's another outlet on Main Street.

H. Stern Jewellers. Havensight Mall. ☎ **800/524-2024** or 340/776-1223.

This international jeweler is one of the most respected in the world, with some 175 outlets. In a world of fake jewelry and fake everything, it's good to know that there's still a name you can count on. Stern is Cardow's (see above) leading competitor on the island. Colorful gem and jewel creations are offered at Stern's locations on St. Thomas. There are two on Main Street, this one at the Havensight Mall, and branches at Marriott Frenchman's Reef. Stern gives worldwide guaranteed service, including a 1-year exchange privilege.

Pierre's. 24 Palm Passage. ☎ **800/300-0634** or 340/776-5130.

Connoisseurs of colored gemstones consider this store one of the most impressive repositories of rare and sought-after collector's items in the Caribbean. It's a 12-year-old branch of a store based in Naples, Florida, and it inventories glittering and mystical-looking gemstones you might never have heard of before. Look for alexandrites, garnets in three shades of green; spinels, pink and red; sphenes, yellow-green sparklers from Madagascar as reflective as high-quality diamonds; and tsavorites, a difficult-to-pronounce green stone from Tanzania. The creative forces behind all this are Jennifer and Gerald Rathkolb, whose training derived from years of gemology and goldsmithing work in Austria and South Africa. Virtually everything for sale here is sold tax free.

LEATHER

The Leather Shop. 1 Main St. ☎ **340/776-0290**.

Here you'll find the best selection from Italian designers such as Desmo, Longchamp, Furla, and Il Bisonte. There are many styles of handbags, belts, wallets, briefcases, and attaché cases, plus reasonably priced bags from around the world.

LINENS

The Linen House. A. H. Riise Mall. ☎ **340/774-1668.**

The Linen House is the best store for linens in the Caribbean. You'll find a wide selection of place mats, decorative tablecloths, and many hand-embroidered goods, much of it handmade in China.

MERCHANDISE FOR LOVERS

Lover's Lane. Raadets Gade 33. Charlotte Amalie. ☎ **340/777-9616**.

Despite the fact that this store expends a lot of effort to cloak its merchandise with an aura of "sex within the confines of marriage" respectability, some of the inventory here is earthy and in some cases, raunchy. That doesn't prevent a visit here from being amusing and, if you're in the mood for it, a lot of fun. And in some cases, day visitors from cruise ships moored offshore make a visit here a required stopover, usually to perk up the sometimes-tame roster of shipboard activities during any of their vessel's "fun days at sea." Set one floor above street level of a building beside Veteran's Drive, within an ever-so-tasteful decor of muted grays and mirrors, the shop sells provocative lingerie, massage aids of every conceivable type, and all the toys you'll need to make your erotic fantasies come true.

MUSIC

Modern Music. Across from Havensight Mall and cruise-ship docks. ☎ **340/774-3100**.

An aptly titled store, Modern Music features nearly every genre of music, from rock to jazz to classical, and definitely Caribbean. It was opened nearly 10 years ago by New Jersey cold-weather refugee Chris Hansen. You'll find new releases from Caribbean stars such as Jamaica's Byron Lee and Virgin Island's The Violators, as well as new releases from U.S. stars such as R.E.M. and Garth Brooks. They also have two other stores: at **Nisky Center** (☎ **340/777-7877**) and at **Four Winds Mall** (☎ **340/775-3310**).

3 Other Top Things to See & Do

EXPLORING CHARLOTTE AMALIE

Sandwiched among the shops are a few historic buildings worth exploring. Most can be covered on foot in about 2 hours. Before starting your tour, stop off in the so-called **Grand Hotel,** near Emancipation Park. No longer a hotel, it contains a visitor center along with shops.

You can't miss **Fort Christian,** dating from 1672, rising from the harbor and dominating the center of town. Named after the Danish king Christian V, the structure has been everything from a governor's residence to a jail. Many pirates were hanged in the courtyard of the fort. Some of the cells have been turned into the rather minor Virgin Islands Museum, displaying Native American artifacts of only the most passing interest. Admission is free, and the fort is open Monday through Friday from 8am to 5pm.

Seven Arches Museum, Government Hill (☎ **340/774-9295**), is a 2-century-old Danish house, completely restored to its original condition and furnished with antiques. You can walk through the yellow ballast arches and visit the great room with its view of the busiest harbor in the Caribbean. You can also view the original separate stone Danish kitchen above the cistern. The admission of $5 includes a cold tropical drink served in a walled garden filled with flowers. It's open Tuesday through Saturday from 10am to 3pm.

NEARBY ATTRACTIONS

West of Charlotte Amalie, Route 30 (Veteran's Drive) takes you to **Frenchtown** (turn left at the sign to the Admirals Inn). This was settled by a French-speaking people who were uprooted when the Swedes invaded and took over their homeland in St. Barts. They were known for wearing *cha-chas,* or straw hats. Many of the people who live here today are the direct descendants of those long-ago immigrants. This colorful fishing village contains several interesting restaurants and taverns.

The **Estate St. Peter Greathouse Botanical Gardens,** at the corner of Route 40 (St. Peter Mountain Road) and Barrett Hill Road (☎ **340/774-4999**), decorates 11 lushly planted acres of grounds at the volcanic peaks on the northern rim of the island. It's the creation of Howard Lawson DeWolfe, a Mayflower descendant who, with his wife, Sylvie, bought the estate in 1987 and set about transforming it into a tropical paradise. A virtual Garden of Eden, it's riddled with self-guided nature walks that will acquaint you with some 200 varieties of plants and trees from all over the world, including an umbrella plant from Madagascar. You'll see a rain forest, an orchid jungle, a monkey habitat, waterfalls, and reflecting ponds. From a panoramic deck you can see some 20 of the Virgin Islands, including Hans Lollick, an uninhabited island between Thatched Cay and Madahl Point. The house itself is worth a visit, its interior filled with works by local artists. It's open daily from 9am to 5pm, charging an admission of $8 for adults and $4 for children.

For a Jules Verne–type thrill, consider the ✪ *Atlantis* **submarine,** which takes you on a 1-hour voyage to depths of 150 feet, unfolding a world of exotic marine life. You'll gaze on coral reefs and sponge gardens through 2-foot windows on the air-conditioned 65-foot-long sub, which carries 46 passengers. You take a surface boat from the West Indies Dock, right outside Charlotte Amalie, to the submarine, which lies near Buck Island (the St. Thomas version, not the more famous Buck Island near St. Croix). Divers swim with the fish and bring them close to the windows for photos. The fare is $72 per person. Children ages 4 to 12 pay $27, and teens (ages 13 to 17) are charged $36. Children under 4 are not permitted. The *Atlantis* operates daily from November through April and Tuesday through Saturday from May through October. Reservations are imperative. Hours and days vary depending on the arrival of cruise ships. For tickets, go to the Havensight Shopping Mall, Building 6, or call **340/776-5650** for reservations.

✪ **Coral World Marine Park & Underwater Observatory.** 6450 Coki Point. ☎ **340/775-1555.** Admission $17 adults, $10 children. Daily 9am–5:30pm.

This aquarium, a 20-minute drive from downtown off Route 38, is St. Thomas's number-one tourist attraction. Set in a 4½-acre park site, it was destroyed by Hurricane Marilyn in 1995 but rebuilt. The marine complex features a three-story underwater observation tower 100 feet offshore. Through windows you'll see sponges, fish, coral, and other underwater life in its natural state. In the Marine Gardens Aquarium, saltwater tanks display everything from sea horses to sea urchins. An 80,000-gallon reef tank features exotic marine life of the Caribbean; another tank is devoted to sea predators, with circling sharks and giant moray eels, among other creatures. The entrance is hidden behind a waterfall of cascading water.

The latest addition to the park is a semisubmarine that lets you enjoy the panoramic view and the underwater feeling of a submarine without truly submerging. Coral World's guests can take advantage of adjacent Coki Beach for snorkel rental, scuba lessons, or simply swimming and relaxing. Lockers and showers are available.

Also included in the marine park are a cafe, duty-free shops, and a tropical nature trail. Activities include daily fish and shark feedings and exotic bird shows.

Paradise Point Tramway. Rte. 30 at Havensight. ☎ **340/774-9809.** Admission $10 per person round-trip, children half-price. Daily 9am–5pm.

This tramway, opened in 1994, affords visitors a dramatic view of Charlotte Amalie harbor on a ride to a 697-foot peak, although you'll pay dearly for the privilege. The tramway operates four cars, each with a 10-person capacity, for the 15-minute round-trip ride (board at Havensight). The tramways, similar to those used at ski resorts, transport customers from the Havensight area to Paradise Point, where riders disembark to visit shops and a popular restaurant and bar.

BEACHES

Many people on a quick visit prefer to spend their time on the beach instead of looking at the minor attractions or going shopping. (Or maybe your significant other is dying to shop and you want to take off on your own.) St. Thomas has some of the best beaches in the Caribbean. You can reach all of them relatively quickly in a taxi from Charlotte Amalie, and have a taxi driver return and pick you up at a designated time. All the beaches in the Virgin Islands are public.

THE NORTH SIDE

Magens Bay, 3 miles north of the capital, once was hailed as one of the world's 10 most beautiful beaches, but that reputation has now faded. Although it still has a certain allure, it is not as well maintained as it should be and is often overcrowded, especially when 10 cruise ships are in port. Changing facilities are available, and snorkeling gear and lounge chairs can be rented. Administered by the government, this beach is less than a mile long and lies between two mountains. There is no public transportation to reach it. From Charlotte Amalie, take Route 35 north all the way. Admission is $1 for adults and 25¢ for children under 12. The gates to the beach are open daily from 6am to 6pm (after 4pm you'll need insect repellent).

In the northeast near Coral World, **Coki Beach** is good, but it too becomes overcrowded when cruise ships are in port. Snorkelers are attracted here, as are pickpockets—so protect your valuables. Lockers can be rented at Coral World, next door. An East End bus runs to Smith Bay and lets you off at the gate to Coral World and Coki.

Also on the north side, the beach at **Renaissance Grand Beach Resort** is one of the island's most beautiful, with the resort in the background. Many water sports are available at this beach, which opens onto Smith Bay and is near Coral World. The resort itself (☎ **340/775-1510**) offers windsurfing; if you're not a guest of the hotel, you pay $35 per hour. The beach lies right off Route 38.

THE SOUTH SIDE

On the south side near Marriott's Frenchman's Reef Beach Resort, **Morningstar** lies about 2 miles east of Charlotte Amalie. This is where you can wear your most daring swimwear. Or you can rent sailboats, snorkeling equipment, and lounge chairs. The beach can easily be reached by a cliff-front elevator at Frenchman's Reef.

At the Bolongo Beach Resorts Club Everything, **Limetree Beach** has been called a classic, and it lures those who like a serene spread of sand. You can feed hibiscus blossoms to iguanas and rent snorkeling gear and lounge chairs. There is no public transportation, but the beach can easily be reached by taxi from Charlotte Amalie.

One of the most popular beaches, **Brewer's** lies in the southwest near the University of the Virgin Islands and can be reached by the public bus marked FORTUNA heading west from Charlotte Amalie Road.

Near the airport, **Lindberg Beach** has a lifeguard, toilet facilities, and a bathhouse. It, too, lies on the Fortuna bus route heading west from Charlotte Amalie.

THE EAST END

Small and special, **Secret Harbour** lies near a collection of condos whose owners you'll meet on the beach. With its white sand and coconut palms, it's a cliché of Caribbean charm. No public transportation stops here, but it's an easy taxi ride east of Charlotte Amalie heading toward Red Hook.

One of the finest on St. Thomas, ✪ **Sapphire Beach** is set against the backdrop of the desirable Doubletree Sapphire Beach Resort & Marina complex, where you can get lunch or order drinks. Windsurfers like it a lot, and snorkeling gear and lounge chairs can be rented. A large reef lies near the shore, and there are good views of offshore cays and St. John. The beach of fine white coral sand opens onto beautiful views of the bay. To reach it, you can take the East End bus from Charlotte Amalie, going via Red Hook. Ask to be let off at the entrance to Sapphire Bay; it's not too far to walk from there toward the water.

4 Where to Dine

Even if you're over just for the day from San Juan, chances are you'll be on St. Thomas for lunch. The island offers a wide selection of restaurants, but we'll review only a few choice ones.

IN CHARLOTTE AMALIE

Beni Iguana's Sushi Bar. In the Grand Hotel Court, Veteran's Dr. ☎ **340/777-8744.** Reservations recommended. Sushi $4.50–$6 per portion (2 pieces); salads $7.95–$12.45; main courses $6–$15.95; combo plates for 4 to 5 diners $25–$35 each. AE, MC, V. Daily 11:30am–10pm. JAPANESE.

St. Thomas's only Japanese restaurant is a change of pace from the Caribbean, steak, and seafood restaurants nearby. Along with a handful of shops, it occupies the sheltered courtyard and an old cistern across from Emancipation Square Park. Select a table outside, or pass through wide Danish colonial doors into a red- and black-lacquered interior devoted to a sushi bar and a handful of simple tables. Most meals begin with a selection of sushi (freshwater eel, tuna, yellowtail, or amberjack), which the chefs dub "edible art." Follow that with a salad or a roll of seafood wrapped in rice—a perennial favorite is the "13" roll, stuffed with spicy crabmeat, salmon, lettuce, cucumbers, and scallions. Todd Reinhard, an American carefully trained in the art of Japanese cuisine, is your host.

Greenhouse. Veterans Dr. ☎ **340/774-7998.** Main courses $6–$21; breakfast $2.50–$6.95. AE, DISC, MC, V. Daily 8am–2am. AMERICAN/CARIBBEAN.

Fronted by big sunny windows, this waterfront restaurant attracts cruise-ship passengers who have shopped and need a place to drop. The food is not the island's best, but it's perfectly satisfying if you're not too demanding. A breakfast menu of eggs, sausages, and bacon segues into the daily specialties, including much American fare and some Jamaican-inspired dishes. A pretty good freshly grilled mahimahi is served here with a Florida key lime ginger butter and Jamaican jerk seasoning, or you might order one of the specialties such as barbecued pork ribs, again with Jamaican jerk spices. Happy hour is daily from 4:30 to 7pm. This is one of the safest places to be in Charlotte Amalie after dark.

Hard Rock Café. 5144 International Plaza, the Waterfront, Queen's Quarter. ☎ **340/777-5555.** Reservations not accepted. Main courses $7.95–$16.95. AE, MC, V. Mon–Sat 10am–9pm, Sun 10am–3pm. AMERICAN.

Occupying the second floor of a pink-sided mall overlooking the ships moored in Charlotte Amalie's harbor, this hot spot is a member of the international Hard Rock chain. Entire walls are devoted to the memorabilia of such artists as John Lennon, Eric Clapton, and Bob Marley. Throughout most of the day, the place is a restaurant, serving barbecued meats, salads, sandwiches, burgers, fresh fish, and steaks. Its burgers are the best in town, but people mainly come for the good times.

✪ **Hervé Restaurant & Wine Bar.** Government Hill. ☎ **340/777-9703.** Reservations requested. Main courses $17.75–$24.75; lunch $5.50–$16.75. AE, MC, V. Mon–Sat 11:30am–3pm and 6–10pm. AMERICAN/CARIBBEAN/FRENCH.

Located next to Hotel 1829, Hervé has quickly surpassed all competition in town. A panoramic view of Charlotte Amalie and a historic setting are minor benefits—it's the cuisine here that matters. Hervé P. Chassin, whose experience has embraced such stellar properties as the Hotel du Cap d'Antibes on the French Riviera, is a restaurateur with a vast, classical background. Here in his own unpretentious setting, he offers high-quality food at reasonable prices.

Study the menu in a room decorated with classic black-and-white photographs of St. Thomas at the turn of the century, or opt for a table on a large open-air terrace or in an intimate wine room. Contemporary American dishes are served with the best of classical French, along with Caribbean touches. Start with the pistachio-encrusted brie, shrimp in a stuffed crab shell, or conch fritters with mango chutney. From here, you can let your taste buds march boldly forward with such temptations as red snapper poached with white wine, or a delectable black-sesame-crusted tuna with a ginger/raspberry sauce. Well-prepared nightly specials of game, fish, and pasta are featured. Desserts here are equally divine—you'll rarely taste a creamier crème caramel or a lighter, fluffier mango or raspberry cheesecake.

✪ **Virgilio's.** 18 Dronningens Gade (entrance on a narrow alleyway running between Main St. and Back St.). ☎ **340/776-4920.** Reservations recommended. Main dishes $16.95–$39.95. AE, MC, V. Mon–Sat 11:30am–10:30pm. NORTHERN ITALIAN.

The best northern Italian restaurant in the Virgin Islands, Virgilio's neo-Baroque interior is sheltered under heavy ceiling beams and brick vaulting. A well-trained staff attends to the tables. Owner Virgilio del Mare serves meals against a backdrop of stained-glass windows, crystal chandeliers, and soft Italian music. Everything appears on the menu, from stuffed grape leaves to a delectable house special *cinco peche*—clams, mussels, scallops, oysters, and crayfish simmered in a saffron broth. The lobster ravioli here is the best there is, and such classic dishes as rack of lamb are served with a distinctive flair, this one filled with a porcini mushroom stuffing and glazed with a roasted garlic aïoli. The marinated grilled duck is served chilled, and you can even order an individual pesto pizza. Fresh fish is also a feature.

Virgilio's Wine Cellar & Bistro. 16 Dronningens Gade. ☎ **340/774-8086.** Main courses $18.95–$38.95. AE, MC, V. Mon–Sat 11:30am–10:30pm; wine bar, 11:30am–1am. ITALIAN.

Set in the brick-lined cellar of an 80-year-old building, this cozy wine bistro was conceived as a less expensive clone of its neighbor, Virgilio's, which is administered by the same team and which lies across the street (see above). The cellar contains the closest thing in St. Thomas to the kind of sophisticated wine bar you might have expected in London. The 1,000 vintages of wine, including Italian, Californian, and French vintages that tend to impress many connoisseurs, sell for between $3.75 and $6.50 a glass. You can visit just for a drink, or stop to consume an entire Italian-inspired meal in the street-level dining room. Begin with any of about 17 kinds of pasta that include ravioli, cannelloni, and manicotti. Main courses feature well-flavored chicken cacciatore, osso buco, three different preparations of veal chops (breaded and baked, grilled, or stuffed with prosciutto, mozzarella, and porcini mushrooms). There's also lobster, prepared virtually any way you want. Technically, both the Wine Cellar and Virgilio's main restaurant maintain separate kitchens, but in fact, there's a lot of communication between the two, and some sharing of ideas.

IN FRENCHTOWN

Alexander's. Rue de St. Barthélemy. ☎ **340/776-4211.** Reservations recommended. Main courses $13–$21.50. AE, MC, V. Mon–Sat 11:30am–10pm. AUSTRIAN/GERMAN.

Alexander's, west of town, will accommodate you in air-conditioned comfort at one of its 12 tables with views through picture windows overlooking the harbor. The Teutonic dishes are the best on the island. There's a heavy emphasis on seafood, and the menu includes conch schnitzel on occasion. Other dishes include a mouthwatering Wiener schnitzel and homemade pâté. For dessert, try the homemade strudel, either apple or cheese. Lunch consists of a variety of sandwiches, salads, and smaller versions of the main courses offered at dinner. At both lunch and dinner, the menu offers 10 to 13 different pasta dishes, although we prefer those at Virgilio's (see above). Alexander's also has a Bar and Grill, open daily from 11am to midnight, and Epernay, a wine bar open Monday through Friday from 4 to 11pm (until 11:30pm on weekends).

✪ **Craig & Sally's.** 22 Honduras, Frenchtown. ☎ **340/777-9949.** Reservations recommended. Main courses $14–$29. AE, MC, V. Wed–Fri only 11:30am–3pm, Wed–Sun 5:30–10pm. INTERNATIONAL.

Set in an airy, open-sided pavilion, this Caribbean cafe is operated by a husband-wife team who escaped from the snowbelt, Craig and Sally Darash. All the eclectic cuisine is created by Sally, who maintains a firm grip in the kitchen. Craig is the greeter and coordinator, and he confides that the food is not "for the faint of heart, but for the adventurous soul." His affection for fine wines has led him to create the most extensive and sophisticated wine list on St. Thomas. Views of the sky and sea are complemented by a cuisine that ranges from pasta to seafood, with influences from Europe and Asia. Roast pork with clams, filet mignon with macadamia-nut sauce, and grilled swordfish with a sauce of fresh herbs and tomatoes are examples from a menu that changes every day. The lobster-stuffed twice-baked potatoes are examples of creative cuisine at its most inspired.

Appendix

A   Basic Spanish Phrases & Vocabulary

English	Spanish	Pronunciation
Good day	**Buenos días**	*bway*-nohss-*dee*-ahss
How are you?	**¿Cómo está usted?**	*koh*-moh ess-*tah* oo-*sted*?
Very well	**Muy bien**	mwee byen
Thank you	**Gracias**	grah-see-ahss
You're welcome	**De nada**	day nah-dah
Good-bye	**Adiós**	ah-*dyohss*
Please	**Por favor**	pohr fah-*vohr*
Yes	**Sí**	see
No	**No**	noh
Excuse me	**Perdóneme**	pehr-*doh*-ney-may
Give me	**Déme**	*day*-may
Where is . . . ?	**¿Dónde está . . . ?**	*dohn*-day ess-*tah*?
the station	**la estación**	lah ess-tah-*seown*
a hotel	**un hotel**	oon oh-*tel*
a gas station	**una gasolinera**	oon-uh gah-so-lee-*nay*-rah
a restaurant	**un restaurante**	oon res-tow-*rahn*-tay
the toilet	**el baño**	el *bahn*-yoh
a good doctor	**un buen médico**	oon bwayn *may*-thee-co
the road to	**el camino a/hacia**	el cah-*mee*-noh ah/*ah*-see-ah
To the right	**A la derecha**	ah lah day-*reh*-chuh
To the left	**A la izquierda**	ah lah ees-ky-*ehr*-thah
Straight ahead	**Derecho**	day-*reh*-cho
I would like	**Quisiera**	key-see-*ehr*-ah
I want . . .	**Quiero . . .**	*kyehr*-oh
to eat	**comer**	ko-*mayr*
a room	**una habitación**	oon-nuh ha-bee tah-*seown*

Do you have . . . ?	**¿Tiene usted . . . ?**	tyah-nay oos-*ted*?
a book	**un libro**	oon *lee*-bro
a dictionary	**un diccionario**	oon deek-seown-*ar*-eo
How much is it?	**¿Cuánto cuesta?**	*kwahn*-to *kwess*-tah?
When?	**¿Cuándo?**	*kwahn*-doh?
What?	**¿Qué?**	kay?
There is (Is there . . . ?)	**(¿)Hay (. . . ?)**	eye?
What is there?	**¿Qué hay?**	kay eye?
Yesterday	**Ayer**	ah-*yer*
Today	**Hoy**	oy
Tomorrow	**Mañana**	mahn-*yawn*-ah
Good	**Bueno**	*bway*-no
Bad	**Malo**	*mah*-lo
Better (best)	**(Lo) Mejor**	(loh) meh-*hor*
More	**Más**	mahs
Less	**Menos**	*may*-noss
No smoking	**Se prohíbe fumar**	say pro-*hee*-bay foo-*mahr*
Postcard	**Tarjeta postal**	tar-hay-ta pohs-*tahl*
Insect repellent	**Rapellante contra insectos**	rah-pey-*yahn*-te *cohn*-trah een-*sehk*-tos

More Useful Phrases

Do you speak English?	**¿Habla usted inglés?**	ah-blah oo-*sted* een-*glays*?
Is there anyone here who speaks English?	**¿Hay alguien aquí qué hable inglés?**	eye *ahl*-ghee-en kay *ah*-blay een-*glays*?
I speak a little Spanish.	**Hablo un poco de español.**	*ah*-blow oon *poh*-koh day ess-pah-*nyol*
I don't understand Spanish very well	**No (lo) entiendo muy bien el español.**	noh (loh) ehn-tee-*e hn*-do myee bee-ayn el ess-pah-*nyol*
The meal is good.	**Me gusta la comida.**	may *goo*-sta lah koh-*mee*-dah
What time is it?	**¿Qué hora es?**	kay *oar*-ah ess?
May I see your menu?	**¿Puedo ver el menú (la carta)?**	*puay*-tho veyr el may-*noo* (lah *car*-tah)?
The check please.	**La cuenta por favor.**	lah *quayn*-tah pohr fa-*vorh*
What do I owe you?	**¿Cuánto lo debo?**	*Kwahn*-toh loh *day*-boh?
What did you say?	**¿Mande? (colloquial expression for American "Eh?")**	*Mahn*-day?
More formal:	**¿Cómo?**	*Koh*-moh?
I want (to see) a room . . .	**Quiero (ver) un cuarto (una habitación) . . .**	Key-*yehr*-oh vehr oon *kwar*-toh

for two persons	**para dos personas**	pahr-ah doss pehr-*sohn*-as
with (without) bath.	**con (sin) baño.**	kohn (seen) *bah*-nyoh
We are staying here only . . .	**Nos quedamos aquí solamente . . .**	nohs kay-*dahm*-ohss ah-*key* sohl-ah-*mayn*-tay
one night.	**una noche.**	oon-ah *noh*-chay
one week.	**una semana.**	oon-ah say-*mahn*-ah
We are leaving tomorrow.	**Partimos (Salimos) mañana.**	Pahr-*tee*-mohss (sah-*lee*-mohss) mahn-*nyan*-ah
Do you accept traveler's checks?	**¿Acepta usted cheques de viajero?**	Ah-*sayp*-tah oo-*sted chay*-kays day bee-ah-*hehr*-oh?
Please send these clothes to the laundry.	**Hágame el favor de mandar esta ropa a la lavandería.**	*Ah*-ga-may el fah-*vhor* day mahn-*dahr ays*-tah rho-pah a lah lah-*vahn*-day-ree-ah

NUMBERS

1	**uno** (*ooh*-noh)	17	**diecisiete** (de-*ess*-ee-*syeh*-tay)
2	**dos** (dohs)	18	**dieciocho** (dee-*ess*-ee-*oh*-choh)
3	**tres** (trayss)	19	**diecinueve** (dee-*ess*-ee-*nway*-bay)
4	**cuatro** (*kwah*-troh)	20	**veinte** (*bayn*-tay)
5	**cinco** (*seen*-koh)	30	**treinta** (*trayn*-tah)
6	**seis** (sayss)	40	**cuarenta** (kwah-*ren*-tah)
7	**siete** (*syeh*-tay)	50	**cincuenta** (seen-*kwen*-tah)
8	**ocho** (*oh*-choh)	60	**sesenta** (say-*sen*-tah)
9	**nueve** (*nway*-bay)	70	**setenta** (say-*ten*-tah)
10	**diez** (dee-ess)	80	**ochenta** (oh-*chen*-tah)
11	**once** (*ohn*-say)	90	**noventa** (noh-*ben*-tah)
12	**doce** (*doh*-say)	100	**cien** (see-en)
13	**trece** (*tray*-say)	200	**doscientos** (*dos*-se-en-tos)
14	**catorce** (kah-*tor*-say)	500	**quinientos** (*keen*-ee-ehn-tos)
15	**quince** (*keen*-say)	1000	**mil** (meal)
16	**dieciseis** (de-*ess*-ee-sayss)		

B Menu Terms

SOUPS

caldo gallego	Galician broth	**sopa de fideos**	noodle soup
caldo de gallina	chicken soup	**sopa de guisantes**	pea soup
sopa de ajo	garlic soup	**sopa de lentejas**	lentil soup
sopa de cebolla	onion soup	**sopa de pescado**	fish soup
sopa clara	consommé	**sopa de tomate**	tomato soup
sopa espesa	thick soup	**sopa de verduras**	vegetable soup

FISH

almejas	clams	**langostinos**	prawns
anchoas	anchovies	**lenguado**	sole
anguilas	eels	**mejillones**	mussels
arenque	herring	**merluza**	hake
atún	tuna	**necoras**	spider crabs
bacalao	cod	**ostras**	oysters
calamares	squid	**pescadilla**	whiting
cangrejo	crab	**pijotas**	small whiting
caracoles	snails	**pulpo**	octopus
centollo	sea urchin	**rodaballo**	turbot
chocos	large squid	**salmonete**	mullet
cigalas	small lobsters	**sardinas**	sardines
gambas	shrimp	**trucha**	trout
langosta	lobster	**vieiras**	scallops

MEATS

albondigas	meatballs	**gallina**	fowl
bistec	beefsteak	**ganso**	goose
callos	tripe	**higado**	liver
cerdo	pork	**jamón**	ham
chuleta	cutlet	**lengua**	tongue
cocido	stew	**paloma**	pigeon
conejo	rabbit	**pato**	duck
cordero	lamb	**pavo**	turkey
costillas	chops	**perdiz**	partridge

VEGETABLES

aceitunas	olives	**guisantes**	peas
alcachofa	artichoke	**judías verdes**	string beans
arroz	rice	**nabo**	turnip
berenjena	eggplant	**patata**	potato
cebolla	onion	**pepino**	cucumber
col	cabbage	**remolachas**	beets
colifior	cauliflower	**setas**	mushrooms
ensalada	salad	**tomate**	tomato
esparragos	asparagus	**zanahorias**	carrots
espinacas	spinach		

FRUITS

albaricoque	apricot	**limón**	lemon
aquacate	avocado	**manzana**	apple
cerezas	cherries	**melocoton**	peach
ciruela	plum	**naranja**	orange
datil	date	**pera**	pear
frambuesa	raspberry	**piña**	pineapple
fresa	strawberry	**plátano**	banana
granada	pomegranate	**toronja**	grapefruit
higo	fig	**uvas**	grapes

DESSERTS

buñuelos   fritters
compota   stewed fruit
flan   caramel custard
fruta   fruit

galletas   tea cakes
helado   ice cream
pasteles   pastries
torta   cake

BEVERAGES

agua   water
agua mineral   mineral water
café   coffee
cerveza   beer
ginebra   gin
jerez   sherry
jugo de naranjas   orange juice
jugo de tomate   tomato juice

leche   milk
sangría   red wine and fruits
sidra   cider
sifon   soda
té   tea
vino blancho   white wine
vino tinto   red wine

BASICS

aceite   oil
ajo   garlic
azucar   sugar
hielo   ice
mantequilla   butter
miel   honey
frito   fried

mostaza   mustard
pan   bread
pimienta   pepper
queso   cheese
sal   salt
vinagre   vinegar

Index

Page numbers in italics refer to maps.

FROMMER'S® COMPLETE TRAVEL GUIDES

(Comprehensive guides with selections in all price ranges—from deluxe to budget)

Alaska
Amsterdam
Arizona
Atlanta
Australia
Austria
Bahamas
Barcelona, Madrid & Seville
Belgium, Holland & Luxembourg
Bermuda
Boston
Budapest & the Best of Hungary
California
Canada
Cancún, Cozumel & the Yucatán
Cape Cod, Nantucket & Martha's Vineyard
Caribbean
Caribbean Cruises & Ports of Call
Caribbean Ports of Call
Carolinas & Georgia
Chicago
China
Colorado
Costa Rica
Denver, Boulder & Colorado Springs
England
Europe
Florida

France
Germany
Greece
Hawaii
Hong Kong
Honolulu, Waikiki & Oahu
Ireland
Israel
Italy
Jamaica & Barbados
Japan
Las Vegas
London
Los Angeles
Maryland & Delaware
Maui
Mexico
Miami & the Keys
Montana & Wyoming
Montréal & Québec City
Munich & the Bavarian Alps
Nashville & Memphis
Nepal
New England
New Mexico
New Orleans
New York City
Nova Scotia, New Brunswick & Prince Edward Island
Oregon
Paris
Philadelphia & the Amish Country

Portugal
Prague & the Best of the Czech Republic
Provence & the Riviera
Puerto Rico
Rome
San Antonio & Austin
San Diego
San Francisco
Santa Fe, Taos & Albuquerque
Scandinavia
Scotland
Seattle & Portland
Singapore & Malaysia
South Pacific
Spain
Switzerland
Thailand
Tokyo
Toronto
Tuscany & Umbria
USA
Utah
Vancouver & Victoria
Vermont, New Hampshire & Maine
Vienna & the Danube Valley
Virgin Islands
Virginia
Walt Disney World & Orlando
Washington, D.C.
Washington State

FROMMER'S® DOLLAR-A-DAY GUIDES

(The ultimate guides to comfortable low-cost travel)

Australia from $50 a Day
California from $60 a Day
Caribbean from $60 a Day
England from $60 a Day
Europe from $50 a Day
Florida from $60 a Day
Greece from $50 a Day
Hawaii from $60 a Day
Ireland from $50 a Day

Israel from $45 a Day
Italy from $50 a Day
London from $70 a Day
New York from $75 a Day
New Zealand from $50 a Day
Paris from $70 a Day
San Francisco from $60 a Day
Washington, D.C., from $60 a Day

FROMMER'S® MEMORABLE WALKS

Chicago
London

New York
Paris

San Francisco

FROMMER'S® PORTABLE GUIDES

Acapulco, Ixtapa/
   Zihuatenejo
Bahamas
California Wine
   Country
Charleston & Savannah
Chicago

Dublin
Las Vegas
London
Maine Coast
New Orleans
New York City
Paris

Puerto Vallarta, Manzanillo
   & Guadalajara
San Francisco
Sydney
Tampa Bay & St. Petersburg
Venice
Washington, D.C.

FROMMER'S® NATIONAL PARK GUIDES

Grand Canyon
National Parks of the American West
Yellowstone & Grand Teton

Yosemite & Sequoia/
   Kings Canyon
Zion & Bryce Canyon

THE COMPLETE IDIOT'S TRAVEL GUIDES
(The ultimate user-friendly trip planners)

Cruise Vacations
Planning Your Trip to Europe
Hawaii

Las Vegas
Mexico's Beach Resorts
New Orleans

New York City
San Francisco
Walt Disney World

SPECIAL-INTEREST TITLES

The Civil War Trust's Official Guide to
   the Civil War Discovery Trail
Frommer's Caribbean Hideaways
Israel Past & Present
New York City with Kids
New York Times Weekends
Outside Magazine's Adventure Guide
   to New England
Outside Magazine's Adventure Guide
   to Northern California

Outside Magazine's Adventure Guide
   to the Pacific Northwest
Outside Magazine's Guide to Family Vacations
Places Rated Almanac
Retirement Places Rated
Washington, D.C., with Kids
Wonderful Weekends from Boston
Wonderful Weekends from New York City
Wonderful Weekends from San Francisco
Wonderful Weekends from Los Angeles

THE UNOFFICIAL GUIDES®
(Get the unbiased truth from these candid, value-conscious guides)

Atlanta
Branson, Missouri
Chicago
Cruises
Disneyland

Florida with Kids
The Great Smoky
   & Blue Ridge
   Mountains
Las Vegas

Miami & the Keys
Mini-Mickey
New Orleans
New York City
San Francisco

Skiing in the West
Walt Disney World
Walt Disney World
   Companion
Washington, D.C.

FROMMER'S® IRREVERENT GUIDES
(Wickedly honest guides for sophisticated travelers)

Amsterdam
Boston
Chicago

London
Manhattan

New Orleans
Paris

San Francisco
Walt Disney World
Washington, D.C.

FROMMER'S® DRIVING TOURS

America
Britain
California

Florida
France
Germany

Ireland
Italy
New England

Scotland
Spain
Western Europe

WHEREVER YOU TRAVEL, *H*ELP IS NEVER FAR AWAY.

From planning your trip to

providing travel assistance along

the way, American Express®

Travel Service Offices are

always there to help.

American Express Travel Service
Offices are found in central locations
throughout Puerto Rico.

Travel

http://www.americanexpress.com/travel